WITHDRAWN

HERALDS OF PROMISE

Edwin Forrest in the title role of John Augustus Stone's *Metamora*. Oil painting by Frederich Styles Agate, circa 1830. National Portrait Gallery.

Heralds of Promise

THE DRAMA OF THE AMERICAN PEOPLE DURING THE AGE OF JACKSON, 1829–1849

Walter J. Meserve

Contributions in American Studies, Number 86

GREENWOOD PRESS
NEW YORK · WESTPORT, CONNECTICUT · LONDON

Library of Congress Cataloging-in-Publication Data

Meserve, Walter J.
  Heralds of promise.

  (Contributions in American Studies, ISSN 0084-9227 ;
no. 86)
  Bibliography: p.
  Includes index.
  1. American drama—1783–1850—History and criticism.
2. United States in literature. I. Title. II. Series.
PS343.M47 1986   812′.3′09   85-21846
ISBN 0-313-25015-4 (lib. bdg. : alk. paper)

Library of Congress Catalog Card Number: 85-21846
ISBN: 0-313-25015-4
ISSN: 0084-9227

First published in 1986

Greenwood Press, Inc.
88 Post Road West
Westport, Connecticut 06881

Printed in the United States of America

The paper used in this book complies with the
Permanent Paper Standard issued by the National
Information Standards Organization (Z39.48-1984).

10 9 8 7 6 5 4 3 2 1

For
Mollie Ann Meserve,
An American Dramatist

CONTENTS

LIST OF ILLUSTRATIONS

PREFACE

My mother once told me that she enjoyed reading the prefaces of the books I wrote. I am not sure that she ever read more than the preface, although I may misjudge her, and I never asked. Knowing that she liked my prefaces, however, made me feel good in the past and makes me pause a moment now. My mother died at the end of October 1984, after I had completed one version of this book which, unknown to me at the time, was to undergo drastic revision—from *Spectacles for a Developing Nation* to *Heralds of Promise*—during the next six months. She was well past her ninety-fifth birthday by that fall, and we felt more pride in the life she had lived than sorrow at her passing.

The previous spring my wife, Mollie, and I had paid Ma a surprise visit at the nursing home on Cape Elizabeth, Maine. We had been in New York doing some library research when Mollie decided that in order to understand a character in a play she was writing she needed to see where this person lived in suburban Boston and learn something about her neighborhood and her home. Once you are in Boston, of course, it is only a couple hours to Cape Elizabeth and, as we were driving, we soon headed "north of Boston." Ma was watching television when we arrived. Although obviously interested in her program, she visited with us in a more coherent manner than we had come to expect during the past two or three years. She knew us and gave us her attention; then, always a lady, she thanked us politely for dropping by and told us to come back again sometime. Our visit was over, and Ma was back with her television program or somewhere. That was that! Now, on to something else. Everybody has things to do. Perhaps I have no reason for a preface now, and you have a book to read while I have more books to write.

All good plays have that obligatory scene. Histories should, too, and I have debts to confess and obligations to acknowledge before I conclude these prefatory comments. For the opportunity to take a two-year leave from Indiana University to complete this second volume of my history of "The Drama of the American People," I am exceedingly grateful to the National Endowment for the Humanities for a Fellowship for Independent Study (1983–1984), to the John Simon Guggenheim Memorial Foundation for a Guggenheim Fellowship (1984–1985), and to Indiana University for a sabbatical leave (1983–1984), a Summer Faculty Fellowship (1984) and a Research Leave Supplement (1984–1985). I was also appointed a Fellow of the Indiana University Institute for Advanced Study for 1984–1985. Such freedom to research and write provided a scholarly and spiritual luxury that I have found most appealing, and I leave it with regret, knowing, however, that I am well into the writing of the third volume of my projected six-volume history.

Over the past years I have used the resources of many libraries, and I wish to acknowledge the following collections which have been particularly helpful in the preparation of this volume: the Boston Athenaeum; Rare Books & Manuscripts, Boston Public Library; Harvard Theatre Collection, Harvard University; Harris Collection, Brown University; Billy Rose Theatre Collection, The New York Public Library at Lincoln Center; the Gratz, Society and Dreer Collections, Historical Society of Pennsylvania; Rare Book Division, Library of Congress; Atkinson Collection, University of Chicago; Clement Library, University of Michigan; Hoblitzelle Theatre Arts Library, University of Texas at Austin; Huntington Library, San Marino, California; Samuel Stark Collection, Stanford University; George W. Poultney Collection, University of San Francisco; Drama Library, University of Washington; the Enthoven Collection, Victoria and Albert Museum, London.

Throughout this book I have quoted from letters and manuscripts which are, in each instance, identified and acknowledged in footnotes. Permission to quote from letters in Rare Books & Manuscripts, Boston Public Library, has been given "by courtesy of the Trustees of the Boston Public Library." Permission to quote from materials identified in the notes of this book has been kindly granted by the Historical Society of Pennsylvania, the Harvard Theatre Collection, the J. Peter Coulson Collection of San Marcos, Texas, and the General Research Division, Astor, Lenox and Tilden Foundations, The New York Public Library. The quotation from the last scene of *Tutoona* by George Washington Harby is reprinted through the courtesy of the American Jewish Archives, Cincinnati, Ohio.

In any research that one undertakes there are always those scholars, past and present, whose works and words have been of inestimable value. I never met George C. D. Odell and corresponded only once with Arthur Hobson Quinn, but I have relied upon their works with the high admiration and respect their scholarship richly deserves. If I complain that Odell rarely identified and tended to disparage the works of American playwrights and apparently disliked melodrama, it is a minor quibble with a trusted authority. Professor Quinn's history of American drama will always remain a standard reference, well written and carefully researched. One does not replace his work but rather adds to it as new evidence for judgment becomes available, hopefully enhancing the history of American drama that inspired him to pursue his distinguished scholarship.

I must also acknowledge a debt to my own teachers, colleagues and students. Dr. Edward Wagenknecht has been an inspiration to my scholarship for nearly forty years, a length of time that undoubtedly shocks us both. I have relied on the opinions and friendship of Dr. Gerald Weales for more than a score of years and valued the judgment of my colleague at Indiana University, Dr. Richard Moody, for nearly that long. Dr. J. Peter Coulson, a former student, has always been extremely generous with his findings. New friends are also to be valued. It was my tremendous good fortune to meet Dr. Robert H. Walker of George Washington University, editor of the American Studies Series for Greenwood Press. Through his great insight and wisdom, brought to an appropriate focus upon my manuscript with just the right amount of that "willing suspension of disbelief," he has contributed immeasurably to my joy and satisfaction in writing this book.

I wish to thank three graduate students of Indiana University: Paul Constantine for his library research, Jerry Dickey for his typing, and especially, Ken Hanes, who has not only worked as typist and research assistant but miraculously solved the mystery of my abominable handwriting.

Walter J. Meserve

HERALDS OF PROMISE

AN AMERICAN POTENTIAL

In 1647 a book was published in London entitled *The Day Breaking, If Not the Sun Rising of the Gospel with the Indians in New England*. This book was probably written by John Eliot, the self-appointed apostle to the Indians of New England, but rather than the contents of the volume, which are fairly dull, it is the thoughtful atmosphere suggested by the title that attracts attention: *The Day Breaking, If Not the Sun Rising*! For those who see the beginning of an American drama only on the shores of Cape Cod during the summer of 1916 when Eugene O'Neill started writing for the Provincetown Players, as critics and historians so often contend, any argument for an American drama worthy of thoughtful consideration and existing during the Age of Jackson is automatically subject to searching questions. Such is the argument of this study, however—presented with something of the messianic enthusiasm that prompted John Eliot to title his work as he did as well as with abundant evidence for both skeptics and persistent believers in a developing American drama. *The Day Breaking, If Not the Sun Rising*—of playwriting in America!

During the Age of Jackson, essentially the 1830s and 1840s, theatre audiences experienced a flurry of playwriting activity in America that not only reflects the attitudes and dreams of Jacksonian America in farce, spectacle and heroic melodrama but provides a brief vision of the American playwrights' potential, a potential that might have reached quite golden heights of achievement had the character of that period in history been different. Before the morning clouds of social, political and cultural obstinacy and expediency obscured the view, there was an instant in the millennial passing of time during which the rising sun of dramatic literature in America was clearly visible, even radiant, and then it disappeared. This noteworthy instant occurred during the generation of Jacksonian influence. Prior to 1829 there were only formative beginnings with very few memorable plays; after 1849 there was a noteworthy decrease in the activity of American playwrights until the Civil War was over and playwrights such as Augustin Daly, artists of quite a different order from their predecessors, appeared on the scene. The accomplishments and disappointments of this "instant" of dramatic productivity during the Jackson Era provide the material for this study.

The American potential in dramatic literature rests upon the argument (1) that during the twenty-year period 1829–1849, designated for convenience as the Age of Jackson, there were more plays written by American dramatists of proven distinction or acknowledged potential than during any similar period before 1870 and (2) that because of the times, the attitudes of the people and the demands of theatre audiences, none of the dramatists were encouraged to provide the national drama that many critics and enthusiastic supporters of both Jacksonian and Whig views urgently desired.

The Age of Jackson is a useful, generalizing phrase for a generation that initiated and experienced certain political and social movements that have since become more patently associated with Jacksonian America than history bears out. Jackson, the man, is that powerful symbol of the years that show the imprint of his leadership. John William Ward illustrated this point clearly as he described Jackson's dynamic relationship to the contemporary ideas of Nature, Providence and Will.[1] According to Vernon Louis Parrington in *Main Currents in American Thought*, Jackson was "the first man of the people . . . the visible embodiment of their vague aspirations."[2] As a noble and inspiring figure, a man with a sense of humor, a capacity for listening as well as an ability to speak and a natural gift for understanding people, Jackson had tremendous charm—charisma, if you will—for young and old. He was known for his great intuitive faculty, and a man of iron will, he obviously enjoyed manipulating people and their opinions. Intelligent, independent, a man of integrity and fundamentally realistic, Jackson was also ambitious for power, fiercely determined in his basic goals and skillful as well as arbitrary in obtaining them. He would not be intimidated. Like others of his bearing and wit, Jackson chose roles to play at different times in order to achieve his desired ends. His strong concerns for a balance of class power, the rights of the common man and a universal freedom, and his preference for the beauty of rural life over the corruption in cities are clearly evident in the concepts of the aggressive democracy he preached.

This was the man on the pedestal, astride his gallant charger, his hair flying in the wind, heroic and spectacular, now sculptured in bronze for future generations to admire. Theatrical in life, he was the hero of a number of contemporary dramas, while his beliefs and concerns became the subject matter for many playwrights during the 1829–1849 period. It is strange that historians of ideas and politics have never taken full advantage of this body of dramatic literature to illustrate the man and his period.

Beyond generalizations, however, those years of Jacksonian influence embody ideas more far-reaching than Old Hickory's personal and public concerns.

Although it might be argued that an average person living during the Age of Jackson could be characterized as basically patriotic and inclined toward the practical, there were obviously other distinctive points of view championed by both Democrats and Whigs that pitted the common man against the aristocrat, the poor against the wealthy and the businessman against the workingman. Jackson's government by the people and his concern for economic equality, for example, aroused the moneyed aristocracy who feared a potential they saw in democratic freedom. Democrats, on the other hand, were fearful of the rapid progress that seemed potentially exploitive and strained cherished traditions. Uncertainties and anxieties touched most people as problems were created by a new understanding of the use of power—in politics, in the persistent social changes, in the written and spoken word. Jackson, with his fundamental acceptance of intuitive reason in the Transcendental sense, as opposed to an understanding brought about through training, and his faith in the wisdom of the common man, quieted some of these fears. The enchantment he stimulated among his followers, however, provoked a disenchantment among certain intellectuals and aristocrats—among writers in general, many of whom espoused Whig principles. The true expression of Jacksonian America speaks to its varied people—the elitists in temperament or by tradition, the workingmen and their liberal champions, the middle-class moralists—and their aspirations, whether vague or particular, Democratic or Whig.

Theatre as it is understood by modern man is a temporal art. It is also "an expression of community," in the words of J. L. Styan, a "feeling of the pulse of an age or a moment in time." A play, Styan explains, "is a social event or it is nothing."[3] To be successful, a play must be appreciated by a gathering of people at a given moment in a theatre when the house lights go down, the curtain parts or rises, and the actors and actresses appear upon the stage. If that appreciation materializes, it will have sprung from the interest the audience found in the form, the wit and the thought of the play and the efforts of the performers. Playwrights, if they wish to see their works performed, must always write with an eye for this practical nature of their art. Such concern was particularly important in Jacksonian America as playwrights, constantly trying to touch the temper of the times, selected their subject matter with a keen sense of urgent expediency.

A feeling for freedom appeared to dominate the period, although fears of exploitation brought different views to the concept. The "common man" is another pertinent phrase that illustrates Jackson's beliefs in human rights and the workingman. Just as the concept of freedom appeared in numerous plays featuring America's past, Roman heroes and the recent Greek revolution, the idea of the common man was almost continually before a theatre audience's eyes in one form or another. Closely related to the anti-intellectual atmosphere fostered by an intelligent but surprisingly ill-read president, this idea emphasized the superiority of the common sense of the common man over wisdom built upon a knowledge of Latin or "law learning." Among many Jacksonians, demagoguery, deception and a certain cunning were greatly admired. Davy Crockett, in myth and reality, illustrates this attitude which was popular on the stage in characters such as Colonel Nimrod Wildfire in *The Lion of the West*. Although not all stage Yankees were Democrats (Major Jack Downing, for example), with his lower-class bragging, innate shrewdness and wit, his common sense and disparagement of book learning, the stage Yankee is an excellent illustration of Jacksonian myth. The character of Mose the fire b'hoy is common enough, but his city background wrenches him from the Jacksonian ideal, while the problems inherent in the rapid growth of cities were a very real concern for many living at this time. Perhaps the most widely recognized emphasis in drama upon the common man theme appears in the conditions Adam Trueman, the Yankee, imposes upon the Tiffanys in *Fashion*: "You must sell your house and all these gew gaws, and bundle your wife and daughters off to the country. There let them learn economy, true independence, and home virtues, instead of foreign follies" (V, 1).

One of the most interesting concepts of any time in history and one of the most difficult to define in any broad and acceptable sense is that of self. How do people regard themselves? As an advocate of independence in art and life, Ralph Waldo Emerson advised his readers and listeners to "embrace the common." He explained in "The American Scholar" that "the world is nothing, the man is all, in yourself is the law of nature." Many people were impressed by Emerson's concept of self-reliance in which he urged man to be "his own star" and "a non-conformist" and by his belief in "representative men" on whom lives might be modeled. The persuasiveness of these ideas is revealed in the Jacksonian American's belief in a manifest destiny and his acceptance of himself as one of the chosen people. He paid little attention to Emerson's reservations about man's ability to keep his head and maintain control.

> Things are in the saddle,
> And ride Mankind.
> * * *
> There are two laws discrete,
> Not reconciled,—
> Law for man, and law for thing;
> The last builds town and fleet,
> But it runs wild,
> And doth the man unking.[4]

Nature, as Emerson described it in "Fate," was not a sentimentalist and did not pamper mankind.

Emerson preached one attitude toward life that Jacksonian Americans could adopt. In *The Popular Mood of Pre-Civil War America*, however, Lewis O. Saum argues that Emerson did not represent the view of the common man and that the common man's belief in a spiritual providence created in him a mood of humble submission and a dependence upon established religion that was not a hallmark of Jackson's presidency.[5] By suppressing the self the common man could envision an order and a discipline or decorum introduced to his personal world by a spiritual force and his own constant indulgence in hard work. Although the common man may not have realized at this time that he was on the road to capitalism, this was the argument of Calvin Cotton, an editor of *True Whig*, who explained in one of his Junius Tracts (no. VII, "Labor and Capital") that "this is the country of self-made men." By and large this was an erroneous thesis, but it was effective propaganda at the time for the exploitive wish fulfillment that helps illustrate the age.[6] It was also excellent subject matter for melodrama in the theatre. In any event, Jacksonian America included all manner of believers—from self-reliance to self-suppression—whose spiritual and temporal lives responded to similar types of performances on American stages.

Early in the century it became clear that theatres would be identified by tne kinds of entertainment they provided. The Park Theatre in New York, for example, catered to sophisticated audiences who enjoyed classical drama and the best plays from England and Europe. Its management infrequently produced plays by American playwrights and then mainly if the playwright had a reputation in literature. The Bowery Theatre, on the other hand, was known for its blood-and-thunder melodrama, while William Mitchell's Olympic Theatre existed largely on spectacles, burlesques and farces. Audiences responded to the theatre of their taste—the elitists, the working class and the growing middle class for which morality was a criterion for good drama. The common quality in all theatre was the hero of the play, whose spectacular accomplishments onstage reinforced the believers in self-reliance, provided the "self-made man" with a model and created a romantic escape for the self-suppressed. In tragedies the hero or heroine brought audiences the highest sensibilities worthy of imitation; in melodrama the protagonist's heroism and frequent patriotic enthusiasm underlined the nationalism of the day; in farce his extravagant impulses provided the confined or indulgent self with vicarious pleasure.

Another widespread attitude in Jacksonian America promoted education and reform. The American lyceum movement which was estimated to have 3,000 associations by 1835, the movement toward formal education for women, the temperance movement and the various utopian ventures with entrepreneurs such as Robert Owen, Frances Wright and Arthur Brisbane—all pointed toward a concern for human rights and better living that is associated with the age. In "An Essay on Education" (1841), Caleb Atwater claimed "that the richest portion of our estate lies in the intellect of our people."[7] He was not alone in that opinion. The previous year's records showed some 3,248 academies and grammar schools and 47,207 primary schools in America. It was, in part, a pervasive sense of mission that epitomized Jacksonian America. In 1835, for example, the American Tract Society resolved to supply its standard evangelical volumes to the entire population of America. Lecturers and pamphleteers enjoyed unprecedented popularity. William Alcott's moral *Lectures to Young Men* caught the public fancy with its first issue in 1833 and reached its twenty-first edition in 1858. Sex manuals also had their place.[8] Part of this determined instruction was thrust upon the public by liberal reformers, both Democrats and Whigs, while the common man had difficulty finding time either to be educated or to take part in reform movements except, perhaps, the temperance movement. These, however, were popular attitudes or moods of the period which the theatre with its vast potential for moral instruction and social comment eagerly reflected in its productions.

The times and the attitudes of the people always dictate theatre fare, and successful playwrights take advantage of current events and the public mood. Between 1829 and 1849, plays emphasized the power of the common man and the heroic qualities that all Americans could admire, the spectacles they could enjoy or the moral statements they felt it necessary to make. Such were the touchstones for the clever American playwright. But the playwright's task was not easy. Just as the times and attitudes provided the material for American dramatists, the public mood also created great barriers to their progress. Not simply antagonistic toward theatre in general, people placed those barricades specifically and deliberately in the pathway of a developing American drama, ironically prohibiting the emergence of a dramatic literature during this recognized period of national emphasis.

For numerous reasons relating to the temperament of the people and their prevailing moods—elitism, anti-intellectualism, religious prejudice, a devotion to work coupled with a lack of time for leisure, a disparate population without traditions of theatre attendance—American dramatists were not encouraged. Although many critics and essayists discussed a national literature and a national drama, they were, like other contemporary American intellectuals and commentators, unable to evaluate realistically the failures and accomplishments of Jacksonian America. That is a judgment in which historians seem to agree. Travelers and writers from across the Atlantic Ocean, however, were only too eager to assess America and its culture. Although some of them obviously treasured their prejudices, their observations on literature and theatre provide strong evidence for some of the frustrations forced upon American dramatists.

The popularity of disparaging American literary efforts was given tremendous impetus when British critic Sydney Smith, writing for the *Edinburgh Review* (January 1820), assured himself a place in the histories of American literature with his rhetorical question: "In the four quarters of the globe who reads an American book or goes to an American play?" From those who were shocked as well as those who sympathized with Smith answers were soon framed. In *The Forest Rose* (1825), playwright Samuel Woodworth responded by creating an English cad who retreated from the action of the play as well as from America with the warning that his enemies would get harsh treatment when he published his "Six Months in America."

In 1827 Frances Trollope published her *Domestic Manners of the Americans* and, in one way or another, impressed people. Apparently, she went to the theatre in America a number of times—and was never pleased. In Cincinnati she seemed indignant at the casual attitude of the audience which filled only a third of the house. On another occasion she left before the end of the third act of Forrest's *Hamlet*, and she did not enjoy Junius Brutus Booth as Lear at the Chestnut Street Theatre in Philadelphia. What shocked her most, however, was the "incessant spitting," the "mixed smell of onions and whiskey" and the fact that one man in a box "deliberately took off his coat." The climax of her disenchantment came at the Chatham Theatre in New York where in the first row of the dress box she observed a "lady performing the most maternal office possible."[9] Mrs. Trollope's observations and reactions, however, clearly identified the theatre at this time, and throughout the period editors of literary magazines would occasionally question why anybody would want to write for this theatre.

Other visitors who attended the theatre in America witnessed similar behavior to that which repulsed Mrs. Trollope but did not always share her conclusions. In *The Autocratic Journey, Being the Outspoken Letters of Mrs. Basil Hall, Written during a Fourteen Month's Sojourn in America, 1827–1828*, the writer seemed to disapprove on principle of nearly everything she encountered, but she enjoyed James Hackett in *The Comedy of Errors* and commended a performance of *Marie Stuart* at the French Theatre in New Orleans.[10] Richard Cobden went regularly to the theatre during his visit to America in the mid-1830s and was favorably impressed. He enjoyed the novelty of child actors, found theatre in Philadelphia equal to that of Manchester and accepted the fact that at the Bowery Theatre "the mechanic class were all without coats, seemingly as though it were fashion"—which of course, at the Bowery, it was.[11]

Thomas Hamilton, *Men and Manners in America* (1833), found "detestable manners and morals" among Americans and a country "uncongenial for the growth of philosophy and literature." Although he thought the acting of Forrest "coarse and vulgar," he admitted that he was without rival as an actor who completely enraptured his audiences. Hamilton also revealed an astute sensitivity to the conditions endured by American arts and letters. Feeling that Americans tended to reprint everything from England without distinguishing good literature from bad, he stressed the fact that native literary talent was not fairly treated by American critics, that it needed protection from foreign competition.[12]

The argument between free trade and protectionist tariffs continued throughout the Jacksonian Era, one of the prominent results being the Tariff Bill of 1833, a compromise effort to reconcile the South and West, where lower tariffs were favored, with the North and Northwest, whose people demanded higher tariffs. Occasionally, the argument extended to the activity in literature and the arts, where pleading for kindness to American plays by critics and editors suggested a protectionist attitude. Hamilton's observation was surely intriguing because it called attention to comparisons that were constantly being made among the elite to the detriment of American creativity. Who among Americans could compare with the English writers? Cooper might be linked with Scott or Irving with Goldsmith, but there were no writers in America comparable to Keats, Shelley, Byron, Coleridge or Carlyle. Extending this observation to the drama—where giants existed in neither country at this time—for snobbish American audiences the nationality of the dramatist was likely to be far more important than the produced play. Consequently, the farces and melodramas of John Buckstone, Charles Dance, Edward Fitzball and Douglas Jerrold were demanded over the American work of Louisa Medina, Joseph S. Jones, Nathaniel H. Bannister, or Joseph Field, although the comparative merit of each could be well argued. In the eyes of theatre managers in America (mainly Englishmen) Sheridan Knowles and Edward Bulwer-Lytton were without peers in America while Robert Montgomery Bird, Epes Sargent and Nathaniel Parker Willis were forced out of the theatre.

Few foreign visitors made as perceptive observations as Hamilton, but their comments frequently help reveal the conditions surrounding drama and theatre in America. In *A Diary in America with Remarks on Its Institutions* (1839), for example, Frederich Marryat noted that stock actors (not the stars) in America were "better than our own," that the love of novelty even at legitimate theatres such as the Park Theatre provided a major inducement to theatregoers, that theatre managers imported foreign stars as they do "manufactured goods or fashions from Paris," that theatres presenting farces or melodrama were seldom visited by the "aristocratic portion of the citizens," and that costumes and scenery for productions at the National Theatre in New York were seldom exceeded "even in our great theatres." Marryat also underscored that characteristic of Jacksonian America that made theatre a very risky venture. "Americans have few amusements," he wrote; "they are too busy." "Theatre is almost their only resort [for amusement], and that is not as well attended as it might be, considering their means."[13] Michael Chevalier made a similar observation in *Society, Manners and Politics in the United States* (1839): "The American can support a constant and unrelaxing devotion to labor; he does not feel the need of amusement and recreation."[14] After stating that Americans have "no national character yet, nor can have, for a length of years," Harriet Martineau advised that some leisure time for amusement would be desirable and left it at that.[15] It was a foregone conclusion that American playwrights would have problems.

In Jacksonian America there were three American playwrights from the generation past whose plays, at least one or two of them, were occasionally performed in New York theatres—John Howard Payne (1791–1852), Samuel Woodworth (1795–1842) and Mordecai M. Noah (1785–1851). Each was established as a playwright well before Andrew Jackson reached the White House; each illustrated a different problem for the American dramatist or for the development of an American dramatic literature. Payne, the best writer of the three, made his living as a playwright during an extended sojourn in England which ended in July of 1832. Landing in New York, he was welcomed home in a manner appropriate to the author of "Home, Sweet Home." His joy, however, was not long lasting. Becoming extremely bitter that his plays, particularly *Brutus* and *Charles II*, were being performed in both America and England, and that the lack of copyright protection prevented him from profitting from his labor, he gave up writing plays.[16]

There was a good reason for Woodworth's continued acceptance in theatre during these decades. In 1825 he had written *The Forest Rose*, which remained a popular play for Yankee actors until the early 1860s. Woodworth, however, continued to write plays during the early 1830s. *The Cannibals; or, The Massacre Islands* opened on February 20, 1833, at New York's Bowery Theatre with good publicity, and when Woodworth's benefit was announced for the twenty-fifth, an enthusiastic reviewer urged everyone to attend. "For the honor of our country—for the love of native genius—for the cause of literature, for every laudable consideration let Woodworth have a bumper on Monday evening. . . . How can we expect domestic plays of sterling merit without we encourage and reward those that have the talent and industry to create them? Let us be just ourselves, wipe away the reproaches of traveling Trollopes and convince the world that, with proper encouragement this is not the climate where 'genius sickens, and where fancy dies.' "[17] Based on Morrel's *Four Voyages to the Pacific Ocean* and Mrs. Morrel's personal narrative of the last trip, the play provided ample opportunity for popular spectacle—the discovery of the Massacre Islands, the landing and battle with the cannibals, the eruption of the volcanic mountain and the climactic return. As the play appears to have followed the chronology of the voyage, however, it became more narrative than dramatic. Reviewers lauded factual aspects and spectacles, but the play was not successful.

Woodworth's *The Foundling of the Sea* was written for a contest sponsored by George Handel Hill and was first performed at the Park Theatre on May 14, 1833. Although the awarding committee was not impressed with any of the submissions, Hill paid Woodworth the prize of $400 and kept the play in his repertory. Like Woodworth's *Blue Laws; or, Eighty Years Ago*, a satiric farce that played at the Bowery Theatre in March of 1835, *The Foundling of the Sea* has not survived. The suggestion of another Woodworth play appears in the December 3, 1836 issue of the *Spirit of the Times*: "Barry has produced Woodworth's new play called *The Massacre; or, The Malay's Revenge*, taken from a M.S. play of George Coleman the Younger, at the Tremont, Boston."[18] Although the relationship of this work to *The Cannibals*, which had been written nearly four years previously, is unknown, a knowledge of contemporary practice in the theatre suggests that the two could easily have been the same play. By this date, moreover, Woodworth had stopped writing plays. In 1835 he had contracted a disease of the eyes which worsened in 1836, and by early 1837 he suffered an attack of paralysis which shattered his nervous system and made it impossible for him to study or to concentrate his attention for any length of time.

A gentle and kind man who seemed to have faith in everyone, Woodworth is remembered in literature as the author of "The Old Oaken Bucket" and in

American dramatic history mainly for *The Forest Rose* which, while adding considerably to the fortunes of some actors and theatre managers and bringing pleasure to many people, undoubtedly brought its author little pecuniary advantage. Judging from his early work, Woodworth had both the talent and the industry to write domestic plays of merit—whether appropriately "sterling" to satisfy the critic in 1833 it will never be known. The critic was right, however, in lauding Woodworth as one who might have stilled the harsh criticism of "traveling Trollopes."

In the history of American Jews, Mordecai M. Noah holds a distinctive position as a leader. Andrew Jackson had considerable faith in the political astuteness of this man, who served the president in New York political offices as well as in the position of editor on the New York *Enquirer*. Noah's views on immigration and slavery and other issues of the day have become political history in America as have his efforts on behalf of American Jews. Although his active work as a playwright was never more than an avocation and ended in 1820, he remained a firm friend of the drama in America, and was occasionally recognized by playwrights and critics. Earlier in his life he had been thought sufficiently important in the theatre world to be attacked in one play and sneered at in another. When in 1819 Noah wrote a disparaging review of an anonymously published play entitled *Wall Street; or, Ten Minutes Before Three*, the second edition of the play was sarcastically dedicated to Noah, calling him a fool. More than a century later, Harry Sackler wrote *Major Noah* and identified his hero as "the first truly American playwright."[19] The point might be argued but, amateur or not, in 1819 Noah wrote a play which was produced in theatres again and again in Jacksonian America: *She Would Be a Soldier*. After one entry (Bowery Theatre, April 22, 1845), George C. D. Odell commented on the script's "surprising vitality . . . amid the wrecks of other American dramas."[20]

It is not difficult to understand the attraction of *She Would Be a Soldier* for Jacksonian audiences. The play had nearly everything that was appealing on the stage at this time: a romantic and melodramatic plot with a heroine who masquerades as a soldier; spectacles in the form of dances, pastoral music, fife and drum corps, parades and military splendor; a lecherous Frenchman, a foppish Englishman and an intelligent Indian; and some of the better trappings of melodrama including a court-martial, with patriotism smoothly blended into all scenes. In addition to these novelties, Noah created a lively and imaginative heroine who was returned to the stage periodically until 1868. Why he did not continue to write for the stage undoubtedly relates more to his own personal ambitions than the conditions of the American theatre, although they must also have been a factor in his decision. In spite of being intimate with theatre people and a friend of New York theatre throughout his life, Noah appeared neither motivated nor able to create support for native playwrights.

All three dramatists—Payne, Woodworth, Noah—might have continued their efforts or made even more important contributions to the American drama, for the skills they showed in their earlier dramatic successes were in demand throughout the Age of Jackson, but they were not encouraged. If America had a potential for dramatic literature among its writers prior to Jackson's administration, what happened to it during these years? To begin with, what was the attitude of the American theatre toward native writers when Jackson took office? How many plays written by Americans, for example, were produced during the first half of 1829? These were certainly exciting days for native Americans who for the first time were admitted en masse to the White House to cheer "the people's champion" on inauguration day, March 4, 1829.

There was not much to cheer about, however, in theatrical circles. By September of 1829 a theatre critic in Philadelphia noted that in New York all the theatres but one had been closed and expressed the wish that the same be done in Philadelphia, in preference to "keeping in miserable half-starved existence, half a dozen houses."[21] New Yorkers, however, had had an opportunity to see Frances Wright's *Altorf* on January 22 at the Park Theatre, prefacing six nights during which she engaged the theatre for her lectures. At the Bowery Theatre, William Dunlap's *A Trip to Niagara* drew a scathing review from the editor of *The Irish Shield and Monthly Milesian*: "the most satiating *namby pamby* production, that ever disgusted an audience; words without ideas, scenes without connexion of probability; low jests and mawlish sentiment clothed in the poorest language."[22] The Lafayette Theatre, starting as a small circus theatre in 1825, had the largest stage and the most lavish scenery of any New York theatre in 1828, only to be destroyed by fire April 10, 1829. In January of that year, however, an adaptation of James Fenimore Cooper's 1827 novel, *The Red Rover*, held the stage for a few nights. (Never as popular in America as in England, Cooper's stories were particularly attractive across the Atlantic where Edward Fitzball's adaptation of *The Pilot* ran 200 nights at the Adelphi Theatre in 1825.) An anonymous play entitled *The Battle of New Orleans; or, Lafitte the Pirate*, appeared on January 8 at the LaFayette Theatre, which produced Dunlap's *The Glory of Columbia* on February 11, and M. M. Noah's *She Would Be a Soldier* on February 23.

In Philadelphia theatres the most produced American playwright in 1829 was Richard Penn Smith. Among his several plays staged this year was *The Eighth of January* at the Chestnut Street Theatre, where it played at least three nights in January, and *A Wife at a Venture*, which was produced at the Walnut Street Theatre on July 25. A production of *The Disowned* at the Chestnut was reported in *The Ariel* as "better than any original play which has been brought out here in some years."[23] Noah's *She Would Be a Soldier* appeared on the stage of the Arch Street Theatre in mid-May, viewed by some Indian chiefs who "appeared to derive but little amusement from the playing."[24] *Brutus* and *Thérèse, the Orphan of Geneva* by John Howard Payne were produced on the same bill at the Walnut Street Theatre in January.

A few American plays appeared in print during the first half of 1829. Amira Thompson (Carpenter) published *The Lyre of Tioga* in which she used some of her childhood experiences in the valley of the Tioga River to create "a sacred drama of the book of Esther." "Obey the holy mandate of the sun," she wrote in the epilogue, "and search the Scriptures, for in them ye find Promise of pardon and eternal life."[25] It is a brief play, twenty pages, undramatic and intensely moralizing. Scenes from *Kathleen O'Neil; or, A Picture of Feudal Times in Ireland* by George Pepper, editor of *The Irish Shield and Monthly Milesian*, were published in the January and March issues of the magazine; audiences had viewed the play at the LaFayette Theatre on May 10, 1827. Dr. James McHenry, writer, critic, and persistent playwright, had the courage to publish his tragedy, *The Usurper*, which had already appeared on the Arch Street stage. Although the reviewer in *Ladies' Literary Port Folio* found the printed version of *The Usurper* much superior to the acting text as a result of "judiciously pruning and curtailing,"[26] the editor of *Ariel* illustrated yet again his intolerance for enthusiastic beginners by noting "uproarious bursts of laughter [that] bore ample testimony to the merits of the play and the exertions of the performers."[27]

A general accounting of American dramatists whose plays were produced in the theatres of New York and Philadelphia during the 1829–1830 season clearly reveals the American dramatist's tentative position in the theatre. Admittedly, this was a weak theatre season with several theatres closed, but American theatre was seldom other than a risky venture. There were, however, at least eight Americans whose plays were being performed and who had written more than one professionally produced play: William Dunlap, Mordecai M. Noah, Richard Penn Smith, John Howard Payne, Robert Montgomery Bird, George Washington Park Custis, James McHenry and John Augustus Stone. Frances Wright's play *Altorf*, was infrequently produced, and the same could be said for Lorenzo da Ponte's *Almachilde*, and *Irma; or, The Prediction* by the New Orleans playwright, J. M. Kennicott. James Hackett performed in two plays this season, *The Times; or, Life in New York* and *The Indian Wife*, which were written especially for him, but they remained anonymous works along with the current dramatizations of Cooper's *The Wept of Wish-ton-Wish* and *The Borderers* and such Indian plays as *Naramattah*.

This was also a season—1829–1830—when Americans were becoming aware of some new native playwrights. Just before Christmas *Sertorious* by David Paul Brown was brought out at the Chestnut Street Theatre in Philadelphia. Joseph M. Field made his first appearance as an actor in New York at the Park Theatre where two of his plays were produced in July: *The Wigwam; or, Templeton Manor*, an adaptation of Cooper's *The Pioneers*, and *Down South; or, A Military Training*. In Boston, where Field had previously worked, Joseph S. Jones was establishing his reputation, duly noted in *The Dramatic Mirror; or, Critical Remarks upon the Theatrical Representations in Boston*, a newspaper to be published every day at midnight after the performances at the Tremont Theatre where Jones acted and wrote some of the farces. A noble, if very idealistic, endeavor, the newspaper first appeared on September 15, 1829, and published its last issue on October 10, 1829. Another actor, Charles W. Taylor, was also making his name as a playwright, particularly for his popular nautical drama, *The Water Witch*, an adaptation of Cooper's novel, which opened in New York on March 21, 1830. Jonas B. Phillips was yet another promising playwright whose work first appeared in 1830.

Although it is difficult to assess accurately the impressions that American playwrights were making in the theatre of 1829–1830, it is clear that in spite of writing that seldom went beyond "adequate," a national drama was contemplated and being created. Playwrights attempted poetic tragedy, adapted fiction and wrote melodrama, farce and burlesque. Subject matter for their plays strayed through American history, politics, current social events and issues and ancient scenes. Although these American dramatists were scarcely a significant force on the American stage, like actors who carry an evening with audiences, they were beginning to be aware of distinct needs which only they could satisfy. They were also attracting either strong positive or negative comments that suggested their potential, an American potential!

Prior to 1829, playwriting in America was little better than a casual interest for those who heeded the siren call of the stage. John Howard Payne is one exception, and he was forced to pursue his career in England. Other Americans who wrote plays during the early decades of the nineteenth century illustrated the directions that playwriting would take in America but generally lacked the talent and persistent determination displayed by playwrights of the second quarter of the century. Some of these were actors such as John Blake White (1781–1859), whose *Foscari* and *The Mysteries of the Castle* attracted moderate attention in 1806. Joseph Hutton (1787–1828) was the most prolific of the actor-playwrights, with five published plays by the time of his death. Playwrights with admitted peripheral interest included Samuel B. H. Judah (1799–1876), who wrote exciting melodramas such as *The Mountain Torrent* (1820) and *The Buccaneer* (1827) before concluding his playwriting career in 1833 with *The Maid of Midian*, a dramatic poem in four acts. Isaac Harby (1781–1828) fashioned his work on traditional models with *The Gordian Knot* (1807) and *Alberti* (1819). Shortly after his death, his brother, George Washington Harby, carried on this interest in playwriting with a strong nationalistic flair.

The single outstanding example of a dramatist with this casual interest in playwriting is James Nelson Barker (1784–1858), whose *Superstition* (1824) marked not only a high point in the development of American drama but, unfortunately, the end of his avocation in the theatre. An avid supporter of Andrew Jackson, he was rewarded with the position as collector of the Port of Philadelphia (1829–1838) and later served Van Buren as comptroller of the treasury. For some reason his interest in politics inspired him to write poetry rather than plays, and the American theatre lost a potentially fine dramatist. By the 1820s, however, there were a number of people, poets or writers with journalistic interests, who discovered a momentary attraction to the theatre. James Wright Simmons (1790–1858) attempted poetic tragedy with *Manfredi* (1821) and *Valdemar* (1822), but his was a slight and forgettable endeavor. George

Pope Morris, the author of *Briar Cliff* (1826), and James Lawson, whose verse drama *Giordano* was performed at the Park Theatre in 1828, were New York editors as well as poets.

Without question there was a growing interest in a national drama by the time Jackson won the presidency. Critics like Samuel Woodworth, James Kirke Paulding, Lawson, Morris, John Neal, Robert Walsh and William Leggett were beginning to mention a national drama. An actor, Edwin Forrest, provided the first open challenge to American dramatists with the announcement of his prize play contest in November of 1828 in *The Critic*, a journal recently started by Leggett, who would become a close friend of Forrest and a fiery supporter of Andrew Jackson. There was obviously a need for American dramatists: American actors needed them; theatre managers might profit by their works; the new nation wanted a distinguishable literature of which drama would be a part. In 1829 the potential appeared to be available. George Washington Parke Custis, for example, wrote *The Indian Prophecy* in 1827 and would write at least eight more plays. Both Robert Montgomery Bird and Richard Penn Smith were starting promising careers in drama. James Hackett was beginning to see the need for plays by Americans, while a new generation of actors arriving yearly from England—many to spend the rest of their lives in America—determined to increase their advantage in the theatre by writing plays. It was truly an auspicious time, for a newly inspired nation and for its native dramatists. The potential was there, and that twenty-year period before 1849 produced the kind of playwrights and the plays that might have flung America into the whirlwind of world theatre with considerable effect. Yet it did not happen. The "man and the moment," the playwrights and their times, must not have been destined for that result.

By 1850 times had changed again. With few exceptions, those Jacksonian American dramatists whose works suggested that desired potential in 1829 had either died or, for one reason or another, stopped writing. From 1850 until the Civil War, plays by American dramatists mainly continued to exploit spectacle and laughter, that need for public diversion that was generally satisfied by the plays of the actor-playwright. During these years it was business as usual for H. J. Conway, James Pilgrim, and John Brougham, with the added excitement of a seven-year visit by the Irish playwright Dion Boucicault. If there was one distinctive quality of American drama during the 1850s, it was the slowly developing awareness onstage of American society in plays by O. B. Bunce, William Hurlbert, J. C. Swayze and William W. Brown. Stage adaptations of *Uncle Tom's Cabin* might also be noted, but in this accumulative play spectacle was more important than comment. There was also a continuing literary presence in the occasional works of William Gilmore Simms and Julia Ward Howe, and of George Henry Boker, whose amibitions would be partially satisfied by the approval of a future generation.

Slowed by the startling influence of Marx and Darwin, the explosive expansion westward and the social upheaval that led inevitably to war, American drama suffered a loss of momentum during the Civil War period. One important event during these war years was the appearance in 1863 of *Leah, the Forsaken* by Augustin Daly, whose *Under the Gaslight* (1867) revealed the kind of dramatic skill and personal determination that America would require to begin its intrusion into world drama. Once the Civil War was past, dramatists and businessmen contended more effectively than ever before in America in that battle of the survival of the fittest, and entrepreneurs emerged in both areas of endeavor. It was soon discovered that dramatists and theatre artists could make a living by their art, and by the 1870s American dramatic literature was struggling to its feet through the efforts of Bronson Howard, Bartley Campbell, J. J. McCloskey, Steele Mackaye, Clay Greene and Edward Harrigan. After a generation of lost progress in the development of American drama, the potential that seemed imminent in 1829, only to struggle to no avail during the Age of Jackson and then lie dormant for another generation, was at last beginning to be recognized and encouraged.

The influence of England and Europe upon American drama and theatre during the first half of the nineteenth century can be clearly seen in the form and substance of American drama, in imitation and in the lack of it. With few exceptions this was not a memorable period in the history of western theatre and drama. It is sufficient to note here, however, that serious playwriting was no more appreciated in England than in America. Most of the romantic poets wrote for the stage, but only Lord Byron had any success, while one of the most admired playwrights was Joanna Baille. It was clearly an age for melodrama, and Americans enjoyed adaptations of numerous plays from the German of August von Kotzebue and the French of Pixerécourt, Victor Ducange and Dumas *père*. Among the English playwrights popular in America were the actor-playwrights John Sheridan Knowles, Edward Bulwer-Lytton, Douglas Jerrold and a score of lesser dramatists such as Edward Fitzball and John B. Buckstone. None of these carries much weight in the history of world drama, which during these years produced few plays of lasting quality. In Germany the two playwrights with lasting fame, Heinrich von Kleist (1777–1811) and Georg Büchner (1813–1837), could not contend during their lifetimes with the popularity of Ernest Baupach (1784–1852). Romantic drama, developing from the melodrama of the first quarter of the century, is characterized by the work of the French dramatists, particularly in the statement made by Victor Hugo (1802–1885) in *Hernani* (1830) and in the plays of Alfred de Vigny (1797–1863), although Vigny's work was virtually ignored by his contemporaries. As in other countries, melodrama ruled in Russia with the more memorable plays of Alexander Pushkin (1799–1837), Mikhail Lermontov (1814–1841), and Nikolai Gogol (1809–1852).

Solidly reflecting the theatrical interests of England and Europe, theatre in America during the second quarter of the nineteenth century gave its native dramatists not only problems similar to those experienced by playwrights in other western countries, but a distinctively American set of barriers to success that would exist only during the Age of Jackson.

NOTES

1. See John William Ward, *Andrew Jackson, Symbol for an Age* (New York: Oxford University Press, 1955).

2. Vernon Louis Parrington, *Main Currents in American Thought*, vol. 2, 1800–1860, *The Romantic Revolution in America* (New York: Harcourt, Brace and Company, 1930), 146.

3. J. L. Styan, *Drama, Stage and Audience* (New York: Cambridge University Press, 1975), 11.

4. From Ralph Waldo Emerson's "Ode, Inscribed to W. H. Channing."

5. Lewis O. Saum, *The Popular Mood of Pre-Civil War America* (Westport, Conn.: Greenwood Press, 1980), 27–54.

6. See Edward Pessen, *Riches, Class and Power Before the Civil War* (Lexington, Mass.: D. C. Heath, 1973).

7. Caleb Atwater, "An Essay on Education," in *The Faith of Our Fathers*, eds. Irving Mark and Eugene L. Schwaab (New York: Octagon Press, 1976), 81.

8. See Donald G. Walters, ed., *Primers for Prudery: Sexual Advice to Victorian America* (Englewood Cliffs, N.J.: Prentice-Hall, 1974).

9. Frances Trollope, *Domestic Manners of the Americans* (New York: Dodd, Mead & Company, 1827), 232, 300.

10. Una Pope-Hennessey, ed., *The Autocratic Journey, Being the Outspoken Letters of Mrs. Basil Hall, Written During a Fourteen Month's Sojourn in America, 1827–1828* (New York: G. P. Putnam's Sons, 1931), 255.

11. Elizabeth H. Cawley, ed., *The American Diaries of Richard Cobden* (Princeton, N.J.: Princeton University, 1952), 197.

12. Thomas Hamilton, *Men and Manners in America* (Philadelphia: Carey, Lea & Blanchard, 1833), 296, 243, 35, 202.

13. Frederich Marryat, *A Diary in America with Remarks on Its Institutions*, ed., Sydney Jackman (New York: Alfred A. Knopf, 1962), 252, 453, 454, and 452.

14. Michael Chevalier, *Society, Manners and Politics in the United States* (Boston: Weeks, Jordan and Company, 1839), 207.

15. Harriet Martineau, *Society in America*, vol. III (London: Saunders and Otley, 1839), 6.

16. Yet he was not completely forgotten. The *North American Magazine* I (February 1833), 213–15, published a "scene from an unpublished play" by Payne, a scene from *The Spanish Husband* which was eventually published in volume V of *America's Lost Plays*, 1940.

17. *New York Traveller, Spirit of the Times, and Family Journal*, II (February 23, 1833), 3.

18. *Spirit of the Times*, VI (December 3, 1836), 1.

19. New York *Herald Tribune*, February 24, 1929, 12.

20. George C. D. Odell, *Annals of the New York Stage*, vol. V (New York: Columbia University Press, 1931), 111.

21. *Ladies' Literary Port Folio*, I (September 9, 1829), 312.

22. *Irish Shield and Monthly Milesian*, I (January 1829), 30–31.

23. *Ariel*, III (May 2, 1829), 5. Founded upon *Le Cassier* (1826), by Jouslin de la Salle and Saint Maurice, the plot of *The Disowned* revolves around a profligate young man whose love for a girl over the objections of his rich uncle brings about an attempted murder and the death of the girl.

24. *Ariel*, III (May 16, 1829), 14.

25. Amira Thompson, *The Lyre of Tioga* (Geneva, New York, 1829).

26. *Ladies' Literary Port Folio*, I (April 22, 1829), 150–51.

27. *Ariel*, III (May 30, 1829), 22.

2

"THE WANT OF A NATIONAL DRAMA . . ."

Almost any statement establishing the beginnings of an American national drama can draw criticism. Writing in 1960 about *Mid-Century Drama*, Laurence Kitchin, an English critic, entitled his chapter on drama in America "The Potent Intruder."[1] An earlier English critic, William Archer, advised scholars to look for the origins of American drama on the shores of Cape Cod in the summer of 1916 when Eugene O'Neill started writing for the Provincetown Players. American drama historians with greater sympathy for slowly developing traditions relate those beginnings to James Herne's production of *Margaret Fleming* in 1890, which William Dean Howells found "epoch-marking."[2] The Duyckinck brothers, however, those mid–nineteenth-century editors of a two-volume *Cyclopedia of American Literature*, found in America only pale imitations of English plays, nothing distinctively American, nothing worthy of critical evaluation. Lewis Strang was only a little more generous when he noted in his chapter on "Playwrights in America" in *Players and Plays of the Last Quarter Century* that until *Fashion* appeared in 1845 "all was darkness and stagnation as far as the American drama was concerned."[3] Describing playwriting activities during the 1830s, Walter M. Leman plucked from his *Memories of an Old Actor* the somewhat contentious idea that "if there was no *American Drama*, there was what was called *Yankee Drama*."[4] Looking backward, it all depends upon a critic's interests and point of view, but nothing changes the fact that by 1829 there was a growing demand for a national drama.

The most important essay urging a national drama during this early period was written by James Kirke Paulding for Robert Walsh's new *American Quarterly Review*. Titling this work "American Drama," Paulding based his commentary on sixty American plays that he had in his possession. "The want of a National Drama," he wrote, "is the first thing that strikes us in this inquiry."

It was this tone describing a definite need to be fulfilled that would be repeated again and again in Jacksonian America. In this instance Paulding argued for a national drama that would appeal to national feelings, focus on domestic incidents and display "a generous chivalry in the maintenance and vindication of those great and illustrious peculiarities of situation and character by which we are distinguished from all other nations." There was an assertive quality as well as a pleading tone to Paulding's essay, and both characteristics would be repeated during the coming years, though not always to the advantage of this admirable quest.

More forcefully and astutely than his contemporaries, Paulding outlined the problems facing American dramatists. He felt a general decline in the "dignity and usefullness of the stage," caused, he contended, by the tendency of theatre managers to cater to low public tastes, the excesses of the star system and the lack of a national drama. The general tone of his observations, however, was optimistic. He clearly envisioned a potential for an American national drama which, he argued, must have "national encouragement." That was a first requisite for producing a national drama. The second involved a more delicate plea: "a little more taste and liberality in the managers of our theatres." The third required "the presence of competent performers, collected in companies of sufficient strength to give effectual support to a new piece, and sufficient talent to personate an original character, without resorting to some hacknied model."[5] In addition to other barriers to success, these three areas of concern—lack of encouragement, management and audience control, and inadequate performers—haunted the progress of the American playwright until well after the Civil War.

The lack of anything becomes a will-o'-the-wisp. There was, however, "little encouragement for dramatic writing" in America in 1829. With some bitterness concerning his own playwriting, archcynic, writer and critic John Neal so stated and added in his customary temper that America had done little for the drama except import bad English actors, build second-rate theatres and produce English plays without regard for "expense or propriety."[6] It is easy to point out negative attitudes toward American playwrights and their work. "We never will allow," complained a critic in *The Irish Shield and Monthly Hilenan*, "that the cackling of the stupid geese of the Hudson is as melodious as the song of the tragic swans of the Thames."[7] Reviewing *Tortesa the Usurer* by the popular New York essayist Nathaniel Parker Willis, a writer for the *Boston Quarterly Review*, a newly established organ for Democratic intellectuals, referred to the work as "a pleasant pastime for an hour when one has no serious calls upon his time or attention and he would be sinning but moderately."[8] This was a period when critics expressed their opinions with a forthright disregard for human feelings and apparently enjoyed the sometimes venomous give-and-take of journalistic combat, but more damaging than the expressed criticisms were the negative assumptions. "Let a thing be never so good," warned a critic for *Ariel*, "if it is of American origin, it runs great risk of failure from that cause alone—so strongly is this community tinctured with a rage for foreign novelties."[9] Such anti-American attitudes were difficult to overcome: hence, the pleas for tolerance and generosity by Paulding and others.

Special pleading, however, breeds the problems that are inherent in this weak form of argumentation. There is always the undeniable good sense expressed by a writer for the *National Register* as early as 1817 that "we are not in the least disposed to encourage nonsense because it is native."[10] Yet there must be opportunity—for either success or failure. Although generous reviewers understood and promoted this necessary approach to good playwriting, it was generally disregarded by theatre managers. To offset strong anti-American attitudes in 1829 Edwin Forrest asked Propser M. Wetmore to write a prologue for *Metamora* which would nudge his first-night audience with a gentle challenge:

> While thus your plaudits cheer the stranger lay,
> Shall native pens in vain the field essay?
> To-night we test the strength of native powers,
> Subject, and bard, and actor, all are ours—
> 'Tis yours to judge, if worthy of a name,
> And bid them live within the halls of fame![11]

An epilogue for the play written by James Lawson, poet and playwright, made a forthright plea. Clearly apprehensive of the critic who "looks so severe" and works "to find a fault," Lawson appealed to the audience:

> Here come I, then, to plead with nature's art,
> And speak, less to the law, than to the heart.
> A native bard—a native actor too,
> Have drawn a native picture to your view; . . . [12]

Obvious and ingenuous, yet often repeated, this technique accomplished little in promoting either a particular play or the cause of an American national drama.

Another questionable yet frequently practiced technique to promote actors and plays was the ancient art of puffing, creating unwarranted praise for a work, something along the line of Curtis Chunk's comment about his former girl-friend Jedidah who, he came to realize, had "been marked at for more than her heft" (*The Stage-Struck Yankee*, sc. i). Critics for the *Spirit of the Times* were as guilty as others and generally favored the so-called legitimate dramas, that is, conventional tragedy and comedy. When Nathaniel Parker Willis' *Bianca Visconti* was produced at the Park Theatre in 1837, the *Spirit* wrote: "We will risk our judgment and our taste on the production of its complete and triumphant success. . . . Take our word for it; it is altogether a most exquisite thing, and will be personated in the style of excellence that will astonish everyone."[13] Throughout this period, as throughout much of the history of drama, critics and essayists complained about puffing. The editor of the *Boston Weekly Magazine* in 1817 identified the "well trained house-dogs who shew their teeth to all but their master . . . the highest bidder" and realized the consequences in a useless contemporary dramatic criticism.[14] Upon assuming the editorship of *Ariel*, Edmund Morris stated his contempt for puffing.[15] The editor for the *Spirit of the Times* chose to rise above the "general system of puffing," or at least pretended to hold this position.[16] Ten years later, in the *Brooklyn Eagle* of February 8, 1847, Walt Whitman condemned the "miserable state of the stage" and described all dramatic notices at the Bowery, Chatham and Olympic theatres as "the slaves of the paid puffing system."[17]

Sympathetic to cries for an American national drama and eager to help, editors and critics sometimes made claims of merit that did not find support in the production. As puffing became more common in dramatic criticism, it became confused with an editor's honest desire to encourage American playwrights, with the result that theatre patrons looked to actors and theatre managers (also guilty of extravagant advertising) for their standards. The answer was simple, but it took nearly a hundred years to be realized. The "New York Gossip" columnist in *Brother Jonathan* struck the right tone in 1842: "Let literary men devote their pens more carefully to dramatic criticism, and I fancy the public interest would be brought back to theatricals, and legitimate drama would no longer be obliged to give place to the circus."[18]

For this earlier time, however, the plea for generosity from critics which became associated with puffing involved a more delicate moral concern than paid dishonesty. Writing about a performance of Richard Penn Smith's *The Deformed* in early 1830, the critic for *Ariel*, a conservative, moral English-oriented magazine, stated that the play had "met with very kindly critics and is pronounced a successful effort of the American muse." As he continued, however, the writer posed an astute question concerning American playwrights. "How far we are polite enough, and old enough as a nation, to patronize playwrights, is a question which seems likely to be tested by the experience of this author."[19] It was a good point. Given its position as a developing nation, what could America afford to do? What should its critics do? Should they be generous or severe? Can one be encouraging and yet not patronizing? Here was a problem, obviously, but one that Smith's experience in 1830 would not test adequately. It was not the time, nor was Philadelphia the place. The testing, in fact, would have to be done by mass activity, and later in the history of the nation.

Although reviewers did not always contend intelligently with the appropriate questions or even hold to the standards which they emblazoned across the pages of their essays and journals, the nation under the protracted sway of Jacksonian democracy did not lack for critics and journal editors. Two of the most important critical commentators on American dramatic literature when Jackson took office were John Neal and Robert Walsh.

A man of very strong opinions and fiery disposition, John Neal (1793–1876) was an established novelist and critic in 1829. During an earlier two-year association with William Blackwood in England, he had written the essay for which American readers knew him best: a five-part evaluation of 120 American writers.[20] It is consistent with Neal's temperament that he allotted the greatest space to John Neal. Returning to America in 1827, he settled in Portland, Maine, and started a weekly magazine, *Yankee*, on January 1, 1828, changing the name the following August to *The Yankee; and Boston Literary Gazette*, which became a monthly in December of 1829. Neal's criticism was highly regarded by Poe as well as Longfellow, Whittier, Hawthorne, Lowell and Whitman. Having met and befriended James Hackett, Neal made a second attempt to write for the stage—*Otho* had appeared in 1819—in response to Hackett's request for a Yankee farce to support his success in *The Lion of the West*. The year was 1834, and Hackett cautiously but finally rejected Neal's three-act melodrama entitled *Our Ephraim; or, The New Englanders, a What-d'ye-call it?* The hero was, indeed, a genuine Yankee, but by this time Hackett could afford to be selective. Neal's own publication of his play in *New England Galaxy* in 1835–1836 confirms Hackett's observation that Neal was "a clever man but a very *bad* dramatist."[21]

In the August 1829 issue of *Yankee; and Boston Literary Gazette* Neal started a series of five essays on "The Drama." The first essay was concerned with "Strictures Of Dramatic Writing, Theatrical Representation And The Laws of the Drama, generally interspersed with remarks on writers and performers, in illustration."[22] Neal thoroughly enjoyed the drama, finding it a "generous, highhearted offspring" of man. Understanding the limitations forced upon native writers in 1829, he expected little but saw good potential and obviously wanted a national drama, "a drama that is peculiar to our country and dramatic of ourselves." As an iconoclast he asked for comedies and tragedies written in "common language"—"not perhaps of common every-day life, such as we hear in the market place or by the way-side; but in the language of that life which is intended to be pictured for us." "Catastrophe," he wrote, "will be more of a domestic nature," in this country where "all men are alike in their crowns and scepters." As a playwright, he felt that the "purposes and powers" of the drama should "be consecrated to the great uses of morality." These were meaningful "strictures" for contemporary playwrights and reveal the insight necessary for the beginnings of a substantial dramatic criticism.

Neal's low opinions of native American plays resulted from his insistence that truly American characters be presented. To his mind there were none in 1829, only "wretched automata"—identified by dress or a phrase or two, and no life that could be recognized. He also criticized writers for imitating the English—"we are not like the English"—and for neglecting the unities. Mainly, however, he emphasized language. Men, he complained, do not talk poetry— and "when a person talks beautifully in his sorrow, it shows both great preparation and insincerity." Sixty years later W. D. Howells would be considered an innovator for saying the same thing. "Our writers," Neal explained in his second essay on "The Drama," "if they hope to be distinguished for *truth*, will avoid poetry whenever the characters are much in earnest."[23] His final essay on "The Drama" summarized his own wishes for American drama. He wanted fewer stage effects—no ghosts, no grotesque murders. Here he obviously disagreed with the theatre of his time and contradicted himself in his own work. He wanted humble life as a source of genuine tragedy, morality without preachment, the love of father and daughter or father and son rather than sexual love. He wanted actors to speak in prose.

Eventually, all of his desires would be fulfilled, but audiences were not ready in 1829. "Nothing short of a thorough *revolution in plays and players, authors and actors*," he wrote, "can save the drama from general abhorrence and contempt." [24] Such a statement is vintage Neal. Revolutions in art and politics generally do not occur with the vigor or speed he demanded, particularly where there are so many distinct elements of society involved. In 1829 John Neal was one of the early firebrands of a revolution that was still in progress sixty years later.

Robert Walsh (1784–1859), editor and journalist, constantly defended in print what he considered to be the best interests of America. During a time of powerful editors, the influence of people such as Neal, Sarah Josepha Hale, George P. Morris, Nathaniel Parker Willis and Epes Sargent has never been adequately assessed. No less influential than his contemporaries, from 1820 through 1836 Walsh voiced his opinions with the intense energy and marked intellect that identified his lifelong work. He edited the *National Gazette and Library Register* throughout this period, held a professorial chair of general literature at the University of Pennsylvania from 1819 to 1828, and edited the *American Quarterly Review* from 1827 until 1836. It was for the first volume of this magazine (June 1827) that James Kirke Paulding wrote an article on "American Drama," an assignment by Walsh which underscored his own importance to the genre. A political as well as literary force, Walsh's thoughts are well illustrated in *Didactics: Social, Literary, and Political* (1836), a two-volume collection of his essays written from 1810 through 1836. Two of the essays in volume 1 deal with theatre: "The Stage" and "Tragic Acting." Like other editors and journalists, Walsh wanted a well-regulated stage and responsible actors who would "engage the minds of a large portion of the community." "The theatre," he wrote in "The Stage," "will subsist and flourish, in spite of all reasoning levelled at its morality. It is connected with the habits of civilized society, and has, indeed, prevailed at all times and in all nations not absolutely barbarous." [25] His perceptive observations bear rereading.

Throughout the Age of Jackson, certain magazine editors stated their policy with regard to theatrical productions and American plays in particular. Edmund Morris, editor of *Ariel*, took a serious view of drama and constantly tried to maintain the high standards in which he obviously believed: "We would not have our readers suppose that we are opposed to theatre, as such, but only to the abuse of the name. . . . But when managers, to attract a crowd, draw lotteries because there is no other attraction and play plays which would make a virtuous woman blush, utter oaths and imprecations with all the native grace of stable boys, then we say the theatre is not what it ought to be, and consequently should not be encouraged."[26] Good drama was also moral drama to Morris, and he resented the tendency toward salacious opportunism that appealed to some theatre managers. Paulding had shared Morris' irritation.

More sympathetic to the call for a national drama and optimistic toward an American potential, the editor of the *North American Magazine* provided the following policy statement in 1832 under the heading "Dramatic Literature":

Like every other department of American literature, the Drama, until a very recent period, had never soared beyond the tamest mediocrity. The feeble and crude essays of writers unacquainted either with theatrical effects or the human heart, have, heretofore, secured for us in Europe little save derision and abuse. Plays, manufactured from popular novels, can never advance or adorn a national dramatic literature. Daring thought, earnest feeling, the strength and independence of our republican institutions must pervade every intellectual enterprise of this country, or all our exploits will be contrasted, to our detriment, with the elaborate achievements of the old, established, and haughty monarchists beyond the waters. We rejoice to see the spirit of a great people awakening; we rejoice to witness the emanations of intellect, that retires awhile from professional toils and devotes its energies, apparently as a divertisement, to the foundation of a difficult but beautiful department of literature. We welcome all aspirants to the honor of dramatists: and shall cheerfully devote a portion of our time and work to a just examination of their several productions.[27]

Unfortunately, that just examination did not materialize during the Age of Jackson and is now long overdue.

Of the newspapers and magazines that reviewed theatre productions, none had broader coverage than William Porter's New York publication, *Spirit of the Times*, which first appeared in 1831 and continued throughout the Age of Jackson. With its attention to the various theatres in New York and its correspondents from other cities as well as a willingness to reprint theatre reviews from American and London newspapers, it is an extremely valuable resource. While attempting to maintain high critical standards, it also acknowledged a generosity towards American playwrights whether their interests were strictly literary or leaned towards a commercial reward. Perhaps the general tolerance for puffing in the mid-1830s stimulated the editor of the *Spirit of the Times* to clarify that paper's approach to dramatic criticism. "The opinion seems to be getting relevant in certain circles that an editor should never touch on theatrical matters but to commend, and that when he cannot praise he should hold his peace." The *Spirit* editor clearly disagreed and proceeded to state his intentions in reviewing theatrical performances:

1. to give all strangers to our boards a generous welcome,
2. to notice *comparatively* the different theatrical establishments,
3. to discuss the demerits as well as the merits of our stock companies,
4. to treat the performance of stars with true candor, and

5. to advocate the productions of Dramatic Writers before they are presented to the public, and as we shall indulge most liberally in praise of whatever we think there is even a remote chance of success, so we shall be slow to condemn any play after its enactment, unless we are convinced of its having received at the hands of those attempting its personation such diligent study and effective representation as can leave no question in our minds of its utter worthlessness or its entire unfitness for the stage.[28]

The final item clearly suggests a very favorable disposition toward American playwrights which is forthrightly given and borne out in countless reviews in the pages of the *Spirit*. Distrustful of theatre managers and lax performers and determined to be fair to American playwrights, the editor promised "to render this paper a medium of correct theatrical intelligence throughout the United States and to secure for the contents of its columns confidence in their honesty and impartiality." It was a cogent statement, promising artistic integrity thoroughly in keeping with the persuasive philosophy of Jacksonian America: to gain customers and make a profit.

As always, however, "correct theatrical intelligence," or any response to a work of art, depended upon the attitudes and beliefs of the critics. The country was changing in 1829. Not only was a new society being born but also a new independent economic order where private morality and business morality were at odds. Consequently, conflicts abounded and the disenchantment of intellectuals, which appeared to begin in 1829 with Jackson's administration, epitomized some of the problems. Oliver Wendell Holmes described the New England intellectuals as a "great procession of the unloved" who hid their affections behind a wall of pretense.[29] Writers of all literary genres shared this feeling of disaffection, and while some literary critics were calling for a national literature, others looked for excellence only among the English writers. In all seriousness, the editor of *Ariel* could defer to England. "We prefer dependence for a little longer on the Mother Country for plays and players," he confided to his readers in 1830. "When we conquer all our forests, it will be time enough for our population to *play*."[30] The view was thoroughly consistent with the anti-intellectual, worker-oriented agrarian philosophy of Jacksonianism, but it was devastating for the development of an American drama.

The American playwright was also held hostage by moralists who made their opinions clear throughout the century, as critics, fathers and preachers. Edmund Morris' strong sentiments were echoed by a writer in *The Hopkinsian Magazine* who decried the "innocent amusement" presented in theatres as promoting intemperance, extravagant, false notions—"Where vice is held up to applause and virtue is degraded"—and lasciviousness. "I charge you," the writer warned his readers, to "bid [your son] *beware of the theatre*."[31] Writing his *Letters on Practical Subjects to a Daughter* (1834), William Buell Sprague could accept the theatre as a possible place to study human characters but objected to the vulgarity, licentiousness and impropriety that one frequently found there and concluded that young ladies should not attend the theatre.[32] It was common for

critics to demand morals in plays and to complain if they found none. One reviewer of Epes Sargent's *Change Makes Change* charged that the play did "not
propound one moral, nor does it display any knowledge of the world beneath
the surface."[33] His conclusion that the only purpose of the play was "to amuse"
was, in his mind, a thorough condemnation. Although the stage and the pulpit
shared many goals and techniques, the antagonism of the church toward the
theatre was frequently an issue in various publications, and no one tried to make
his point more dramatically than the Reverend Lyman Beecher when he changed
the Tremont Theatre in Boston to the Tremont Temple.

Although the lack of encouragement for native dramatists bothered certain
critics and undoubtedly had an effect upon the literary people who attempted to
write for the stage, those dramatists who had few illusions concerning the power
of critics found difficulties elsewhere. The art of playwriting has always been
an elusive quality to understand or to assess—for the moment, for an actor, for
a theatre manager, or for a particular audience. Basically, of course, one writes
for an audience, but what was the American audience? Was it completely unen-
lightened as some critics contended, elitist as the Park Theatre management
pretended, or simply demanding of spectacular amusement? Clearly, it was all
of the above, and theatre managements in America soon determined their audiences and sought to please them. Playwrights also had to learn this lesson for,
as B. Franklyn, Jr., explained in 1832, "there are no patrons of literature and
learning in America."[34] Thus the kind of drama produced by American playwrights was controlled, as it has always been, by the people they had to please.
"It is the play-going community that must decide whether the native dramatists
shall receive an equivalent [patronage] for the exercise of their abilities," declared the *Spirit of the Times*.[35] Or, from another point of view, "it is in the
people to restore the theatre to its primitive purity and decorum. Managers, to
make money, must cater to poor public taste . . . to suit the fashion of their
customers, or to attract by novelty."[36]

It became easy for critics to blame audiences for the kind of plays produced
and, consequently, for the difficulties a potentially good dramatist must face.
Writing about the "Decline of the Modern Drama"—always a popular topic in
dramatic criticism—a critic for the *New England Magazine* complained that it
was "to the pit and gallery that he [the playwright] must appeal." Seeing "no
reason to doubt that there is as much dramatic talent extant in this as there has
been in any human age, excepting that of Shakespeare," the critic indignantly
blamed a "vicious and depraved" public taste for the decline he envisioned.[37]
The *Spirit of the Times* added its condemnation of "the apathy and the gross
ignorance of the public that really degrades the drama."[38] Such comments are
scattered through theatre criticism during the Age of Jackson and refer to the
blatant popularity of spectacular melodrama that epitomized the theatre of the
period and the boisterous farce that scandalized the moralists.

In whatever manner the theatre, the play or the actor or actress was identified, the trappings of spectacular melodrama were usually prominent. Hundreds

of apocalyptic melodramas appeared on the stage of the Bowery Theatre between 1835 and 1850 with leading actors playing the avenger or the villain whose
acts would be enhanced by witch or ghost scenes and primeval rituals. Here is
a sample comment from the theatre critic of the *Spirit of the Times*: "The rage
for spectacle and pageant is at its height at this house. After interest felt in
Ivanhoe began to flag, another grand equestrian drama was produced, called
Marmion, founded upon the poem, of course. The piece embraces all the ac-
cessories of terrific combats, tableaux, red fire, etc., and requires for its representation a stud of over thirty horses. We need not say that it has been successful."[39] The previous month another important spectacle was presented on
the stage of the Howard Athenaeum in Boston where "Jack Sheridan, the celebrated teacher of boxing, appeared in the character of Rolla in *Pizarro*. It was
a droll personation surely, and the pugilist no doubt felt keenly that he was not
in his favored element."[40] Spectacle of any kind was clearly a drawing card
for audiences, as another reviewer for the *Spirit* noted in February of 1849:
"Our worthy citizens have a perfect mania for gigantic performances, musical
festivals, monster concerts and all that sort of thing, and the success of an entertainment depends more upon the size of the wording of the bill than in the
intrinsic merits of the performance."[41]

Spectacles existed in the theatre because spectacle was demanded by audiences. Generally, this was translated into melodrama at eight, but farces and
extravaganzas were also appreciated. Although interest in stage classics, particularly the plays of Shakespeare, was governed by the performer who created
the spectacle, some contemporary critics felt that audiences whose snobbery made
them view spectacular melodrama and melodramatic plays as terms of reproach
were only fooling themselves. "Is not *Macbeth*," wrote a critic in the *Spirit of
the Times*, "a melodramatic play, in the strictest sense of the term? We have
music, spectacle, combats, supernatural agents, ghosts and machinery, all essential to and productive of *effect*. Is not *Hamlet* a mix of melo-drama? O, no!
that is Shakespeare. So it is not the name of the play, but the name of the writer,
that decides it."[42]

No matter how sophisticated certain critics would have theatre audiences be,
no matter how much certain elements of society demanded the legitimate drama—
that is, tragedy and English comedy—the people to whom theatre really appealed wanted something else: spectacle, melodrama, farce, excitement! Successful actors and actresses flourished in Jacksonian America because they were
entertainers. Forrest and Cushman, for example, were essentially melodramatic—strong, direct and representative of masculine America. Managers of
theatres had to please, not the editors, reviewers and armchair critics of the
theatre, but audiences. Otherwise, they went bankrupt, as an astonishing number of managers did every year. Even Bostonians, who could take artistic offense as quickly as any people in America and whose English-leaning idiosyncrasies and elite self-awareness were well advertised, could not falsify theatre
conditions, according to the correspondent for the *Spirit of the Times*:

[Bostonians] decry New York because she patronizes the melo-drama, and ornaments the stage with *quadrupedal* performers from cattle-fairs, rope-dancers, political-speeches, natural curiosities, contortionists, French legs, wild beasts and learned pigs, blue light and brimstone. They call vociferously for the "*legitimate drama.*" "Give us the *legitimate drama,*" they cry, "and have done with this gagging melo-drama!" The newspapers echo the cry, and waste ink and paper in long tirades against the very useful, but very, *very* vicious melo-drama, and *Madame Kickshoes* is reviled because the public will have her show her legs in an excellent ballet. The poor manager, thus beset, wonders at the transcendancy of the age, and forthwith bows to the sovereign will of the people.[43]

The sarcasm in the correspondent's tone is well balanced by the truth of his statement. With melodrama and farce theatre managers kept their doors open, and dramatists could do no better than to respond to the same drummer.

If there was a "tyranny of the majority," in the words of Tocqueville, it did not affect the power, wealth and status of fashionable society, which generally kept to itself. In an admirable work entitled *Riches, Class and Power Before the Civil War*, Edward Pessen explodes the myth that has guided historians to believe that Emerson's preachments concerning self-reliance actually combined with Ned Buntline's romantic stories and the efforts of the "damned mob of scribbling women" that haunted Nathaniel Hawthorne to produce a society of self-made wealthy men.[44] By and large, it did not work that way. A class society did, however, create the need for distinct theatres in large cities like New York. On the one hand, there was a fashionable society that founded clubs, gave spectacular balls and fêtes, went on excursions, organized elaborate musical evening entertainments and enjoyed Italian opera and the offerings of certain theatres such as the Park Theatre and the National Theatre. These very wealthy people included few writers and dramatists. In his watercolor entitled "Fashionable New Yorkers at the Park Theatre" (November 1822), John Searles included only Mordecai M. Noah and James K. Paulding from the recognized literary world, both of whom were eminent figures in politics. Among the playwrights in Jacksonian America, only Charles J. Ingersoll and Robert T. Conrad had incomes substantial enough to be listed in Pessen's study.

In contrast to the demanding inhabitants of the pit and gallery, fashionable society made other choices for entertainment, choices which rarely promoted a native American drama. From among the members of that wealthy society history has the advantage of the observations of Philip Hone, who kept a diary from 1828 to his death in 1851 and detailed much of the social, political and popular events of the day.[45] Theatre was one of Hone's passions, and at one time he lived diagonally across the square from the Park Theatre. Throughout this period he went to the theatre, mostly the Park or the National, but almost never to see an American play or an American actor or actress. Mainly, he showed his fascination for English drama and English performers—Kean, Charles Kemble and Fanny Kemble, Tyrone Power, James Wallack, Ellen Tree, Macready, and the plays of Sheridan Knowles. He had a good word for *Fashion* and Mrs. Ritchie who was, of course, part of New York society, and he admired Josephine Clifton. He did not, however, like Nathaniel Parker Willis' *Bianca Visconti* (August 25, 1837) in spite of paying "uninterrupted and critical attention to it."

Never did he discuss the popular melodramas or farces such as *A Glance at New York*, although he understood that "the people will be amused; they must have some way of passing their evenings besides poking the fire and playing with the children." For him, at the time of this observation (November 11, 1841), the theatre did

not seem to be exactly the right thing. When it revives a little and raises its head, the legitimate drama, good honest tragedy, comedy and opera, has to encounter a host of competitors, ready to administer to a vitiated public taste. The good is mixed up with the bad. Shakespeare and Jim Crow come in equally for their share of condemnation, and the stage is indiscriminatingly immoral, irreligious, and what is much worse, unfashionable. But the good folks as well as the bad must be amused, and at the present time lecturers are all in the vogue.

Hone's attitude, however, was not frivolous, and he enjoyed dining with and listening to the stories of Thomas Rice, the impersonator of Jim Crow, and Samuel Lover, the author of the story entitled "Handy Andy," as much as he did his evenings with James Wallack and Sheridan Knowles. He did not enjoy Edwin Forrest, perhaps because of Forrest's pro-Jackson politics as much as his acting, and described the Astor Place Riot in some detail, noting the problem existing between Macready and Forrest "but with no cause, that I can discover, except that one is a gentleman, and the other is a vulgar, arrogant loafer, with a pack of kindred rowdies at his heels" (May 8, 1849).

Although Hone was nationalistic in defending his American rights according to his Whig principles and could feel pride in the popularity of American actors in England—once even, "to help along a lonesome evening," visiting Palmo's Opera House to see the "Ethiopian Serenaders" (August 4, 1837)—he and his social class not only largely ignored attempts by American dramatists but by their habits of theatre attendance actively discouraged such efforts. While it might be expected that an intellectual and fashionable class would promote the nationalistic literature of which the drama should be a part, the divided politics of Jacksonian America seemed to force Holmes' "unloved" generation away from a nationalistic endeavor that might otherwise have held some appeal. Unfortunately, as it was, the elite neither tolerated the commercial efforts of the journeyman playwrights nor encouraged the literary efforts of their own upper class.

Writing plays to suit the tastes of audiences is part of the successful playwrights' task. Pleasing critics is not always the same thing, although generally necessary, but playwrights in Jacksonian America faced another melancholy fact that was frequently decried by the critics. The star system required that a playwright who was serious about getting a play produced "must compose pieces not so much for the purpose of 'holding up to nature' as to suit the fancies of actors, a thing about as ridiculous as would be the writing of books to suit the tastes of compositors."[46] Critics resented the fact that actors became the arbiters of dramatic taste in America and frequently had the final word by emphasizing that flagrant abuse by actors that added another burden to the playwright's art and another barrier to his or her success.

A portion of a review of N. P. Willis' *Bianca Visconti* illustrates this problem, describing accurately many theatre performances of this period and showing why serious writers had artistic difficulties creating for their contemporary theatre.

Now followed many scenes developing the plot of the tragedy, which was most barbarously murdered for the simple reason that those to whom parts were assigned had not condescended to commit them to memory, and thus passages were omitted, and line after line, utterly marred, and in fact, the sense perverted or rendered nonsense. An author subject to such an ordeal as this was must have some stamina, we take it, to escape unscathed. But fortunately, so outrageous was their imperfection in this instance, that the audience, though ignorant of the text, were pretty well assured they were not listening to poetry or reason, and attributing the fact to the true cause, their sympathies for the suffering author were greatly excited and rendered them lenient to any real imperfection the play might present.[47]

Willis had similar complaints about *The Kentucky Heiress*, and his was not a singular experience.

Some years earlier a critic for *The Ariel* argued that actors frequently introduced "extraneous matter, not only ill-timed and out of place, but frequently offensive and injudicious."[48] Burlesquing actors in his play entitled *The Candid Critic*, Epes Sargent pictures his playwright suffering as he sees "the children of my brain / Dismembered, mangled, strangled, torn and swallowed / By those word butchers" (Sc. 1). The editor of the *Parlour Review and Journal of Music, Literature and Fine Arts* wrote in "Thoughts on Theatres as They Are:

It is no wonder that we find the field of dramatic literature utterly abandoned by the master-spirits of the age, that acting itself is so little improved as an art, and that the very existence of our national drama is at stake. Indeed, no author of spirit or talent will submit to the degrading and vexatious treatment he is absolutely sure of encountering at the hands of our theatrical dictators—the trifling criticisms, the unmannerly objections, and, worse than all, the tasteless mutilations his piece is certain of suffering till, like Deiphobos, in Virgil, the poet can scarcely distinguish one original feature of his offerings. It is degrading that an author should have more to apprehend from the actors than from the audience—yet it is so.[49]

One of the principal causes of "the degradation of the dramatic literature of the present day," according to the editors of *New England Magazine* in 1835, was "the prevailing practice of writing exclusively for popular actors or Stars."[50] Years later, people were saying the same thing, even theatre people. At the first annual dinner of the American Dramatic Fund Association in the spring of 1849, Thomas Hamblin, a theatre manager of considerable reputation, said that the star system had militated against the drama and caused its decline. "For a number of years past," he said, "it has been the custom to invite an audience to see some great actor *instead of the play*, and all parts of the play have been disregarded except that which the 'bright particular' star of the evening was to perform."[51] Such complaints, however, did not change the theatre.

If critics, audiences, and callous actors were not enough to intimidate the fledgling American dramatists, there was the additional problem, peculiar to America at this time, of the theatre manager who was more frequently than not an Englishman who employed English actors and actresses to perform English plays. In 1836 the *Spirit of the Times* published a long article listing the English managers of American theatres. The Park, the Bowery, the Franklin, the National, and the Richmond Hill in New York were managed by Englishmen, as were the Tremont, Warren and Lion in Boston, four theatres in Philadelphia and two in New Orleans. The writer concluded that "out of sixty theatres in the United States that are open for definite periods annually there are not above ten Americans associated in their management."[52] Although the custom decreased as years went by, it was better business for these managers to go to England each year to recruit actors and actresses and to produce English plays free of royalties (there being no international copyright agreement in America) than to pay American dramatists to write for their theatres. It is equally logical that resentment of this activity was not confined to American playwrights. American actors and actresses, of whom there were relatively few who could be termed stars, felt abused by the system and its managers, although it must be pointed out, as did the editor of the *Spirit*, that English managers and English actors and actresses did a great deal to build the American theatre.

The American people, too, were partially to blame for the condition of the theatre—if "blame" is the proper word—because the Anglophile snobbery that responded favorably only to English literature also demanded English plays and performers. Other Americans had different views. The Ferren Riot in July of 1834, which Edwin Forrest helped to quell, and the Astor Place Riot of 1849, in which he played a part, were inspired by nationalistic sentiments. It was a difficult and ambivalent situation which is clearly revealed in the *Spirit*'s declaration in 1837 that it would welcome strangers to its theatre while showing an abundant tolerance for American playwriting efforts.

The problem was not so much the number of plays written in England versus the number of plays produced by Americans as the simple preference of American theatre managers and certain audiences for English plays. Hundreds of dramatists wrote for the English stage, but plays by the following found their way most frequently across the Atlantic: Douglas Jerrold, Richard Brinsley Peake, Sheridan Knowles, W. T. Moncrieff, Thomas Noon Talfourd, J. R. Planché, B. F. Rayner, Edward Bulwer-Lytton, George Dibdin, John Maddison Morton, Charles Selby, John Buckstone, Edward Fitzball and John W. Marston. During this same period in America there were upwards of seventy-five Americans who had some interest in seeing their plays produced. Of these, nearly thirty could be considered serious playwrights who wrote at least four plays that were staged.

Throughout this period one of the most serious handicaps for a developing American literature, including the drama, was the lack of adequate copyright protection. From the 1820s until 1891 when America signed an international copyright agreement, American writers and dramatists vigorously protested the lack of protection for their artistry and periodically assailed congressmen for their cavalier attitudes. It was a cause that attracted dozens of supporters during the Age of Jackson, writers such as James Fenimore Cooper, John Neal, Robert Montgomery Bird, Henry W. Longfellow, even English writers like Charles Dickens, who visited America, in part, to protest the stealing of his stories by American publishers. This lack of copyright protection also developed a minor industry in which the pirating of other people's work became a fine art. All writers felt the need for protection, but dramatists experienced a particular agony as they generally received only a pittance for works that made fortunes for actors and managers like Edwin Forrest and Thomas Hamblin.

In an essay published in 1836 the *Spirit of the Times* explained this agony in blunt terms:

The question we hold is yet to be decided, whether native dramatists can successfully compete with their contemporaries abroad. In the present state of the American laws of copy-right, in our opinion, they cannot, without the additional outlay consequent upon the production of original pieces here be met by a corresponding degree of support from that many-headed monster, the public, of whose patriotic feeling and taste, sooth to say, we have no very exalted opinion.[53]

It was a foregone conclusion that American dramatists could not compete unless they took certain precautions which were even then seldom effective. Joseph Jones, a popular dramatist of the period, defended his position in a letter dated "Boston, October 1855," printed in a preface to the 1855 publication of *Moll Pitcher; or, The Fortune Teller of Lynn*, a four-act melodrama: "I have objections to publishing my plays; one, that they were written to be acted to the people and not to be read by them; another that by publication I lost my ownership, copyright giving no protection against representation upon the stage." His experiences were similar to those of other successful playwrights, and he explained that his play *The Carpenter of Rouen* "had not only been acted in nearly every theatre in America without consent, but in many of the theatres of Great Britain. The author has never received one dollar of remuneration." At a time when profit was exalted and the common man was arguing through labor reform movements that work should be rewarded appropriately, why should the efforts of the playwright be slighted? "It is often asked," Jones continued, "why there is no standard America drama. One of the best answers is, nobody will pay for it." In 1855 Jones' "pecuniary interests" were not in the theatre, but he was indignant that the inventors of "Patent corkscrews" had protection denied playwrights who might with their work create a "Home Drama which would become creditable to our literature, and profitable to authors, managers, and actors."[54] Such were the opinions of a man of the theatre, a man thoroughly involved in the Jacksonian business world and a writer with pride in his work and a realistic view of his objectives.

The most avid dramatist among the proponents of copyright protection for America was Cornelius Mathews, whose contemporary popularity earned him the title of "Father of American Drama." At a dinner for Charles Dickens at the City Hotel in New York on February 19, 1842, the twenty-four year old Mathews delivered an impassioned speech on the desirability of a copyright agreement, a topic very dear to Dickens. "What, sir," Mathews said, "is the present condition of the field of letters in America? It is in a state of desperate anarchy—without order, without system, without certainty."[55] In June he gave another speech, "An Appeal to American Authors and the American Press on Behalf of International Copyright." He helped found the Copyright Club in 1843, and prepared an essay on "The Better Interests of the Country in Connexion with International Copyright."[56] Although Dion Boucicault receives much of the credit for the passage of a law (August 18, 1856) which gave the dramatist "The sole right to print, publish, act, perform or represent" a dramatic composition, Mathews was supporting a law in 1844 "That Dramatic Pieces (as defined in Sec. S. 2 of the Bill) should be protected against theatrical representations as well as against being reprinted.[57] For nearly twenty years, beginning in 1838, Mathews voiced his opinions about copyright, a national literature, New York society, politics, theatre, and man's condition in general with a self-assurance that brought him friends and foes alike.

By 1849, copyright protection was a burning issue and one argued with some rancor by the *Spirit* under the heading "Dramatic Copyright": "The appeals of such an unfortunate class of people as authors rarely meet with anything like sympathy from the grave and reverend seigneurs who direct the affairs of our mighty nation." After berating negligent congressmen, the *Spirit* editor complained that "there is in our country no copyright whatever for dramatic productions—no protection against the stealing and reproduction of any piece which may emanate from a native brain. It may with justice be said that as yet we have no dramatic authors, or at least but few, who have made any sensation, or coined money in the theatrical world." He went on to explain the control by actors such as Forrest, the fear of dramatists to publish their works and the resulting loss to the reading public. "As long as the present state of things continues," the *Spirit* threatened, "we shall present the singular spectacle of a nation reputed among the best educated in the world, destitute of a dramatic literature."[58] There is no question that a lack of copyright had some effect on the establishment of a dramatic literature in America. At this time, however, it was only one of several deterrents to the drama, and partial copyright relief would come in the next decade.

At the beginning as at the end of the Age of Jackson there was an expressed need for a national drama. Other than an understanding of the barriers impeding a playwright's progress—the star system, English theatre managers, demanding audiences, critics with religious, moral and Anglophile persuasions, and an irritating lack of concern by Congress to establish adequate copyright protection—little was accomplished to encourage a fulfillment of that frequently expressed need. Yet plays were written that reveal a substantial and exciting potential for the establishment of an American drama. How did it happen? With such a slight possibility for either fame or fortune in the theatre, perhaps the major question should by "why?" Why did people keep writing plays?

Perhaps the simplest answer is the best. As the writer in the *American Masonic Register and Literary Companion* stated, "We might as soon change the nature of man, as obliterate his love for the drama."[59] People wrote plays because plays were necessary for the theatre in which they believed, because they had something to say and because there were people who went to the theatre to be entertained and stimulated. Throughout this twenty-year period from 1829 to 1849, the theatre in America endured many hardships. Theatres closed almost as frequently as they opened, but the theatre was still a primary source of relaxation for Americans even if many of them, either from religious conviction or commercial obsession, considered it a waste of time. Comparatively speaking, a lot of people went to the theatre in those days. In early 1845 the *Spirit of the Times* reported that the

Chatham Theatre had an audience on New Year's night of twenty-seven hundred and ninety-eight persons. The Bowery three thousand and five. The Olympic thirteen hundred, and the Park one thousand and eleven. The Opera seven hundred and fifty. The American Museum fifteen hundred. Peale's five hundred—in all nine thousand eight hundred and fifty-three, and to which probably some ten thousand persons attended other various places of amusement, such as balls, concerts, etc. during the day—a total of nineteen thousand eight hundred and fifty persons.[60]

This was, of course, an accounting on a good night in New York, but there can be no escaping the fact that audiences did exist and that there was a market for plays. So, plays were written; the challenge was for production and profit, a condition and risk thoroughly in keeping with the spirit of Jacksonian America and ever compatible with the theatrical spirit.

Even Robert Montgomery Bird, embittered by his experiences with Edwin Forrest, acknowledged the need for an American drama, and eventually, there would be profit for the dramatist. Although Epes Sargent's dramatization of the

Norma story did not prove successful onstage, it did attract the attention of P. T. Barnum.[61] If some people were bothered by the character of the theatre which, although consistent with the times, by its nature indulged practices that could be considered distasteful or even abhorrent, this quality should not have been overwhelming. Samuel Ward, writing for the *New York Review*, explained this situation very clearly: "The highly wrought fiction and the wild drama accord well now with our existence of increasing excitement. . . . But we are, unhappily, prone to judge all productions of the mind by the touchstone of their effect upon sensations habituated to unnatural excitement."[62] Given the situation, what artistry was better equipped than that of the theatre to exploit these sensations in which many Jacksonians delighted? There were many plays to be performed and eager audiences, even if a part of the citizenry were repelled and the "master-spirits of the stage" refused to contribute to that delight.

There can be no argument that many Americans felt the challenge and the need for a national literature. For this, Sydney Smith deserves a certain amount of recognition and, probably, gratitude. In spite of a stuffy attitude toward lower-class American theatre—such as his disgust at the Bowery Theatre's handbill announcing *Othello; or, The Jealous Nigger* (August 4, 1837)—Philip Hone made this entry in his diary on October 30, 1838: "Whoever reads an American book? was the impertinent question of an English coxcomb." America needed "the expression of a nation's mind in writing," as William Ellery Channing described it in his "Remarks on National Literature";[63] yet Jacksonian America, which might appear fertile for the growth of a national literature, held such divergent views about literature in general, about a national literature, about education even, that the necessary encouragement for dramatists came very slowly.

It is a fact that many writers and artists aligned themselves with the Jacksonian Party—Hawthorne, Bryant, Whitman, Paulding, Hiram Powers, Edwin Forrest, Frances Wright. Some even promoted a political literature and the *Democratic Review* stated clearly in 1837 that "the vital principle of an American national literature must be democracy."[64] Although the wealthy aristocracy in America did not include many writers, those who could cling to the edges of this social elite tended to create a literature derivative of England and Europe. They were generally Whigs who were criticized as being tame and reliable rather than bold and speculative and probably agreed with John Quincy Adams' view that literature was by nature aristocratic.[65] Those members of both political parties who promoted the reforms—such as in education, which could have stimulated an interest in literature and the arts—characteristic of Jacksonian America were invariably members of an upper class, such people as Frances Wright and Robert Dale Owen. The working people seldom had the time or the inclination to participate in or take advantage of the work of the activists for human rights and principles. The indifference, antagonism and conflicting ideas that resulted were not conducive to the promotion of a national literature or drama during the Age of Jackson.

There were, however, noticeable instances of the "national encouragement" that James Kirke Paulding called for in his article on "American Drama" in Walsh's *American Quarterly Review*. Although critics realized the great attraction that anything English held for Americans and could see "how often authors have New York on their paper and London on their mind; and how often actors stand mid Gotham scenes and talk as though they were in Cornhill on the Strand," they could be optimistic.[66] The nation was still young. "The turn which dramatic literature is taking here," wrote the editor of *Ariel* in 1831, "tho to be sure in its infancy, promises well for that species of composition."[67] James Rees, the author of *The Dramatic Authors of America* (1845), a frequently fascinating and valuable, although not always reliable, reference work, was an early champion of the American dramatist. Cornelius Mathews was also very positive about the future of American arts and letters and a larger reading public.

When *Such As It Is* by Joseph M. Field opened at the Park Theatre on September 4, 1842, and failed, the reviewer for the *Spirit of the Times* made some revealing observations:

The comedy is the author's first serious effort as a dramatist, and contains much that is ingenious in plot and impressive and beautiful in language; there are some palpable hits at the follies of the times, and occasional flashes of wit which tell well. But it is written too much like the real life to meet with success upon the stage, where everything must be extravagant, vivid, and broad, to produce interest and effect. Had the author employed more time in maturely digesting and strengthening his plot, and condensing his language, he would have much improved it. We trust he will not be discouraged from making another effort, for many worse productions have been played night after night, and called successful.[68]

This is both the encouraging criticism that the *Spirit* promised native playwrights and a forthright reflection of the requirement of Jacksonian America that playwrights produce spectacle—"extravagant, vivid, and broad"—in some form of farce or melodrama if they wanted to succeed.

At another time, the *Spirit*, noting that Epes Sargent had produced two successful plays with Ellen Tree and Josephine Clifton, felt free to draw certain bold and optimistic conclusions:

The old world, step by step, has been compelled to acknowledge that America can produce authors in almost every branch of literature, not unworthy to cope with her own distinguished children. Our actors have won the applause of those who have beheld Siddons, Kemble, and their talented successors. Our dramatists are last in the field. Let us hope that they are not long destined to be the least; and it is to be desired that, as our other writers (with one or two exceptions) cannot be accused of borrowing assistance from their predecessors "over the water" there may be no ground afforded by the supposition that our dramatists are compelled to seek it.[69]

It would be a long wait before the "old world" would take that necessary final step, but Sargent was one of a dozen American playwrights of the period whose plays inspired hope. As guarded optimism, honest assessment or obvious puffing, such comments can be accepted as part of a national encouragement for native dramatists. As incidents of positive criticism from Jacksonian America, they suggest the generous attitude for which Paulding hoped.

There were also other indications of encouragement. Prize play contests, usually created by actors, stimulated the writing of many plays. Certain theatre managers also were especially kind to native authors. Writing about the Arch Street Theatre in Philadelphia in 1833, for example, the editor of the *North American Review* stressed a little known fact:

Considerable attention has been paid by the managers of this establishment, during the past year, to the presentation of novelties and new pieces ranging under the head of *national drama*. . . . Among the number of *original* pieces brought out at this house, . . . may be enumerated the tragedies of *Oralloossa* by Dr. R. M. Bird; *Dion*, by Dr. T. E. Ware; *Camillus*, by J. B. Phillips, Esq.; *The Ancient Briton*, by J. A. Stone, Esq.; the melodrama *William Penn*, by R. Penn Smith; *Crossing the Delaware*, by A. Turnbull. And the Comedies *The Green Mountain Boy*, by J. S. Jones, Esq. (redramatized in London, and produced during the present engagement of Mr. Hackett); *Rip Van Winkle, Mr. Dubikins*, and *The Kentuckian*, by J. K. Paulding, Esq.[70]

The list continued as the writer mentioned other plays by native writers produced at the Arch Street Theatre that year. Even more important to native playwrights than the words of critics, who were seldom influential in promoting or harming the popularity of a play, these theatre productions were a positive incentive for playwrights.

Throughout the second quarter of the nineteenth century there was a repeated concern for an American drama—a hope and a belief. Margaret Fuller expressed that concern as well as any:

The drama cannot die out: it is a stream that will sink in one place, only to rise to light in another. As it happened successfully in Hindostan, Greece (Rome we cannot count), England, Spain, France, Italy, Germany, so it has yet to appear in New Holland, New Zealand, and among ourselves, where we too shall be made new by a sunrise of our own, when our population shall have settled into a homogenous, national life, and we have attained vigor to walk in our own way, make our own world, and leave off copying Europe.[71]

With belief in their art and the occasional encouragement thrust in their direction, American dramatists fought the good fight, losing the battle but creating startling plays that heralded great promise for the future. Accepting the times, they wrote for actors and actresses, staged the life around them that appealed to audiences, dramatized America through American characters and ideas as well as with foreign themes, and abandoned America, as their imaginations dictated, to write about distant lands and people. The result was a spectacular achievement, on the stage and in theory, that serves as a legacy of the Jackson generation in the development of an American drama.

NOTES

The chapter title is derived from James Kirke Paulding's 1827 essay, "American Drama."

1. Laurence Kitchin, *Mid-Century Drama* (London: Faber and Faber, 1960). Chapter IV, 56–71.

2. W. D. Howells, "Editor's Study," *Harper's New Monthly Magazine*, LXXXIII (August 1891), 479.

3. Lewis Strang, *Players and Plays of the Last Quarter Century*, vol. II (Boston: L. C. Page, 1903), 116–17.

4. Walter M. Leman, *Memories of an Old Actor* (San Francisco: A. Roman Co., 1886), 8.

5. *American Quarterly Review*, I (June 1827), 331–57.

6. *The Yankee; and Boston Literary Gazette*, N.S., II (August 1829), 58.

7. *The Irish Shield and Monthly Hilenan*, X (December 1829), 467–68.

8. *Boston Quarterly Review*, July 1839, 390.

9. *Ariel*, III (May 2, 1829), 5.

10. *National Register*, IV (July 12, 1817), 30.

11. The Prologue was written by Prosper M. Wetmore and spoken by Mrs. Barrett, New Park Theatre, New York, December 15, 1829.

12. The Epilogue was written by James Lawson and spoken by Mrs. Hilson, New Park Theatre, New York, December 15, 1829.

13. *Spirit of the Times*, VII (August 26, 1837), 1.

14. *Boston Weekly Magazine*, I (January 25, 1817), 62.

15. *Ariel*, V (October 22, 1831), 219.

16. *Spirit of the Times*, VII (December 9, 1837), 1.

17. Reprinted in Cleveland Rogers and John Black, eds. *The Gathering of the Forces* (New York: G. P. Putnam's Sons, 1920), II, 310–11.

18. *Brother Jonathan*, December 31, 1842, 538. Quoted in Odette C. Salvaggio, "American Dramatic Criticism, 1830–1860," Ph.D. diss., Florida State University, 1979, 28.

19. *Ariel*, III (February 20, 1830), 176.

20. "American Writers," *Blackwood's Magazine*, XVI (September 1824), 304–11; (October 1824), 415–28; (November 1824), 560–71; XVII (January 1825), 48–69; (February 1825), 186–207.

21. Benjamin Lease, *That Wild Fellow John Neal and the American Literary Revolution* (Chicago: University of Chicago Press, 1972), 186, reproduces Hackett's letter.

22. "The Drama, No. I," *The Yankee; and Boston Literary Gazette*, N.S., II (August 1829), 57–68; quotations from pages 58, 59, 60 and 61.

23. "The Drama, No. II," 139.

24. "The Drama, No. V," 318.

25. *Didactics: Social, Literary, and Political* (Philadelphia: Carey, Lea & Blanchard, 1836), Vol. 1, "The Stage," 103.

26. *Ariel*, III (December 26, 1829), 141.

27. *North American Magazine*, I (November 1832), 1.

28. *Spirit of the Times*, VII (December 9, 1837), 1.

29. Oliver Wendell Holmes, *Elsie Venner* (New York: Grosset & Dunlap Publishers, 1883), 1–5, discusses the Brahmin caste of New England.

30. *Ariel*, III (February 20, 1830), 176.

31. *Hopkinsian Magazine*, III (February 1829), 329.

32. William Buell Sprague, *Letters on Practical Subjects to a Daughter* (New York: D. Appleton & Co., 1834), 128.

33. *Anglo-American, A Journal of Literature, News, Politics, Drama, Fine Arts*, V (October 11, 1845), 596.

34. "Impediments to Knowledge, Literature and Science in the U.S.," *Atlantic Journal and Friend of Knowledge*, I (Winter 1832), 124–26.

35. *Spirit of the Times*, VI (July 2, 1836), 241.

36. *American Masonic Reporter and Literary Companion*, I (April 11, 1840), 250.

37. "Decline of the Modern Drama," *New England Magazine*, VIII (February 1835), 105–7.

38. *Spirit of the Times*, XVII (April 10, 1847), 76.

39. *Spirit of the Times*, XVI (March 28, 1846), 60.

40. *Spirit of the Times*, XVI (February 28, 1846), 12.

41. *Spirit of the Times*, XVIII (February 10, 1849), 612.

42. *Spirit of the Times*, XVII (April 10, 1847), 77.

43. *Spirit of the Times*, VIII (September 15, 1838), 1.

44. Edward Pessen, *Riches, Class and Power Before the Civil War* (Lexington, Mass.: D. C. Heath, 1973).

45. Allan Nevins, ed., *The Diary of Philip Hone, 1828–1851* (New York: Dodd, Mead & Company, 1936).

46. *American Masonic Register and Literary Companion*, June 1, 1844, 62.

47. *Spirit of the Times*, VII (September 2, 1837), 1.

48. *Ariel*, IV (December 11, 1830), 134.

49. "Thoughts on Theatres as They Are," *Parlour Review and Journal of Music, Literature and Fine Arts*, I (March 10, 1838), 38.

50. "Decline of the Modern Drama," *New England Magazine*, VIII (February 1835), 105.

51. *Spirit of the Times*, XIX (April 21, 1849), 108.

52. *Spirit of the Times*, VI (July 2, 1836), 234.

53. *Spirit of the Times*, VI (July 2, 1836), 241.

54. Letter dated Boston, October 1855, and published as a preface to *Moll Pitcher; or, The Fortune Teller of Lynn* (Boston: W. V. Spencer, 1855).

55. Theatre Collection, New York Public Library, *IL p.v.6. no.6.

56. Theatre Collection, New York Public Library, *IL p.v.8. no.8.

57. Letter to Rufus Griswold, February 21, 1844, Gratz Collection, Case 6, Box 32, Historical Society of Pennsylvania.

58. *Spirit of the Times*, XVIII (January 20, 1849), 576.

59. *American Masonic Register and Literary Companion*, I (April 11, 1840), 250.

60. *Spirit of the Times*, XIV (January 11, 1845), 552.

61. Letter, Society Collection, Case 19, Box 9, Historical Society of Pennsylvania.

62. *New York Review*, V (1839), 439.

63. William Ellery Channing, "Remarks on National Literature," *The Christian Examiner*, XXXVI (January 1830), 269–94.

64. *Democratic Review*, I (October 1837), introduction.

65. Arthur M. Schlesinger, Jr., *The Age of Jackson* (Boston: Little, Brown & Company, 1950), 372.

66. *Literary World*, September 29, 1849, 278.

67. *Ariel*, V (October 22, 1831), 219.

68. *Spirit of the Times*, XII (September 10, 1842), 336.

69. *Spirit of the Times*, VII (December 16, 1837), 1.

70. *North American Review*, III (November 1833), 72.

71. Margaret Fuller, "The Modern Drama," in *Papers on Literature and Art*, vol. 1 (New York: Wiley and Putnam, 1846), 102.

3

WRITING FOR AN ACTOR
DEMAGOGUE: EDWIN FORREST

It was an actor's theatre in Jacksonian America; moreover, it was largely a theatre of English actors. Few Americans became recognized stars—Edwin Forrest, Josephine Clifton, Charlotte Cushman and vehicle actors like Thomas D. Rice, George ("Yankee") Hill, James Hackett and Dan Marble—while the country welcomed frequent visits by English performers. Many were the top stars from London—Charles Kean, Master Burke, Charles Kemble and Fanny Kemble, Tyrone Power, Sheridan Knowles, Ellen Tree, Fanny Ellsler, and William Macready. Others were the journeyman performers who infiltrated the American theatre in such a manner that they not only controlled, to a large extent, the bill of fare for an evening's entertainment but discouraged Americans from trying to become actors. Harry Watkins, an actor and occasional playwright, undoubtedly voiced the opinion of many Americans against the "bloody Englishmen who have got possession of our best theatres": "I am actually driven out of my native city by Englishmen."[1]

It was also a popular time for actors in America, or, at least, a time for performers whether in theatres, on lecture stages, from pulpits or behind the scenes of social and political intrigue. Even Andrew Jackson enjoyed performing among his political friends and adversaries and took pleasure in explaining to confidants the purpose of any unexpected behavior on his part. By using power and popularity, Jackson could exercise the techniques of the demagogue to his advantage.[2] Actors, preachers, lecturers and reformers did the same thing, and to some degree, audiences in theatres and from all levels of society responded favorably to such treatment. With the developing lyceum movement the period was an extremely popular one for lecturers, too much so for Epes Sargent, who wrote to Henry W. Longfellow on November 10, 1840, that "the city is overrun with lecturers."[3] Speaking in public was a means to power whether it was

Frances Wright on education, John Gough on temperance, the Reverend Beecher on religion, or Davy Crockett on politics. Lecturers like William Valentine became actors; actors like Charles B. Parsons became preachers; and storytellers were everywhere. James Hackett, "Yankee" Hill and Dan Marble were all storytellers on and off the stage. It was a time when entertainment, education and moral instruction were intermingled and tinctured with elements of persuasion that were readily accepted or even demanded.

With this popularity of the spoken word, the performer held a position of power. Because American actors, however, were thrust aside by their visitors from across the Atlantic Ocean, they had to create new ways to attract attention and gain this power. One of these ways, at least momentarily, worked to the advantage of the aspiring American playwrights who were beginning to realize that they must write for particular actors and actresses if they were to see their plays performed. People seldom went to the theatre because a certain person had written a play. Actors and actresses or spectacular novelties attracted audiences in Jacksonian America, and probably always will. John Augustus Stone wrote *Metamora* for Edwin Forrest; James Kirke Paulding wrote *The Lion of the West* for James Hackett; Robert T. Conrad wrote *Conrad of Naples* for James E. Wallack; Nathaniel Parker Willis wrote *The Kentucky Heiress* for Josephine Clifton. Many playwrights, in fact, wrote or tried to write for Edwin Forrest. Theatre managers might also require the services of playwrights. Charles W. Taylor, for example, adapted much of the current popular fiction for the management of the Bowery Theatre during the early 1830s. William Mitchell, manager of the Olympic in New York, had a stable of actor-playwrights during the 1840s—Joseph M. Field, Alexander Allan, Charles Walcot and Benjamin Baker. The temple and its high priests attracted the worshippers, and it was only logical and necessary that materials for the service be constantly replenished on the terms demanded by the parishioners.

If this was a melancholy situation for playwrights, it was nonetheless a fact and one frequently decried by critics of the drama. Lacking a core of dramatists, the American actor or actress had to devise some means of encouraging native playwrights to help satisfy the perennial need for new material. For a time playwriting competitions provided an answer. The first open challenge to American dramatists was delivered by Edwin Forrest in the form of an ad placed in the New York *Critic* (November 28, 1828), announcing a playwriting contest: For "the best tragedy, in five acts, of which the hero, or principal character, shall be an aboriginal of this country." It was a shrewd and innovative approach for an actor attempting to advance his career at this particular time in history. With nationalism a key issue in the minds of those who elected Andrew Jackson president of the United States of America, 1828 was a crucial year. People wanted to see themselves as citizens of a united nation, and Americanism was being trumpeted as a creed. Literature was also becoming recognized as a viable part of the new nation's profile, and writers were beginning to discuss copyright laws and to express themselves through American characters and with American themes. What better place than the theatre to advertise a country and to exploit the admirable and spectacular idiosyncrasies of its people? Forrest's ad obviously appealed to the burgeoning concept of Americanism, the belief in native heroes and the hope for a strong national literature. It was singularly appropriate for this man at this particular moment.

In America during the late 1820s Forrest was the rising native actor. A typical man of Jacksonian America and not yet firmly established in his profession, Forrest sought the advantages of a patron playwright. His immediate objective, however, was to find a vehicle for his own talents, and he was successful. From the 1828 contest and his subsequent contests there are nine plays recognized as the Forrest Prize Plays: *Metamora; or, The Last of the Wampanoags* (1829) by John Augustus Stone; *Caius Marius* (1831) by Richard Penn Smith; *Pelopidas; or, The Fall of the Polemarchs* (1830, not produced) by Robert Montgomery Bird; *The Gladiator* (1831) by Bird; *Oralloosa* (1832) by Bird; *The Ancient Briton* (1833) by Stone; *The Broker of Bogota* (1834) by Bird; *Jack Cade* (1835/1841, first produced as *Aylmere*) by Robert T. Conrad; and *Mohammed, The Arabian Prophet* (1851, not produced by Forrest) by George H. Miles. These plays, of course, represent only a small percentage of those written in response to Forrest's contest announcements, and in this fashion Forrest stimulated the development of American drama. The dramatists whose work he chose, however, did not prosper. Of the winning writers who contributed plays to Forrest—Stone, Smith, Bird, Conrad, Miles—not one was encouraged to the kind of sustained literary effort that might have produced a distinctive dramatic literature in America.

This epic gesture on Forrest's part was almost completely self-serving. Its major importance for the development of American drama rests upon the work of Robert Montgomery Bird and the stimulus Forrest's several contests gave other actors and managers to create similar prize play contests. Making one of his numerous ad-lib comments, this time with reference to Forrest's production of Bird's *Oralloossa* on December 7, 1831, George C. D. Odell wrote: "I hope the reader sees what Forrest was doing for the American dramatist."[4] But the reader should also remember that Stone died young and a pauper, that Bird responded to Forrest's treatment by refusing to write more plays, and that Forrest was always the major winner in any of his contests.

The idea of a playwriting competition, however, was a good one. Six months after *Metamora* opened, James Hackett offered "a premium of two hundred and fifty dollars for the best comedy in three acts, in which the principal character shall be an original of this country."[5] From the two plays submitted Hackett chose James Kirke Paulding's *The Lion of the West*, which provided him with a vehicle in the character of Colonel Nimrod Wildfire. In 1832 the Park Theatre produced Caroline Lee Hentz' *Werdenberg; or, The Forest League*, a prize play in a contest held by William Pelby of Boston.[6] When George Handel Hill offered $400 for a five-act comedy with an original Yankee character, thirteen plays were submitted, and the judges chose Samuel Woodworth's *Foundling of the Sea*, which was first produced at the Park Theatre on May 16, 1833. A typical vehicle actor, Hill was described by the *Spirit of the Times* as a performer "whose constant care is to increase his store."[7] At that time (1838) he was going to England to get more plays. In the late spring of 1836 the young actress Josephine Clifton had returned from a successful tour in England and offered $1,000 for a tragedy. James Wallack was equally generous in offering a prize for a play founded on events in American history. Wallack's contest, however, stirred some unpleasant suspicions that not all playwriting contests were wisely handled. When a disappointed contributor discovered that his play had been rejected without being read, Wallack had to publish a letter explaining that "a committee of literary gentlemen" had not considered any of the plays submitted worthy of presentation and that no award had been given.[8] Enthusiasm for play contests waned a bit in consequence of this and other bad publicity. Prizes were not always paid, and judges for some contests were either not identified or considered inadequate.

The need for new material, particularly for vehicle actors such as the Yankee or Irish impersonator, remained a persistent problem, and playwriting contests continued. In the fall of 1845 Dan Marble offered $500 for "a play written for him and illustrative of American character." Consistent with its editorial policy, the *Spirit* used this announcement to say that "now we should be proud of sending good American plays, as players, to London, and while we cultivate a tone for, and proficiency in dramatic personation, should not neglect the encouragement of dramatic production."[9] A few weeks later, the *Spirit* listed N. P. Willis, Epes Sargent and Mrs. Mowatt as the best American dramatists to compete for the prize, and by March of 1846 had heard of at least twenty people in the competition. In spite of the number of people writing for actors, however, the plays were frequently of poor quality. H. O. Pardey, manager of the National Theatre in New York, awarded a prize of $1,000 to Harry Watkins for a weak effort entitled *Nature's Nobleman, the Mechanic; or, The Ship's Carpenter of New York*, which was produced on December 2, 1850. Barney Williams, a successful actor of Irish roles whose career started in earnest in 1847, needed a large repertory of plays, but the many submissions to the prize contest he sponsored in 1855 were so poor that not one of them was considered worthy of production. As encouraging for the dramatists these play contests may appear to have been, with the exception of Forrest's contests no playwriting competition produced any memorable American plays.

The winning play of the first American playwriting competition, *Metamora; or, The Last of the Wampanoags* by John Augustus Stone, opened on December 15, 1829, at the New Park Theatre in New York. The *New York Mirror and Ladies Literary Gazette* reviewed the performance:

The Indian tragedy was performed, for the first time, on Tuesday evening last for the benefit of Mr. Forrest. A considerable interest having been excited, long before the rising of the curtain, the house was completely filled. The prologue, spoken by Mrs. Barrett, was received with enthusiastic applause, and everything indicated, on the part of the audience, a desire to give the author a favorable reception. The actors, both male and female, were eminently successful in their endeavors to do justice to their several parts, and during the progress of the play received the most unequivocal proofs of the approbation of their delighted spectators. Independent of the undoubted merit of *Metamora*, the manager had afforded a gratifying exhibition of scenery, dresses, decorations, etc.[10]

Although historians regard this play as a landmark in the development of a national drama, not all contemporary reviewers shared this writer's pleasure in the evening's performance.

Writing about "The New Tragedy of *Metamora*—a Bird's Eye View of Mr. Forrest's Performances," a reviewer explained that American dramatists could never match the quality of English plays and then castigated *Metamora* as "an incongruous medley of dullness and insipidity, without a single redeeming atonement of language, sentiment, situation, or incident. . . . When such a meager and miserable dramatic abortion as *Metamora* is hailed with applause, why, then, should any American dramatist give himself the trouble of writing elegantly, or painting poetically, for an audience whose apprehension is never touched by the impassioned eloquence of the tragic muse? So much for the author," the writer concluded, and proceeded to condemn the acting of Forrest and everything about him with the exception of the "possession of one attribute of genius—*ambition*."[11]

Metamora, however, survived both opening night and its critics to become a substantial part of Forrest's acting repertory. For the next forty years, Forrest played *Metamora* across the country, generally to capacity audiences whose enthusiastic response never seemed to change. Whatever the critics wrote, Forrest and innumerable managers made money. Describing Forrest's engagement at the Arch Street Theatre in Philadelphia a year after the New York opening, a reviewer noted that "immense crowds have been attracted by Forrest, who has displayed his usual round of characters, interspersed with an occasional representation of *Metamora*, a tragedy by the way, as wholly worthless as any ever acted upon any stage, and utterly unworthy of the great and original incidents it professes to delineate. It never fails, however, in that sterling merit of drawing overwhelming houses, to the solid profit of both managers and actor."[12]

For all the money that Forrest made from acting Metamora, he obviously tired of the role. John Ellsler, a contemporary theatre manager and actor, remembered overhearing an incident in December of 1857: "Sitting in the box office one day, and hearing the oft repeated query: 'When is Mr. Forrest going to play *Metamora*?' he [Forrest] gave vent to an expression of disgust. 'It seems to me that people have an idea that I can play nothing but *Metamora*.' He growled out the name savagely. 'I utterly despise the play, but for God's sake, as the people like it, put it on, and let's get it over.' "[13]

Although over the years critics and scholars have argued the merits of *Me*-

tamora as a dramatic composition, such arguments can never suggest the significance of the play in the history of American drama or American theatre. As a theatrical presentation, *Metamora* belonged to Forrest, who was "proprietor of the tragedy." It was his play because it was created for him, and he paid for it. That concept of ownership was understood in 1829. After Forrest's death in 1872, other actors tried the role without distinction, and the play remained unpublished in its entirety until 1966, although two scenes—"The Council Scene" and the final scene—were printed in *A Library of American Literature from the Earliest Settlement to the Present Time*.[14]

Regardless of its literary merits, which are few, *Metamora* is something of a milestone in the history of American drama. George C. D. Odell had good reasons for feeling that *Metamora* "despite the crudity of the writing, advanced the cause of the American dramatist."[15] Commenting on *Metamora* nearly twenty years after its opening, in an essay entitled "The Modern Drama," Margaret Fuller called it "a favorite on the boards in our cities which, if it have no other merit, yields something that belongs to the region, Forrest having studied for his part the Indian's gait and expression with some success." Fuller saw *Metamora* as "quite good enough for the stage at present" because it provided the spectacle that audiences demanded.[16] For sixty years, *Metamora* was part of that spectacle on which America and its drama focused, and its inclusion in *A Library of American Literature*, which excerpted few plays, only emphasizes that point. Beyond the sphere of theatre, Roy Harvey Pearce found added significance for *Metamora* as the "richest evidence of the imbalance between the convention of the noble savage and the idea of savagism."[17]

Forrest organized his contest carefully and with the sense of spectacle that was part of his nature. Those selected to judge the plays were Fitz-Greene Halleck, a popular writer; James Lawson, an editor and playwright; William Leggett, a poet, the editor of *The Critic* and a playwright who a year earlier had been himself writing a play for Forrest; Prosper M. Wetmore, a poet; and James G. Brooks, an essayist and poet. Chairing this distinguished committee was William Cullen Bryant, who in July of 1829 had become editor of the New York *Evening Post*. Fourteen plays were submitted.

With the spectacular success of *Metamora* everyone appeared to gain—audiences, managers, and especially Forrest—everyone except the playwright. In 1828 John Augustus Stone (1800–1834) had a slight reputation as an actor and a playwright. Born in Concord, Massachusetts, he had started acting character parts at the Washington Garden Theatre in Boston in 1820 and continued to play either eccentric comics or old men throughout his career, first in New York (1822–1828) and then mainly in Philadelphia. His first play, *Restoration; or, The Diamond Cross*, was performed in New York in 1824. Three years later he published *Tancred; or, The Siege of Antioch*, which dramatizes certain disputes among the Christian leaders at the time of the First Crusade in 1097. Although Joseph Jefferson praised the dramatic quality and language of the play and Philip Hone saw a production at the Park Theatre (May 31, 1830) which he thought eloquent in language and interesting in action, no features identify it as the work of the author of *Metamora*.

An excellent vehicle for Forrest's robust acting style and forceful personality, *Metamora* has structural qualities of considerable merit. The frequently uninspired language notwithstanding, the action, certain characters and some of the long monologues have strong dramatic appeal. The setting is, of course, America. In Act I, scene 1, Mordaunt, Oceana's father, awaits the arrival by ship of Fitzarnold, whose marriage to Oceana is designed to conceal Mordaunt's role among the regicides of King Charles. The scene is "wild, picturesque, half dark," among rocks near a "rude tomb" with "slow music" playing. Its gothic qualities are reinforced by the imagery in Mordaunt's opening speech—"the sun has sunk behind yon craggy rocks"—by his anguished plea, his anxiety concerning his future and his decision "to force her gentle will." At his exit, Oceana approaches, sentimentalizing her dead mother, and is interrupted by Walter, her lover. She tells of being saved from a panther by an Indian chief whom Walter identifies as Metamora—"our people love him not, nor is it strange; he stands between them and extended sway."

Metamora then appears above them on a rock, exits, is admired again by Walter—"the white man's dread, the Wampanoag's hope"—and comes to them. In four speeches Metamora explains something of himself and his debt to Oceana as well as his problem with the white man: "Metamora has been the friend of the white man; yet if the flint be smitten too hard, it will show that in its heart is fire." His goodness, strength of mind and purpose and his nobility are forcibly established, and before he leaves he gives Oceana an eagle plume from his headdress.

Maiden, take this; it means speed and safety; when the startling whoop is heard and the war hatchet gleams in the red blaze, let it be found in thy braided hair. Despise not the red man's gift; it will bring more good to you than the yellow earth the white man worships as his god. Take it—no Wampanoag's hand will e'er be raised against the head or hand that bears the eagle plume. (I,1)

Like other speeches this carries a majesty of image and rhythm which is strengthened by the irregular stresses. The act ends with Fitzarnold's appearance as a rival of Walter for Oceana's hand and the critical news that "the Indian tribes conspire from east to west and faithful Sassamond has found his grave!"[18]

Characters and their conflicts are clearly established in the first act. Mordaunt is the cowardly villain whose deeds penetrate both the Indian–white man conflict and the romantic subplot. By appearance, action, speeches, and the reactions and words of others, Metamora is shown to be a spectacular hero. For mother, God and the Indian's country, he is also a defender of love, honor and all that would be admired in a hero living in Jacksonian America.

The remaining four acts of the play carry the conflicts to their appropriate and theatrical climaxes while giving Forrest maximum opportunity to be a star.

Enticed to the white man's council, Metamora is accused of Sassamond's murder and condemned through the witness of a traitor whom Metamora kills before fleeing. By chance, and unknowingly, the English capture Nahmeokee, Metamora's wife, who refuses to identify herself until Metamora appears, accepts the peace compromise delivered previously by Walter and agrees to be a prisoner while Nahmeokee is returned to the Indian camp. The English are treacherous, but in the final act Metamora escapes his prison and kills Fitzarnold, helping the romantic subplot reach its appropriate climax, only to discover that the Narragansetts have been beaten and that defeat is certain. Believing only in "Death, or my nation's freedom!" Metamora, alone with Nahmeokee, mourns the death of their child, killed by the English, and the desertion of his Indian warriors. As he hears the English approach, he stabs Nahmeokee and faces the guns which will kill him:

My curses on you, white men! May the Great Spirit curse you when he speaks in his war voice from the clouds! Murderers! The last of the Wampanoags' curse be on you! May your graves and the graves of your children be in the path the red man shall trace! And may the wolf and panther howl o'er your fleshless bones, fit banquet for the destroyers! Spirit of the grave, I come! But the curse of Metamora stays with the white man! I die! My wife! My queen! My Nahmeokee! (V, 5)

Metamora's end may be eloquently operatic, but the curse adds the appropriate romantic touch to the form recognized by contemporaries as heroic tragedy. Although the love plot becomes less important toward the end of the play, it is emphasized as Metamora, the hero in all action, dispatches the villain. Oceana is slightly more enterprising than the typical pale and helpless heroine of the period drama, but she has the appropriate sentimental speeches and appropriate fear of the villain. Nahmeokee is another dramatic type of the day, the strong and forceful woman who usually meets with disaster. Metamora was Stone's greatest creation, a dramatic and noble figure whose understanding of humanity and sensitivity to the demands of love and honor made him an ideal hero for Jacksonian America. His straightforward approach to problems and his use of the physical and the violent were surely attractive to a people who bragged about meeting life head-on and worked hard for what they believed. The theatrics of the play had great appeal, too—battles, soldiers, fire, treachery, disguise, the mysterious Mordaunt, the long-lost son discovered—all the trappings of successful melodrama complete with symbolic language, theatrical devices, sentiment and appropriate music throughout. As numerous reviewers noted, *Metamora* could be considered a thing of shreds and patches, but it had an abundance of stage effect, and it played night after night and year after year with great success.

Like most dramatists, Stone used history to his advantage. His reference to the regicides of King Charles was sure to be recognized by his audience. Barker had used the regicides in *Superstition* (1824); Cooper's novel *The Wept of*

Wish-ton-Wish (1829) included Goff the regicide in the plot; and Hawthorne would use him in the story of *The Grey Champion*. King Philip or Metacom (Metamora), the second son of Massasoit, became Sachem of the Wampanoags after the death of his elder brother in 1662. His war with the English, King Philip's War, lasted scarcely a year, beginning on June 18, 1675, when the Wampanoags presumably provoked the Swansea settlers to action in response to constant marauding. Although the Narragansetts had fought beside the English in the Pequot War of 1637, they joined King Philip in 1675 and met disastrous defeat in the Great Swamp Fight on December 19. As the war began to turn against Philip, various bands of Indians fled westward. By the end of May 1676, Captain Benjamin Church and a group of scouts were harrying Philip and his followers in swamps near Taunton, Massachusetts, and Bridgewater, Connecticut, and on August 1 after surrounding his camp, captured his wife and son. On August 11 they shot Philip as he tried to escape. From this history and his knowledge of the theatre, Stone created *Metamora*.

Stone wrote at least five plays after *Metamora*, all of which were performed: *Tancred, King of Sicily; or, The Archives of Palermo* (1831); *The Demoniac; or, The Prophet's Bride* (1831); a complete revision of *The Lion of the West*, which James Kirke Paulding requested when the play lacked a successful leading character; *The Ancient Briton* (1833); and *The Knight of The Golden West; or, The Yankee in Spain* (1834), which provided George Handel Hill with one of his favorite Yankee characters, Sy Saco. Two other plays of unknown date— *Fauntleroy; or, The Fatal Forgery* and *La Rogue, the Regicide*—were performed in Charleston; *Touretoun*, known only by this title, is also attributed to Stone. In all, Stone may have written eleven plays; two won Forrest's prize contests, and two became vehicles for well-known actors of the period. This is not a poor record for any dramatist, but Stone did not fare well in the American theatre.

In 1835 a writer in the *New England Magazine*, commenting on the "Decline of the Modern Drama," used *Metamora* to illustrate the absolute need for playwrights to write for a star. He noted that Stone's subsequent pieces were utter failures and their names forgotten because "there was no star to sustain them." [19] The irony of this statement appears in the fact that both *The Lion of the West* and *The Knight of the Golden West* were popular in theatres, although Stone's work on *The Lion of the West* was probably unknown. Whether or not they wrote for a star, however, dramatists were frequently forgotten or considered unimportant. About Stone as an individual little is known. Walter M. Leman remembered him as a man of "singular temperament" who committed suicide when partially insane. [20] Stone was, no doubt, despondent and in ill health when he jumped from the Spruce Street Wharf in Philadelphia into the Schuylkill River on May 29, 1834. Newspapers recorded the event. James Hunter, editor of the Albany *Daily News* and a friend of Forrest, praised Stone's "successful efforts . . . to elevate and establish permanently the dramatic character of our country."[21] Forrest himself erected a monument over Stone's grave: "By His Friend Edwin Forrest."

The Ancient Briton, a historical tragedy and a winner of one of Forrest's contests, opened at the Arch Street Theatre on March 27, 1833. It has never been published, although the editor of the *North American Magazine* published some excerpts, unidentified by act or scene, and a general commentary. In events preceding the action of the play, Brigantius has been captured and sent to Rome, leaving in Britain his wife, Monadia, and a son and daughter, Ottodate and Albiona. Upon his return Brigantius finds his country in turmoil as a result of Paulinus' decision to conquer the island of Mona, the stronghold of Druidical power where Albiona has been placed in service of the Druids. Immediately, Brigantius rushes off to rescue his daughter and, returning home with her, finds his wife dead as a result of his son's intimacy with the treacherous Roman rulers. Maddened at this loss, Brigantius vows revenge and the subjugation of Britain, which he accomplishes by joining the revolt of the Icenians under Queen Boadicea.

The writer in the *North American Magazine* found the plot of *The Ancient Briton* "better maintained" than that of *Metamora* and the language, "though more energetic than graceful," better fitted to the characters. Stone's ear for rhythm was clearly not the best, and his words and lines, though mainly very dramatic, are occasionally hackneyed and ill-constructed. Alert to theatrical needs, Stone always appeared to have Forrest in mind.

> Brigantius: This rugged bosom mark, these sinewy arms!
> Were these limbs form'd in silken vesture clad,
> To be the jest of Roman revellers?
> This head, that often I have raised unawed
> Beneath the fasces and the eagle's wing—
> Britons! Should this in mockery be crowned,
> While strains lascivious chimed with Nero's lyre?

Obviously not! One critic, perhaps more concerned with history than theatre, complained that Stone did damage to the role Boadicea played in history but sustained her spirit well. Although he believed "that Stone's play would be successful," he was not overly enthusiastic. "Till a happier era in the drama dawns," he wrote "let us be justly proud that an American actor has the ability and judgment to foster the genius of his countrymen, and some of those countrymen, the intellect to confer such honors, as have been heretofore denied, upon their native land."[22] Nearly a decade later James Rees, playwright, critic and historian, declared *The Ancient Briton* "the best of Mr. Stone's productions."[23]

Among the Philadelphia intellectuals who, in 1829, seemed destined to contribute to American dramatic literature, none was more active in the theatre than Richard Penn Smith (1799–1854). It would have been surprising, too, had Smith not written for Edwin Forrest. Growing up in very favorable circumstances, Smith was the grandson of William Smith, the first provost of the college which became the University of Pennsylvania, and the son of William Moore Smith, "a gentleman of polished education and a poet of considerable reputation in his day."[24] A center of culture and commerce, Philadelphia provided Smith with the opportunities that accompanied family wealth and reputation and his own intellectual curiosity. Privately tutored during most of his adolescence, Smith began to study law in 1818, a career he interrupted in 1822 to purchase and edit the newspaper *Aurora* for five years. During this period and until 1835 he concentrated his efforts on the writing of fiction and drama. Thereafter, until his death in 1854, he lived in comfortable semiretirement, occasionally practicing law, and for a while serving as secretary to the comptrollers of public schools.[25]

A fellow Philadelphian, James Rees, described Smith as a man whose "favorite study is the drama" and who had "an extensive acquaintance" with the drama of all nations, especially the "dramatic history of England and France."[26] Smith's interest in literature spanned some twenty-five years, as recorded in a number of bound volumes in the Historical Society of Pennsylvania. A well-read and romantic youth, Smith wrote poetry—including a poem entitled "To a Lady Who Accused Me of Impurity of Mind" (June 1820), and a long poem on "Francesca di Remini" (1821). There is also a scene of rather light and appealing dialogue from an unfinished play about "Angelica and Lisette," an older woman who does not want to get married and a young woman who does. Other playwriting efforts from this period include a one-act farce entitled *The Pelican* (1825); *The Lost Man; or, The Cock of the Village*, in which the hero acts upon the maxim that "scarcity makes a market"; *Shakespeare in Love*, "an interlude from the French of Alexandre Duval"; and an unfinished play, *The Solitary; or, The Man of Misery*, created for its scenic effect. *Quite Correct*, a comedy in two acts, from a story by Theodore Hook, was produced in 1828.

In his contemporary literary world, Smith was one of a number of educated and intellectual people who wrote fiction and poetry, edited journals, and were interested in the theatre—among them Samuel Woodworth, George Pope Morris, George Pepper, Sarah Josepha Hale, Nathaniel Parker Willis, and Epes Sargent. Although Smith's knowledge of the theatre came from his reading of plays and clearly showed the influence of English and European dramatists, he was also associated with a fascinating group of Philadelphia intellectuals including James Nelson Barker, Robert Montgomery Bird and Robert T. Conrad, all of whom loved the theatre. Whereas the most successful American dramatists of the past—William Dunlap and John Howard Payne—had been intimately associated with the theatre, either in the United States or in England, Smith was different. Not exactly a dilettante but without a real dedication to the theatre, he displayed some evidence of talent, had a modicum of success and then stopped writing. Throughout the century, others of his intellectual persuasion would take his place with more or less comparable success.

Drama historians remember 1829 as the year of Stone's *Metamora* at the Park Theatre in New York, but in Philadelphia Smith was the native playwright of distinction. Of the twenty plays he wrote, at least five were produced that year. The first was *The Eighth of January*, which opened on that date in 1829 to celebrate Andrew Jackson—victor at New Orleans in 1815, newly elected president in 1828—by contrasting Charles Bull, the American soldier, with John Bull, his loyalist father who refuses to fight for either side. Composed rapidly for a particular occasion, the play reaped whatever success it received onstage mainly by merit of its theme. *The Disowned; or, The Prodigals*, first produced in Baltimore in March, was brought to the Chestnut Street Theatre a few weeks later. "The plot is bad," wrote the critic for the *Ariel*, "and is not worked up into any very good scenes; neither is the language remarkable for anything but carelessness in the selection of it." [27]

In July, Smith's *A Wife at a Venture* was performed at the Walnut Street Theatre as written by "a Gentleman of this City." The play is a confused farce set in Bagdad with action determined by the Caliph's new law that every honest Mussulman must become either a husband or a soldier or pay a fine of one-third his estate. Disguise is important in the play, which relies for its appeal upon the Irish character Dennis O'Whack, played by Joseph Jefferson, who is married to a man one moment and threatened with execution the next. One performance of this play was followed by a "Grotesque African Dance" and three songs. Such were the theatre bills in Philadelphia and the competition a dramatist was forced to endure.

The Sentinels; or, The Two Sergeants, an adaptation of a play by D'Aubigny, was performed in mid-December,[28] and *William Penn*, concerned with problems of justice and jealousy within an Indian tribe and showing his continuing interest in American history, was first produced at Christmas of 1829. Although Smith produced an odd mixture of English for his Indians and allowed Penn to preach unmercifully, he showed his ability to write good comic dialogue in scenes with Hickory Oldboy, Benjamin Bobstay and Timothy Twist.

Oldboy: Verily, friend Timothy, here is an opportunity to dispose of some of your venture. Exhibit your merchandise, and it will be hard if you find not a purchaser in the number.

(Twist displays various articles—wearing apparel, trinkets, looking glasses. Indians delighted; females get the glasses.)

Twist: (To an Indian.) Allow me, to fit you with the latest fashion of Bond Street.

(Helps him on with a coat. Indian struts about. Twist turns to Whiska with a pair of red hose and slippers.)

Look here, damsel. Doth not the color take thine eye?

Whiska: Pretty, pretty, pretty! What for!

Twist: They are hose, damsel, and if thou wilt permit me, I will show thee the use of them. Should they fit, they shall be thine.

(Makes sign.)

Whiska: Bad man! Indian girl's red cheek grows redder with shame.

Oldboy: Hum! Timothy, try the military boots and spurs; they might delight her more. Art thou going it again, Christian? (II,3)

It is unfortunate that Smith did not exercise his comic skills more frequently, because he appears to have had a lively sense of humor which, with his interest in language, might have produced successful comedy. In addition to these five plays produced in 1829, Smith translated *The Bombardment of Algiers* from the French of Frédéric du Petit-Mèrè.[29]

In 1829 Smith must have experienced certain encouragement in his playwriting career. His dramatization of Cooper's novel *The Water Witch; or, The Skimmer of the Seas* was performed at the Chestnut Street Theatre in December of 1830, although it could not match the popular version by Charles W. Taylor which had been produced at the Bowery Theatre in New York in March of 1830. *The Deformed; or, Woman's Trial*, a version of *The Divorce; or, The Mock Cavalier*, written in 1825, was first performed in February of 1830 at the Chestnut Street Theatre. Using as a subplot Thomas Dekker's *Honest Whore* and William Dunlap's earlier adaptation of that work entitled *The Italian Father* (1799), Smith employed blank verse to create his central figure, a man misshapen in body and driven to self-defeating acts by his desire for beauty and affection. On January 8, 1830, Smith repeated his task of the previous year with another history play produced at the Chestnut Street Theatre: *The Triumph of Plattsburg*. Based on the American victory on Plattsburg Bay in September of 1814, the play provided the conflict and spectacle demanded of plays dealing with the War of 1812. It also showed Smith's ability to create strong patriotic melodrama as well as his talent for writing comedy.

The single play for which Smith might have had real expectations on the American stage was *Caius Marius*, a tragedy in blank verse produced January 12, 1831, as one of Forrest's Prize Plays. After an earlier version, submitted to Francis Wemyss in 1828, was not produced, Smith revised his play under Forrest's direction. Letters which Forrest wrote to Smith during the autumn of 1830 indicate the actor's interests, but not the full extent of his demands upon the script, although his request for a change of the conclusion of Act II, leaving him alone on stage with an appropriate exit speech, is a technique intimately associated with Forrest's acting style. Only twenty-five years old in 1831, Forrest enjoyed a reputation on the American stage of such gathering momentum that any dramatist would have wanted to hitch his wagon to this rising star. Smith obviously revised his work to fit Forrest's peculiar powers and, consistent with Forrest's practice, gave up all rights, including publication, to his play. Unfortunately for Smith, Forrest acted *Caius Marius* only a few times in his career, although he did allow F. B. Conway to perform the role twice in 1858.[30]

Contemporary response to Smith's work varied considerably, and the production of *Caius Marius*, in spite of advance publicity, was not successful. Although the Philadelphia *Daily Chronicle* of January 17, 1831, thought the play "decidedly superior to any native tragedy which has been brought upon the American stage," the audience must have been meager; Smith's author's benefit netted him only $96.42.[31] The *Irish Shield and Literary Panorama* vigorously attacked the "undeserved magnificence of scenery" for *Caius Marius* which it termed "an abortion of genius" and decidedly inferior to *Metamora*.[32] When George Pope Morris, the editor of the *Inquirer*, defended the play, the editor of the *Irish Shield* ridiculed him for supporting such a glaring "medley of barefaced plagiarism and puerile absurdity." "On the negative merits of *Marius* we would wish to grapple with such an intelligent writer as Mr. Robert Walsh [editor of the *American Quarterly Review*]; as there is no glory in vanquishing literary sciolists."[33] Such was the tone of literary and dramatic criticism of this period. Surely, it was not a time for tenderhearted playwrights. As for the play, the scenery was evidently effective, as were the costumes, and Forrest's acting was generally applauded, while the supporting players were obviously inept and youthful.[34]

By all reports Richard Penn Smith had a classical education which would have given him the opportunity to read Plutarch's *Lives*, where the fullest account of the life of Caius Marius (157–86 B.C.) appears. He may also have read Thomas Otway's *The History and Fall of Caius Marius* and talked his ideas over with David Paul Brown, a good friend, whose *Sertorius*, concerning a young soldier under Marius' command, opened at the Chestnut Street Theatre on December 14, 1830. Whatever resources he used—and it may be assumed that he studied his material carefully—Smith took as many liberties as he desired with history. He had also chosen his subject well. Jackson's election to the presidency has frequently been called a second revolution in America, and around the Western world there were other revolutions—in South America, in Greece, in France. Like Jackson, Marius, who gained much of his popularity historically by insisting upon land grants for his soldiers, became in Smith's play a hero of the people.

Act I shows Marius' defiance of the Roman senate, particularly Metellus who hates him, and gave Forrest strong speeches in defense of the people and against tyranny.

> The people are the fountain of all power
> Which springing from that source, direct, is pure,
> But when cut off—the stream confine'd within
> A narrow channel, it becomes corrupt—
> A wild destructive torrent that o'erwhelms
> Whate'er oppose its fury. Yes, my friend,
> The people's rights must be restor'd to them
> But no mild measures can affect that end. (I,3)

This would have been a popular democratic speech at this time in the history of America as Marius goes to the senate to assist in passing the agrarian laws.

Such was the influence of Forrest in Smith's play that every scene in which Marius appears ends with a forceful speech by the hero.

The main conflict of the play lies between Metellus and Marius, while the subplot follows the love of Metellus' daughter and Marius' son. With the backing of the people, Marius retains his position as consul, in spite of opposition which would crush him for his arrogance and pride. Like Jackson, Marius is honorable; he fights for Rome, for the people. Suddenly, in Act III, Sylla, another military force, refuses to obey Marius, and the tables are turned. Marius is banished, only to be brought back to aid a weak senate when trouble in Rome creates a dangerous situation. Old but still full of revenge, Marius confronts and stabs Metellus. His cause again failing, however, Marius sees himself as "sick to death," but when Sylla enters with the soldiers, rushes to attack him, falls and dies slowly: " 'Tis done; and Sylla now this world is thine; / But for me, freedom, freedom, freedom with the Gods." (V,6).

The language in this play could inspire, especially as delivered by such an actor as Edwin Forrest, but the character of Marius was undoubtedly not as noble as Forrest wished. Marius is not a Metamora. Although like Metamora, Marius is defeated, he does not stand as high in defeat and lacks Metamora's noble motivation and fascinating savagery. Moreover, Smith's work suffers, as did the work of most of the writers of his background, from sparsity of action. The great crises in Act III which change the direction of the play are not dramatized. They are explained in words, and more words, on life, liberty and freedom, forcefully delivered by Forrest. Whatever spectacle existed, it was created primarily by triumphant entrances and processions, but it was not ultimately satisfying to Jacksonian audiences.

After *Caius Marius*, Smith devoted less time to original drama and concentrated on adaptations and translations of farce and melodrama, forms which better suited his particular talents. *My Uncle's Wedding* was a slight farce which failed when produced as an afterpiece at the Arch Street Theatre in October of 1832. A year later, in November of 1833, *Is She a Brigand?* appeared at the same theatre. Altered from the French play by Theaulon, Dartois, and Francis, *Clara Wendel; où, La Demoiselle Brigand*, Smith's version shows a heroine who gains her objective by assuming the character of the brigand for whom she has been mistaken. *The Daughter*, translated from Laroche's *Clara; où, La Malheur et La Conscience*, played in May of 1836 in Philadelphia. His last play, *The Actress of Padua*, also performed in 1836, was a translation of Victor Hugo's *Angelo, Tyran de Padoue*. This play had the best stage record of any of Smith's plays in spite of his decision to publish it as a story, *The Actress of Padua and Other Tales* (1836). In a preface to this volume, he argued, perhaps out of pique, that few would go to the theatre to see such a play and that no one would read a printed drama. Hugo's melodrama concerning the wife and the lover of a tyrant, both of whom yearned for another man, had the popular amount of intrigue, romance, revenge, sacrifice and escapism. Smith's reaction to the theatrical world, however, was typical of those with his literary interests, and he seemed disdainful of this final effort.

Like James Fenimore Cooper and Robert Montgomery Bird, Smith wrote adventure fiction; and *The Forsaken*, a novel in two volumes, went through several editions. Smith also published, in 1836, "Colonel Crockett's Tour in Texas," as a pseudo-biographical, popular tale which abounded in humor and acute observations. It may be unfortunate for the history of American dramatic literature that Smith chose to write for Forrest rather than for his popular contemporaries on the comic stage, James Hackett or "Yankee" Hill.

Of all the aspiring dramatists from Philadelphia's literary and social elite, none achieved a satisfying career in the theatre. None had the talent, the discipline or the theatre connections to be successful. Smith came close to success, but his interest was fleeting; David Paul Brown was equally deserving. There was one, however, who had the potential to go beyond even his own considerable achievements. This was Robert Montgomery Bird (1806–1854), a dramatist with the necessary skill, the understanding and the opportunity. Evaluating Bird's career, Arthur Hobson Quinn, premiere historian of American drama, described him with perceptive accuracy:

His life was a brave struggle for the right to create, and had he lived in a time when the American playwright received fair treatment, it is not easy to put a limit to his possible achievements. For he had a rare sense of dramatic effect, a power to visualize historic scenes and characters, to seize the spirit of the past out of the mass of facts and, in a few brief lines, to fuse those facts into life. Before he was thirty years old he had lifted romantic tragedy to a higher level than it had reached in English since Congreve and had written several plays which even to-day can be placed on the stage with effect.[35]

Quinn omits here only one important point. Bird knew how to write for a successful actor of his day—Edwin Forrest, who was at first his life and salvation in the theatre, and later his nemesis.

By January of 1829, Bird had either completed or written portions of at least ten plays. Most of these were comedies, and *The City Looking Glass* (1828) gives some indication of the talent he would show in later plays. *The Cowled Lover* (1827) and *Caridorf* (1828) are melodramas of little distinction. Bird's serious career as a dramatist began in 1830 when *Pelopidas* was accepted by Forrest. Prior to this date Bird served his own style of apprenticeship to the dramatic muse and did it well. He was without question one of the remarkable men of his generation. His aggressive and responsive mind carried him into the fields of medicine, science, music, art, history, politics and pedagogy as well as literary criticism, poetry, fiction and drama. Had he been destined to concentrate on any one of these areas of scholarly or creative endeavor, he would surely have distinguished himself, but his appetite for variety demanded a focused but limited activity in several careers. In literature, he determined that he would begin as a poet and dramatist, then turn to fiction and write history towards the end of his life. As a dreamer, a romantic and an idealist, however, he did not assess accurately the ravages of life, nor did he understand the workings of the practical theatre. Like his contemporary writers, he wanted to write good plays which he assumed an intelligent and responsive theatre manager would be eager to produce.

The American theatre, however, was run by people who may or may not have enjoyed good theatre but who knew for a certainty that they must please audiences. Like Bird, Edwin Forrest was another youthful, ambitious man, equally determined concerning his career and perhaps with fewer scruples, although Forrest's dealings were no worse than those of any other entrepreneur within the accepted theatre traditions of his day. Both were men of strong opinions. Forrest admired William Leggett, Bryant's hot-headed assistant on the *Post* in 1829, and underwrote Leggett's venture with the *Plaindealer* in the amount of many thousands of dollars. A Democrat and supporter of Van Buren's policies in 1838, Forrest was sufficiently political to be nominated for a seat in Congress, which prompted Philip Hone to sneer: "He may be a leader to the Pitt party [Bowery Theatre] but no statesman" (October 15, 1838).

Bird was clearly inspired by the concepts of Romanticism that were underscored in the writings of his literary contemporaries—the idealism of Emerson and Thoreau, the gothic quality of Poe and Hawthorne, the wide adventurism of Cooper and Kennedy. Trying to bring these characteristics to American dramatic literature, he failed in the degree of his ambition, but his accomplishments were distinctive. Within the voluminous records and notes he kept during his apprentice years he outlined his dreams and objectives. He wanted to demonstrate that superior "gift of poetry and a knack for dramatic effect" which distinguish acted drama from mere closet drama.[36] There was, he realized, a desperate need for an American drama which to be successful must stimulate a cooperative effort between the authors of fine plays and the creators of inspiring theatre.

During his planned lifetime Bird projected at least fifty-five plays. After his initial flurry of dramatic activity, however, he wrote only four: *Pelopidas* (1830), *The Gladiator* (1831), *Oralloossa* (1832), and *The Broker of Bogota* (1834). He also revised *Metamora* for Forrest, although the actor claimed not to have used this version. All four plays were accepted as Prize Plays by Forrest, and although *Pelopidas* was not produced, Forrest made considerable money and reputation from *The Gladiator* and *The Broker of Bogota* and acted in *Oralloossa* until 1847. It would appear to have been an ideal arrangement—a fine dramatist and a talented actor, both beginning promising careers. Unfortunately, the root of all evil was again shown to be money. When *Pelopidas* did not, in the final analysis, suit Forrest, the two men agreed orally that a new play would be substituted. Bird was to receive $1,000 for writing *The Gladiator*, and $2,000 if it proved successful. Although no contracts were signed, Bird believed that the same agreement would apply to *Oralloossa* and *The Broker*. Bird and Forrest were, indeed, friends at this time and in 1833 traveled together through the South and West. As a favor, Forrest had even loaned Bird $2,000.

With the success of *The Gladiator*, Bird thought his debt had been cancelled.

Then in 1837, Forrest demanded repayment. To this date, Bird had been paid only $1,000 each for the last three plays and nothing for his work on *Metamora*. Forrest, on the other hand, had made many thousands of dollars as a consequence of Bird's work and, having paid for the plays, would not allow them to be presented by other actors. A letter from Forrest dated 1869 explains his position:

The heirs of the late Dr. R. M. Bird have neither right, title, nor any legal interest whatever in the plays written by him for me, *viz*; *The Gladiator*, *The Broker of Bogota* and the play of *Oralloossa*.

These plays are my exclusive property, by the right of purchase, and for many years by the law of copyright.[37]

The law of American copyright, unfortunately, did not protect the dramatist when Bird was writing plays. Such protection did not come until 1856, two years after his death.

In 1853, *The Gladiator* reached its one thousandth performance and became the first play written in English to have that many performances during the lifetime of its author. By that date, however, it was slight comfort to Bird. Forrest's tactics and his demand in 1837 for repayment convinced Bird that his career as a dramatist should be ended. He confided his feelings to a kind of diary which he called *Secret Records*. "What a fool I was to think of writing plays!" he wrote. "To be sure, they are much wanted. But then novels are much easier sorts of things and immortalize one's pocket much sooner."[38] He then concentrated upon the writing of novels, three of which were dramatized, but not by his hand. *Nick of the Woods*, one of the most successful romantic adventure novels of the period, was adapted to the stage three times and entertained audiences for a quarter of a century.

Pelopidas is a historical play based on an account in Plutarch's *Lives*, with the addition by Bird of a love plot. Forrest rejected it for the obvious reason that Pelopidas was not central to the entire action of the play, although his victorious attempt to wrest control of Thebes from the Spartan tyrants formed the basis of the plot. *The Gladiator* was much better suited to Forrest's talents.

Always a scholar, Bird again used Plutarch as a major source for *The Gladiator*, along with the histories of Appian, Adam Ferguson and N. Hooke. Over his research Bird laid the imagination of the dramatist and the shrewdness of a man of politics. Tyranny and slavery were important issues in America, where within the past generation a dispute had been stilled by violence. Even as Bird pondered his thesis, William Lloyd Garrison's issues of the *Liberator* were being read, the first appearing in January of 1831. In choosing a man of independent spirit, a Thracian bound by slavery, as his hero, Bird showed his sensitivity to the society around him. Spartacus, a powerful and sentimental hero set against one of the most powerful tyrannies in history, was an ideal voice of the people. Honorable, patriotic and with a sense of humanity, he epitomized the romantic hero. He was Edwin Forrest and Andrew Jackson rolled into one, and the success of the play was assured.

The Gladiator was first performed on September 26, 1831, at the Park Theatre in New York and was immediately successful. The reviewer for the *Ariel* expressed a common sentiment toward this work by the twenty-five year old playwright. "As a literary performance, we know of nothing of the kind, which will compare with it. It is poetical, and well adapted to the stage, where we have no doubt it will be long a favorite." [39] Less than two years later the role of Spartacus was considered to be Forrest's best, next to Metamora. [40] Although during his English tour in 1836 Forrest performed Spartacus with mixed response, most critics finding the acting better than the play, several pointed out the impassioned and beautiful language and the noble concept of the drama. It appeared as a surprise to many that the pleasure of the evening could be produced by an American actor performing in a play written by an American. One immediate result was the unanimous election of Bird to the English Dramatic Author's Society.

The Gladiator held the stage for forty years because Forrest acted the title role. For its comments on war, tyranny and slavery, however, it deserved its popular appeal. The noble commitment and sacrifice of its strong hero, who acted on his own beliefs and could make the grand gesture with an admirable fusion of abandon and dignity, were worthy of imitation. Yet the play has obvious weaknesses in construction: it reaches its greatest climax, for example, at the end of Act II and suffers from falling action in Acts IV and V. Contemporary critics saw the faults clearly. [41] The play does, however, have the advantage of some excellently contrived scenes and an exceptional use of language.

The Gladiator opens in Rome, in a street where Phasarius, a successful and arrogant gladiator, boasts of his prowess and with his friends contemplates revolt. There is, however, a newly arrived gladiator, Spartacus, a Thracian captive, a man of great skill and strength but of equal anger and misery who refuses to take the gladiator's oath. When Spartacus sees his wife, Senona, and his son about to be sold as slaves, he begs his owner, Lentulus, to buy them. "And you will swear?" asks Lentulus. "I will," replies Spartacus, "To be a cutthroat and a murderer— / What'er you will,—so you will buy them." Lentulus agrees.

The Roman Prator is Crassus, a sensitive man with a sense of honor whose fondness for his niece, Julia, prompts him to seek a more noble suitor for her than Florus, Lentulus' son whom she loves, and to refuse her permission to attend the games she adores. At the arena Spartacus counsels the other gladiators: "If ye care not for life, why die ye not / Rather like men, than dogs?" (II,2). The games begin; Spartacus is brought in, and he speaks:

> Well, I am here,
> Among these beasts of Rome, a spectacle.
> This is the temple, where they mock the Gods
> With human butchery,—Most grand and glorious

> Of structure and device!—It should have been a cave,
> Some foul and midnight pit, or den of bones,
> Where murder best might veil himself from sight.—
> Women and children, too, to see men die,
> And clap their hands at every stab! This is
> The boastful excellence of Rome! I thank the Gods
> There are Barbarians. (II,3)

To the Romans, of course, Spartacus is a barbarian, but Crassus is impressed by his bold speech. After Spartacus shows his skill in killing, there is the climactic event: Spartacus versus Phasarius. Although this scene, in which the two brothers recognize each other, is too long, the result is a dramatic and spectacular moment, well motivated and foreshadowed, as the gladiators revolt, urged on by Spartacus:

> Death to the Roman fiends, that make their mirth
> Out of the groans of bleeding misery!
> Ho, slaves, arise! it is your hour to kill!
> Kill, and spare not—For wrath and liberty!—
> Freedom for bondmen—freedom and revenge!— (II,3)

These are meaningful and compelling lines, well structured for strength of character and beauty of delivery.

Act III explores the consequences of the revolt. Ashamed of what has happened, Crassus plans to attack, but on a plain in Campania he is beaten by the gladiators who, envigorated by their victory, now show different objectives. Spartacus urges caution. But Phasarius wants to sack Rome; and the schism between the brothers widens when Phasarius demands Julia as his reward and disaster becomes inevitable. In battle with the Romans Phasarius is badly defeated, and Spartacus' wife and child are killed. Overwhelmed with frustration and bitterness, Spartacus rages among the Romans; Crassus, with some feeling for this "valiant madman," wants him alive, even as he charges into Crassus' tent, where he dies. In the printed play Crassus had the curtain speech:

> Thy bark is wreck'd, but nobly did she buffet
> These waves of war, and grandly lies at last,
> A stranded ruin on this fatal shore.
> Let him have burial; not as a base bondman,
> But as a chief enfranchised and ennobled.
> If we denied him honor while he lived,
> Justice shall carve it on his monument. (V,7)

Forrest, of course, eliminated this final speech in his acting version. Although the physical action in the final acts supports the strong speeches by Spartacus— such as the one beginning "Men do not war on women" (IV,3)—the play loses some of the focused power promised in early scenes; Bird elaborated too much on Phasarius' betrayal, the Julia-Florus love plot and the philosophical distinction between Romans and barbarians. Still, *The Gladiator* was a masterful vehicle for Forrest.

Bird continued to indulge his interest in the barbarian in his next play *Oralloossa*, based on an event in the early history of Peru. Again, he researched his story thoroughly, creating a son, Oralloossa, for Itahualpa the Inca, whose execution by Pizarro prior to the rebellion of Diego de Almagro motivated the assassination of Pizarro. Repeating his earlier concept in *The Gladiator*, Bird wanted to show that any plans of a great leader could be undermined by the selfish ambitions of an unprincipled individual. Forrest produced the play at the Arch Street Theatre in Philadelphia on October 10, 1832. Although in March of that year it had been praised by the editor of the *Ariel*, it received only moderate reviews and was not the success that audiences expected.

Once again Bird had concentrated on the timeliness of tyranny and had used Oralloossa as the symbol of individual freedom. By showing the assassination of Pizarro in Act II, however, Bird again provided the greatest climax of his play long before its end—as in *The Gladiator*—and tried to create a tragic atmosphere through some means not clearly defined in the play. Critics also found the third act "one wild scream of exultation—the triumph of a regicide rather than a monarch" and compared it unfavorably with *The Gladiator*.[42] Although the fourth act, in which Oralloossa is betrayed and begins his fall, was spectacularly conceived, the faults of the play were much too prominent to bring Forrest the popularity he needed. According to one reviewer,

The plot of *Oralloossa* is complex in the extreme, the author having in the formation of it worked up incidents and events, which might with propriety constitute the subject for three or four dramas. Of its poetical merits we would say but little. In the overweening anxiety which the author has taken to store his play with incidents, it seems to have escaped him that a good drama must possess something more than continued bursts of passion, and vigorous and continued action, to constitute it a legitimate tragedy; and one may therefore look in vain for those poetic beauties in *Oralloossa*, which have contributed not a little to make *The Gladiator* so permanent a favorite.[43]

In this instance Odell's repeated praise of Forrest's aid to native dramatists seems to be justified. Without Forrest, this play would surely have disappeared after its initial production, like so many other plays written during this time.

Before he wrote his next and final play, *The Broker of Bogota*, Bird studied Forrest's acting style much more carefully and developed his dramatic skills accordingly. He also took more time to create this play; *Oralloossa* had admittedly been written very quickly. *The Broker of Bogota* was produced first in New York on February 12, 1834, and in Philadelphia on June 11. Its success speaks more to Bird's talent as a dramatist than any of his other plays. One must also praise Forrest for performing a play that lacked, as James Rees correctly observed in the *Dramatic Mirror*, the "drums and trumpets" which were the foundation of most popular successes of this period.[44]

Edwin Forrest as Baptista Febro in Robert Montgomery Bird's *The Broker of Bogota*.
Theatre Arts Library, Harry Ransom Humanities Research Center, The University of
Texas at Austin.

A romantic play of profound human interest, the most finished and inspired
of Bird's writing, drama or fiction, *The Broker* is the story of Baptista Febro,
a broker and a severe, if unwise, but loving parent who is distraught with the
situation in his household—a daughter who has a lover of whom he does not
approve and a profligate son. Like all human beings, Febro's virtues can be his
faults and his weaknesses assets. With his character clearly presented in the
early scenes of the play, Febro's catastrophe bears down upon him inevitably

and relentlessly. He acts as only he can act, and he is abused by friends, by family, by foe and by the Roman concept of justice which must be served. The villain of the play, Cabarero, practices his black art to a remarkable degree, but it would be to no avail were Febro not what he is. Although Febro's death is highly romanticized in the tradition of the day, the steps leading to it are compelling and frightening, filled with the pathos that infuses romantic tragedy.

It is a comment on mid-century audiences, presumably conditioned to the denouements of romantic melodrama and the current efforts at reform, that some of Bird's ideas were considered unbearable. The *Spirit of the Times* explains:

The whole plot of the play is founded on the disobedience of children and the disastrous results which follow. It contains the very common story of a hot-headed youth plunging into vice, and ending an inglorious career by suicide; but the framework is so full of horrible details, that it becomes revolting to the senses, and is fatal to the tragic effect; however sublime the composition, it seems incredulous. Bad as we know depraved nature to be, horrible as we know the character of crime may become, yet the cool deliberate calculation of a father's death by ignominious condemnation is beyond the range of contemplation.[45]

Later events and a greater national maturity toward art would alter such attitudes, but at this time the domestic situation was the current subject of a much more romanticized and pleasurably optimistic view than Bird had presented.

In the traditional way Bird had set his play in eighteenth-century New Granada, but audiences soon realized that the action of *The Broker of Bogota* could take place anywhere and at any time. Febro has disinherited his son, Ramon, who is now found undesirable by Mendoza, the merchant and father of Juana to whom Ramon was betrothed. Distraught and needing money, Ramon becomes the willing victim and dupe of Cabarero, a villain of considerable talent whose approach to money provides a comment on Bird's contemporary society:

Money, 'tis the essence of all comfort and virtue. Thou carest not for gold! Give me gold, and I will show thee the picture of philosophy, the credential of excellence, the corner-stone of greatness. It is wisdom and reputation—the world's religion, mankind's conscience; and what is man without it? Pah! 'Tis as impossible honesty should dwell easily in an empty pocket, as good humor in a hollow stomach, or wit in a full one. Didst thou ever see integrity revered in an old coat, or unworthiness scorned in a new? (I,1)

Febro also believes in money, but he is brought down by his sense of pride as head of a family and his stubborn and authoritarian nature. When Cabarero makes it appear that Febro, the broker, has robbed himself, Febro is furious. He would have forgiven Ramon, but now he must defend himself in the viceroy's court. There, however, he refuses to speak; Ramon, too, stands silent, although knowing the truth. Eventually saved from further persecution by Juana, who has forced Ramon to bring Cabarero to the viceroy and confess, Febro learns that his daughter has been wooed by the viceroy's son in disguise, and he is happy, for a brief moment, until he succumbs to the agonies to which he has been subjected when he is told that Ramon, in shame, has jumped to his death. Both hero and victim, and opposed by "a devil-born destroyer of men's sons" whose indifference to moral values in society provides the basic intrigue, Febro broods about his own idiosyncrasies which allow him to be the victim of circumstantial misfortunes. The role of Febro was an excellent vehicle for Forrest, whose range of emotions could endow the impassioned broker with substance and pity. He would not, of course, allow another actor the final speech, but the viceroy's intoned moral concerning "the rigid sire and disobedient son" did survive for the reader.

Without Forrest, Bird would never have enjoyed the reputation, brief as it was, that history accords him. Without Bird, Forrest would not have had two very popular roles in his repertory. It is unfortunate that they could not have worked longer together, that it was an actor's theatre, that there was not copyright protection for the playwright, that the times were such that only individual efforts, in the theatre and in the nation, were highly praised. Given the character of the theatre during the 1830s, however, Bird's plays are remarkable, both for their contemporary success in the theatre and for their value as literature, in an art form which could boast few distinguished works.

Another aspiring playwright, if only for a brief time, who contributed to Edwin Forrest's well-being was Robert T. Conrad (1810–1858). Journalist, editor, lawyer, judge, orator, poet and politician, the son of a publisher and a wealthy man who served one term as mayor of Philadelphia, Conrad wrote at least three plays, one of which, *Jack Cade*, after revisions and changes of title, became a Prize Play in Forrest's repertory. Conrad was a man of wide interests—writing and speech central to all of them—but the theatre seemed to present a sentimental fascination that he could not escape and for which he maintained an enthusiastic optimism. Addressing an audience at the Walnut Street Theatre, Conrad showed his eager and naive pleasure in the American theatre where he saw no "serpent tempted." "For every mood the drama has a mood," he explained; "who can't be happy here?"[46] He, however, did not spend all of his life writing for the stage.

Bright and energetic, Conrad was admitted to the bar very early in life, but worked with the *Daily Commercial Intelligentsia* from 1832 until poor health and the consequences of his political leanings led him back to the less strenuous practice of law in 1838 and finally to the General Sessions in 1840. Throughout the 1830s he maintained an interest in playwriting and after leaving the judgeship became the editor of *Graham's Magazine* and an associate editor for the *North American Review*. In 1854 he was elected mayor of Philadelphia and two years later was appointed judge of the Quarter Sessions. During a relatively brief life, he balanced careers in law, literature, politics and the theatre, with moderate achievements in all.

Conrad's first work, a tragedy entitled *Conrad of Naples* or *Conrad, King of*

Naples, was first produced in Philadelphia in January of 1832. Critical response was good, and the play was eventually produced in other American cities, but never in New York. According to the *Spirit of the Times* it was a tragedy of great power, with an interesting and well-managed plot and characters that were natural and forcibly drawn. "The character of Conrad, the hero of the piece, is full and strongly marked, and requires, perhaps, as much histrionic ability to perform it as any other character in the whole range of drama. He is really a noble personage."[47] James Wallack acted the main role in Philadelphia, but it was not taken up by other actors, and the play has not survived. Another of Conrad's efforts which has also not survived is *The Heretic*, written, according to Conrad, for Forrest, who never staged it but sold the manuscript to Edwin Adams, who acted it at the Arch Street Threatre and played the leading character, Adrian de Teligny, with Mrs. Drew in the cast.[48]

The history of Conrad's best-known play, *Jack Cade*, exposes the mid–nineteenth-century American theatre in miniature. At the suggestion of Francis Wemyss, Conrad wrote the tragedy for Augustus A. Addams, an actor notorious for his excessive drinking habits who, on opening night (December 7, 1835) was too drunk to perform. Two days later, David Ingersoll performed the role, and although Addams appeared in the play on February 1, 1836, it was not successful until five years later when Conrad revised it for Edwin Forrest. Title changes also confuse the stage history of the play. Its earliest title was either *Jack Cade* or *The Noble Roman*. When Conrad revised his work for Forrest, who first produced it in May of 1841, it was variously called *Aylmere; or, The Kentish Rebellion*, *Aylmere; or, The Bond Man of Kent* and finally *Jack Cade, the Captain of the Commons*, or simply *Jack Cade*. It was published at least twice, once by Conrad under the title *Aylmere; or, The Bond Man of Kent and Other Poems* (1852).

The role of Jack Cade was a favorite with Forrest throughout his acting career and was acted by others after his death. When the play was first announced for Forrest, however, the *Spirit of the Times* had some misgivings about Jack Cade's having "the essential requisites of a hero of tragedy," but felt comfortable with the "refined judgment, classic taste and brilliant imagination of Judge Conrad."[48] After production, however, the *Spirit* appeared to question its previous faith in the judge. It found the play "full of errors and gross anachronisms," excessive in histrionics, shocking in its details and given over to "claptrap," with lines "written expressly to gather applause from the least discriminating portion of the audience." The play was also "too tragic—there is the greatest variety of deaths in it—death by burning, death by poisoned daggers, death by starvation, death by the sword, death from a broken heart, and death by knocking out the brains with a blacksmith's hammer;—and in this last case you are to hear the infliction of the blows and the yell of the dying wretch and to see the murderer rushing on the scene with his ponderous weapon dabbled in blood."[50] Such was the refined judgment, classic taste and imagination of Conrad, and if it adversely affected the squeamish, it appealed to Americans generally, as it had to the Romans and Elizabethans. "With all its faults," the *Spirit* admitted, *Aylmere* was a very effective *acting* play, a fact accepted by two generations of American playgoers.

The 1852 publication of *Aylmere* in five acts is not the version acted by Forrest, although the story is the same. Conrad explained in the introduction:

It is imagined in the play that the leader of the commons was originally a villein by the name of Cade; afterwards a fugitive known as Aylmere; then after an absence abroad, returning to England, he excites an insurrection for the double purpose of avenging his own wrongs and abolishing the institution, *villeinage* which made him a bondman. After his triumph he assumes his original name. The tragedy as originally written and now presented to the reader comprises much that was not designed for and was not adapted to the stage.[51]

The Lacy Edition of *Jack Cade, the Captain of the Common*, in four acts, is, indeed, a much better play, with excessive dialogue omitted and sharpened action and issues dramatically focused upon Aylmere, improvements obviously demanded by Forrest.[52]

In 1450 the times are severe in London and Kent. Lord Say is a tyrant, a cruel, prideful and arrogant man. Jack Cade, whose father Say killed, has returned to England with his wife, Marianne, and child, after studying medicine in Italy. As Aylmere, he has a purpose:

> I heard the genius of my country shriek
> Amid the ruins, calling on her son—
> On me! I answered her in shouts, and knelt—
> E've there in darkness, 'mid the falling ruins,
> Beneath the echoing thunder peal—and swore,
> (The while my father's pale form, stain'd with
> The death prints of the scourge, stood by and smiled)
> Then the air seemed thick with vengeance, clouded with blood,
> I swore to make the bondman free! (Lacy ed., I,4)

It will not be an easy task, however. When Lord Say hears of Aylmere, he orders the firing of the Widow Cade's cottage. With her death in the blaze, Aylmere makes another vow, and Act II has a strong ending. As Aylmere, his wife and child hide from the law in the forest, there is gossip that Aylmere is really Mortimer, the true heir to the English throne. By chance, Aylmere meets Say in the forest; they fight, and Aylmere is captured and sentenced to death. Later Aylmere escapes, only to find his child dead and his wife insane. Returning to his band of rebels, he declares that he will be Mortimer "Until our claims are molten in the glow / Of kindled spirits" (IV,2). With the success of the rebellion, Aylmere achieves "freedom for the bondman" before he dies of a wound from Lord Say's poisoned dagger.

Along with *Metamora* and *The Gladiator* this play was clearly a fine vehicle for the talents of Edwin Forrest. It reflects well the persistent images of Forrest in the theatre and Andrew Jackson in the political arena—the defenders of the common man, heroic caretakers of individual liberty.

NOTES

1. Maud and Otis Skinner, eds., *One Man in His Time, the Adventures of H. Watkins, Strolling Player, 1845–1863, from His Journal* (Philadelphia: University of Pennsylvania Press, 1938), 217, 90.

2. See Edwin C. Rozwenc's introduction to *Ideology and Power in the Age of Jackson* (New York: Doubleday & Company, 1964).

3. Letter, Harvard Theatre Collection.

4. George C. D. Odell, *Annals of the New York Stage*, vol. III (New York: Columbia University Press, 1928), 613.

5. *Ariel*, IV (May 15, 1830), 13.

6. Caroline Lee Hentz (1800–1856) was a popular novelist and the author of several plays, none of which had much success in the theatre. *De Lara; or, The Moorish Bride* was produced in Boston and Philadelphia in 1831; *Werdenberg; or, The Forest League* played at the Park Theatre in New York in April 1832. Both were selected as prize tragedies by William Pelby. James Rees mentioned *Zara* and *Lamorah; or, The Western Wild*, which he found an "excellent Indian Play" (*Dramatic Mirror*, I [September 11, 1841], 33–34).

7. *Spirit of the Times*, VIII (May 26, 1838), 152.

8. *Spirit of the Times*, VII (November 25, 1837), 452.

9. *Spirit of the Times*, XV (November 8, 1845), 440, 446.

10. *New York Mirror and Ladies Literary Gazette*, December 19, 1829, 21.

11. *Irish Shield and Monthly Hilenan*, X (December 1829), 467–68.

12. *Ariel*, IV (December 11, 1830), 133.

13. Effie Ellsler Weston, ed., *The Stage Memoirs of John A. Ellsler* (Cleveland: The Rowfant Club, 1950), 112.

14. E. C. Stedman and Ellen M. Hutchinson, eds., *A Library of American Literature from the Earliest Settlement to the Present Time*, vol. VI (New York: Charles L. Webster & Company, 1892), 67–71. The complete play is printed in *Dramas from the American Theatre, 1762–1909*, ed. Richard Moody (New York: World Publishing Company, 1966), 199–227.

15. Odell, *Annals of the New York Stage*, III, 449.

16. Margaret Fuller, *Art, Literature and the Drama* (Boston: Roberts Press, 1875), 115, 121.

17. Roy Harvey Pearce, *The Savages of America* (Baltimore: Johns Hopkins Press, 1953), 176.

18. Sassamond was one of the Indians who attended John Eliot's Indian School in Harvard Yard and left to become, eventually, secretary to King Philip, the Indian chief. Sassamond's death—he was found floating in a pond one morning—led some to call him the first Indian Christian martyr because, it was argued, he tried to convert Philip and was killed for his attempt. Others have suggested that, being a scribe and literate, he tried to cheat Philip and met his just reward. Stone used his death to good effect, but it is unlikely that the name meant much to his audience.

19. *New England Magazine*, VIII (February 1835), 106.

20. Walter M. Leman, *Memories of an Old Actor* (San Francisco: A. Roman Co., 1886), 84.

21. Quoted in Moody, ed., *Dramas from the American Theatre*, 200.

22. *North American Magazine*, I (November 1832), 29, 32, 35.

23. *Dramatic Mirror*, I (October 2, 1841), 64.

24. Henry Simpson, *The Lives of Eminent Philadelphians* (Philadelphia: W. Brotherhead, 1859), 899.

25. See "Biography of Richard P. Smith," *Burton's Gentleman's Magazine and American Monthly*, September 1839, 119–21.

26. *Dramatic Mirror*, I (October 9, 1841), 71–72.

27. *Ariel*, III (May 2, 1829), 5.

28. *The Sentinels* was plotted around the condemnation to death and exile of two French sergeants, their exchange of lots and the scheming of the evil commanding officer who wants to execute the sergeant whose sweetheart he wishes to marry.

29. Ware and Schoenberger, editors of volume 13 of *America's Lost Plays*, state that *The Bombardment of Algiers* was not produced, but the copy in the Historical Society of Pennsylvania lists a date of January 4, 1829, and indicates that Joseph Jefferson played Osmin, a eunuch of the harem.

30. The manuscript of the play was lost until purchased at auction in 1956 by the University of Pennsylvania. See Neda McFadden Westlake's edition of *Caius Marius* (Philadelphia: University of Pennsylvania Press, 1968).

31. Westlake, *Caius Marius*, 25.

32. *Irish Shield and Literary Panorama*, III (January 14, 1831), 8.

33. *Irish Shield and Literary Panorama*, III (January 21, 1831), 29.

34. *Ariel*, IV (January 22, 1831), 157.

35. Arthur Hobson Quinn, *A History of the American Drama from the Beginning to the Civil War* (New York: Appleton-Century-Crofts, 1943), 248.

36. Curtis Dahl, *Robert Montgomery Bird* (New York: Twayne Publishers, 1963), 51.

37. Reprinted in Quinn, 246.

38. Quoted in Dahl, 69.

39. *Ariel*, V (November 12, 1831), 236.

40. *Spirit of the Times*, II (February 9, 1833), 3.

41. See, for example, *The American Monthly Magazine*, II (December 1833), 351.

42. *North American Magazine*, I (January 1833), 189–92.

43. *Federal American Monthly*, I (January 1833), 65–66.

44. *Dramatic Mirror*, I (August 28, 1841), 17.

45. *Spirit of the Times*, XVII (April 3, 1847), 72.

46. Handwritten note in Dreer Collection, Historical Society of Pennsylvania.

47. *Spirit of the Times*, II (April 7, 1832), 3.

48. Letter, n.d., to the *Transcript*, Harvard Theatre Collection.

49. *Spirit of the Times*, XI (April 3, 1841), 60.

50. *Spirit of the Times*, XI (May 29, 1841), 156.

51. *Aylmere; or, The Bondman of Kent and Other Poems* (Philadelphia: E. H. Butler & Co., 1852), 308.

52. Robert T. Conrad, *Jack Cade, the Captain of the Commons* (London: Thomas Hailes Lacy, n.d.)

4

THE PLAYWRIGHTS AND THE STARS

The 1839 publishing venture of Samuel Colman—Colman's Dramatic Library, a series of American plays—was greeted with marked enthusiasm by literary people. Although short-lived, publishing only three plays, Colman's venture was similar to Samuel Kettell's three-volume *Specimens of American Poetry*, which ten years earlier had been published as an "attempt to do something for the cause of American literature."[1] Colman's enterprise, however, clearly illustrates an obvious misunderstanding of the inextricable relationship between drama and theatre. By separating the drama from the theatre in their minds, he and his contemporaries committed a practical error comparable to denying a musical composer access to a piano or an architect a space to fill. The disconcerting situation amounted to ambivalent encouragement for American dramatists throughout the nineteenth century, with predictable results: literary people wrote with an eye toward publication; practical playwrights wrote for the contemporary stage. It took many years for these two views to merge; some say it happened only with the writings of Eugene O'Neill. One may fault Samuel Colman's understanding and insight, but he was not alone, and his idealism was admirable. "It is believed," Colman wrote in the first volume of Colman's Dramatic Library "that much of native genius, now in obscurity, would be introduced to the public if this enterprise is successful."[2]

The plays of Nathaniel Parker Willis (1806–1867) were a wise and popular choice for Colman's Dramatic Library. Willis' first play, *Bianca Visconti; or, The Heart Overtasked* (1837), had won $1,000 in a competition offered by Josephine Clifton, who acted the leading role. Moderately successful on the stage, it was praised by the editor of the *Federal American Monthly* as a "successful tragedy" in American drama, which is "more lean and wretched than the drama of any of the cultivated nations."[3] This was the beginning of an intense if short-lived association with the theatre for Willis, whose popularity abroad as an American writer was second at this time only to that of Washington Irving and James Fenimore Cooper. Although primarily an essayist, Willis was also a journalist, an editor and the author of poetry, plays and short stories. According to Henry A. Beers, an early biographer, from January of 1842 to June of 1844, Willis was "beyond a doubt, the most popular, best paid and in every way most successful magazinist that America had yet seen."[4] The theatre, however, brought him little satisfaction, and his association with Edwin Forrest brought him physical injury and considerable trouble.

James Russell Lowell struck an appropriate chord in "A Fable for Critics" in which he described Willis: "There's Willis so natty and jaunty and gay, / Who says his best things in so foppish a way." For modern historians of American letters Willis' popularity has not lasted; yet his contribution to dramatic literature of the 1830s and 1840s deserves recognition for its own merit as well as an illustration of the problems a writer might encounter in creating for the theatre. In one area of literary endeavor Willis achieved the greatest possible popularity; in another he failed. Obviously, talent had something to do with it. Beers states that Willis' "genius was undramatic" and that *Tortesa the Usurer* and *Bianca Visconti* "are book plays, merely."[5] Analysis of the plays, however, does not bear out this opinion, and modern productions of *Tortesa* reveal that it retains considerable attractiveness for audiences.

In Jacksonian America, successful playwrights created heroic figures consistent with their perceived reality, their aspirations, and the dreams of the public they were trying to please. Because it was basically a masculine world that the theatre had to reflect, they provided heroes: Metamora, Spartacus, Nimrod Wildfire, Jonathan and Mose. These stage heroes were generally youthful, intense, idealistic and without subtlety. Humanitarian, yet lacking a concern for tradition or gentility, they boasted natural habits and basic tastes. Later, through the shock of an awareness brought about by political and social upheaval, the American stage more consistently supported protagonists that were female as well as male—but not at this time. Throughout the period there were, of course, exceptions, perhaps begun by *She Would Be a Soldier*, although the heroine exhibited masculine qualities. Actresses such as Josephine Clifton and Charlotte Cushman, who had good reputations during the 1830s, gained part of their stature by acting male roles. Mazeppa was, for example, a male role frequently acted by a woman. In Epes Sargent's *Bride of Genoa*, Clifton acted the male lead in the Boston production, and Charlotte Cushman took the same role in New York. Willis, however, wrote his best parts for women, and this in itself would have worked against his success in the American theatre of his day.

Willis—the name to which he answered to friends, relatives and his wife— was an elegant man, in appearance and in prose style. Literary and personal affectations were basic to his nature. An educated and conceited young man, always in love and fond of wine and fast horses, he purposefully offended his more sober-minded associates in the literary and editorial worlds. He pretended to write, for example, at a rosewood desk in a crimson-curtained sanctum. After his graduation in 1827 from Yale College, where he composed a comedy which was produced by the Limonia Society, he edited the *Legendary*, the *Token* and the *American Monthly Magazine*, published scenes and sketches and was at the age of twenty-five famous in the demanding literary circles of New York City. From 1831 to 1834, he traveled abroad, where he wrote many sketches, some of them published in one of his better known collections, *Pencillings By the Way* (1835). As he became involved with George Pope Morris, Park Benjamin and Horace Greeley in the numerous editorial skirmishes that characterized the editorial world at that time, he matured as an editor and a writer.

During the early period of his intensely popular and successful career, summer of 1837 to early spring of 1839, he wrote three plays, two of which are among the best written during the era. Unfortunately, however, one of Willis' most publicized experiences in the theatre was his confrontation in 1850 with Edwin Forrest. Earlier in his life Willis had enjoyed Forrest's acquaintance and had even written in a letter to a friend, J. B. Van Schaich, his "Alcibiades," that Forrest "is a splendid fellow, by Heaven, I adore him." [6] Subsequent events would alter that opinion. The second Mrs. Willis was a good friend of Catherine Sinclair, whose scandalous divorce from Forrest came to trial late in 1851. The previous year, when slanders against Mrs. Sinclair were being wildly publicized, Willis took occasion in print to express his disbelief. For his gallant defense of Sinclair, Willis was accosted by Forrest in Washington Square, knocked down and, until police came to his aid, beaten with a whip. Although the frank character of editorial opinion was common in New York, Forrest's response was extreme. Lawsuits followed, but editors, Willis among them, generally remained dauntless in expressing their opinions regardless of actions or attitudes directed toward the Fourth Estate.

Bianca Visconti was first produced at the Park Theatre on August 25, 1837, and for reasons that must relate to Willis' popularity as a writer, the *Spirit of the Times* prepared audiences for its success. The day after this opening, August 26, the puffing became more obvious: "We will risk our judgment and our taste on the production of its complete and triumphant success." [7] The next issue of the *Spirit* carried a full review and the plot of the play in which the acting of Josephine Clifton and Henry Placide, for whom Willis wrote the part of Pasquali the whimsical poet, was abundantly praised. [8]

Willis took the germ of his plot from the life of Francesco Sforza, a fourteenth-century condottiere who married the daughter of Philip Visconti and became Duke of Milan. Generally well-structured for stage effect, the plot is embellished with some excellent dialogue and a few distinctive scenes. Two minor characters, for example, provide fine wit and comedy and have important roles in the plot—Pasquali the poet, and Fiametta, Bianca's waiting woman and friend of Pasquali. The play opens with their conversation.

Fiametta: Why dost thou never write verses upon me?

Pasquali: Didst thou ever hear of a cauliflower struck by lightning?

Fiametta: If there were honesty in verses, thou wouldst sooner write of me than of Minerva thou talkest of. Did she ever mend thy hose for thee?

Pasquali: There is good reason to doubt if Minerva ever had hose on her legs.

Fiametta: There now! She can be no honest woman! I thought so when thou saidst she was most willing at night.

Pasquali: If thy ignorance were not endless, I would instruct thee in the meaning of poetry. . . . (I,1)

It is a fine opening scene: light wit, exposition presented easily, a complication suggested by Fiametta's observation that Bianca dotes on Gulio, her page. Scene 2 shows Sforza ready to attack Milan if Bianca's bedridden father does not finally arrange his long-promised marriage to Bianca. Warned by Sarpellione, the ambassador to Milan of King Alfonso of Naples, that there is a true heir to the dukedom of Milan, a boy whose identity is secret, Sforza, a practical soldier who has fought on many sides in the wars among the city-states of Italy, says that he will share his power with the boy.

After an opening scene in Act II in which Pasquali is challenged by the villainy of Sarpellione, Willis reveals Bianca's insecurity and loneliness with considerable sensitivity and spirit. Showing her a ring engraved with these words, "he who loves most, loves honor best," Sforza leaves a confused bride on his wedding night to wander the ramparts as a soldier. Bianca wonders if he loves her, wonders if he can "find pleasure in simplicity like mine" (II,4), and with a sweet innocence decides to renounce her childhood romantic adoration of Sforza and try to win him as a woman. Scene 2 in Act III is particularly well conceived to show the character of Sforza, who through a playful dueling practice with Gulio, discovers that this page, though unaware of his parentage and his destiny, is the son of the dying Visconti and should be the next duke. Tempted to the extreme in their swordplay, Sforza struggles with his emotions and wins: "As I am true to honor and that child, help me, just heaven" (III,2). Before the bridal feast, Bianca defends Sforza against the evil sneers of Sarpellione. Then the announcement: Visconti is dead. Bianca thinks only of Sforza becoming the duke; he, knowing that her brother lives, glories in her majestic bearing.

At the beginning of Act IV, Willis again uses Pasquali and Fiametta for foreshadowing and for humor. Later, Bianca rejects the news that Gulio is her brother, yet remains aware that her fondness for him has always warred with her love for Sforza. When she overhears Sarpellione hire a man to kill Sforza while he sleeps, she reacts in a manner that seems foreign to her character and ponders some way to entice Gulio to sleep in Sforza's place during his afternoon nap. In Act V Bianca listens to Sforza explain that he struck down his trained falcon because it was poised to kill Bianca's nightingale, and overwhelmed by his sensitivity to her desires, decides that Sforza must be made duke. In a sentimental scene in which her emotions are torn in both directions, she allows Gulio to be murdered in Sforza's place. The final scene (V,3) is confused and long as Bianca, in the tradition of heroines in heroic tragedy, loses her sanity—"And I killed my brother / To make you Duke!"—and lives only long enough to crown Sforza before dying of a broken heart.

For all its weaknesses, *Bianca Visconti* shows a sensitivity to human nature that generally did not appear in the work of Willis' contemporaries. As a first effort, it was remarkable. Readers could enjoy the plot expressed through the characters and the beauty of many of their lines. For theatregoers of the 1830s, however, the play lacked the basic requirement for success: spectacle. The editor of the *Federal American Monthly* expressed it clearly: "There is hardly incident enough in the first three acts to keep up that melo-dramatic influence which the artificial appetite of the present day delights in. The author seems to have scorned the *clap-trap* which has become the chief merit of many modern playwrights."[9] This writer and others, although with some misgivings, were forced to conclude that *Bianca Visconti* was more a literary composition than a drama for the stage. Such was the tenor of the times. When the Reverend Zouch S. Troughten based his tragedy, *Nina Sforza*, on the same theme, the performance at the Chestnut Street Theatre in Philadelphia was reviewed in the *Dramatic Mirror* as "replete with poetic gems" but also "better adapted to the closet than to the stage."[10]

Three months after the opening of *Bianca Visconti*, the Park Theatre management premiered another play by Willis written for Miss Clifton. A five-act comedy entitled *The Kentucky Heiress*, it was unashamedly promoted by the *Spirit of the Times* on November 18, 1837, and again a week later, largely on the basis of Willis' published sketches and "the dashing style of Miss Clifton in comedy." When the play failed, the *Spirit* blamed the actors, even Miss Clifton, in the part of Honoria Trevor: "There is not a five-act comedy in the English language that could have survived such a cast, much less such wanton and unpardonable disregard for the text."[11] The play, however, was admittedly written to order and in great haste. Willis obviously created a number of distinctive individuals but did not have the interest nor the time to arrange them in a respectable plot with confrontations appropriate to their characters. "There was a Kentucky heiress, more wolfish than Nimrod Wildfire, paired with an English nobleman [Lord Barksdale], polished, bland and plausible: a London coxcomb of the first water dancing attendance on a toothless maiden aunt—a fighting Western Colonel without brains, and a Yankee with a superabundance of them, besides a cicerone, a boots, and an enormous gentleman in straw." With this comment the *Spirit* appeared to absolve itself from its earlier puffing and declared that the play "died a natural death, and deserved its fate."[12] Willis may have learned a lesson. He afterward left American subjects to those who saw more potential in them. He also devoted more time to creating his next work for the stage.

Tortesa the Usurer was first produced at the National Theatre in New York on April 8, 1839, with James Wallack, for whom the play was written, in the title role. One may find several sources for Willis' inspiration—*Romeo and Juliet*, *The Winter's Tale*, *La Sepolta Viva* by Domenico Maria Manni—but Willis wrote his own play, the real charms resting upon the clever delineation of characters. Although Wallack starred as Tortesa, there are four other parts in the play that are attractive: Zippa, the glover's daughter; Angelo, the painter; Tomaso, the wine-loving servant; and Isabella, the heroine of the play. Angelo, the excessively romantic hero and excessively absorbed painter, suggests shades of the young Willis who seemed always in love, seldom serious and usually vocal in his adulations. From London, Willis once wrote to Van Schaich: "I should like to know if all my red hot verses are quite used up for curling purposes. Somebody pines for me, I trust." [13] He was much the ladies' man, according to Beers, and this play reveals an apparent understanding of women and their ways. It is, in fact, a woman's play. As Angelo moons like a stricken youth and Tortesa turns himself, and his character, inside out for the love of women, Zippa and Isabella control most of the action of the play. Tortesa's humane reversal in the final act depends entirely on the climax Willis contrived for his play.

Tortesa, the usurer, is the happiest man in Florence. By dint of his great wealth, he has made a bargain with Count Falcone, who faces disaster from his ill-managed estate. "So, briefly, there's the deed!" he tells Falcone as he returns his lands to him; "You have your lands back, and your daughter's mine—so ran the *bargain*!" Later, he boasts of that *bargain*: "I have bought with money / The fairest daughter of their haughtiest lien!" Exulting in his accomplishment, Tortesa explains his triumph to Zippa, who also has a strong appeal for him:

> I marry this lord's daughter
> To please a *devil* that inhabits me!
> But there's an angel in me—not so strong—
> And this last loves you!

This revelation stirs a thought in Zippa's soft and simple heart; she feels pity for Isabella, who must marry this hard-hearted monster.

There is yet another complication for the arrogant machinations of Tortesa, a conniving but not unscrupulous man who tries to keep his heart and head unaware of each other's existence. Angelo, the painter commissioned to paint a portrait of Isabella, falls overwhelmingly in love with her. In his speech, Angelo sounds like the youthful Willis writing to his friend, Van Schaich:

> *Angelo*:   In a form like yours,
> All parts are perfect, madam! yet, unseen,
> Impossible to fancy. With your leave
> I'll see your hand unglov'd.

Isabella: (Removing her glove.)   I have no heart
            To keep it from you, Signor! There it is!
Angelo: (Taking it in his own.)
            O, God! how beautiful thy works may be!
            Inimitably perfect! Let me look
            Close on the tracery of these azure veins!
            With what a delicate and fragile thread
            They weave their subtle mesh beneath the skin,
            And meet, all blushing, in these rosy nails!
            How soft the texture of these tapering fingers!
            How exquisite the wrist? How perfect all! (I,3)

At this point Tortesa, who has overheard, rushes in to defend his honor and
that of his betrothed, but is repulsed by Isabella:

My *troth* is yours!
But I'm not wedded yet, and till I am,
The hallowed honor that protects a maid
Is round me, like a circle of bright fire!
A savage would not cross it—nor shall you!
I'm mistress of my presence. Leave me, Sir! (I,3)

Furious, Tortesa leaves, and the act ends with the triangle complete. It is, indeed, a well-conceived and finely structured first act. Willis must have enjoyed
himself thoroughly as he composed Angelo's gushing lines of admiration, mix-
ing man and painter, and manipulating his lovers like a writer of Restoration
comedy.

Willis handles his romantic plot with considerable grace and assurance while
adding a good change of pace with Tomaso, Angelo's gluttonous servant, who
provides exposition, a vital role in the plot, and good low humor—too low for
one critic who found the scene of the drunken Tomaso with Isabella "the most
objectionable portion of the play. . . . our feelings recoil within us in disgust." [14] In Act II Zippa discovers that Angelo, an object of her affections,
loves a "lady" and feels that she can take revenge on this "fickle Angelo" by
marrying Tortesa. Isabella also shows her character. Because the Duke of Florence has decided to help Falcone by returning his lands to him and arranging
another marriage for Isabella, Falcone now prohibits her marriage to Tortesa.
Isabella is livid:

I'll die first! Sold and taken back,
Then thrust upon a husband paid to take me!
To save my father I have weigh'd myself,
Heart, hand, and honor against so much land!—
I—Isabella! I'm not hawk nor hound,
And, if I change my master, I will choose him! (II,3)

These are strong words that make complete nonsense of the love and honor
theme of heroic tragedy, and Isabella chooses Tortesa. It is a comic twist, clearly

in character, but Isabella is not through designing her own life. She must find out if Angelo, the man, really loves her; Zippa must make the same discovery, and the two women must talk. Act III is weighed down with discoveries and discussions and little real action, but the conclusions are important. Zippa learns that although she and Angelo had good times together, "His *soul* was never mine!" Isabella will take a potion to feign death: "And from my sleep I wake up Angelo's / Or wake no more!" (III,2).

The guests assemble for the wedding of Tortesa and Isabella in the "sumptuous drawing room" of the Falcone Palace. Then the news! "She's dead!" Wedding music changes to funeral music, as the procession moves, followed by Angelo and by Zippa, who taunts Tortesa with hints that Angelo will steal the body. Later, the drug having worn off, Isabella appears in the street, cold and irritated that Angelo did not keep "*one* night of vigil near me, / Thinking me dead." When Isabella finds herself on her father's doorstep and is refused entrance, a drunken Tomaso happens by, offers her a drink and takes her to Angelo's house where he "deposits her in Angelo's bed." Presumably, an understanding is reached before the opening of the fifth act in which the two lovers, rejoicing together, are interrupted by Tortesa. To foil the jilted groom, Isabella assumes the attitude of her portrait behind the empty frame and fools her tormentor, but her presence is revealed by the discovery of her bridal veil, and Angelo, in consequence of his conspiracy is led away to the duke. At the final curtain, however, he is saved by Isabella and by Tortesa, who sensed "a new feeling here" as he places his hand upon his heart.

Like all poetic drama of this period, the play is overwritten, and the final scene is irritatingly long as Isabella temporizes with Tortesa and Angelo before choosing the painter and allowing Tortesa the joys of Zippa. The play may also be faulted for excessive intrigue and the inconsistencies of Tortesa's character. *Tortesa the Usurer*, however, seemed to excite the entire spectrum of critical response. If a critic found Tomaso disgusting in one scene, he could praise his "frequent sallies of wit and sprightly repartees" in another.[15] Reviewing the production, the *Spirit* thought the play "the heaviest dramatic effort of its author, but likewise one of the best plays ever written in America."[16] Although "the overcrowded . . . unnecessary and impertinent intrigue" bothered the writer of "Literary Reviews" in the *Literary Examiner and Western Monthly Review* as did the improbable effect of Isabella's assuming the place of a portrait, he preferred it to "any American play."[17] An overabundance of asides—for humor, exposition, plot action—might be added to the list of frailties. There is also no moral in the play for the moralist, nor was there a sense of earnestness for the serious playgoer. All critics, however, saw it as more readable than most plays, although they questioned its dramatic quality and structure. Such detractors as the critic for the new liberal democratic journal of Orestes Bronson, the *Boston Quarterly Review*, focused more on the author than the play: "Let him sport on gilded wings his summer days; too soon will come the frost, the killing frost and no one will dream of asking, 'Where is he?' "[18]

Although few students of American literature still read the essays of Nathaniel Parker Willis, 150 years ago he entertained a generation who are better understood for their enjoyment of his sporting ways. There were also those who enjoyed *Tortesa* and reveled in scenes and characters as well as speeches that still delight. Clearly, the same frivolous and sporting nature that made some of Willis' essays pleasant reading found expression in his play, which Samuel Colman did well to include in his Dramatic Library. Yet Willis was not a successful dramatist in the theatre of his day.

Among the theatre items in the *Spirit of the Times* for December 16, 1837, the following note appeared: "Mr. Sargent has now produced two successful plays, under the auspices of the two most distinguished actresses of the day [Josephine Clifton and Ellen Tree]; he must, therefore, be placed among the foremost in the slowly increasing list of American dramatists, and all friends to the native drama will desire his success."[19] The sixth in his family to carry the name, Epes Sargent (1813–1880) descended from successful Gloucester, Massachusetts, merchants and ship owners and sailed with his father to Russia when he was fifteen years old. He attended Harvard College but did not graduate and, instead, went to work as an editor of newspapers, a journalist, a poet, a novelist and compiler whose interest in American writers and in American drama remained a force throughout his life. He wrote only four full-length plays, several sketches and dramatic criticism but had a marked influence upon drama in America. Although he lived for a time in New York, he is generally associated with Boston, where he edited several newspapers, foremost among them the Boston *Transcript*. At his death, the *New York Times* (January 1, 1881) described him as an extraordinarily industrious man who wrote with "great diligence, talent and versatility." A distinguished American drama at this time would have required a careful fusion of talent and industry, guided by a persistence inspired by failure as well as success. Sargent had the potential and the interest. A serious playwright who wrote for popular actors and actresses in the fashion of the day and produced two or three good plays, he was still not a success in the theatre.

The Bride of Genoa opened at the Tremont Theatre in Boston on February 13, 1837, with Josephine Clifton in the role of the hero, Antonio Montaldo. Set in Genoa in 1593 and based on the historical character who became the Doge at the age of twenty-two (two years younger than the author of the play), *The Bride of Genoa* has a romantic and ordinary plot in which the common-born hero falls in love with the daughter of Count Castilli and, after considerable struggle, reaches both his political and romantic ideals. It played for five nights in Boston and netted Sargent a profitable benefit. At the Park Theatre in New York with Charlotte Cushman supporting Miss Clifton (November 18, 1837), the five-act tragedy, now called *The Genoese*, was criticized as a youthful effort with more promise than actual achievement. It was, however, a fine beginning for Sargent, who published his play in *The New World*.[20]

By September of 1837, Sargent had a new play in rehearsal with parts for

Ellen Tree and James Murdock, who were predicting its "extraordinary success."[21] This was *Velasco*, which opened at Boston's Tremont Theatre in November of that year. Several years later Rees predicted that this play would "form quite an event in the annals of the stage."[22] In the meantime critics of the New York production in December of 1838 were both pleased and surprised—pleased that the piece was so successful and surprised that "the inexperience and retiring modesty of the amiable author" could produce a tragedy "that yields to few of the modern school in boldness of conception and dramatic power."[23] *The Expositor* thought a "pruning knife might be exercised with advantage," but enjoyed the "subtle thoughts and graceful images" as well as the "exquisite richness of diction" in the play.[24] Looking back at the production, even Odell had kind words: "The American drama suddenly looked up."[25] At the opening of the 1849–1850 season of the Marylebone Theatre in London, *Velasco*, with E. L. Davenport in the lead role, ran for longer than the week originally determined, and the *Spirit of the Times* quoted three newspaper reviews from the London press that praised the tragedy. From the *London Dispatch* (September 30, 1849): "The author has elaborated a drama as replete with general interest as it is remarkable for some of the best situations the tragic stage can command. The last scene was very perfectly acted and, together with the concluding tableaux, produced a powerful effect."[26]

Sargent found the idea for his play in the life of Le Cid and placed the action of *Velasco* in Burgos, Spain, about 1046. The play opens with the return from a period of banishment of Velasco, who had once angered King Ferdinand of Castille, by interrupting his argument with another. Now, fresh from victories among the Moors, Velasco makes the most of his presentation at court as a mysterious vizored knight. The heroine of the play is the delightful Izidora, betrothed by her father, Gonzalez, to Hernando. She is, however, not pleased with her engagement. Appearing at the court on the arm of her brother, Julio, she is enchanted by the vizored knight and shows her thoughtful yet lighthearted nature in a response to Julio's question: "What is love?"

> A cloud steep'd in the sunshine! An illusion,
> On which concentrate Passion's fiercest rays!
> Your Lover's little better than a Pagan;
> On the heart's shrine he rears a human idol;
> Imagination heightens every charm,
> Brings down celestial attributes to clothe it,
> And dupes the willing soul, until at length,
> He kneels unto a creature of the brain—
> A bright abstraction! But the cynic Time
> Who holds the touchstone to immortal Truth,
> Soon laughs him out of his prodigious folly! (I,2)

Before the final curtain her attitude toward love will change, but now, Velasco, having looked fondly on her in the past, is disturbed by her betrothal and asks the king to help arrange his own marriage to Izidora.

Love appears triumphant until Act II, in which Sargent introduces that concept of honor, which in tragedies of this character must be appeased before love can be satisfied. Sargent, however, wrote melodrama rather than tragedy, building the inevitable catastrophe upon the machinations of the villain, Hernando, rather than the characters of the lovers. Trying to satisfy his own basic desires, Hernando fans the ancient feud between Gonzalez and Velasco's father, DeLerma. When Gonzalez, goaded to anger, strikes the older man, DeLerma cries out to Velasco: "To thy trust I yield mine honor!" (II,3). Although Hernando is not a well-developed villain, he seizes his advantage: "Ambition shall complete / What Vengeance has so prosperously begun" (III,1). According to his concept of honor, Velasco kills Gonzalez and is spurned by a shocked Izidora, to whom Gonzalez, at his death, passed his honor with the gift of his dagger. Throughout Acts II, III and IV Hernando tries to intensify the lovers' struggle and basely, though unsuccessfully, employs the conflicting values of love versus honor to satisfy his jealousy. At the king's banquet announcing the wedding of Velasco and Izidora, Hernando gives Julio a vial of poison and uses his smooth tongue to influence Julio's sense of honor: "to save thy sister from a fearful crime / And to avenge thy father" (V,1). These are powerful arguments. At the banquet festivities Velasco succumbs to Julio's villainy, while Izidora, mouthing Juliet's complaint about the last "friendly drop," dies of a broken heart.

Critics of the produced play praised the stage effects and the language which, like that of Willis, was considerably superior to the poetic drama of this period. Those who read the version published in 1838 came to similar conclusions and found *Velasco* a "good play, well-constructed toward an inevitable tragic catastrophe and full of lively incidents."[27] The joie de vivre of Izidora in the early scenes makes her as charming as the youthful Francesca in Boker's *Francesca da Rimini*, and her progress toward maturity and purpose obviously provided a fine role for Ellen Tree. Velasco, too, is very human as he returns home full of triumph, as he loves, as he defends his honor, even as he tries in the final scene to make peace with a maddened Julio. Spectacular incidents and the scenic possibilities helped make this play momentarily popular, but the play also builds upon interesting characters and well-devised decisions, on love and honor—and the presumed impossibility of the two existing together in conflict.

Sargent wrote other plays, but none as well received as *Velasco*. The hero of *Change Makes Change*, which played in New York in 1845, was Nathaniel Bunker, a Down-East Yankee, "cute and knowing, always ready and able to detect whatever is amiss," according to one critic who also dismissed the play as full of "disjointed incidents of a broad and farcical nature" and "localisms." "The play," the critic continued, "does not propound one moral, nor does it display any knowledge of the world beneath the surface; thus its only purpose is to amuse."[28] Among the playwrights who made a little money in the theatre there was nothing wrong with writing to amuse, and *Change Makes Change* may have been an attempt on Sargent's part to conform to the popular trend at Niblo's Theatre. It was not really part of his nature, however, and nearly ten years later, Willis, who considered Sargent "the only dramatist among us," called him "dis-modernized—a knight in armor instead of a gentleman on Broadway."[29] He was discussing Sargent's poetry, but the comment could well refer to his plays.

The Priestess, Sargent's five-act version of Bellini's *Norma*, was performed at the Boston Theatre in March of 1855. It was poorly received, although the correspondent for the *Spirit of the Times* felt that most of the adverse criticism was directed against Sargent individually, and not against *The Priestess*. Even this critic, however, did not find the blank verse pleasing and complained that a "life so stormy in its young freshness should have merged into bright and glorious sunshine."[30] That "glorious sunshine," however, did not exist either for the dramatist or the drama, although *The Priestess* excited some interest among theatre managers. P. T. Barnum, for example, wrote to Sargent on August 27, 1855: "I see you have written a new play. Will you send me a duplicate of it to be performed at the Museum? If so, please name price."[31] These should have been welcome words, but whatever happened, the play was no great climax to Sargent's career as a dramatist, and there are no records of plays written at a later date.

In *Songs of the Sea, with Other Poems* (1847), Sargent included two "Dramatic Pieces," as he called them: "The Candid Critic" and "The Lampoon." Both sketches have to do with critics of the drama and help explain Sargent's reluctance to write more plays. At this time in history much of the criticism, either pertaining to literature or to theatrical performances, could be vitriolic and devastatingly personal. Poe, for one, is well remembered for his venomous pen, and burlesques on page and stage were commonplace. In his two sketches, Sargent, as creative writer, spoke his mind through the hero of "The Lampoon," who explains that only dupes and fools are fooled by "the puniest of all creeping things! The press!"[32]

Sargent's sketch of "The Candid Critic" (a revision of *The Royal Poetaster*, An Historical Drama in One Act, 1841) is based on a historical account of Dionysis of Syracuse, a poet who confined his critics to the quarries. His quarrel with the poet Philoxenus reached a climax when Philoxenus drew his pen through the entire drama Dionysis had asked him to revise. In "The Candid Critic" Philoxenus is not charmed by Dionysis' *Ajax*, which the author complained was "murdered by the players." He admits his dislike and is sent to the quarries where he meets two executioners who, like him, as craftsmen have pride in their work. Moreover, they agree with Philoxenus, admire his honesty and praise him for finding merit only in true artistry. Later, pardoned and returned to the palace, Philoxenus refuses to flatter, but he is now wiser.

> *Dionysis*: Philoxenus, in truth, canst thou discern
> No merit in my *Ajax*? Can I write
> Poetry, think you?

Philoxenus: No. But thou canst act it;
　　　　And that is nobler.
Dionysis: Then I am content.

One has the strong feeling that Sargent, for all his celebrated amiability, did not share Dionysis's contentment and in this admirably clever sketch had a word for actors as well as critics.

In addition to writing plays Sargent contributed to the substance of American drama and theatre as an editor and compiler. By all accounts as well as by the amount of material he left behind, he was a man of great energy and industry. In his long anti-slavery novel, *Peculiar, A Tale of the Great Transition* (1864), about a black African called Peculiar Institution, Sargent enhances a complicated plot with references to theatre, such as the story of Estelle, an actor. Sargent's *Standard Speaker; Containing Exercises in Prose and Poetry for Declamation in Schools, Academies, Lyceums, Colleges* (1852) included his own treatise on oratory and two original speeches: "Spartacus to the Roman Envoys in Ethuria" and "Brutus Over the Dead Lucretia." His editing of the first seven volumes of the forty-three–volume collection of *Modern Standard Drama* (1846–1856) provides a valuable resource for the historian. Later in his life he edited Harper's *Encyclopedia of British and American Poetry*. His absorption with spiritualism is reflected in part of his writing but relates to drama only through the people who shared his interest. Seven years after Mrs. Mowatt's death, Sargent wrote to E. P. Whipple, the literary critic: "Last Tuesday I got for the first time in my life, the absolute proof of independent slate-writing ('spirit-writing') under conditions the most simple, irresistible and conclusive. . . . and I got, 1st, the name of Anna Cora Mowatt, then letters from my brother George and my father." [33]

Clearly a man of imagination and sensitivity whose broad interests carried him into different branches of literature and communication, Sargent emerges in the history of American letters as a minor but noteworthy contributor to dramatic literature and its criticism. If his enthusiasm for theatre soured as the obstacles became overwhelming, his life also spanned difficult times for American letters—a struggle for direction and recognition throughout Jacksonian America, the Civil War and the chaos of Reconstruction. Even during his young manhood, however, when he was doing his best work in the theatre, he did not find the encouragement that James Kirke Paulding had deemed necessary a dozen years earlier. In a letter to Longfellow (November 10, 1840) he wrote: "I find no time for the tragedy—have not even found a subject. . . . The theatres are going down. There are no books in the press. Wall Street looks gloomy and seedy." [34]

The most popular spectacle in the theatre of Jacksonian America was the actor—the visual image and voice of the new country, thunderous and majestic in the case of Forrest, brash and twangy in the Yankees, comic and suspiciously foreign in the Irish. Challenged and obliged to appeal to and feel the talents of this spectacle, most American playwrights during the 1830s and 1840s wrote, at least on occasion, with a particular actor or actress in mind. In contrast to Willis and Sargent and generally with a remarkable lack of pretense, some of these playwrights pictured a common and more recognizably realistic life that they thought people would enjoy seeing in the theatre. They wrote for the pit and the gallery, using the dramatic forms their audiences understood—farce and melodrama—taking scenes and themes from English and French plays, and exploiting current events, popular figures both real and imagined, and any glories or absurdities of the past or present they could discover or invent.

In many instances, playwrights wrote for actors who performed a single role, the Yankee, for example. James Hackett was the first. Stimulated by the success of Charles Mathews, the English impersonator of the Yankee, Hackett discovered the theatrical value of the Yankee character while visiting England and subsequently prevailed upon the younger George Coleman to allow him to change the title of *Who Wants a Guinea?* to *John Bull at Home; or, Jonathan in England*, substituting Solomon Swap for Solomon Grundy. With some grumbling and an obvious pun upon Hackett's name, Coleman agreed. And the race was on among actors. George Handel Hill soon appeared as a Yankee impersonator to be followed by Dan Marble, Joshua Silsbee, John Owens and lesser stars. A great deal has been written about these actors, their different roles and their techniques.[35] They were truly a fascinating lot and had a strong effect upon the development of an American drama.

At a time when novelties and spectacles were in great demand in the American theatre, the novelty of the Yankee character emerged as the most popular. It pleased English audiences as an aberration of America society which they found both amusing and, because it frequently showed rather common and crude peculiarities, truthful. With such a recommendation, Americans with English affectations could also accept the presentations. It also pleased Americans who wanted a native drama and literature by placing on the stage the Yankee characters who were popular in contemporary fiction, poetry and song—the work, for example, of Seba Smith and James Russell Lowell and such songs as "Jonathan's Visit to the Steamboat" (1825) and "Jonathan's Visit to New York City" (1833). As an impersonator of the Yankee (as acted by Hackett, less a New Englander than a general American), the Backwoodsman and the Irishman, the actor exploited those characteristics of Jacksonian America which the common man admired.

Perhaps the Yankee play became the most popular of the vehicle pieces because all of the great Yankee actors were also storytellers. For mid–nineteenth-century America the lecture circuit which frequently featured the storyteller was a meaningful part of many people's lives and was perhaps subconsciously accepted as a respectable substitute for theatre. Literary figures such as Ralph Waldo Emerson earned a good part of their livelihood lecturing across the country. Others, less learned but undoubtedly more entertaining, sometimes hired theatres or were featured during theatre seasons. Dr. William Valentine, the humorist who acted Yankee roles, was a popular and frequent entertainer at places like Niblo's Garden. During some of the disastrous seasons of the 1830s and 1840s, financially pressed managers opened theatres to different forms of entertainment, and audiences could listen to concerts, readings and lecturers or watch panoramas and dioramas in theatres where days or weeks before they might have witnessed traditional theatre fare. People were curious; they reached out—for new lands, for new ideas, for dreams or for a sense of security which they might derive from the stage, the platform or the pulpit.

After the Tremont Theatre in Boston closed in 1843, it was converted into the Tremont Temple, which functioned as a church on Sundays and a lecture hall the remainder of the week. Wags commented on this change from theatre to church, or lack of change, but there has always been an intimate relationship between church or place of worship and theatre or place of entertainment. In their vague and mysterious beginnings there may well have been a common source of inspiration. As audiences in either church or theatre react to what is happening before their eyes, the creator or creators of both events share an atmosphere as well as certain talents. It has not been uncommon, for example, for preachers to become actors or for actors to become preachers. Many theatre artists share a sense of mission—David Belasco with his clerical collar, for example—that is not generally acknowledged. Charles Booth Parsons, the tragedian, left the theatre in 1838 to become a Methodist minister and after 1839 alternated between stage and pulpit.

The relationship between preacher and actor, however, has not always been peaceful, and the antipathy was wonderfully illustrated at the Tremont Temple where the Reverend Doctor Lyman Beecher, upon his first appearance, thanked the Almighty God for having effected this change and prayed that "all theatres might soon become Temples of God, and that Satan, their great head, might immediately be driven back to his appropriate home, the bottomless pit." He also made some pointed comments on the bad character of actors and actresses and the evils that constantly surrounded them. Upon reading this speech in St. Louis, Sol Smith, the renowned theatre manager in the midwest and southwest, took offense and wrote what he called "a friendly letter to the Reverend Doctor Beecher" which was printed in the *Spirit of the Times*.[36] In a telling and generally compelling fashion Smith not only defended himself and his associates but undertook to instruct the Reverend Beecher in some of the basic principles of Christianity. They were—the preacher and the actor—not adversaries but "fellow sinners," Smith declared. The point to be made here is not the exchange between Messrs. Beecher and Smith, nor any continued confrontation between theatres and churches, but the similarity, along with the popular lecturers and humorists, of their positions in the eyes of the people at this time, not to mention the similarity of techniques they all shared.

The stage, the platform and the pulpit, albeit for different objectives on occasion, held similar appeal for the emotions of different segments of American society. Although the aggregate power of the theatre to stimulate emotions was slight in a nation of people who still did not look at entertainment per se as advantageous in the "root hog or die" world they saw before them, that power was developing as a factor in Jacksonian society. The number of riots taking place in American theatre is still uncatalogued, but one must acknowledge the passions that stimulated the Ferren Riot in 1834 as well as the Astor Place Riot in 1849, when the militia was called out and thirty-one people were killed. People chose to become involved in the many public situations involving the stage, the platform and the pulpit—where emotions were aroused and heroes and villains recognized and regaled.

On the stage the vehicle plays were a strong means of identification, and the vehicle actor, acknowledging a larger framework for the storyteller's art, became a visible enactment of a form of literature then popular among the nation's readers. As the nation developed, so did the popular art of mythmaking and storytelling. Davy Crockett is the best-known example, but there were others. A talker, a storyteller with an incredible ego, Crockett described himself as half-hoss and half-alligator. Soon this vision was confiscated by actors, and people saw Crockett portrayed on the stage or platform, just as they read about him or heard songs about him. Also popular in song and tale were the Yankee, the Backwoodsman and the Irishman. Consequently, the Yankee actor and the other vehicle performers were recognized as extensions of the tales of the day, and just as actors sometimes confused both Yankee and Backwoodsman for rural Americans, writers were likewise guilty.

Everyone enjoys a story, and a few exaggerations and extravagant embellishments never hurt in the retelling. Seba Smith, writing for the Portland, Maine, *Courier* in the 1820s, created Major Jack Downing who, dressed in a tall hat, striped trousers, vest and blue coat, influenced the costume of a long line of Yankee figures. Thomas C. Haliburton's Sam Slick, the Yankee peddler, was another, as was Hosea Biglow from James Russell Lowell's *The Biglow Papers*. Just as Davy Crockett confessed his talents—"I'm the darling branch of old Kentuck that can eat up a painter, hold a buffalo out to drink, and put a rifle-ball through the moon"—Sam Slick described himself as "the Yankee peddlar—I can ride on a flash of lightning and catch a thunderbolt in my fist." Bragging was a characteristic that appeared in most of the tales of this caliber along with a certain amount of rural humor, racy dialogue, strong dialect and grammatical absurdities.

In most of the stories there was a strong personal narrative, an approach which was taken over by the actor with scarcely a hesitation. The fact that some of the tales appeared to be taken from real life made them even more appropriate for the actor who quickly put Major Jack Downing and Sam Slick on the stage. Just after mid-century Henry Plunkett (H. P. Grattan) dramatized the chatty old dame from Frances M. Witcher's *Widow Bedot Papers* for Mrs. Barney Williams' acting talents. In 1835, Augustus B. Longstreet had published his *Georgia Scenes*, showing rural Americans in such tales as "The Horse Swap," "The

Gander Pulling'' and ''Georgia Theatrics,'' the narrative of a young farmer faking a bloody fight. The emphasis upon practical jokes, extravagant pranks and homely idioms provided good material for the experienced actor who must help his audience visualize the action. It was the chatty, rambling narrative quality with cacography for the reader and a twangy accent for the listener that gave these characters easy passage from page to stage. It was also clear that American literature and American drama and theatre, or at least elements of both, had similar objectives and techniques at this time.

For a sample of the hero stories popular in Jacksonian America, there is Davy Crockett's ''Coon Story'' (1833), which has the quality of stump speech:

Yes, gentlemen, he may get some votes by *grinning*, for he can *out grin* me, and you know I ain't slow—and to prove to you that I am not, I will tell you an anecdote. I was concerned myself—and I was fooled a little of the dam'dest. You all know I love hunting. Well, I discovered, a long time ago, that a 'coon couldn't stand my grin. I could bring one tumbling down from the highest tree. I never wasted powder and lead when I wanted one of the creturs. Well, as I was walking out one night, a few hundred yards from my house, looking unclearly about me, I saw a 'coon planted upon one of the highest limbs of an old tree. The night was very *moony* and clear, and old Rattler was with me; but Rattler won't bark at a 'coon—he's a queer dog in that way. So, I thought I'd bring the lark down, in the usual way, by a *grin*.[37]

Crockett goes on to describe his technique and the surprising result.

Compare Colonel Nimrod Wildfire's description of an incident in his life from William Bernard's version of Paulding's *The Lion of the West*, called *The Kentuckian; or, A Trip to New York*:

Why, I'll tell you how it was. I was riding along the Mississippi one day when I came across a fellow floating down the stream sitting cock'd up in the starn of his boat fast asleep. Well, I hadn't had a fight for as much as ten days—felt as though I must kiver myself up in a salt bin to keep—''so wolfy'' about the head and shoulders. So, says I, hullo, stranger, if you don't take keer your boat will run away wi you. So he looked up at me ''slantindickular,'' and I looked down at him ''slanchwise.'' He took out a chaw of tobacco from his mouth and, says he, I don't value you tantamount to that, and he flopp'd his wings and crowed like a cock. I ris up, shook my mane, crooked my neck, and neighed like a horse. Well, he run his boat foremost ashore. I stopped my wagon and set my triggers. Mister, says he, I'm the best man—if I ain't, I wish I may be tetotaciously exflunctified! I can whip my weight in wildcats and ride straight through a crabapple orchard on a flash of lightning—clear meat axe disposition! And what's more, I once back'd a bull off a bridge. Poh, says I, what do I keer for that? I can tote a steamboat up the Mississippi and over the Alleghany Mountains. My father can whip the best man in Old Kaintuck, and I can whip my father. (II,2)

On and on Colonel Wildfire rambles, boasting, elaborating in his own particular dialect until he identifies himself as ''Nimrod Wildfire. Why, I'm the yaller flower of the forest. I'm all *Brimstone* but the *head*, and that's *aky fortis*.''

The Yankees in fiction and onstage were also doing the same thing, telling stories. The same pattern can be found in poetry, if one remembers the Fireside Poet, memorialized for future generations in his huge chair in Longfellow Square, Portland, Maine, with a book in his hands, reading to anyone who will listen: "Listen, my children, and you shall hear. . . . " In Lowell's *Biglow Papers* Hosea had humorous adventures and spoke his mind. Whether reading stories or listening to the storyteller, one found that the tales were remarkably alike; yet the dramatization of the writer's concept added to an audience's enjoyment. It did not really matter whether the story was told within the atmosphere of a play or as a monologue from the stage. O. E. Durivage, for example, an actor and the author of *The Stage-Struck Yankee*, appeared on New York stages during the summer of 1848 telling what were billed as "Original Yankee Stories." Newness was, of course, always important to this generation of theatregoers, and therefore, to the tellers of tales. Most of the humorous stories of this period could bear retelling only by the inspired actor, and even he realized the necessity for novelty.

To illustrate further the close tie between the vehicle actor and the platform lecturer in technique and objectives, as well as the similarity between words appearing in countless journals and newspapers of the day and words spoken from the stage, consider the activities of George Handel Hill. Although he worked within the confines of a play, generally embellishing the material that brought him popularity, he also enjoyed giving talks. "The People and Antiquities of New England, Yankeeological Speaking" is the title of a speech which began in this fashion: "It is a pooty ginerally conceded fact, that man is a queer critter, and that when he ain't movin' abeout, he's doin' suthin' else." Hill no doubt ad-libbed the same line in any number of the stage roles that he performed. He also lectured on New England. "As a philosopher, he [the New Englander]," Hill opined,

believes in that individual freedom which protects itself against the usurpations of society; which does not cower to human opinions; which feels itself accountable to a higher tribunal than man's; which suspects a higher law than fashion; which respects itself too much to be the slave or tool of the many. . . . He has the convenient capability of adapting himself to every situation, and it has been said, that if you place him on a rock in the midst of the ocean, with a penknife and a bundle of shingles, he would manage to work his way ashore.[38]

It is impossible to realize the tone of Hill's delivery, and it must have been equally difficult to distinguish the Yankee-Backwoodsman story in a play from the comic monologues on stage or the humorous lectures. "The Varmount Wood-Choppen" was the title of a comic recitation. "We had," it began, "a Wood-choppen frolic at our farm down near Soapstone Swamp. Mammy wanted me to stay at the house an' help make reed-bird apple dumplens and huckleberry doughnuts for supper, but I was arter seein' heow Bill Butternut did his choppen, so I telled her as heow thar wan't chips enough in the oven to scare up a bake, so she let me out into the woods to hunt chips.'' Silas Steele, a prolific dramatist who wrote vehicle plays, included this monologue in his *Book of Plays: for Home Amusement* (1859). One could read comparably humorous scenes in the pages of the *Spirit of the Times*, which printed ''The Visit to the Histrionic Society, Etc.''[39] The comic story of the country hick attending a theatre goes back at least to a poem entitled ''Chuang-chia pu shih kou-lan'' (''Country Cousin At The Theatre'') by Tu Shan-fu in fourteenth-century China. Royall Tyler made a good thing of it in *The Contrast*, and the idea seems to retain its appeal. The rube in the *Spirit* sketch visits ''this ere gret city ov New Orleans'' and meets a friend:

Sez he, ''yere's a ticket to the Stronic Sociation, wot I are orinery member of, and this is my guest ticket.'' I thought he wus a darn feul tu call hisself onnary if he warnt good lookin'. ''Wot is it?'' sez I. ''Why,'' sez he, ''it's a place got up by ammyturs to execute plays in, a kinder theaytur.'' I hed offen hern tell of them places, but I had never bin in one, so I was right keen tu go. Sez he, ''yeu must dress up right smart, and look as 'cute's a nutmeg,' else they won't let yew in.''

The story continues with expected or unexpected results.

With the passage of another generation following the Age of Jackson, the Yankee and Backwoodsman vehicle actors had virtually disappeared, although the star system persisted and there were still such actors as Denman Thompson who for many years recreated the Yankee in *The Old Homestead*. Storytelling continued, however, as it probably always will. Soon after the Civil War comic writers and speakers such as Henry Wheeler Shaw, Edgar Wilson Nye and Mark Twain excited audiences in ways that were strongly reminiscent of the vehicle performers of the 1830s and 1840s, and the innumerable vehicle plays supplied by many known and unknown playwrights.

Because the actor was far more important than the playwright and had a constant need for novelty in an art form which was short-lived, almost by definition, vehicle plays are more notable for quantity than quality. They were not really meant to endure. In 1838 the *Spirit of the Times* noted that only Woodworth's *The Forest Rose* (1825) retained its popularity in the vast repertory of George Handel (''Yankee'') Hill, the actor who followed and soon replaced James Hackett as a Yankee impersonator.[40] ''Friend Woodworth's comedy of *The Forest Rose* is a most capital little affair,'' wrote a critic in the *Spirit*. ''Mr. Hill enacted Jonathan to admiration and 'told such a funny story,' as a little youngster remarked to us, that the audience were kept in excellent humor throughout.''[41] Most other Yankee plays quickly disappeared. After beginning as a storyteller at the Chatham Garden during the summer of 1831, Hill acted in such plays as *The Yankee in Trouble; or, Zephanich in the Pantry* (1832); *The Inquisitive Yankee; or, A Peep in All Corners* (1832); *Ovid and Obid; or, Yankee Blunders* (1834); *New Notions* (1840); *The Tourist* (1840), in which Hill played Ebenezer Fish; *Josh Horseradish; or, The Lying Yankee* (1842); *Of Age Tonight; or, Natur's Nature* (1842), with Hill as Jubal Judex; and *The Vermonter; or, Love and Phrenology* (1842), with Hill as Zephanesh Twang. All of these plays were written for "Mr. Hill's peculiar talents."

Other momentary plays, mainly written by Americans, are associated with the performance styles of different Yankee impersonators: Josh Silsbee in *The Yankee at Niagra, The Yankee in 1776* and *The Yankee Preacher*, all in 1843; James Hackett in *Major Jack Downing; or, The Retired Politician* (1834), based on the popular sketches of Seba Smith, and *Job Fox; or, The Yankee Valet* (1834); Dan Marble in *Sam Patch* (1839) and *A Yankee in Time* (1838). Ideas, plays and acting techniques spread quickly and were as quickly stolen. In *Nullification; or, The Yankee in Charleston*, advertised as a new play by the Bowery Theatre in New York, an actor named Giles played Peletiah Peaceful for several nights in late January of 1833. A week later at the Warren Theatre in Boston, it was announced that Yankee Hill "has got up a new Yankee play called *Timothy Lincoln's Visit to the Capitol of Nullification.*"[42] Current events were also important to the storytelling impersonator. After Great Britain provoked the Opium War (1839–1842) in China, an anonymous play entitled *Yankees in China; or, A Union of the Flags* (1840), featuring Tchoa Kong, Ponkqueha Sing Sing, a New Hampshire opium speculator and a Yankee sailor named Harry Darling, had a satisfactory run of eleven performances at the Bowery Theatre. It was a fast-moving world in America where exictement was a measured quantity, and American playwrights had to turn out the right product in the limited opportunity allowed them.

A few dramatists who contributed to the Yankee vehicles managed to escape anonymity. One was Cornelius A. Logan (1806–1852), the first native-born actor-playwright who wrote Yankee vehicle plays. Born in Baltimore, Logan worked briefly at a shipping house, then went to sea as a common sailor. Upon his return, Logan wrote for the Baltimore *Morning Chronicle*, reviewed plays in Philadelphia, where he first acted in 1825, and started a newspaper with William Leggett. Although Logan had his share of theatre management, he made his reputation as an actor, first in Yankee roles but mainly as a comedian in the West and South, where he became popular as an ardent defender of the stage. Cincinnati became his family home. Unfortunately, his vigor as actor and advocate of the theatre does not display itself remarkably in his plays, which were generally unpolished sketches to be exploited by an actor. That vigor, however, was obviously passed on to his daughter, Olive Logan, whose insightful accounts and forceful opinions color her writing.

It is unwise to judge Logan's plays by too severe dramatic standards. He wrote in response to need or commerce, as did many other actors and managers at this time, and naturally expected that his plays would be used for whatever serviceable purpose actors and managers would find. He probably wrote *The Wag of Maine* for James Hackett, who produced it at the Park Theatre in 1834. Essentially, it existed under this title and in two later revisions by Logan called

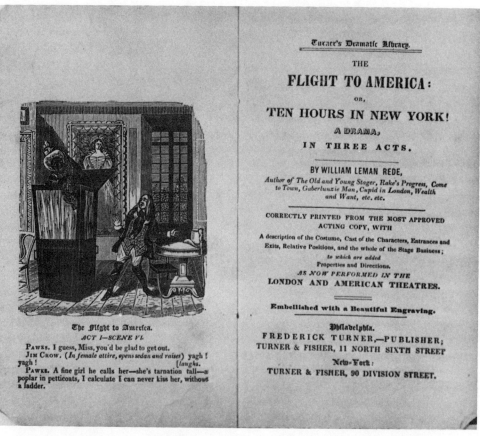

The Flight to America.

ACT I—SCENE VI.

Pawks. I guess, Miss, you'd be glad to get out.
Jim Crow. (*In female attire, opens sedan and raises*) yagh !
yagh !   [*laughs.*
Pawks. A fine girl he calls her—she's tarnation tall—a
poplar in petticoats, I calculate I can never kiss her, without
a ladder.

Tucker's Dramatic Library.

THE

FLIGHT TO AMERICA:

OR,

TEN HOURS IN NEW YORK!

A DRAMA,

IN THREE ACTS.

BY WILLIAM LEMAN REDE,

*Author of The Old and Young Stager, Rake's Progress, Come
to Town, Gaberlunzie Man, Cupid in London, Wealth
and Want, etc. etc.*

CORRECTLY PRINTED FROM THE MOST APPROVED
ACTING COPY, WITH

A description of the Costume, Cast of the Characters, Entrances and
Exits, Relative Positions, and the whole of the Stage Business;
to which are added
Properties and Directions.
AS NOW PERFORMED IN THE
LONDON AND AMERICAN THEATRES.

Embellished with a Beautiful Engraving.

Philadelphia.
FREDERICK TURNER,—PUBLISHER;
TURNER & FISHER, 11 NORTH SIXTH STREET

New-York:
TURNER & FISHER, 90 DIVISION STREET.

Title page of *The Flight to America: or, Ten Hours in New York!* by William Leman Rede.

Yankee Land; or, The Foundling of the Apple Orchard (1842 and 1844), both evidently made for Dan Marble, who acted a fourth version entitled *Hue and Cry* (1846), adapted by William Rede, an Englishman. Like several other English playwrights, Rede had some reputation as an adapter of American material. He had written *The Flight to America; or, Ten Hours in New York* (1836) evidently as a vehicle for T. D. Rice, the American actor of "Jump Jim Crow" fame who was currently enjoying a very popular engagement in England. After the version entitled *The Wag of Maine*, the names of the characters were changed, but the plot, improved as revised, remained essentially the same.

The original play was the usual complicated farce-melodrama revolving around a Yankee character named Mischievous Joe. An Orphan, Joe lived on the Kennebec River in Maine with his guardian, Mr. Rowell, a scoundrel employed as a steward by Sir Charles Anson. Joe's task is to expose Rowell's villainy, help bring the lovers together and discover his own fortunate circumstances. And he is to do this with as much wit and comic action as a good actor could bring to his part. The plot follows Rowell's attempt to marry Lt. Marshall's daughter by threatening to expose Marshall's presumed murder of Sir Charles. It does not matter that her affection lies elsewhere, but Anson's unexpected return complicates Rowell's plans. Shocked by this turn of events, Rowell tries to kill Anson, who is saved by Mischievous Joe at the appropriate melodramatic time. Logan's knowledge of a Maine Yankee was a little shaky, however, and Joe is more Westerner than Down-Easter. The introduction of an English peer on the Kennebec River leans towards the extraordinary when Joe turns out to be the long-lost son of Sir Charles, and one sees more of the tradition of romantic melodrama than of a vehicle play for a Yankee actor.

James Hackett played Mischievous Joe to his advantage, and James Rees, commenting on Hackett's performance in *The Wag of Maine* at the Park Theatre during the 1835–1836 season, noted that "the New York papers pronounced this the best American comedy that has been written."[43] Audiences, however, demanded change. Sometimes, probably more frequently than can be known, only the title of the play and the advertising was changed to promote novelty and entice the unwary to the theatres. Odell occasionally notes that the list of characters for a play suggests a repeat production from a previous year under a new name. Changes sometimes were also very deceptive, purposefully so at this time when plots and characters were plagiarized easily and with impunity. There is the story, probably apocryphal, of the playwright who watched a production of a play four times, trying to determine whether it was a play he had written. A. H. Quinn recorded the first performance of *Yankee Land*, Logan's retitled play, at Philadelphia's Pennsylvania Theatre on January 4, 1837, in which Mischievous Joe improved his Yankee dialect and became Lot Sap Sago.

The Vermont Wool Dealer, a farce in one act and two scenes, may have been written for Dan Marble, who first played it in Cincinnati on June 4, 1838, and kept it in his repertory for the rest of his life. Logan published the play in Cincinnati in 1844. The scene is a New York boardinghouse which boasts an Irish chore boy named Con Golumby and a Negro waiter named Bob. As the play opens, Captain Oakley, a military man, arrives with the girl he intends to marry, Amanda Waddle, and her mulatto maid, Betty, with the singular purpose of meeting Amanda's father and asking his blessings. After some opening comedy as Con tries to take Oakley's shoes off with a bootjack, Deuteronomy Dutiful enters with a trunk on his shoulders, which Oakley manages to knock off accidentally in their confused encounter. It seems that Deuteronomy has seen Amanda, followed her to the boardinghouse and, because she has $55,000, is determined to marry her. The second scene opens with a comedy rountine: Bob and Con discuss their plan to get three glasses of wine and deliver only two. When Deuteronomy's comically blunt proposal of marriage to Amanda is rejected, he contrives to send her a letter which is in due course intercepted by her father. Properly furious, both Waddle and Oakley challenge Deuteronomy to a duel, and Amanda combines her apprehension with a sense of humor. Appealing to Deuteronomy's vanity, she confesses that she will veil herself and steal away with him that night if he will not take part in the duel. Deuteronomy is delighted and sends Bob to tell the duelers that he will not appear, but Con gets drunk and reveals the plot to Waddle who, with Oakley, catches Deuteronomy and a veiled figure that turns out to be Betty. The joke is on the Yankee as Amanda declares her love for Oakley, but Deuteronomy is a good sport and buys champagne for the wedding.

The Vermont Wool Dealer has all the ingredients necessary for a successful vehicle: a Yankee by dialect, but by character tuned to general rural America; an Irish drunk; a witty heroine; a Negro waiter and a mulatto maid; an American military man; and an irate father. The disguise of a veiled black woman passing as white had been successful in *The Forest Rose* and serves as a clear social comment for modern historians. Much of the play's humor springs from the character of Deuteronomy Dutiful, a man who needs "just a few feathers to lie on" for his bed and feels "sheepish" when asked the price of wool. His actions give the opportunity for good physical humor onstage while his vocabulary reveals the quality of his naive pretense. Speaking of his love for Amanda, he assumes that he has "roused the ramifications of your rampant sensibilities, ma'am." Moreover, he is the country bumpkin in the big city. The farce itself, typical of the times and the genre, ends with the hero speaking directly to the audience: "Trusting that some amusement has been derived by friends from the visit to New York of the Vermont Wool Dealer." In another farce, *The Celestial Empire; or, The Yankee in China* (1846), Logan capitalized on America's recent ventures into Asia with a play that Joshua Silsbee acted with some regularity. As Yankee vehicles, Deuteronomy Dutiful and Lot Sap Sago held the stage for a generation.

Logan evidently wrote his last play for himself, and with good results. *Chloroform* appeared in Burton's Theatre on May 5, 1849, and as reported by the *Spirit of the Times* a month later, "has been in the ascendant at this establishment for some nights. . . . Mr. Logan, the author of the burletta and personator of the principal character, whose name is Aminadab Slocum, has gratified all sorts of people by his performance. His part is that of a stump orator, and he has a most powerful and effective voice for declamation with a very lively sense of ridicule. The piece is somewhat broad in humor, but it is certainly amusing."[44] The play dealt with the concept of progress and an anticipation of what the future would bring. The time is 1949, and Edward Slocum, searching through some family papers, discovers the confession of a dentist, stating that in 1849 one Aminadab Slocum died while the dentist was extracting a tooth with the aid of chloroform and that Slocum was buried in a building then being erected. Edward's search produced, not a skeleton, but old Slocum himself, who, like Rip Van Winkle, awakens from a kind of trance and wonders about everything around him. Critics found the work entertaining and filled with buffoonery but not terribly imaginative. "To criticize a burletta would be like dissecting a mosquito," declared a reviewer for *The Literary World*.[45] Evidently, neither critic nor playwright could imagine what would be happening in 1949.

Another successful writer of Yankee plays and a most prolific and popular playwright was Joseph Stevens Jones (1809–1877). Born in Boston, the son of a sea captain who was killed by savages on Donalaska Island in 1819, Jones received a basic education in the public schools of Boston. After brief employment in the counting room of a bank, he went to Providence to start an acting career which would have begun traditionally in the part of young Norval in *Douglas* had not the starring actress, Mrs. Duff, failed to appear. Consequently, Jones escaped that stigma and began his acting as Crack, a comic character, in Knight's *The Turnpike Gate*. Returning to Boston, he acted at the Tremont and Warren theatres before finding employment at the National Theatre as stage manager under William Pelby. About this time he began to study surgery at Harvard Medical School. With the failing management of Thomas Barry at the Tremont, Jones leased the theatre in 1839 and worked as stage manager until the end of the 1840–1841 season, returning to manage the last season of the theatre in 1842–1843. In 1843 he was awarded the Doctor of Medicine degree from Harvard College, and from that time on practiced medicine occasionally, lectured on anatomy and physiology and was generally advertised in the theatre as "the celebrated Dr. Jones." During his career he also acted in Philadelphia and in New York at the Bowery Theatre under the management of Thomas Hamblin. Jones continued to write plays until a year or so before his death when a lingering disease made writing impossible. Described by John B. Clapp in the Boston *Transcript* of December 30, 1910, as "a kindly man, with hosts of friends, vigorous, forceful," Jones left two children when he died in Boston in 1877—Dr. William Jones and a well-known comic actor, Nathaniel D. Jones; a daughter had drowned the previous fall.[46]

Jones' first successful venture at playwriting, *The Liberty Tree; or, Boston Boys in '76* was produced at the Warren Theatre on January 17, 1832. This patriotic play, in which Jones acted the part of Bill Ball, a Yankee, suggested a direction his career would take. From 1837 through 1839 Jones kept a daybook of his activities at the National Theatre: plays, acts, roles, costumes and remarks. In Payne's *Thérèse* and F. S. Hill's *Six Degrees of Crime*, Jones acted spy parts. In a play called *Fashionable Society* he played Cabbage, and he frequently appeared in his own plays—*The Surgeon of Paris* and *The Carpenter of Rouen*. The account book Jones later maintained at the Tremont Theatre provided an interesting record of a theatre manager's life.[47] Usually, Jones produced two plays each night, and to keep the theatre open, secured visiting stars as frequently as possible: Edwin Forrest, Edward Ranger, Kean, Hill, Mrs. Fitzwilliam, Dan Marble, Vandenhoff. His task was difficult, the risk constant. When James Murdock appeared first at the Tremont Theatre on May 18, 1840, the take was $88.50. For Murdock's benefit performance the box office receipts came to $265, but the next night brought in only $70. In the competitive Jacksonian world people worked for themselves. When actors put pressure on their friends and sold more tickets for their own benefit nights, managers suffered.

These were hard times in the theatre, the same in Boston as in New York or Philadelphia—the same actors, the same plays (very few of them American), the same benefits. Jones' blotter for the week of February 1, 1840, shows his weekly expenses: workmen and others (twelve people) at $116; actors, receiving from $4 to $45 a week (23 people) at $353; an orchestra of thirteen people paid $5 to $16 a week totaling $134. The grand total was $603 a week plus expenses for printing, supernumeraries, doorkeepers, police officers, watchmen and various benefits. Jones was able to help himself a great deal with the plays he wrote, but his was a losing battle. His business correspondence also suggests the problems of the theatre manager: firing W. H. Smith (September 26, 1839); arranging to pay Dan Marble $200 a week for five nights (July 7, 1840); arguing with A. W. Fenno, an actor, about free tickets (January 6, 1840); telling H. J. Conway that he will try to revise his play for production but can make no promises (March 3, 1841); explaining to G. H. Andrews that his reasons for not acting were unacceptable and that he will no longer be connected with the theatre (March 22, 1841).[48] Over the years the personnel problems of theatre managers change little, and one could imagine that, for Jones, writing plays, even under conditions prevailing at that time, might have been one of his more satisfying theatrical endeavors.

As a playwright, J. S. Jones was extremely popular, although the number of plays he wrote must remain pure conjecture. James Rees in *Dramatic Authors of America* states that Jones had written more than sixty. Jones himself could not remember the exact number, perhaps as many as 150; several had been very successful in England where *The Carpenter of Rouen* became a stock piece. A good number of his plays were ephemeral entertainments, however, written to help out an actor or manager who wanted to use Jones' name. Some were dramatized novels. The Yankee vehicle plays he wrote were created mainly for George H. Hill, who was the same age as Jones and a very good friend. On one occasion they toured part of New England together. Hill, too, had a craving for another profession—dentistry, which he learned from a New York dentist. He even practiced a little; the engraved plate on his door read "Dr. G. H. Hill/Surgeon Dentist."

Although the number of plays Jones wrote is impressive, he was not the only nineteenth-century playwright to write a play at a drop of a hat. He was, however, one of the first to do so in America. Joseph M. Field was a contemporary while James Pilgrim, John Brougham, Silas Steele and George M. Baker came to the theatre after Jones began to write. Compared with that of many of the prolific playwrights of this period, Jones' work illustrates a broader activity in the theatre. More efficient than most of his peers, he possessed talents that allowed him to help meet the needs of the profession he served. His feeling for comic action onstage and the wit of the native intelligence that pokes fun at all social institutions helped him become a successful writer of farce at a time when actors freely embellished, for good or for ill, any script they used. Jones also loved melodrama, patriotic enthusiasm and spectacle—the kind of theatre demanded by American audiences. Quite simply, Jones supplied this type of entertainment better than most of his contemporaries and frequently mixed the two genres to advantage for actors and for his own theatre management. He was a sensible person, and his divided career between medicine and theatre measures his individuality, his creative industry and the scope of his instincts. He wrote plays as a man of the theatre, separating himself from writers like Robert Montgomery Bird or Epes Sargent, who wrote for the theatre as a means of creative expression. Because he lost control of his plays through publication, he had distinct objections to seeing his work in print. Moreover, he did not write for a reading audience. As he once explained, *Moll Pitcher* was written in two or three days and for its success depended more upon what was done on the stage then what was said.[49] He could have made the same statement for most of his plays.[50]

Jones wrote *The Green Mountain Boy*, a farce in two acts, for George H. Hill, who first played the major character of Jedediah Homebred in Philadelphia in 1833. Although the play pleased audiences for nearly thirty years, the *Spirit of the Times* was not overly impressed with Hill's early production. "The only novelty of the evening was a farce called *The Green Mountain Boy*, but as it has evidently been written for the mere purpose of displaying Mr. Hill in another version of his Yankee character, any criticisms on its dramatic construction would be both unprofitable and unpleasing. The character of Homespun [changed to Homebred in the next issue of the *Spirit*] abounds in the usual Yankeeisms, but the quaint quiet manner in which Mr. Hill delivered them gave more value to the trifles than either their wit or point."[51] The play was immediately popular, however, and the next autumn the *North American Magazine* noted Hackett's current production of *The Green Mountain Boy*, by J. S. Jones, and the fact that it had been "redramatized in London."[52]

Like many other Yankee vehicle plays, *The Green Mountain Boy* carries a plot which seems incidental to the Yankee character. Although Ellen Tomkins loves young Edward Merston, her father, Major Tomkins, is forcing her to marry a supposedly rich English peer named Montague. As a comic contrast to this action, Joe Shakespeare, a lover of poetry, woos an old maid, Miss Squeamish. Jedediah is the shrewd Yankee lad "raised on the north side of the Green Mountains, half a mile t'other side of Widder Simm's House in the town of Danbury." There is also a Negro servant appropriately named Bill Brown with comic possibilities. The melodramatic love plot is enhanced by disguised brothers, an unrecognized son, an English villain, an avenger and a gentle dupe. No character is centrally important, but the impersonator of Jedediah had great opportunities to build upon his unaffected simplicity and his sturdy and independent spirit. Comparable scenes from many melodramas had appeared previously on the stage and would appear again in different plays by different authors.

In *The Green Mountain Boy* the avenger and manipulator of the plot is a man named Sandfield, who exposes Montague and allows Ellen to marry Edward, whom Sandfield claims is his son. Squeamish and Joe Shakespeare also marry. The combinations of characters and incidents would later change, but the recognizable features of many Yankee vehicle plays are clear in *The Green Mountain Boy*: Yankee garrulousness for comic ends, a Negro-Yankee confrontation, a melodramatic plot in which the Yankee actor serves mainly as a plotting device and a comic monologuist.

Hill's reputation as a Yankee actor was growing at a startling pace in the 1830s. Announcing Hill's appearance at the Park Theatre in early 1833, the *Spirit of the Times* noted that Hackett, then in England, "has a powerful rival, and we fear on his return home he will find himself supplanted."[53] Hill was extremely fortunate in having Jones for a friend, and at this point in their careers they supported each other. Because Hill lacked material for his vehicle acting, Jones wrote *The Adventure; or, The Yankee in Tripoli*, which Hill performed at the Park Theatre in the fall of 1835 and at the Tremont Theatre the following June under the title *The Adventures of a Yankee*.

The People's Lawyer, which Hill acted first in Boston in 1839, is the best known of Jones' plays. A generation later it became the primary acting role for another Yankee actor, John E. Owens. Robert Howard is "the people's lawyer," but Solon Shingle, a garrulous old country teamster who wanders in and out of the plot, became so important that the play eventually came to be known as *Solon Shingle*. Though irrelevant to the success of the piece, the plot is relatively simple. Charles Otis, a poor but honest clerk in the office of Hugh Winslow, is asked by this unscrupulous merchant to swear that a man gave Winslow a check from a Mobile bank. Unsure, Charles refuses to swear and is fired by his boss, who then gets bored with his country visitor, Solon Shingle, and leaves in a huff. Charles' coworker, John Ellsley, is as dishonest as his employer and manages to borrow $50 from Solon to replace what he has stolen from the firm. Left alone in the office, a curious Solon Shingle manages to get flour and lamp black all over himself and to find a pistol that he accidentally fires. At the Otis home Charles' sister, Grace, and their mother bemoan the fact that their furniture, including the harp on which Grace plays so beautifully, must be sold to cover their expenses. Charles' sad return is interrupted by John Ellsley who shows him a watch he has stolen from Winslow. He argues with Charles but finally agrees to confess his theft if Charles will write his confession. John then stealthily stuffs the watch into Charles' pocket. Thus set up, the Otis family experiences a little joy as Howard, in workman's clothes, brings money for Grace's paintings. Clearly in love with Grace, Howard remains as the police arrive and arrest Charles for theft, finding the watch and the confession in his pocket.

The second act of *The People's Lawyer* takes place in the courtroom after Winslow tries to gain Grace's favors at the price of dropping charges against Charles. Fortunately, Grace is protected by Howard, whose identity as "the

SOLON SHINGLE

Woodcut advertising *The People's Lawyer* by Joseph S. Jones. From *Scenes from Nineteenth-Century Stage*, selected by Stanley Appelbaum, Dover Publications.

people's lawyer'' and a wealthy man remains unknown to both Winslow and Grace. Solon Shingle, complaining bitterly that his "apple sarse" has been stolen, is invited by Winslow to the court and is sworn in by mistake. On and on Solon rambles about his "apple sarse" until he is removed. Howard then replaces Charles' ineffectual lawyer, gets a confession from John and an acquittal for Charles. On the street outside the courtroom, the audience hears another soliloquy filled with Solon's witticisms. Again in Howard's palatial home, where he and Grace announce their engagement, Solon ambles in with a mouthful of quaint expressions before Grace addresses the audience: "I trust that in the Court you will admit to full practice—the people's lawyer."

By making a spectacle of the Yankee, actors brought some fame to this slight piece. *The People's Lawyer* does, however, show more clearly than most vehicle plays of this type the very close relationship between the theatre and the lecture platform or the published folktales and regional stories. The role of Solon Shingle was essentially a series of monologues, expertly delivered by actors who occasionally appeared on the stage between the acts or after the final curtain of the play to enthrall the audience with ad-lib patter. Lecturers such as Dr. William Valentine and Anna Dickinson were beginning to appear in the theatres about this time and would gain popular acceptance after mid-century. Soon the monologuist would be featured in variety theatres and vaudeville acts across America. The trend was just beginning during the 1830s.

Among Jones' innumerable melodramas three were extremely popular during his lifetime and well illustrate his work in this genre: *The Surgeon of Paris; or, The Massacre of the Hugenots*, a historical drama in four acts (1838); *Moll Pitcher; or, The Fortune Teller of Lynn*, in four acts (1839); and *The Carpenter of Rouen; or, The Massacre of St. Bartholomew*, a romantic drama in four acts (1840). Jones based his plot for *The Surgeon of Paris* on the "sanguinary massacre of St. Bartolomew" in Paris and, according to his printed introduction, did not attempt a "correct picture of the times." He did, however, retain some historical people while adding Michael, the artisan, and Ambrose, the king's surgeon and defender of freedom and right. The beginning scene is one of fear and disaster. As the massacre is plotted, Michael's wife and child are refused the protection of Catherine de Medici, although by the end of the act, these good and innocent people are rescued by a masked surgeon who does not reveal his identity until the final curtain. The complicated story, as poorly told as structured, was explained by a critic for the *Dramatic Mirror* who complained that "there is mystery in the beginning, the middle and the end, and if it were not for the more striking features of scenery, tableaux, etc., we should be induced to ask 'what was it all about?' "[54] This was a time for spectacles, however, comprehensible or not, and Catherine's use of necromancy, poison, secret panels, moving statues and subterranean passages were all that audiences demanded.

Jones boasted—or rather complained, as he received no royalties—that *The Carpenter of Rouen* ran for one hundred performances in London where it became almost a fad. The major conflict in this play is between De Saubigne, the Duke of Rouen, and the carpenter Marteau, a coffin maker who "makes the only suit of clothes husbands never begrudge their wives the expense of." As a carpenter, Marteau is "one of God's noblemen," a mechanic. "At his bidding mountains are overcome, rocks are torn asunder, and all things in nature change to do his command! The Supreme Ruler of the Universe is himself 'The Great Mechanic'!" (I,1). The duke wants to tear down the carpenter's shop, which is situated in the square near the palace; this Marteau refuses to allow. With strong beliefs, Marteau sets himself against the duke, whom he holds responsible for his wife's death at the Massacre of St. Bartholomew. Early in the play he creates his own "secret order" into which he inducts Antoine, a nobleman's son in disguise, as his apprentice. Mystery surrounds the duke and Antoine as it does Madelon, Marteau's daughter, who returns to Rouen after ten years' absence and, as the climax to Act I, recognizes Antoine as her husband. Each of the next two acts begins with songs and scenes from a comic subplot. Meanwhile, secret societies supporting France against the duke spread among the common people. The conflict deepens. Madelon disappears, and Marteau is accused of murder and captured by the duke's men. In the final act Antoine rescues Madelon from the convent where the duke has kept her. Marteau then seizes the duke, who, indeed, did murder the carpenter's wife. The final tableau: "Music. Crash—the whole scene at the back falls, and discovers the Convent Yard with Gibbet, upon which a profile figure of De Saubigne, the Duke of Rouen, dead; coffin at the foot." Who has done this? Marteau: "I—the avenger of a murdered wife—Marteau, the carpenter of Rouen." It is, as the plot suggests, a traditional melodrama filled with action, suspense, mystery, disguises, songs, some comic change of pace, a few memorable lines by a persistent avenger, and elaborate spectacle.

Jones was persuaded to publish *Moll Pitcher; or, The Fortune Teller of Lynn* in 1855 and noted that it had been produced frequently. An early production at the Bowery Theatre entitled *Moll Pitcher; or, The Pirate Priest*, however, was probably a different version and drew a scathing review: "The glorious boys of the Bowery," wrote a critic for the *Dramatic Mirror*, "scratched their heads, uneasily, looked vacantly, and yawned unmercifully. [The Pirate] grinned like death's head upon a mopstick and fought like a skeleton at arms . . . but it was a miserable attempt made to sustain a miserable affair. . . . We predict Moll's fate will be suddenly precipitated, her sufferings will not be of long durations, and we advise the author to prepare a sermon for her funeral."[55]

The Pirate Priest is a more accurate description of the action of the play than is the published title. Maladine, a priest and archvillain, a marked and mutilated man, on whom Moll swears vengeance, dominates the action. Moll herself is something of a witch, a hag, a mysterious figure who deals with the devil. Also an avenger of evil deeds, she prowls the waterfront telling fortunes. The plot line follows a love theme, and Moll, always appearing unexpectedly, hears things and sees things in order to help virtue thwart Maladine's villainy.

"Man is a betrayer; I live to protect woman" (II,1), Moll declares. This she does, finally rescuing the bridegroom from a charge of murder by accusing Maladine who, in turn, blames one of his own cohorts, who shoots him on the spot. Moll then identifies herself as Mary Diamond (a heretofore unheard of name for the audience), once seduced by the same Maladine who now dies in agony begging for her mercy. As Jones honestly acknowledged in his preface, the merits of the play depended upon "the manner in which the business of the piece is done."

The titles of Jones' plays show both the breadth of his interests and his determination to please Boston audiences. The more melodramatic incidents of history obviously appealed to him, but there is a definite appreciation in most of his plays of such Jacksonian traits as individuality, personal conviction and freedom of spirit. Jones' characters had strong beliefs and would fight for their ideals—the surgeon of Paris, the carpenter of Rouen, the people's lawyer. One of his earlier plays was called *The Liberty Tree; or, Boston Boys in '76* (1832), and his last play was entitled *Paul Revere, and the Sons of Liberty* (1875). Among his prize plays are *The Wheelwright; or, Boston Pride* (1845); *Old Job and Jacob Gray* (1849); *The Last Dollar* (1850); and *The Silver Spoon* (1852).

Zafari the Bohemian, a legend of the court of Spain written for Wizeman Marshall and performed at the Boston Theatre from February 25 to March 1, 1856, suggests Jones' greater ambitions as a dramatist.[56] According to "Acorn" (James Oakes), who commended the play's stageworthiness and found the dialogue "generally smooth and pleasing" and the imagery "spirited," the story was taken from a play by Victor Hugo.[57] Unlike Jones' other plays, *Zafari* is a carefully plotted intrigue in which character is emphasized. Bazan, a chief of the Alcades, has been banished by the king and queen of Spain as a result of the disgrace brought upon him by a woman who claimed that he fathered her child. Plotting revenge against King Charles and his queen, Bazan chooses as his tool Zafari, a strange young Bohemian, a dreamer whose past is unknown even to himself. Presumably, a storm unsettled him: "I may not quell or raise a storm," Zafari says, "but by my knowledge I may prophesy of its coming." To Bazan's advantage, Zafari is in love with the queen. Sworn to loyalty to Bazan, Zafari is introduced to the queen as a young nobleman, and the intrigue begins. As time passes, the queen still refuses to recall Bazan from exile, but her belief and trust in Zafari grows, and she makes him both her secretary and a duke. When Bazan's power within the queen's council increases through the schemings of a priest, Zafari discovers the plottings, kills the priest and controls the council for the queen. For some reason King Charles has never consummated his marriage with his queen, and by the fourth and final act of the play, Zafari and the queen have become lovers. Learning of this, Bazan returns to his homeland and confesses his scheming to the queen, at the same time calling her an adultress. At the climax of the play, Bazan is dragged away as the queen identifies Zafari as "my Lord King Charles."

Unlike other plays by Jones, the action of *Zafari the Bohemian* is slow, has few spectacles and no passionate speeches. The movement of the play, however, is constant, and the intrigue fascinating as Zafari disguises himself to combat a vengeful Bazan, an evil priest and a conniving council. Although Jones was no poet and did not always use language skillfully, *Zafari* is clearly a play in which ideas are important. Existing in three manuscript versions, the play performed in 1856 was longer and more wordy than the 1842 version and gave different names to many of the characters. A still later version shows that Jones edited and developed the produced script; yet *Zafari* is not a play that shows Jones' playwriting talents to their best advantage. What part it played in Jones' own view of his career may never by known.

As a man of strong views, Jones occasionally allowed space in his plays for his own opinions, such as his broadside against lawyers in *Eugene Aram*. Nowhere was he more biting and clearly satirical, however, than in his creation of Jefferson Scattering Batkins in *The Silver Spoon; or, Our Own Folks: A Joiner's Job in Four Parts*. Written for William Warren and first acted at the Boston Museum on February 16, 1852, *The Silver Spoon* was printed in 1911, "revised and reconstructed" with a long introduction. Ridiculing the Great and General Court of the Commonwealth of Massachusetts, it was Jones' only play to have any lasting appeal for audiences. As a member of this Court, the honorable Jefferson S. Batkins from Cranberry Center created enough comic havoc to entertain audiences for years. Warren last performed the major role on April 7, 1883. Through his major character, Jones commented on speech-making among politicians, the importance of money as an influence upon legislators and the inanity of Congressional bills. As a representative solidly "agin' the Boston click," Batkins sponsors a bill "for the encouragement of caterpillars" and for the protection of toads but not frogs. So successful was the play that Jones tried a sequel—*Batkins at Home; or, Life in Cranberry Center*—but this was not well received, nor was his 1871 novel entitled *Life of Jefferson Batkins, Member from Cranberry Center*. Only the original play has survived, and it remains the best illustration of Jones' comic artistry.

The essay of John Bourne Clapp in the Boston *Transcript* of December 30, 1910, attempts to distinguish Joseph S. Jones as "the Clyde Fitch of the days of our grandfathers." The truth in this observation, however, is very slight. Only in their popularity with contemporary audiences were the two playwrights similar. Each age makes its own demands upon the theatre. Jones wrote a few spectacular melodramas which brought him popularity with audiences and also pleased certain actors by giving them vehicles which they made successful. His attitude toward melodrama, however, was different from that which brought "tears and smiles" a half-century later. Although the fact that politics is always fair game for satirists—from *Androborus* to *Knickerbocker Holiday*—provides another opportunity for comparison, Jones' comic approach in *The Silver Spoon* is drastically different in structure and form from Fitch's *The City*. Without comparison with another age, Jones should be recognized for his own distinctive contributions to the American drama of his day in quantity and quality: He

William Warren as Jefferson Scattering Batkins. Photographed by Notman; engraved by H. Velten.

was one of the first professional men of the theatre who left his mark as actor-manager and, more significantly, playwright, and his career should be discussed between the contributions of William Dunlap and John Brougham in that line of development leading to Augustin Daly and David Belasco.

For a generation, George ("Yankee") Hill (1809–1848) was an intensely popular and spectacular Yankee actor, and it was only good common sense, so revered by people in Jacksonian America, that playwrights of the 1830s would write Yankee plays. Hill had, according to Henry Dickinson Stone, a "natural

GEO. H. HILL.
COMEDIAN.

George Handel "Yankee" Hill. Courtesy of the Library of Congress.

nasal twang" which he embellished with a lot of mugging and grimacing to create a very theatrical Yankee for audiences on both sides of the Atlantic Ocean.[58] Of the four American actors who in 1838 were making considerable impression upon the London audiences—Edwin Forrest, George H. Hill, Josephine Clifton and T. D. Rice—each in his or her own fashion brought something uniquely American to England. Prior to this time the English had been able to form some notion of the American character from those novels of James Fenimore Cooper that were adapted for the stage by such Englishmen as Edward Fitzball or T. P. Cooke. The latter's adaptation of *The Pilot* (with music by G. H. Rodwell), enhanced by a comic recitation of "The Nautical Yarn of the Great Sea Serpent," played intermittently from 1830 to 1833. The English also felt that they learned about America from the stories of Washington Irving (sometimes called the "American Goldsmith") or from books like the *Life of Colonel Crockett* but, as explained by an English theatre critic to the *Spirit of the Times*, "the actual sight of a real live Yankee is something of a novelty, and Mr. Hill makes it as amusing as it is new. Some of his Yankeeisms were beyond our comprehension, but the picture altogether was delightfully quaint, humorous and racy."[59] In this manner Hill brought a part of America to England, and it is appropriately ironic that one of his better vehicles was written by the expatriate American playwright, William Bayle Bernard.

Bernard (1807–1875) was born in Boston, the son of the actor-manager John Bernard, and moved to England in 1820. Once involved in English theatre, he made a reputation as a writer of plays about Americans and as an adapter of American plays and fiction to English circumstance and understanding. Several of his plays crossed the Atlantic to become popular in America. Although *The Yankee Peddler; or, Old Times in Virginia* is of obscure parentage, there is no question that it was considered genuinely American by the English. Quinn, in fact, lists an anonymously written *Yankee Peddler* acted at the Park Theatre on September 6, 1834. In spite of the statement by W. K. Northall, the editor of *Life and Recollections of Yankee Hill: Together with Anecdotes and Incidents of His Travel* (1850), that Hill employed Bernard to prepare a new piece for his debut at Drury Lane and that *The Yankee Peddler* was the result,[60] London reviewers of Hill's 1836 performance understood that Bernard adapted an existing vehicle known as *Old Times in Virginia; or, The Yankee Pedlar*.[61] For the historian, however, the chronology of the work is complicated by Samuel French's publication of the play in "The Minor Drama," with Morris Barnett (1800–1856), an English minor dramatist who did not arrive in America until 1854, listed as the author and the earliest production of the play given as St. Louis (1841), featuring Dan Marble as Hiram Dodge.

The subtitle of *The Yankee Peddler* confused the English, who took Hill seriously as an interpreter of "a distinct caste [in America] peculiar to the State of Virginia, and, like our Yorkshire men . . . chiefly distinguished by a shrewd craving under the mask of simplicity."[62] Unlike many Yankee heroes, Hiram Dodge is central to the plot. Appearing at a Southern plantation as a salesman for Fancy Ware, Hiram scares away the Negroes—"now, stand out of the way, you patent, pow-chong, pulverized, pewter-headed puppies!"—and tells jokes about a Negro whose "mouth was so big that he had to get it made smaller for fear he'd swallow his own head" (I,1). He then sees Jerusha, the white serving girl, and starts the preening and wooing process. To gain the favor of the plantation owner, Mr. Fuller, Hiram agrees to ride his horse in a race against the neighbor whom Fuller hates. When he sees Fuller's daughter, Maria, kissing her lover, Charles, another whom Fuller dislikes, Hiram shows his self-reliant and self-serving ingenuity by collecting bribe money from all parties. He is, however, a kind and sentimental Yankee, and hearing that Fuller will give his daughter to the rider who wins the horse race, arranges to have Charles ride Fuller's horse while he rides the other one and throws the race. As expected, all turns out well—for the lovers, for the Yankee and for the play. Hiram, the Yankee, is clever, shrewd and obviously a brash person who made the play popular by his funny speeches and comic action. It was a favorite of all Yankee actors. Yankee Hill even performed the play twice in Paris, although there appears to be no French criticism of Hiram Dodge.[63]

Another Yankee actor, Dan Marble (1810–1849), although a native New Englander, was in performance quite unlike either Hackett or Hill, bringing a Western focus to his impersonation. Walter Leman considered Marble a funny man who took monstrosities of plays which were worse than bad and made them better than good with his acting.[64] Beginning his career as a Yankee storyteller in New York theatres in 1832, Marble appeared at the Buffalo Theatre four years later, presenting his most famous Yankee play, Sam Patch; or, The Daring Yankee, presumably written by E. H. Thompson. The fascination this play held for audiences resulted from its basis in reality. There actually was a Sam Patch from Pawtucket, Rhode Island, who in the late 1820s made a career of jumping—jumping from the bridge above Pawtucket Falls, from the roofs of cotton mills, and then from the top of Passaic Falls, some seventy feet. His last leap occurred on Friday the thirteenth of November, 1829, from a platform built on the top of the Genesee Falls. Here he jumped the distance of 125 feet before a crowd of thousands—out of history and into legend. Four months later a New York farmer, chopping a hole in the ice on the Genesee River near the spot where it empties into Lake Ontario, found the lifeless body of Sam Patch. The playscript of Marble's acting vehicle has been lost, but something of its nature is suggested by the love plot involving the hero who carried the heroine across the river in a storm. The climax, however, was the leap over Niagara Falls, a feat the real Sam Patch accomplished on October 17, 1829. Dan Marble planned his jumps in theatres across the country to appear as spectacular as possible. A second play, Sam Patch in France; or, The Pesky Snake (1843) written by comedian J. P. Addams, has not survived, nor was it as successful as the first play.

Dan Marble created a considerable reputation for himself as a Yankee actor and appeared to enjoy it thoroughly. In London, October 7, 1844, Marble wrote

Dan Marble's letter of 7 October 1844 from London: "The King of the French will be here tomorrow, then I shall have a look at the King & Queen." Courtesy of J. Peter Coulson, San Marcos, Texas.

back to his friends in Buffalo through J. J. Bloomer of the Pantheon Theatre: "The hit I have made in London is very gratifying to me—and I think to all my friends. I have played six nights and have been called out every evening after the play. . . . The King of the French will be here tomorrow, then I shall have a look at the King & Queen."[65] Yankee actors, however, like many others of their profession, generally did not enjoy long lives. Marble's problem was a common one: alcohol. Harry Watkins mentions an incident in which "Marble was so drunk I thought he would be unable to get through the performance. But after drinking some vinegar, he got along well enough; at least the audience couldn't perceive that he had been drinking too much."[66] Marble died of cholera in Louisville, Kentucky, on the night of his own benefit performance. Ironically, the title of the play that evening was *A Cure for the Cholera.*[67]

The Stage-Struck Yankee (1840) by Oliver Everett Durivage was another Yankee play that was basic to Dan Marble's repertory. Durivage, a Boston-born actor and an occasional playwright, was also a journalist, contributing to the *Spirit of the Times* a series of articles on the theatre entitled "The Gagging Concern." During the 1840s he was evidently associated with William Mitchell's Olympic Theatre, for in the fall of 1842 he wrote a burlesque entitled *Richard Number 3*, which became a stock role for William Mitchell. Prior to this time, *Cut and Come Again* by Durivage was advertised as "the principal attraction of the evening" at a Boston Theatre in May of 1841.[68] Durivage's burlesque entitled *The Lady of the Lions* played at the Bowery Theatre in 1842, the Olympic in 1846 and in Baltimore, St. Louis and Albany after mid-century. The characters include Gasser, Clod Meddlenot, Polly Ann Dishabille as the Lady of the Lion, and her parents.

According to Wemyss, Durivage fought in the Mexican War, returned to acting and in 1852, at the time of Wemyss' *Chronology of the American Stage*, was living in Memphis, Tennessee. He may later have gone to New York and written and acted in that city. It is unclear whether he was related to the Boston actor and journalist named John E. Durivage (b. 1813) who in 1854 adapted *Our Best Society* from George William Curtis' *Potiphar Papers* and was highly regarded by critics. Little is known about either of these men. O. E. Durivage apparently wrote for his own convenience and starred in *The Stage-Struck Yankee* when it played in Boston in 1845. Quinn notes a performance at the Chatham Theatre in New York in 1840, and the play was still being staged in the mid-1850s. Indicative of the changes in characters or plot that occasionally overtook plays of this period in history, the *Spirit of the Times* recorded Marble's favorable reception as Zachariah Hotspear in *The Stage-Struck Yankee* at the New Strand Theatre in 1845.[69] In a version published in *The New York Drama* (vol. 4, 1878), however, the hero's name is Curtis Chunk, a Yankee who has just seen his first play. Completely enamored with Fanny Magnet, the star of the play, Chunk is ready to jilt his girlfriend Jedidah, but Fanny sees through this would-be actor and by disguising herself as a servant girl—"the ugliest white gal I ever see"—sends Chunk back to Jedidah.

The Yankee, although exceedingly popular, was not the only native character on whom American playwrights based their vehicle plays. Closely related was the Westerner or Backwoodsman, mainly presented as Colonel Nimrod Wildfire, acted by Hackett and, in a general way, by Dan Marble whose Yankee, dressed "much after the present caricature of Uncle Sam, minus the stars but glorying in the stripes," was not confined to New England.[70] There was also the Irishman. All of these characters had achieved popularity on the American stage before mid-century.

The Lion of the West is a distinctive play in the development of American drama for a number of important reasons. First, it was written for a competition and won the prize offered in November of 1830 by James H. Hackett for "an original comedy whereof an American should be the leading character." Second, the original author was James Kirke Paulding (1778–1860), an established writer who had collaborated with Washington Irving in the *Salmagundi*, had written for contemporary journals such as Robert Walsh's *American Quarterly* and had achieved a good reputation as a satirist (*The Diverting History of John Bull and Brother Jonathan*, 1812) and novelist with *Koningsmarke* (1823) and *The Dutchman's Fireside* (1831). In spite of Paulding's excellent conception in his creation of Colonel Nimrod Wildfire, the story of Cecilia Bramble of Washington, D.C., importuned to elope with a fake count because she has a passion to see Paris, is slight and loaded with excessive sentiment and talk. The scene in which the elopement is subverted and Wildfire forces a confession from the impostor might have satisifed some of the contemporary theatregoers' demands for action, but the play ends, although with great dignity on the part of Cecilia, in a relatively subdued fashion. The colonel's stories intrude theatrically and appropriately; and although some critics showered praise on Paulding's delineation of native manners and character, James Hackett did not immediately consider the play a good vehicle for his art.

A third reason for the importance of *The Lion of the West* rests on the fact that other hands were brought in to serve the play. John Augustus Stone, the author of *Metamora* and a thoroughly professional man of the theatre, wrote a version which was produced in the fall of 1831 and maintained in Hackett's repertory until he left for England in the spring of 1833. While Stone added much more plot and wrote a different story line, he retained and embellished Wildfire's role. His heroine, Fredonia, lives in England with Mr. Bonny Broun, who rescued her as an infant from the arms of a dying British soldier at the battle of Lundy's Lane. Now, nearly eighteen, Fredonia is saved from a conniving fortune hunter named Lord Luminary by Nimrod Wildfire, Bonny Broun's nephew from Kentucky. Chastened but not defeated, Luminary attempts to ruin the reputation of Trueman Casual, the young man Fredonia loves, but is prevented by Wildfire, who shows his accomplishments as a rifleman and backwoodsman. In the final act Casual is wounded in a duel with Luminary, Fredonia finds her real father, and Wildfire introduces his intended: "Miss Patty Snag of Salt Licks . . . there's no back out in her breed, for she can lick her weight in wild cats, and she shot a bear at nine years old."

Apparently still not satisfied, Hackett, on his arrival in England, asked William Bayle Bernard to revise the play once more. It was this version, set in New York and retitled *The Kentuckian; or, A Trip to New York*, that Hackett played in London and retained as a popular role in his repertory for the next twenty years. The Heroine, Caroline Freeman, a merchant's daughter wooed by a fake Lord Granby, must be rescued to marry Percival, a pleasant English merchant. The most important addition to the cast is Mrs. Wollope, a burlesque of Mrs. Frances Trollope, the Englishwoman who made such a nuisance of herself in America—arriving in 1827, finding very little to her taste and returning to England in 1831 to write *Domestic Manners of the Americans*. Constantly at odds with Wildfire, whose wit escapes her, Mrs. Wollope is finally recognized as a conniving sister of the impostor. Although she adds a great deal to the plot and the satire, Wildfire remains the major attraction—"I'm half horse, half alligator, a touch of the airth-quake, with a sprinkling of the steamboat!" He brags, tells stories, insults Negroes, dances a jig, kisses the girls, enjoys fighting and generally creates havoc. "Of all the fellows either side of the Alleghany Hills," he says, "I myself can jump higher—squat lower—dive deeper—stay longer under and come out drier" (I,1). The ridicule rained upon Mrs. Wollope must have been a great source of delight for American audiences. "I have made my observations," she declares indignantly as she exits: "I'll return with them to England; I'll give them to the world, and posterity shall judge between us" (II,3).

The Kentuckian opened at Covent Garden on March 9, 1833, advertised as "an American olla'podrida" by William Bayle Bernard. A critic reluctantly admitted that "we are willing to allow it the credit of considerable humor" and, with some condescension, stated that "the denouement was of course satisfactory to the Yankee taste." Mrs. Trollope "is considered an interloper, as the Yankees prefer independence to luxurious refinement." That opinion may have gone unchallenged, but the critic was mistaken in concluding that the play would not "be an exhibition of long endurance."[71]

Although *The Lion of the West* has been exploited by some historians as a major contribution to American drama by an American writer of stature, James K. Paulding, the facts of the matter suggest a different view. The creation of Colonel Nimrod Wildfire is, indeed, significant, but the presentation by Hackett which made the play popular was twice removed from Paulding. Bernard must also be given credit for his effective and timely satire of Mrs. Trollope. Without these two characters, the play could easily have disappeared along with countless others. It must be remembered, too, that Davy Crockett was then at the height of his extravagant career, a career which legend would make even more extravagant, and that Wildfire was generally regarded, in language and action, as a genial imitation of Crockett. As imitation of any sort may be construed as a certain acknowledgment of popularity, if not always as a compliment, the appearance on the stage of the Olympic Theatre in 1846 of a farce called *The Lioness of the North*, a burlesque now lost, reveals the usual progress of many well-received works of art. The individual peculiarities of the backwoodsman were confused at this date with those of the Yankee, and the vehicle actor should probably bear the responsibility of this fusion of idioms and idiosyncrasies. An evening's entertainment, however, owes its success to the cooperative artistry of actor and writer. It is an interesting fact that William Bayle Bernard finally created the successful acting versions of *The Lion of the West* and *The Yankee Peddler* while his father, John Bernard, provided one of the better explanations of the *Yankee*: "a term denoting character rather than locality, and represent[ing] a certain set of qualities in a particular grade of society."[72]

It was not until almost mid-century that the Irish stage character began to stimulate the writing of vehicle plays in America. Prior to this time there had been a few impressive Irish characters created by American playwrights, but the great surge of vehicle plays came after 1850 with the acting careers of Barney Williams, John Brougham, and others. William Dunlap's *A Trip to Niagara* had been produced in 1828 mainly for its scenic power, as Dunlap admitted. Dennis Dougherty, the Irishman of the play who came to America because he heard that the land was cheap, is a disillusioned immigrant who wants only to go home again; "I've sane the world, and it's cost me all I was wort in the world to see it. And I've sane liberty, of all shapes and colors; and now I'm at liberty to go home again—if I can get there" (III,6). The great Irish actor Tyrone Power (1795–1841) probably did much to stimulate interest in Irish vehicle acting, particularly after his trips to America. Comparable to the English acceptance of Hackett and Hill as realistic interpreters of American character, Americans saw Power as a mirror of the peculiarities of the Irish—such people as Paudeen O'Rafferty, Dr. O'Toole, Sir Lucius O'Trigger or Major O'Flaherty.[73] Power traveled widely in America and published his two volumes of *Impressions of America* in 1836. Usually, he enjoyed what he saw and was well received; it was on his return to England after a second trip to America that he was lost at sea. Americans remembered his acting, however, and several actors tried to imitate his style.

During the early years of his career Barney Williams depended largely on plays from Power's repertory—such as Paddy O'Rafferty in *Born to Good Luck* and Terry O'Rourke in *The Irish Tutor*. By 1846 it was clear that audiences craved a successor to Power, and Barney Williams was trying desperately to fill those Irish shoes, substituting vigor and vitality for the finesse and finish he clearly lacked at this time. Soon he was mentioned whenever Irish roles and Irish plays were discussed. One of his early original roles was that of Jerry Murphy in *Bumpology* by Charles H. Saunders (1818–1857), an actor-playwright from Boston where he first appeared on the stage in 1836. In the fall of 1843, when Williams was playing Jerry Murphy at the Chatham Theatre in New York, Saunders was newly arrived at the Bowery Theatre to which he contributed *Bumpology* and at least four other plays, all slight farces for novelty entertainment.

One of the early Irish plays written by an American was *Handy Andy*, adapted by Thomas Dunn English (1819–1902) from a novel (1842) by Samuel Lover, a Irish writer and lecturer who attracted some popular attention at the Park Theatre in New York in early 1846. English's play opened at the National Theatre in Philadelphia on January 1, 1844. A physician, journalist, editor, ballad writer ("Ben Bolt"), poet and dramatist, English was part of the bustling literary scene in New York. He is remembered during the 1840s for his early friendship with Edgar Allan Poe, who later opened an irreparable break in that friendship with an article on English in his series entitled "The Literati of New York." It was a cruel and unfair article even at a time when bitter comments in print were the norm and typifies Poe's position in many such arguments—with Longfellow, with Mrs. Elizabeth Ellet, with Mr. Osgood, with Margaret Fuller. English wrote a few plays during the 1840s—*Blud Da Nouns; or, The Battle of the Frogs*, a satirical, operatic piece which was successfully produced in 1843; *The Doom of the Drinker* (1844), a melodrama founded on his own experience; and *Handy Andy*, which James Rees described as bold and energetic. English's best known play, *The Mormons*, was produced in 1858.

Handy Andy became a vehicle for W. J. Florence—who during the late 1850s was to become Barney William's chief competitor—and soon afterwards versions of *Handy Andy* were claimed by H. Montgomery (1860) and W. R. Floyd (1862). Andy is "Felius Nullius," an excessively stupid young man who blunders here and there. The action, dealing with a marriage that cannot take place until a deed is found, is motivated by a woman named Mad Nance who rails against Squire O'Grady as a "man of fraud and wrong" and claims that her son is alive and the "heir of his father's title and the broad lands." With a great deal of shadowy activity, Mad Nance eventually finds the deed and claims as her son and the Earl of Scatterbrain, as well as the Duke of Ulster, none other than Andy himself, who accepts his position rather lightly and still plans to marry Oonah, the girl of his country dreams. Lacking a well-defined plot, *Handy Andy* furnished good Irish dialect, farcical stupidity and a few interesting observations. Says Andy, "If a gintleman breaks a horse's neck, he's a bould rider, but a poor sarvint is a careless vagabond for only taking the sweat out of him. If a gintleman drinks till he can't see a hole in a ladder, he's only fresh—fresh, mind ye's—but drunk as a baste is the word for a poor man!" (II,5). It was an unfair world, and those who fled the potato famine in Ireland during the 1840s to come in droves to America were frequently pictured catching the hot end of the iron. *Handy Andy* was a popular play and continued to be performed through the 1860s.

Another actor of Irish characters who was frequently compared with Tyrone Power and, indeed, encouraged that comparison by performing many of the roles that Power had made famous, was John Brougham (1810–1880). A fairly successful actor in London, Brougham made his first appearance in America at the Park Theatre on October 4, 1842. By the following spring, both he and his wife were happily accepted on the American stage, according to a statement in *An-*

John Drew as Handy Andy.

glo-American, A Journal of Literature, News, Politics, the Drama, Fine Arts.[74]
Brougham had written plays in London, the first in 1835, and soon set to work
in America. His better Irish plays would be written after mid-century, and although he was not limited to Irish roles, he wrote most of his plays with an eye

to his own acting career. *Romance and Reality; or, Silence Gives Consent*, for example, opened at the Broadway Theatre in April of 1848. Not a vehicle play as that term is understood, it was a comedy in which love is faced with the usual difficulties, and the characters in the play represent various aspects of society. One of the most interesting characters is Barbara Manly, an enthusiastic "member of the Social Reform Association" who is concerned with freeing herself and all women from the slavery imposed by men. Brougham played Jack Swift, "an impudent roving blade ready for any kind of fun, and as fearless in pursuit of it as an Irishman could be."[75]

Edwin Forrest's historically acclaimed largess toward American playwrights in 1828 seemed to strike the appropriate tone for the creation of the national drama that critics were beginning to encourage. The immediate effect of his announced Prize Play Competition was, indeed, stimulating to the development of American drama, but the long-range effect was hardly the kind of encouragement that playwrights actually needed. Forrest, however, surely deserves far more praise than blame. As a true follower of some of the best remembered concepts of the Age of Jackson, his strong, self-serving entrepreneurship undoubtedly made playwrights, actors and theatre managers more aware of a need and gave them a means to satisfy it. That inadequate laws, corrupt and careless competitions and disgracefully cavalier actors discouraged playwrights was the fault of the times, the demands of society and the perversity of individuals. Although Stone, Bird, Smith, Conrad, Willis, Sargent, Logan, Jones and other playwrights created many memorable plays for competitions and for actors, without exception their experiences did not encourage them to greater accomplishments. Moreover, not until well after the Civil War would American audiences enjoy plays of quality equal to theirs or to works of their nationalistic and poetic contemporaries writing in Jacksonian America.

NOTES

1. Samuel Kettell, ed., *Specimens of American Poetry*, 3 vols. (Boston: S. G. Goodrich & Co., 1829). See Benjamin T. Spencer, *The Quest for Nationality* (Syracuse: Syracuse University Press, 1957), 147.
2. Rufus Dawes, *Athenia of Damascus* (New York: Samuel Colman, 1839), publisher's introductory comment.
3. "Editor's Talk," *Federal American Monthly*, X (October 1837), 353.
4. Henry A. Beers, *Nathaniel Parker Willis* (Boston: Houghton Mifflin, 1885), 262.
5. Beers, 235.
6. February 25, 1838, Gratz Collection, Case 7, Box 10, Historical Society of Pennsylvania.
7. *Spirit of the Times*, VII (August 26, 1837), 1.
8. *Spirit of the Times*, VII (September 2, 1837), 1.
9. *Federal American Monthly*, X (October 1837), 354.

10. *Dramatic Mirror*, II (February 12, 1842), 6.

11. *Spirit of the Times*, VII (December 2, 1837), 1.

12. *Spirit of the Times*, VII (December 23, 1837), 1.

13. Letter dated June 25, 1834, Gratz Collection, Case 7, Box 10, Historical Society of Pennsylvania.

14. "Theatricals," *Expositor*, I (April 13, 1839), 199.

15. *Expositor*, I (April 13, 1839), 199.

16. *Spirit of the Times*, IX (April 6, 1839), 72.

17. *Literary Examiner and Western Monthly Review*, July 1839, 409, 412, 413. The published play was a revision of the acted version. See also "The Drama," *Knickerbocker*, XIII May 1839, 462.

18. *Boston Quarterly Review*, July 1839, 390.

19. *Spirit of the Times*, VII (December 16, 1837), 1.

20. *New World*, IV (1842), 99–103.

21. *Spirit of the Times*, VII (September 30, 1837), 1.

22. *Dramatic Mirror*, I (October 2, 1841), 64.

23. *Spirit of the Times*, VIII (December 29, 1838), 1.

24. *Expositor*, I (December 29, 1838), 45–46.

25. Odell, *Annals*, IV, 280.

26. *Spirit of the Times*, XIX (October 27, 1849), 432.

27. *New York Review*, IV (January 1839), 243.

28. *Anglo-American, A Journal of Literature, News, Politics, the Drama, Fine Arts*, V (October 11, 1845), 596.

29. Letter, November 28, ?, in which Willis assumes that Sargent will "get the prize of $500 which Marble offers," and letter, November 17, 1854, Rare Book Department, mss. acc. 2545, Boston Public Library.

30. *Spirit of the Times*, XXV (March 31, 1855), 79.

31. Letter, Society Collection, Case 19, Box 9, Historical Society of Pennsylvania.

32. *Songs of the Sea, with Other Poems* (Boston: James Monroe, 1847), 195–201.

33. Letter, September 20, 1877, Harvard Theatre Collection.

34. Letter, Harvard Theatre Collection.

35. See Francis Hodge, *Yankee Theatre, The Image of America on the Stage, 1825–1850* (Austin, Texas: University of Texas Press, 1964).

36. *Spirit of the Times, XIII (August 26, 1843), 312.*

37. *See J. S. French, Sketches and Eccentricities of Col. David Crockett of West Tennessee* (New York: Harper, 1833).

38. William K. Northall, ed., *Life and Recollections of Yankee Hill* (New York: W. F. Burgess, 1850), Appendix.

39. *Spirit of the Times*, XIX (June 30, 1849), 218.

40. *Spirit of the Times*, VIII (May 26, 1838), 152.

41. *Spirit of the Times*, II (March 9, 1833), 53.

42. *Spirit of the Times*, II (February 2, 1833), 3.

43. *Dramatic Mirror*, I (October 16, 1841), 83.

44. *Spirit of the Times*, XIX (June 2, 1849), 180.

45. *The Literary World*, June 9, 1849, 498.

46. See the obituary in the *New York Clipper*, January 5, 1878, 326; John Bourne Clapp essay in the Boston *Transcript*, December 30, 1910, n.p., clipping file of Harvard Theatre Collection.

47. Jones' daybook and account books are in Rare Books & Manuscripts, Boston Public Library.

48. Jones' business correspondence is held in the Harvard Theatre Collection.

49. A letter dated "Boston, October, 1855," prefacing the 1855 publication of *Moll Pitcher; or, The Fortune Teller of Lynn*.

50. *Eugene Aram*, a dramatization of Bulwer-Lytton's novel, was produced at the Tremont Theatre on May 17, 1832, with Jones in the part of Jonah Gunn, a comic role which allowed Jones to ridicule lawyers.

Captain Kidd; or, The Wizard of the Sea, first produced in Boston in 1839, is concerned with the identity of the true Lord of Lester, who becomes Captain Kidd. A love theme is enhanced by spectacular sea fights, the humor of Horsebean Hemlock and a Dutchman named Vander Splocken, and the mystery of a witch named Elpsy. Arthur Hobson Quinn classified this play as one of the "wild and strenuous type," and his words are appropriate.

51. *Spirit of the Times*, II (March 23, 1833), 63.

52. *North American Magazine*, II (November 1833), 72.

53. *Spirit of the Times*, II (February 2, 1833), 3.

54. *Dramatic Mirror*, I (October 23, 1841), 87.

55. *Dramatic Mirror*, I (October 23, 1843), 83.

56. The Harvard Theatre Collection holds three manuscript versions of this play, the first dated December 18, 1842.

57. *Spirit of the Times*, XXVI (March 8, 1856), 48.

58. Henry D. Stone, *Personal Recollections of the Drama* (Albany: Charles Van Benthysen and Sons, 1873), 225.

59. *Spirit of the Times*, VI (December 31, 1836), 2.

60. W. K. Northall, ed., *Life and Recollections of Yankee Hill* (New York: W. F. Burgess, 1850), 19.

61. Hodge, *Yankee Theatre*, 192–193.

62. *Spirit of the Times*, VI (December 31, 1836), 2.

63. Brander Matthews, "The American on the Stage," *Scribner's Monthly*, XVIII (July 1879), 323.

64. Leman, *Memories of an Old Actor*, 137.

65. Letter in the J. Peter Coulson Collection, San Marcos, Texas.

66. Maud and Otis Skinner, eds., *One Man in His time*, 38.

67. Stone, *Personal Recollections of the Drama*, 193.

68. *Spirit of the Times*, XI (May 15, 1841), 132.

69. *Spirit of the Times*, XV (March 22, 1845), 32.

70. Joseph Jefferson, *The Autobiography of Joseph Jefferson* (New York: The Century Company, 1889), 20.

71. An unidentified review in the Enthoven Collection, the Victoria and Albert Museum, London.

72. Mrs. Bayle Bernard, ed., *Retrospections of America, 1797–1811* (New York: J. Harper, 1887), 37.

73. *American Monthly Magazine*, III (November 1, 1833), 215.

74. *Anglo-American, A Journal of Literature, News, Politics, the Drama, Fine Arts*, I (April 1842), 22–3.

75. *Spirit of the Times*, XVIII (April 22, 1848), 108.

5

STAGING THE STRUGGLES AND TRIUMPHS OF THE JACKSON GENERATION

At a reception for the English actor Henry Irving, given by the New York Goethe Society on March 15, 1888, Parke Godwin presented a discourse on "The Dramatic Art." As a journalist and translator of Goethe, Godwin talked about the "special attractiveness" of the drama. "Man is," he said, "of all things that man knows, the most interesting to man, and the drama concerns itself with man in the whole round of his being, in all the varieties of his social conditions and in all the subtleties of his individual motives." In consequence of its "immediate contact with the public," dramatic art captures the intellect, senses and feelings of man; it "catches directly this inspiration of popular life."[1] Although his ideas were not new, they were well expressed, while his concern for an art that may catch the spirit of the people was particularly relevant to Jacksonian America when Godwin, as an assistant to William Cullen Bryant on the *Post*, was prominent in the political, social and literary life of New York.

Perhaps no period in the history of the theatre made a more determined effort to reflect the wishes of the society it endeavored to entertain or to sell its product than did the Age of Jackson. For both playwrights and theatre managers it was a challenging time. Running a theatre was an extremely risky business; failure was common, and a sense of humor was doubtless a necessary asset in an uncomfortable situation. If a theatre manager lacked the necessary aesthetic distance, he was sure to be reminded of his folly.

No less than NINE theatres will be in full blast in this city [New York] on the 1st of September [1837], provided some of them live to open, and others close their doors on that day, viz: the Park, Bowery, National, Olympic, City, Franklin, Richmond Hill, Euterpean Hall, and Cooke's Amphi-theatre. Go it, managers, *you* will make fortunes, no doubt. Not more than 99 in 100 usually get "bursted" their first season. Shin-plas-

ters are worth ten cents on the dollar, and you may hire money at five per cent per
month, provided you allow yourselves to be locked up with the money in your pockets,
as security. But that's nothing—only a slight annoyance, so go ahead—who's afraid?[2]

There was a double dare in this comment because the Panic of 1837 was de-
scending upon the commercial world, including the theatre; yet, people constantly took the dare and were subjected to that buoyant attitude of burlesque
so characteristic of some reviewers at this time.

Forced to be extravagantly inventive, theatre managers often found success
by reflecting the topics of the day—political problems, social issues and fads,
newspaper headlines, or current interests in patriotism, reform and the latest
popular fiction. In contrast to the traditional theatre fare of Shakespeare and
other English works that managers placed upon their stages whenever they could
catch the appropriate touring star, the plays that kept theatres open when stars
were not available—the novelties and spectacles that reflected the progress and
problems of Jacksonian America—were written mainly by Americans. These
were the anonymous or soon-forgotten dramatists who regularly dramatized the
travails and high spirits of the developing nation and the worried search of its
citizens for a recognized and homogenous identity. If the northern border of
Maine was in question, if Charles Dickens visited America, if a murder caused
a sensation,[3] the event was sure to be dramatized by that jumble of individuals,
amateurs and professionals, who expressed in jest or seriously the idiosyncrasies of many of the fiercely independent and determined Americans living in
Jacksonian America—patriots, reformers, romantics, hard-headed entrepreneurs and the common man as well as the social snobs whose affectations,
wherever they lived, pointed eastward.

Finding it extremely difficult to compete with the popularity of a Sheridan
Knowles or a Bulwer-Lytton, particularly when the lack of an American copyright agreement allowed any theatre manager to steal what he wanted, the
American playwright was forced to write for the few American actors whose
reputations would allow them to commission plays or sponsor contests or to
provide the occasional spectacles and novelties that filled out an evening's entertainment. In general these playwrights entertained the masses. While fashionable society watched Charles Kemble and William Macready at the Park
Theatre, the Bowery Theatre fascinated other New Yorkers with the plays of
Louisa Medina, Nathaniel Bannister or Ben Baker. Theatre patrons in cities such
as Boston, Philadelphia and New Orleans enjoyed plays by Silas Steele, Joseph
M. Field or Charles Saunders. Starring actors, of course, also played those cities, while fashionable New York audiences could watch the spectacular melodramas and topical farces. The task of portraying the struggle of the Jacksonian
Generation, however, was largely the challenge of the American playwright whose
opportunities for major billing were limited.

The daily life of people, particularly those aspects sharply contrasted in urban and rural environments, was a constant source of fascination in Jacksonian

America. Playwrights burlesqued daily life as much as poets romanticized it, and novelists moralized its idiosyncrasies into absurdities. It was always there for the playwright to exploit as he wished, and plays about city life appeared as one of the earliest forms of native American drama, although they obviously had an English antecedent. Pierce Egan's *Life in London* (1821), dramatized by Egan and others as *Tom and Jerry, or; Life in London*, started a trend in local color melodramas that soon spread to America. James Hackett's production of *The Times; or, Life in New York* (December 1829) by a "gentleman of this city" illustrates the easy migration of this kind of theatre which would continue to be popular in Jacksonian America. *The Mirror's* review explains some of the play's peculiarities: *The Times* "consists of a dozen or so scenes thrown cleverly though loosely together, exhibiting the manners and habits of the worthy inhabitants of this city. . . . There is a pretended English baronet, a Frenchman, two Broadway dandies (a black and a white), a plain merchant and his fashionable wife, a talking speculating Yankee, a brace of young ladies and young gentlemen."[4] Three seasons later, T. D. Rice played the lead character of Hector in *Life in Philadelphia* at the Bowery Theatre. Jonas B. Phillips wrote *Life in New York* (1834), in which he provided recognizable scenes of the city. Bannister used the same title for his benefit at the Franklin Theatre in New York in 1839 and played in *Old Manhattan; or, Wall Street in an Uproar* the following year.

One of Cornelius Logan's very early plays entitled *The Night Hawk*, produced at the Walnut Street Theatre in Philadelphia in November of 1830, shows the direction that this type of city play took in America before reaching an astonishing theatrical climax in 1848 with *A Glance at New York*. Just as the high society diarist Philip Hone apparently avoided Frank Chanfrau's success, some Philadelphians rejected *The Night Hawk*. The *Ariel* reviewer found it "a display of low, vile, and disgusting indecency, coupled with scenes and language which no female ought to hear uttered, much less to utter." It drew good audiences, but of a caliber less sophisticated and discerning than the reviewer might have wished, although the *Ariel* printed the following description of *The Night Hawk* that appeared on handbills:

The bar-room of a Tavern in Race Street, a Norristown gentleman reading the "Mechanic Free Press." Scene 3, A Milliner's Shop; Milliners making love and corsets; a Yankee in a Band-Box. Night Hawk among the Mantua Makers. Act two. Charcoal Jenny blowing a Horn, and taking one—Cordials and Corsets—A tumble over a Fire Plug—Faithful Watchmen—A Bucks County Damsel in Distress—A Yankee's escape from the guardians of the Night. Scene 2, a Serenading Party—Gostport Tragedy—Faithless Sally Brown. Song, a True Lover's Ditty by Mr. W. Chapman—An attempt at the Minstrel's Return from the Wars, with an accompaniment on the Horn, by Charcoal Jenny. Act 3, Past twelve o'clock and a charcoal Morning. A fire; Charcoal Jenny having dined out, exhibits painful concern for the Engines "Vigilant, Neptune, and Humane," and becoming entangled in the Hose, is borne to the fire without any voluntary Locomotion. Scene last. A Ballroom, Jenny in liquor, in disguise, in trouble, and in Petticoats. A country Dance by the Characters and a general Blow up by Powder, id est, pulvarized charcoal.[5]

The Night Hawk appears to have been raucous entertainment put together by Logan for his own benefit. Evidently, it served him well.

On opening night (February 2, 1848) at William Mitchell's Olympic Threatre, the title was *New York in 1848*, but ever afterwards it was called *A Glance at New York*. Ben Baker's little farce immediately caused great excitement in the pit and gallery. Odell declared it "one of the greatest successes ever known in the history of the New York stage,"[6] and by all accounts, it created the kind of entertainment that many Jacksonian theatregoers relished. Not all those at the Olympic Theatre, however, including Baker, who wrote it for his own benefit, either appreciated or understood its attraction. In *Before and Behind the Curtain* William K. Northall noted that people did strange and outrageous things on benefit nights and that ordinarily Mitchell would not have allowed the Mose play to go onstage. Only outstanding acting, Northall claimed, kept this "unmitigated conglomeration of vulgarity and illiteracy" in the theatre for four months, and during the summer of 1848, Mitchell, concerned with "restoring" the atmosphere of the Olympic Theatre, consigned Mose to the "Chatham where we do not object to see it flourish."[7]

A Glance at New York, however, turned out to be a distinctive piece both for American theatre and for American drama with a hero who immediately caught the public fancy. Although Mose, the fire b'hoy, had theatrical ancestors in the works of Egan, Logan and others, his popularity was also tied to an interest in the city firemen, whose competitive spirit in getting water to a fire is still a popular feature of rural fairs in America. *The Fireman's Frolic*, written by a real fireman of Philadelphia, was presented at the Arch Street Theatre in 1831. *Beulah Spa; or, Two of the B'hoys* (1834) and *Fifteen Years of a Fireman's Life* (1841) also suggest something of the background from which Mose erupted. Perhaps Baker was aware of these plays as he must have known Ned Buntline's popular novels of the late 1840s about life in New York—*The B'hoys of New York* and *The Mysteries and Miseries of New York*, followed in 1850 by *The G'hals of New York*.

When the immediate popularity of Mose and the play was sufficient to make people think of comparisons, Cornelius Mathews, editor and dramatist, declared that the character was taken from his novel entitled *Puffer Hopkins*. Baker, however, denied any knowledge of Mathews' novel before writing his play. The only source he would acknowledge was *102 Broadway* by William Henry Herbert, from which he drew Major Gates. He also denied that Mose Humphreys, a newspaper man in New York, was the origin of Mose, in spite of Humphreys' claim. In fact, Baker once explained, most of the parts were not named until the play had been revised after its opening and retitled *A Glance at New York*.

The simplicity of Baker's recital of his creation leaves little room for doubt.

"Mr. Mitchell used to give us a week's notice for our benefits. Mary Taylor was ill, and I depended on Chanfrau for mine that season. I had promised to write the part of a fire boy for him, and we thought that my benefit might be a good time to try it. I made Mose a rough melon, but sweet at the core. In writing the piece I was afraid the Centre Market Boys would take offense at it, and to satisfy them I put the pathos about the baby into it."[8] In its original version A Glance at New York, reminiscent of its English and American forebears, had twenty-four performers—among them Mose; Harry Gordon; George Parsells; Jake and Mike, both sharpers; Major Gates, a literary loafer; Mrs. Morton, president of the Ladies Bowling Saloon; Mary, her daughter; and Jane, a girl from the country. "That piece made me a great gun," Baker explained, "and it made Chanfrau famous in a single night." Six weeks later, March 15, 1848, new scenes and new characters were introduced—Mr. Morton; Ben, the sender of news; Sam, the young thief; Eliza Stebbins, a gal; Jenny Bogent, her friend. This version ran for about fifty performances according to Odell, and the Mose fad was underway. New plays by Baker and others soon appeared as Mose took a glance at other cities and visited other countries around the world. Mainly, Mose was a vehicle for Frank S. Chanfrau, but other actors also tried the part.

Benjamin A. Baker (1818–1890) was a native New Yorker, born in Grand Street near the corner of Edridge. At the age of twelve, after the death of his father, he was apprenticed by his guardian to a harnessmaker but ran away from his job, finally landing in New Orleans where at seventeen he "was seized with the wish to become an actor." His first job was as a lamp-lighter in a theatre in Natchez where he was sent with a company organized by Richard Russell, the manager of the Camp Street Threatre in New Orleans. Baker finally realized his desire to act in Louisville, staying there for two years before returning to New York, where he joined Mitchell's Olympic Theatre as prompter and actor prior to its opening in 1839. Odell notes that Baker was paid $10 a week plus a one-half benefit after a deduction of $100.[9] These were reasonably good times at the Olympic Theatre, the only theatre in New York making money during the 1842–1843 season.

Along with Alexander Allan, Joseph M. Field and Charles Walcot, Baker began to write for Mitchell. His first play, a travesty of the opera Amelia, called Amy Lee; or, Who Loves Best? and first performed on April 13, 1843, was not successful, nor was Peytona and Fashion; or, North against South (April 7, 1845). A Glance at New York, however, changed Baker's life, and he capitalized on his good fortune. During his lifetime he wrote some seventeen or eighteen farces and burlesques, mainly, he said, on "the follies of the day" none of which, "of course, were calculated to live." When the Olympic Theatre closed in March of 1850, Baker went to Boston and afterwards back to New York, on to Washington and then to California, managing theatres and working with starring actors and actresses. For two years he traveled with Edwin Booth as his business manager. When he died in 1890, he was the assistant secretary of the Actors Fund, and the obituaries were full of praise and sentiment for Uncle

Ben Baker, the utility actor and prompter who worte one amazing play and worked with the biggest stars of the nineteenth-century American theatre—Charlotte Cushman, Laura Keene and Edwin Booth. "Few men, occupying a comparatively humble sphere in life, have become so widely known and respected."[10]

The man who gained the most from Baker's creation was the actor Francis S. Chanfrau (1824–1884). Another native New Yorker, Chanfrau received what Wemyss considered a respectable English education and went briefly to the West where he worked as a ship carpenter and joiner before returning to New York. There, after seeing Edwin Forrest perform at the Bowery Theatre, he joined an amateur dramatic association, eventually known as the Forrest Dramatic Association, and finally became a supernumerary at the Bowery. Ironically, it was his ability to imitate Forrest that first brought him recognition and started him on the tour of theatres and cities that led him to the Olympic Theatre in 1848. As Mose the fire b'hoy, Chanfrau became at once the dramatic "lion" of the town: "his likeness pervaded every window, and his sayings were uttered by every urchin in the city as well as by a very great portion of the elder part of the male community." Dressed in the red shirt, plug hat and turned-up trousers of the New York fireman, he became the epitome of the extravagant roughneck who enjoyed physical action and practical jokes and would fight a fire, sing a song, or love a girl with equal zest. In dress, manner, gait, tone and action he was a Bowery b'hoy, and the people loved him in that role—at least for a time. Chanfrau surmised that the intense popularity of Mose in all of its ramifications and revisitations lasted for about three and a half years. With his reputation established, he moved on to other roles—that of Kit Carson, which he played 560 times, and the title role in Thomas De Walden's *Sam*, which he performed 783 times.[11]

The published version of *A Glance at New York*, a local drama in two acts, opens with a "View of the Steamboat Pier, foot of Barklay Street" and a chorus of newsboys, porters, and applewomen singing of the "Jolly Young Waterman":

> The folks are all waiting to see the fast steamer
>   That's coming from Albany down to this pier;
> Ah, here she is! Now, you, sir, ain't she a screamer?
>   In New York, the fastest boats always land here.

As Harry Gordon, the native New Yorker, and George Parsells, the country boy, leave the boat, Harry says: "Here we are in the great metropolis of the Western World . . . where you can purchase amusements of all kinds, from the Astor Place Opera to the far famed 'Hall of Novelty,' " and you can see "how much better it is to live here than in your stupid village in the backwoods." When Harry runs off to get a cab to take them to the Astor House, Jake, a sharper, recognizes the greenhorn and soon talks George out of his silver watch and $10 in exchange for a gilt watch that he swears is gold. A little

Poster for *A Glance at New York*. Courtesy of the Library of Congress.

later, George is again fooled by the "drop" game with this same sharper and loses another $10 before Harry can explain that the "drop" bills from the Globe Bank and the Hoboken Banking and Grazing Company are "worthless as chaff." And so the "better" life begins for George in the big city.

Mose, recognized as an old schoolfellow by Harry, enters talking to the audience:

(Smoking, he spits) I've made up my mind not to run wid der machine any more. There's that Corneel Anderson don't give de boys a chance. Just 'cause he's Chief Ingineer he thinks he ken do as he likes. Now, last night when de fire was down in Front Street, we was takin' 40's water; I had hold of de butt, and seed she was gittin' too much for us; and I seys to Bill Sykes: "Sykesy, take de butt." Seys he, "What for?" Seys I, "Never you mind but take de butt." And he took de butt; so I goes down de street a little, and stood on 40's hose. Corneel Anderson cum along and seed me. Seys he, "Get off de hose!" Seys he, "If you don't get off de hose, I'll hit you over de gourd wid my trumpet!" Seys I, "What—I won't get off de hose!" And he did hit me over de gourd! (I,2)

Harry interrupts Mose's soliloquy, introduces George and, for excitement, suggests they go to the Ladies Bowling Saloon where, disguised in the plain white pants, blue blouses and little black caps ladies wore when bowling tenpins, they discover George's friend, Jane, who had captured Harry's heart during his recent stay in the country, and her aunt, Mrs. Morton, whom she is visiting in New York. The women immediately penetrate the men's disguise, and Mose cannot hide the fact that he is "a man and no mistake—and one of de b'hoys at dat!" He grabs Mrs. Morton around the waist and kisses her (I,3).

The next stop for the three pleasure seekers is Loafer's Paradise, "a dirty Bar-room," because Mose is "itchin' for a regular knock-down and drag-out." At the Bar they meet some "foo-foos," or, as Mose explains, "an outsider, a chap wot can't come de big figure" which is "three cents for a glass of grog and a night's lodging" on one of the benches. Major Gates has this problem, and Harry obliges him and would be off, but Mose still yearns for a fight. Fortunately, Jake, who "speechifys" while Mike picks pockets, begins his act. His opposition to all governments and all laws is vigorously applauded, but his insensitivity to "foo-foos" raises the ire of Mose, who starts a brawl with Jake as the scene ends.

(Front Street—Music Hurry—Dark Stage—George runs across from L to R, followed by a Loafer, beating him—Harry Crosses, fighting Loafer—Mose enters.)

Mose: Them fellows have been followin' me long enough. Now I'm goin' in!

(Enter two fellows who attack Mose. He knocks them down, and after one or two rounds, they fight each other. Mose runs off, laughing. The two men roll about the stage, fighting till they discover their mistake—Then they run off.) (I,vi)

And Act I ends.

In Act II there are six scenes, more incidents, more greenhorn jokes and more characters. Even Mose is conned into holding a baby for a woman who immediately runs away, but this incident gives him a chance to tell about the time he saved a baby from a fire. "The fire-boys may be a little rough outside, but they're alright here. (Touches breast.) It never shall be said dat one of de New

York boys deserted a baby in distress'' (II,1). Mose's gal, Lize, appears and wants to see "George Christy play de bones.'' She sings a song and makes a date with Mose. "She's a gallus gal—she is,'' says Mose; "I've strong suspicions, I'll have to get slung to her one of these days'' (II,2). George loses money to Major Gates in another version of the "drop'' game, buys a day-old newspaper and gets conned into bidding against himself at a mock auction. Preparing for a visit to Waxhall (Vauxhall Gardens), Lize and her friend Jenny sing "Oh Lud, Gals'':

> *Lize*: Here we are, as you diskiver,
>   All the way from roaring river—
>   My wife dies—I'll get another
>   Pretty yaller gal—just like t'other
>   Oh Lud, gals, give me chaw tobacco!
> *Jenny*: Oh, dear—fotch along de whiskey,
>   My head swims when I get tipsy.

(Baker stated that Mitchell questioned the language in this play but was persuaded to accept it.) As all gather at the Vauxhall Gardens, they watch a group dance "a Gallopade,'' and have dinner. Having fallen in love with Jane's friend, Mary, George is tempted to remain in New York, and Mrs. Morton is busy planning two weddings—Harry and Jane's and George and Mary's—when Mose gets a message that Sykesy wants him. "Look here,'' Mose explains to the audience as he gets ready to leave, "Ladies and gentlemen—don't be down on me 'cause I'm going to leave you—but Sykesy's got in a muss, and I'm bound to see him righted, 'cause he runs wid our machine, you know—and if you don't say no, while I'll scare up this crowd again tomorrow night, and then you can take another GLANCE AT NEW YORK.'' And Chanfrau-Mose did just that or something similar for the next three or four years.

The fad spread and Baker quickly wrote another Mose play for the Chatham Theatre. *New York As It Is* was entirely different from *A Glance at New York*, Baker said, but "in the same style.'' Odell notes that it was staged by Chanfrau (April 17, 1848) and provides a synopsis of its scenes:

Views of Chatham Square and the Chatham Theatre; the old Dutch church; the Interior of the Soup House with Teniers' picture of crowded, sweating humanity, and Mose raising what he calls a "plug mess''; City Hall; a chamber in the house of Mr. Meadows with a song, "Come Miss, Stir your Stumps''; the Catherine Fish Market, with a race between the Steamers *Oregon* and *Vanderbilt*, and with songs and a "nigger Dance for Eels and much special business for the Slippery Joe''; a Ladies' Gymnasium, and finally, the Old Bowery in Flames with Mose and the Fire Company in operation. "Mose dashes into the Burning Building, appears at the window with the child in his arms. She is saved, Grand Tableau.'' [12]

This play, too, created a sensation, and the *Spirit of the Times* described the scene as the people came to the theatre to see Mose. So great was the interest that the play preceding *New York As It Is*—*The Brigand*—was interrupted as people pushed into the theatre and caused those already seated to crawl or jump over the footlights onto the stage. "The police and attackers of the theatre hereupon commenced to clear the front of the stage, amid the most deafening cheers; and some of the young 'B'hoys' were to be seen springing forward on the heads of their different groups of friends, from the stage, whom they joined in the pit, amid continued laughter."[13] The *Spirit* surmised that over a thousand people were either refunded ticket prices or turned away from the theatre.

Both plays, *A Glance at New York* and *New York As It Is*, had similar appeal: a rather particular view of New York or any big city life garnished with songs, jokes, monologues by Mose, and a number of farcical situations. If the jokes and the songs were a little rowdy for uptown audiences, it was not by error. The appeal was clearly made to a certain class of citizens. Men disguised as women appeared in both plays; one play had a monologue about a baby. There were dances in both plays and scenes of real places and events. Each play was a collection of farcical episodes loosely held together by a picaresque heroic figure. The actions of George and Harry may provide a slight plot for *A Glance at New York*, but they are hardly the main figures.

A Glance at New York can easily be compared to *The Lion of the West* or *The People's Lawyer* or other Yankee plays in which the major character intrudes into a farcical or melodramatic plot and claims the audience by his mannerisms, vocabulary, dress and outrageous actions. New scenes could easily be added to such a play, and were, as audiences changed and made different demands. Cities other than New York could be featured, and were, as in *A Glance at Philadelphia* and *Philadelphia As It Is*. At Burton's Theatre in Arch Street, where John E. Owens was the starring comedian, an imitation featuring local scenes with Jake, the sharper, at one time called *Jakey*, rivaled the success of the New York play.[14] The most attractive feature of all of these plays was, of course, that rowdy character from a certain level of society who enjoyed a certain attitude toward life. Audiences liked what they felt was a realistic presentation and the humorous interaction of the character with different aspects of society. The order of events really did not matter, and the result was something akin to a musical review.

Mose kept moving with or without the help of his creator. Most Mose plays are anonymous, but Baker wrote *Mose in China* for Chanfrau, and Odell credits W. B. Chapman with the authorship of *Mose in California*.[15] A year after Mose's sensational opening, the Chatham Theatre was leased by Chanfrau's friends and renamed the National.

The new National, having made "Mose" the peculiar tenant of the establishment, relies upon him to draw together his host of admirers, and consequently we have that worthy at one moment "runnen wid de masheene" over the rattling pavement of our city, and in a few seconds we find him shining among the glittering mines of California. The earthly career of this popular character has, however, a limit, and the best thing we can do is to suggest his further transplantation to paradise, and when he grows disconcerted with our city, we trust to find Mose among the angels.[16]

In this fashion the *Spirit of the Times* explored Mose's continuing popularity.

There would be an end to Mose's earthly career, but the season of 1848–1849 might well be dubbed the Mose Season in New York. In the fall of 1848 *The Mysteries and Miseries of New York* from the Ned Buntline novel, adapted specifically for Chanfrau by Henry W. Grattan Plunkett (H. P. Grattan), opened at the National Theatre. Plunkett (1808–1889), a Dubliner by birth who first appeared in New York as Hamlet at the Park Theatre, spent twenty-three years in America writing a number of plays, working as an actor and managing theatres in New York and Memphis. In early June a sequel to *The Mysteries and Miseries of New York* called *Three Years After*, probably written by W. B. Chapman, opened with more adventures for Mose and was followed three weeks later by Chapman's *Mose in a Muss*. By September of 1849, an anonymous play entitled *Mose, Joe and Jack* at the Bowery Theatre presented scenes of the Jersey City Ferry, the Battery, the American Museum, St. Paul's Church, Five Points, the interior of the Tombs and the exterior of the Bowery Theatre.

Quite distinct from the masses who followed the adventures of Mose and his friends, there was a New York society which had greater ambitions for its future. Like all social groups this one had its problems which playwrights were quick to recognize while taking advantage of its fashions and fads. Among the representations onstage of this society no play was more popular than *Fashion* by Anna Cora Mowatt Ritchie (1819–1870), whose own social background was sufficiently high society that her play opened first at the Park Theatre and found an appeal among that theatre's more sophisticated audiences. As the work of a talented but amateur playwright, *Fashion* has all of the virtues and faults that critics have never tired of pointing out. It was, however, shrewdly created by someone who understood the theatre better than might be expected of a social aristocrat who made her debut as a professional playwright by scattering currently popular themes, characters and situations in a reasonably appealing manner throughout her play.

Mowatt's family came straight from Knickerbocracy, as Nathaniel Parker Willis identified high society in New York. Her mother's grandfather had been one of the signers of the Declaration of Independence. She belonged, indeed, to an enterprising family. When her father lost his money in a South American venture, he soon recouped his fortune as an agent for a French wine company in Bordeaux, where he was living when Mowatt was born, the ninth of fourteen children. Although she was only six years old when her family returned to New York, she had enjoyed theatre in Paris as well as the amateur theatricals practiced by the family. Her mature life started early, when at fifteen she married James Mowatt, a young lawyer. Soon she was writing. *Pelazo; or, The Caverns of Cavadonga* (1836), an epic poem, was one of her first projects. An early dramatic creation, *The Gypsy Wanderer; or, The Stolen Child*, labeled an operetta, tells the story of a woman whose child is stolen by gypsies. Filled with hatred, the woman forbids all contact with gypsies until her niece befriends a little gypsy girl who, of course, turns out to be the stolen child.

Always bothered by consumptive symptoms, Mowatt was sent to Europe in 1837 to recover. In Paris she again attended the theatre, became a devotee of Rachel and, before returning to America in 1840, completed a six-act drama in blank verse entitled *Gulzara; or, The Persian*, for which she commissioned a French scene painter to do the designs. Wealth had its advantages, and once back in New York she arranged a lavish production of *Gulzara*, playing the lead character herself. The scene was the harem of Sultan Suliman where the jealousy of an old favorite slave toward the new one, Gulzara, provided material for the plot. Epes Sargent, a friend of the family, found striking passages in the play and published it in *The New World*, of which he was an associate editor.

Life, however, was an uneven adventure for Mowatt. In 1841 her husband lost his fortune, and Mowatt, after talking matters over with Sargent, decided to undertake a career as a public speaker in Boston, whose people, it was felt, would be most receptive to her talents. Her first recitation in October of 1841 was a substantial success. Clapp wrote that "she exhibited the most beautiful moral spectacle of which human nature is capable." [17] The following spring Mowatt fell seriously ill again, a victim of excessive work and consumption. At this time her friendship with Sargent inspired her to consider the current interest in mesmeric healing. Although Mowatt was treated by William Francis Channing, a mesmeric healer, Sargent hypnotized her when she had chest pains and apparently relieved her distress. She also became interested in Swedenborgian philosophy and continued her writing, publishing in *Godey's*, *The Democratic Review*, *Ladies Companion* and *Graham's*. These years—from September of 1842 until February of 1845—were to be the most productive of her life as a writer, resulting in eleven books, including two novels: *The Fortune Hunter* (1842) and *Evelyn* (1845). It was during February of 1845 that she completed *Fashion*, which Sargent immediately took to Edmund Simpson, the manager of the Park Theatre.

Fashion; or, Life in New York opened at the Park Theatre on March 24 and ran for at least eighteen performances. As a kindness and as a gesture from one of the literati of New York, Epes Sargent wrote a prologue in verse in which he noted the prevailing prejudice against native American playwrights.

> "*Fashion*, a comedy"—I'll go: but stay—
> Now I read farther, 'tis a *native* play!
> Bah! home-made calicos are well enough,
> But home-made dramas *must* be stupid stuff![18]

This was delivered by William Crisp, the actor who played Count Jolimaitre, in the guise of a New Yorker looking for an evening's entertainment. While Sargent's thoughts were self-indulgent and a little bitter, Mowatt was more instructive in her preface to the London edition of *Fashion* (1850): "The Comedy of *Fashion* was intended as a good-natured satire upon some of the follies incident to a new country, where foreign dross sometimes passes for gold, while native gold is cast aside as dross; where vanities rather than the virtues of other lands are too often imitated, and where the stamp of *Fashion* gives currency even to the coinage of vice."[19] Few were in a better position to know New York society, and no one had the wit and skill to satirize it more effectively onstage.

Not only was *Fashion* a commercial success in 1845, it provided something of a landmark in the progress of American drama and theatre, for it encouraged that necessary cooperation between professional theatre people and the literati. As a woman and a member of the social and literary aristocracy, Mowatt was still a neophyte in the theatre who should not have understood the rules. She was, however, a fair writer and an intelligent and well-read person who loved the theatre, and, of course, *Fashion* was first produced at the Park Theatre, not at the Bowery Theatre. It was properly puffed, and weeks before *Fashion* opened, critics anticipated its production as an opportunity for Simpson to recoup his fortune. They also took advantage of the situation to describe the condition of American dramatic literature as "an unplowed field for genius."[20]

After opening night even the indulgent viewers had reservations, for good and specific reasons. Clearly reflecting the popular interest in spectacular melodrama, the *Spirit* noted that Mrs. Mowatt "possesses few qualifications for dramatic writing, as she lacks the essentials—vigor and ingenuity." "The dialogue of *Fashion*," the critic continued, "is unpolished, spiritless and disjointed; the satire is dealt out in unconnected items, much after the manner of newspaper squibs; the plot is entirely too light for the dialogue, and the action, although not encumbered by an underplot, is cut up by unnecessary deviations." "The piece, taken as a comedy, is a dreadful failure."[21] Other reviewers emphasized the acting, generalizing that acting could make or break a play, or praised the American authorship and the American theme. Regardless of these particular reactions to the play, even accepting the *Spirit*'s contention that "without the acting *Fashion* would be intolerable," the nationalistic plea prevailed.[22] Most critics touched on the idea that here was a play that might stimulate American theatre, and from all sides the cry arose for meaningful American drama—not, of course, a new idea, merely a popular one. Other plays, other dramatists—Stone, Bannister, Medina, Field, Bird, Jones—had created similar reactions, but Mowatt's personal background and particular achievements in writing *Fashion* conveyed a recognizable stimulus for the development of an American drama. It was that strange mixture of nationalism and snobbery permeating America at this time that gave this play its status.

Edgar Allan Poe reviewed *Fashion* twice in *The Broadway Journal*, giving the play some prestige in the eyes of historians. At first Poe found the play "theatrical but not dramatic," a "pretty well-arranged selection from the usual routine of stage characters and stage manoeuvres." With this sound criticism, he compared *Fashion* to other American plays, enjoying the play's simple plot, its spirited and tense comedy and finding it "in many respects . . . superior to

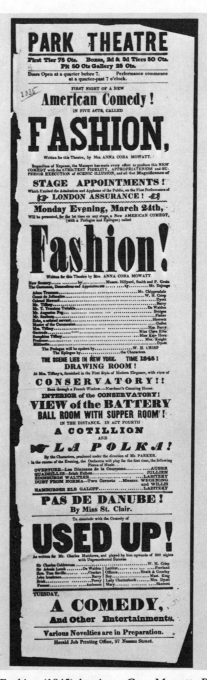

Program of *Fashion* (1845) by Anna Cora Mowatt. By permission of the Harvard Theatre Collection.

any American play,'' although he did not consider it representative of high dramatic art.[23] The play did absorb his interest, however, for in his second review he confessed to having seen every performance to date. He also moderated his first observation that *Fashion* was a bad imitation of *The School for Scandal* and noted that in satirizing fashion as fashion Mrs. Mowatt had taken an original approach.[24] Other critics adopted a nationalistic and conciliatory view which may have worked more to the play's advantage than they imagined. ''Although,'' began the editor of *Arthur's Ladies Magazine*, ''we by no means consider *Fashion* as equal to many of the sterling old English comedies, our approval of it is cordial, because it is American and inspires a love of country; and because we see in the hearty reception that it has met, an earnest [desire] that new laborers are about to come into the field of dramatic literature, and give it a new and better life.''[25]

With caution and moderation or extravagant flamboyance, many reviewers tried to see *Fashion* as a key to the future of American dramatic literature. The times were not right, however; nor was the play a sufficient exemplum. Rather than providing a key to the future, *Fashion*, as Poe pointed out, merely suggested that there was hope—a hope, however, that had been equally underscored by the works of a handful of dramatists during the past twenty years and yet gone unrecognized. By chance, *Fashion* caught the wandering attention of thoughtful reviewers and has since become a focal point for modern historians. Like all of her peer playwrights, however, Mowatt wrote *Fashion* to succeed onstage, not in the library. Even by design it would not meet the vague standards chosen by contemporary magazine editors and literary critics. It was, indeed, a fusion of melodrama and farce exhibiting the follies of fashionable life in New York. As a play of 1845, *Fashion* held something for everyone—moral commentary, a nationalistic theme, a city versus country conflict, love episodes, a melodramatic villain, society caricatures, witty epigrams, a country Yankee, an American hero, a Negro servant, patriotic sentiments, a temperance issue, a French count and a French maid, and satire throughout. For what *Fashion* lacked in spectacle—although there is a ballroom scene—a variety of action, style and characters compensated.

Fashion begins as a typical drawing-room comedy. Zeke, the new Negro servant in the Tiffany household, meets Millinette, the French maid, and asks her the usual question: ''What I wants to know is your publicated opinion, privately expressed, ob de domestic circle'' (I,1). Mrs. Tiffany, having risen quickly in the world from milliner to snob, apes foreign cultures, practices *French without a Master* with alarming results, and clutters her drawing room with such pretenders to modernity as T. Tennyson Twinkle and Augustus Fogg. She is also trying to arrange the marriage of her daughter, Seraphina, to Count Jolimaitre who finds, he says, ''but one redeeming charm in America—a superlative loveliness of the feminine portion of creation—and the wealth of their obliging papas'' (I,1). Adam Trueman, the Yankee, has no patience with either foreigners and their manners or deception anywhere. ''This *fashion*-worship has made heathens and hypocrites of you all!'' he tells Mr. Tiffany (II,1). When Gertrude, the governess, is outrageously importuned by Jolimaitre, Trueman protects her with a fervor even he does not understand.

By Act III all of the situations and conflicts are carefully prepared: an extravagant Mrs. Tiffany versus a financially beleaguered Mr. Tiffany; Tiffany versus Snobson, his blackmailing clerk; Count Jolimaitre versus Seraphina and Gertrude. The eventual pairing will involve Millinette and Count Jolimaitre, whom she recognizes as a past beau, and Gertrude and the American soldier, Colonel Howard, a direct descendant of Colonel Manly in Royall Tyler's *The Contrast*. Trueman becomes central to all of these situations. The act ends as Gertrude realizes that the Count is an impostor and that she must save Seraphina from his grasp—a strong melodramatic climax. The spectacle of the play appears in Act IV, the ball scene, where Gertrude attempts to trap Jolimaitre and Millinette and is herself discovered by Trueman as her trap fails. Immediately, she is turned out of the house by Mrs. Tiffany and rejected by Trueman. Fortunately, there is a fifth act in which to right all wrongs and join the proper hands. A letter in Gertrude's possession establishes her identity with Trueman, who begs forgiveness and then settles the affairs of everyone else: Snobson is charged with forgery but is allowed to leave; Millinette and Jolimaitre will marry; Gertrude and Howard will marry; and the Tiffanys must go to the country to learn "economy, true independence, and home virtues, instead of foreign follies " (V,1).

Fashion is the true center of the wit and enterprise of the play. "A woman of fashion *never* grows old!'' says Mrs. Tiffany; "Age is always out of fashion'' (I,1). Fashion, according to Trueman, is "an agreement between certain persons to live without using their souls! To substitute etiquette for virtue— decorum for purity—manners for morals!'' (IV,1). Trueman also provides the clear moral of the piece: don't be led astray by dreams of wealth or deceived by false fashions. Such views, presented within the popular framework of "life in New York'' and with a wit that was not generally practiced among American dramatists, were particularly attractive to Jacksonian audiences. Other dramatists tried to imitate Mowatt's work but without her success, and she herself did not write another play of comparable effect.[26]

Encouraged by her reception as a platform reader and by her playwriting success, Mowatt embarked upon a career as an actress. Her debut as Pauline in *The Lady of Lyons* took place at the Park Theatre (June 13, 1845). "Of Mrs. Mowatt and her acting,'' wrote Edgar Allan Poe, "we have to speak only in terms of enthusiastic admiration. . . . No actress in America is her equal for she reads not theatrically but with the emphasis of Nature.''[27] His detailed description of her physical appearance, even to the "profusion of rich auburn hair,'' places her among Poe's idealized women. For the next five years Mowatt acted upon the major stages of America and England. It was an exhausting life. Consider the 1846–1847 theatre season, for example: mid-July at Niblo's in New York, early August in Buffalo, August 20 back in New York at the Park Theatre, end of August in Philadelphia, mid-September back at Niblo's—so tired, she wrote in her *Autobiography* (1854), that she fell asleep behind the screen, playing Lady Teazle in *School for Scandal*—a rest of three weeks in October, then engagements at Boston, New Orleans, Mobile (in that order) and at the Park in New York for ten days in early May. By this time she had mastered twenty roles.

In late 1847 Mowatt sailed for England, where she had considerable success. "Since the first appearance of Charlotte Cushman in London," wrote a reviewer for the *Spirit of the Times*, "no artist has made a more successful hit than our countryman, Mrs. Mowatt. She has been completely successful both as an authoress and actress."[28] In 1851 Mowatt's husband died, and she soon returned to America, "welcomed [at Niblo's] most enthusiastically by a densely crowded and fashionable audience, a majority of whom were ladies."[29] After continuing her acting career in America, she retired from the stage on June 3, 1854, at Niblo's Garden. "That evening," she wrote to a gentleman of that theatre, "must close my dramatic career, and I rejoice that it will end where it began—in the city which you have rightly termed 'the home of my family.' "[30]

That same year she married William F. Ritchie of Virginia aristocracy and began to write works of fiction. Most interesting for theatre people is her *Mimic Life; or, Before and Behind the Curtain* (1855), three strongly autobiographical stories dealing with the theatre. When she sailed for France in August of 1860, she had left Ritchie, for reasons that involved her attitudes toward religion, slavery and his personal life. Although repeated illness still haunted her life, she continued to travel and to make new friends in Europe where she spent her last years. She died in London on July 29, 1870. In March of that year she had written to her old friend Henry W. Longfellow, "I am hopelessly an invalid, always confined to the house," signing herself Anna Cora Mowatt Ritchie.[31]

Fashion became Mowatt; it seemed to epitomize her style and personality. Her other play, the only one worth noting, *Armand, the Child of the People* (1847, acted in England with the subtitle *The Peer and the Peasant*), was a romantic drama written partly in blank verse and set in the time of Louis XV. Although it seems a contradiction to her work in *Fashion*, in fact it represents a popular theatre mode in both America and England. To save his daughter Blanche from the clutches of the king, the Duke of Richelieu gives her a potion to suggest death and places her in a convent—away from the king as well as away from Armand, her lover. Her escape is as romantic as the climax of the play in which the king is persuaded to arrange her marriage to Armand. The play was reasonably successful in America and in England, where a critic described it as lively and intense with continuous interest. Lacking great passion or bursts of poetry, the play contained "living and suggestive outlines of character, scenes of pathos whose power is testified by the emotions of the audience, and a pervading simplicity, truth and loveliness, both of thought and language which act as a charm and are full of fascination."[32]

With her success in these two plays it is somewhat surprising that Mowatt did not write more for the theatre in which she concentrated so much of her energy. Perhaps her acting gave her sufficient satisfaction—and certainly more financial reward—and in her own generation, it appears to have been the way in which she was best remembered. One critic described her as "the most gifted and versatile American lady who ever, for a series of years, adopted the stage as a profession."[33] An American, a lady, an impressive actress, an observant writer, Mowatt focused her wit and her knowledge of the theatre to create one play which appealed to her contemporaries and has pleased later audiences. Her art and activity have become a landmark in the development of an American drama.

The parvenue and the urban low life, identifiable heroes of rural society and city eccentrics, frontier romances, social and political adventuring, personal and national peculiarities of any dimension—these were the topics Jacksonian playwrights explored and placed on the stage from any available source—history, newspapers or the latest published fiction. It was the same on both sides of the Atlantic Ocean, and in the theatrical world ideas went quickly back and forth as the English and Americans easily stole, swapped, adapted and borrowed each other's spectacles and peculiarities. Actors and managers frequently crossed the Atlantic, bringing and taking ideas and capitalizing on snobbery and the fascination of the foreign and exotic in both countries and, as often as not, making fortunes. During a visit to England in 1836, Dan Rice jumped and sang Jim Crow to the tune of £16,000. Fanny Elssler made more money during one week in New York than in an entire season in Paris. There were bandwagons, and playwrights necessarily joined them, shaping their talents to the popular fads and fashions, struggles and triumphs, of the day. The idea was to please audiences whose sense of spectacle and degree of curiosity or snobbery were reasonably the same in English or American theatres. Covent Garden, for example, created the *Pictorial Records of 1837–38* with spectacles of the Coronation of the Emperor, the Assault on Jerusalem, the Arrival of the *Great Western* of New York and the Ruins of the Royal Exchange.

William E. Burton (1804–1860) came to America from England in 1834, stayed and gained a considerable reputation as an actor and theatre manager in Philadelphia and New York. He was also a successful writer and editor who contributed to the principal periodicals of his day, wrote and edited Cary and Hart's "Living Souvenir" for several years, and in 1836 started the popular *Gentleman's Magazine*. As an actor, Burton was a low comedian of broad humor who winked, wiggled and grimaced at the audience, often smacking his lips to gain attention. As a playwright, he had established his reputation in London the year before he came to America with *Ellen Wareham* (1833). The most popular play Burton wrote in America was *The Toodles* (1848), in which he portrayed Timothy Toodles, a role that gave him a reputation for years. In a number of other plays Burton shrewdly capitalized upon current events and the theatrical fads of the day. *Fashion; or, How to Write a Comedy* (1845) was his reaction to Mrs. Mowatt's success; in *A Glance at Philadelphia* (1848), he took comic and commercial advantage of Baker's farce; *New York Directory; or, The Cockney in America* (1849) gave Burton in the role of Thomas Augustus Picadilly an opportunity to look over New York City; *The World's Fair; or, London in 1851*, that year, was, like many plays of its day, a response to a contemporary event. As a dramatist Burton belongs to America more than England, and Allardyce Nicoll does not attempt to claim him as he does John Brougham in *A History of English Drama*.

When Charles M. Walcot, one of the house playwrights for William Mitch-

Mr W. E. BURTON, AS TOODLE,

as originally played by him, over Six Hundred nights, at the various theatres in the United States.

"NO. MA'AM. NO! I AM NOT A DAMAGED ARTICLE."

William F. Burton, actor and playwright. Courtesy of the Library of Congress.

ell's Olympic Theatre, took his character Giovanni to Texas in March of 1844, he was following a popular fad of this time which may have originated with W. T. Moncrieff's *Giovanni in London* (1817). Eventually, Giovanni went to the country, to Ireland and to Brittany and, with the help of W. S. Landor, to Naples. J. R. Planché wrote about *Giovanni the Vampire* (1821), and long after Walcot brought this character to America, F. F. Cooper, an Englishman, dramatized *Giovanni Redivivus* (1864). With *The Don Not Done; or, Giovanni from Texas*, Walcot had built upon his own comic extravaganza of the previous season called *Giovanni in Gotham*. The transatlantic voyages of characters such as Jonathan and Giovanni and their swift adoption by writers of either country provide a telling comment on the close relationship that existed between English and American theatre.

A comparable theatrical phenomenon appeared in a series of plays that always began with "Did You Ever Send Your Wife to . . . ?" Turner's Dramatic Library of Acting Plays published *Did You Ever Send Your Wife to Brooklyn?* (n.d.), a farce presumably written by Joseph Sterling Coyne, an Englishman. Although Nicoll does not mention this play, he does list a play by Coyne entitled *Did You Ever Send Your Wife to Camberwell?* (1846). It may well be that Coyne never sent his "Wife to Brooklyn," but the plot is always the same slight, nonsensical fare.[34] Why it happened may never be known, but as the century progressed, variations of this little farce became a fad in America. *Did You Ever Send Your Wife to Harlem?*, *Did You Ever Send Your Wife to the Greenwich Theatre?*, *Did You Ever Send Your Wife to Williamstown?*, *Did You Ever Send Your Wife to Troy?*, *Did You Ever Send Your Wife to San Jose?* and so on to many other places. Probably no theatre management ever changed more than the title. The original farce remained Coyne's, but many American hands tampered with it.

Periodically, Jacksonian Americans attempted to distinguish a fashionable life of their own. *The Moderns; or, A Trip to the Springs* suggested such an attempt, theatrically, in 1831. Nine years later at Niblo's Garden, Moncrieff's *Foreign Airs and Native Graces*, an English play, stimulated some of the thoughts that Royall Tyler had tried to inspire in *The Contrast*, albeit from a different point of view, thoughts that Mowatt and Joseph Field, in *Foreign and Native* (1846), continued. At the Olympic Theatre Alexander Allan made light of the idea of fashion in *Saratoga Springs* (1843); George H. Andrews, an actor, wrote *Punch in New York* for his benefit in 1847, and two years later W. K. Northall created a travesty with the same title for Burton's Chamber Street Theatre. Because New York was the major theatre center in America, it was understood that here would be the touchstone for understanding American society. Playwrights used that city extensively—primarily, of course, because the inhabitants comprised their major audiences. Plays appeared with such titles as *The New York Merchant and His Clerks* (1843) and *The New York Milliners* (1848).

New York in Slices (1848) illustrates yet another source of inspiration for the predatory playwright. The idea for this anonymous play came from a column in the New York *Tribune* written by George G. Foster from July through November of 1848, and the production of the play at Burton's Theatre on October 9 of that year shows something about the quick reaction of theatre managers to popularity of any sort. Gaslight Foster, as he was sometimes known, was an active journalist in New York from 1845 to 1856 and delighted in creating portraits of New Yorkers—the elite, the Bowery b'hoys, the bums or the prostitutes.[35] Even before his essays appeared in book form—*New York in Slices, By an Experienced Carver* (1849)—audiences were enjoying his characters on the stage: Craball, Nabem, Slybutts, Bob Drygoods and Mrs. Noseup. It was the task of the stage carpenters and mechanics to stage pictures of the Steamboat Landing, the New York Exchange in Wall Street, Streets by Daylight, Trinity Church, Bar Rooms, Streets at Night, a Den in a Five Points Boarding House, the Astor Place Opera House and a Fancy Dress Ball. Not all parts of the play were flattering to New York, however, and one indignant critic complained that *New York in Slices* was "a mass of incongruous ingredients rolled into form somewhat after the manner of an apothecary's pill, by a strong physical exertion, and a slight mental speculation. . . . New York is represented," he huffed, "not, as once the custom, by members in congress or assembly, but by a pickpocket, and a mere utilitarian companion—a bank forger." With obvious pain, the critic protested the "cutting up, or rather hacking of the philosophy of our city."[36]

Politics was an aspect of society that playwrights of this period usually regarded as part of the larger scene rather than for itself. James E. Heath's *Whigs and Democrats; or, Love of No Politics*, a comedy in three acts, played at the Walnut Street Theatre in Philadelphia in 1839 but was not popular, primarily because the dramatist, admittedly an amateur, was more interested in delivering a message than in entertaining audiences. Heath (1792–1862) wanted, he wrote in his preface, "to hold up to ridicule the dispicable acts of demagoguism" and to show that America had "the characters, customs and sentiments" for great drama.[37] A talky love story, the play dramatizes the struggle between a Whig and a Democrat—a practical politician and an idealist—with the heroine given to the winner of the election (the idealist): "I will never belong," he says, "to any party whose creed would confound all distinction between public profligacy and private virtue; or whose principles would rebuke dishonesty among individuals and yet tolerate and applaud it in governments" (II,1). As auditor for the state of Virginia from 1819 to 1849, Heath had experience to support his satire on rural politics, and although he did not take his playwriting seriously, it was rumored that he lost his job in 1849 because of this play. In 1828 he had written a romance, *Edge Hill*, and was once praised by Poe as "almost the only person of any literary distinction" living in Richmond.[38] Although Heath showed a certain wit and facility in writing dialogue, he seemed to be more comfortable writing polemic than dramatic action.

Henry J. Finn (1790?–1840), a successful comic actor, is remembered in histories of American drama for writing *Removing the Deposits* (1835) to capitalize on Jackson's argument with Nicholas Biddle. He may also have written another play produced that season at the Bowery Theatre and entitled *Moonshine; or, Lunar Discoveries*, based on a hoax published in the New York *Sun* describing discoveries on the moon. Finn appeared in this play as "the new universally popular Major Jack Downing," the Yankee character created by Seba Smith. During his association with the Tremont Theatre in Boston, Finn had written two plays for his benefit in April of 1829—*Peter Finn; or, A Trip to See the Sea* and *Massachusetts Railroads*. He probably wrote other plays that did not survive. A native of Cape Breton, Finn portrayed Yankee and Canadian characters with success until his death in the fire that destroyed the steamer *Lexington* in Long Island Sound.

Always eager to respond to, comment on and, hopefully, make money from the pleasures and pains that a society struggled to escape from or endure, playwrights constantly adapted successful current fiction and created the melodramas that provoked the patriotic spirit or provided the blood and thunder that stimulated man's coarser sensations. Nowhere was this accomplished with greater success than at New York's Bowery Theatre under the management of Thomas Hamblin (1800–1853). Although Philadelphia had early proved itself sympathetic to native playwrights, New York had appeared indifferent until Hamblin, an English actor of some reputation, arrived in 1825. Five years later he was enjoying theatre management, and in 1832 a writer for the *Spirit of the Times* noted that Hamblin's success was, in part, due to his patronage of native playwrights.[39] It was a point worth making, and Hamblin continued this practice, which combined good business and good politics, throughout his career, particularly at the Bowery Theatre.

A persistent and undaunted individual whose Bowery Theatre burned four times during his management, Hamblin inspired many laudatory comments during his years in the American theatre. "Bold and brilliant enterprise and the name of Thomas S. Hamblin are synonymous," wrote one critic.[40] During the 1830s Hamblin produced more plays by American dramatists than did any of his management colleagues. That he paid the writers a pittance was as consistent with Jacksonian philosophy as the practice of Edwin Forrest. More effectively than Forrest or other actors who solicited plays, however, Hamblin encouraged American playwrights by producing their melodramatic and patriotic spectacles. Further evidence of Hamblin's undaunted character and individuality appears in his startling private life. Frequently made public, the more scandalous parts appeared in *A Concise History of the Life and Amours of Thomas S. Hamblin (Late Manager of the Bowery Theatre) as communicated by his legal Wife, Mrs. Elizabeth Hamblin, to Mrs. M. Clarke*, although the information here deserves all the scrutiny reason demands from the fact that this Mrs. Hamblin died in 1849, four years before Hamblin. Because he produced plays that did not have the literary merit they wanted, Odell and some other historians have rather little good to say about Hamblin and his Bowery Theatre. Describing the opening of the 1833–1834 theatre season at the Bowery, for example, Odell berated Hamblin for becoming "mad with blood and thunder" melodrama. Such were the prejudices of this devoted and inestimably valuable historian of American theatre. Generally condescending to any play by an American, he felt that the appearance of melodrama and spectacle on the playbills of any theatre was a sure indication of that theatre's decline.

Not only did spectacular melodrama satisfy the appetites of many American theatre audiences, it was, along with farce, the form of drama that the majority of early nineteenth-century English, European and American dramatists were capable of writing. By the latter part of the nineteenth century, such American dramatists as Augustin Daly, Bartley Campbell, Steele Mackaye and David Belasco would bring this form to a high level of artistry—a level successfully maintained by modern playwrights.

Mazeppa; or, The Wild Horse of Tartary was a sensation on the American stage from the early 1830s until the death of Adah Isaacs Menken (1868), the most spectacular performer of the title role. It is most unlikely that the version performed was written by an American although John Howard Payne translated Leopold and Cuvelier's *Mazeppa; où, Le Cheval Tartare* in 1825. This popular melodrama, however, carried Hamblin's Bowery Theatre throughout the 1833–1834 season, answered the demands for excitement of countless American audiences and fueled an interest in equestrian drama that lasted throughout the century. Although the play is generally exciting, all actions pale when compared with the "gorgeous" and "splendid" grand spectacle of Mazeppa's ride "up and down those vast platforms while strapped along his [the horse's] back without power to move or save himself."[41] The play provides opportunities for tremendous spectacle, and an 1837 production featured Cooke's Equestrian Company, a stud of horses and the 1,100 supernumeraries.[42]

One of the most successful purveyors of spectacle on the American stage in Jacksonian America, Louisa Medina (1813?–1838), a playwright by profession, enjoyed an astounding career by dramatizing current fiction which, in contrast to the works of some of her journeyman peers, usually provided the major attraction of an evening. Although some contemporary historians—Rees and Wemyss—tended to ignore her work, other commentators were enthralled with her successful association with Thomas Hamblin. Odell, while maintaining that melodrama was not part of the legitimate drama, records Medina's success in New York, mainly at Hamblin's Bowery Theatre. Without question Louisa Medina created for the American stage some of the most popular blood-and-thunder melodramas of the 1830s. Although her career was brief, 1833–1838, her plays held the stage for a generation after her death and reveal her remarkable ability to extract from contemporary fiction the most appealing and dramatic sequences which she then embellished with the kind of theatricality that entranced theatregoers.

Information concerning Louisa Medina's life is meager. Born in Europe about 1813, the daughter of a Spanish businessman fortunate enough to be able to provide her with a formal education, she claimed to have written for London publications at the age of twelve and to have spent the next five years traveling and studying in Ireland, France and Spain. An exceptional young woman, upon her arrival in America in either 1831 or 1833, she immediately showed her literary talents as a teacher of French and Spanish and as a writer of poems and stories that she contributed to journals. She also began to write plays, working almost exclusively with Hamblin during his management of the Bowery Theatre. Although Hamblin's propensity for annoying people appeared to be overdeveloped, much of it stemmed from his frequently publicized amours and his habit of speaking frankly, if not always wisely. His casual contempt for the Yankees he entertained at the Bowery Theatre did not endear him to Americans, and his support of native dramatists was motivated solely by commercial instincts. His interest in Medina, however, was personal as well as professional.[43] Beginning with his divorce decree from his first wife, which prevented him from marrying again before her death, Hamblin placed his personal problems before the public by forming liasions with other women. Louisa Medina was the second of three women associated with Hamblin after his divorce: Naomi Vincent, who died in childbirth in 1835; Medina, whom he may have married in 1837 after the birth of her child named Louisa Medina Hamblin in 1836; and the popular actress Mrs. Shaw, whom he did not claim publicly as his wife until a year after his first wife's death.[44]

In addition to contributing to Hamblin's amours, Medina wrote plays that provided him with good acting roles and major successes for his Bowery Theatre. From 1833 until her death five years later, she is credited with writing some thirty-four plays. Evidently, the strain was too much. In early 1837 she was reported to be very ill, and she died in New York of apoplexy on November 12, 1838, a young but quite distinguished playwright, a significant contributor to the popular melodrama of her day. Her writing techniques bear analysis while her plays stand among the first to be given long runs on the American stage. Little is known about her personally, but Lester Wallack called her "one of the most brilliant women I ever met. She was very plain, but a wonderfully bright woman, charming in every way."[45]

Only eleven of Medina's plays have been documented from stage histories, and only three of these—*The Last Days of Pompeii* (1835), *Nick of the Woods* (1838), and *Ernest Maltravers* (1838)—were published. Some mention of other plays, however, indicates that she was a consistent contributor to the Bowery Theatre whenever plays were required of her. For example, when Isaac A. Van Amburgh, the Great American Lion Tamer, performed at the Bowery Theatre in the mid-1830s, the entire stage was turned into a den of living animals, according to an advertisement, and Medina wrote a play for the occasion called *The Lion Doomed*, in which the hero was to be cast into a den of lions.[46] Her first play at the Bowery, *Wacousta; or, The Curse*, opened on December 30, 1833, and was a popular success. An adaptation of John Richardson's novel, the play capitalized on the current interest in American Indians both on the stage and in fiction. She repeated her success the next September (1834), with *Kair-*

risah; or, The Warrior of Wanachtihi. Indicative of the popularity of American frontier and Indian life onstage, Hamblin also produced, during the fall of 1834, *Guy Rivers; or, The Gold Hunters*, evidently a dramatization of William Gilmore Simms' novel of rural life in Georgia; *Outallissi; or, The Indian Counsel Chamber*; and a version of Cooper's *The Wept of Wish-Ton-Wish*. Medina's adaptation of Bulwer-Lytton's *Last Days of Pompeii* opened on February 9, 1835, and except for one night in March ran continuously for twenty-nine performances, according to Rosemarie Bank, the longest run to that date in New York theatre history. "Medina's three-act play concentrates solely on the story of Glaucus and Ione, which with its baths, feasts, games, erotic religious ceremonies, boat trips, mysterious witches, and gladiatorial games, not to omit the earthquake itself, provided ample opportunity for the spectacle the Bowery did so well. Moreover, the story is full of the betrayals, jealousies, misunderstandings, dangers, and would-be seductions beloved by melodramatists."[47] Three months later the Bowery mounted Medina's *O'Neil the Rebel*, which Odell described as "a far more important piece of the same thrilling quality."[48]

Medina's adaptation of Theodore S. Fay's 1835 novel, *Norman Leslie*, which opened on Janury 11, 1836, was excellent fare for the Bowery Theatre audience. This story of murder, false accusations, disgrace and final triumph of Norman's virtue features a carnival masquerade, an Italian palazzo, Russian and Spanish dances, a duel, an exciting trial scene and Norman's spectacular rescue of the heroine from a burning house. A month later audiences were still responding to its stirring action which critics ascribed to the efforts of the adapter rather than to Fay.[49] *Rienzi*, Medina's second dramatization of a novel by Bulwer-Lytton, played nearly the entire month of June of 1836 at the Bowery Theatre, where it offered spectacular scenery as well as good roles for Hamblin as Rienzi and Mrs. Flynn as Nina. On September 16, 1836, soon after the beginning of the next season at the Bowery Theatre, Medina offered *Lafitte, Pirate of the Gulf*, based on James H. Ingraham's novel published earlier that year. Critics noted that the performances of this nautical drama were crowded nightly from pit to ceiling with audiences that responded eagerly to the theatre machinery needed to create such spectacles. Ten years later the play was again drawing capacity audiences at the Bowery Theatre.[50]

With these successes it is surprising that only after Medina's next recorded work, an adaptation of Bulwer-Lytton's *Ernest Maltravers*, did she apparently gain the serious consideration of reviewers. After the opening of this play at Wallack's National Theatre (March 28, 1838), the New York *Mirror* printed the article that brings to posterity almost everything known about the young playwright. The article begins with praise for the acting of Wallack, Hamblin and "the young debutante"—a younger sister of Josephine Clifton, calling herself Miss Louisa Missouri, whose death at seventeen of brain fever caused considerable scandal, particularly after Miss Clifton tried to implicate Hamblin and Medina. The writer for the *Mirror* then turned his attention to Medina and confessed that we are surprised to learn that she [Medina] has written in the space of five years no less than thirty-four successful dramas. These embrace a wider range of subjects [history, American frontier, romance and adventure] than has been attempted by any other modern dramatist. Some of them have been played for sixty consecutive nights, and all of them distinguished by marks of publick approbation. . . . Her power of composition is said to be astonishingly rapid. She is partial to startling and terrible catastrophes. Her knowledge of stage effects is very great, and there is an impassioned ardour in her poetry, which enhances the thrilling interest of her pieces.

This writer, who appears genuinely impressed and admits to a certain astonishment, made particular reference to Medina's departures from her sources, departures which were described as "evidence of the fertility of her invention—which is one of the highest attributes of true genius."[51]

In her adaptation of *Ernest Maltravers* Medina not only escaped from Bulwer-Lytton's heavy philosophizing but changed the novel considerably, reforming the villain (played by Hamblin) and providing a fine role for Miss Missouri as Alice. Returning to his "paternal home," Ernest Maltravers, "heir to the oldest and wealthiest family in Cumberland," meets Richard Davil, a poacher and robber, who takes Ernest to his home where Ernest falls in love with and secretly marries Davil's daughter, Alice. All is not right with Davil, however; he is "a younger brother with a sad past" who becomes violent as time passes. Nor are things right with Ernest. Having been led astray by a presumed friend who persuades him that Alice is a wanton, Ernest leaves for Maltravers Hall. Immediately—as things tend to happen in this play—Ernest casts off Alice who, herself deceived by Ernest's false friend, follows Ernest to Maltravers Hall. Here, she interrupts the robbery planned by her father in which Ernest's father is murdered. The revelation toward the end of Act II that Davil is the brother of Ernest's father is climaxed by Davil's confession that Alice is Ernest's sister.

The third act takes place in the Lake Como area of northern Italy where Alice, presumably driven mad by her discovery, travels with her father. There, amid the beauties of song and scenery, Ernest finds her; the villainy of his false friend is revealed; a letter from Davil's wife, given to the lovers at a propitious moment, explains that Ernest and Alice are merely first cousins. Their happiness as man and wife is suggested in the final act through some interesting scenes involving birds and songs. Medina also showed her talent for the spectacles of successful melodrama with the typical gothic attributes of strange scenery, insane characters and darkened woods with old mansions. To the modern ear, however, Medina's dialogue is sometimes unwieldy. For example, in the final scene Davil instructs Ernest:

Ernest Maltravers, approach, sole remaining scion of my father's home, listen to the last words of Richard Maltravers; fear not to take yon fainting form within your arms. I, whose curse brought death and woe, now speak of peace and blessings; take her—take her; she is pure as heaven's own stainless angels. (III,3)

Fortunately, Medina's theatrical techniques were not as heavy and pretentious as Davil's words. She knew how to select the most dramatic episodes from the works she adapted to the stage, and her audiences appreciated her efforts.

Medina's adaptation of Bird's 1837 novel, which she called *Nick of the Woods; or, Telie, The Renegade's Daughter* (1838), quickly became one of the most successful melodramas of the period. It was also well received in London, where John T. Haines made some revisions. Like *Ernest Maltravers*, however, which was once termed "worse than trash," *Nick of the Woods* also had its detractors.[52] From St. Louis a critic referred to it as "a most miserable piece of trash called *Nick of the Woods*. The novel itself, is common place enough," the critic continued, "heaven knows—but this piece—O Lord!"[53] Indian plays, however, were a theatrical staple during the 1830s, and *Nick of the Woods* combined frontier adventure with romance, revenge and an abundance of spectacle.

The protagonist of *Nick of the Woods* goes by several names: Jibbenainosay, Bloody Nathan, Nick of the Woods, the Avenger, Reginald Ashburn and the Spirit of the Waters. To add to this inherent confusion, the play follows a complicated double story line: (1) Bloody Nathan's continuing attempt to avenge himself upon the Indians, particularly Wenonga, who killed his bride and his family, and (2) a complicated legacy involving a Virginia estate. Nathan, a former Quaker with a thirst for blood, carries his desire for revenge throughout the play and dies at the climax like Cooper's Natty Bumppo answering the last roll call in *The Prairie*: "My Alice awaits me there—I come—I come." The play is set in the woods, at a stockade and in an Indian camp. On their westward journey, Roland Forrester and his cousin and bride-to-be, Edith Forrester, join a group of immigrant travelers among whom are Braxley, the man who cheated them of their legacy by destroying their uncle's will; a horse thief named Ralph Stackpole; and Telie Doe, a maiden of the forest, presumed daughter of a "white Indian" but, in truth, the daughter of Roland's rich uncle. The villains are the Indians and Braxley along with Abel Doe, Telie's "father," who tries to kill Roland and does manage to kidnap Edith. Fortunately, Nathan appears frequently on the spot, killing Indians whom he mysteriously marks with an "X" and rescuing Edith. In a spectacular climax to Act II, effecting yet another rescue of Edith, the Jibbenainosay "comes down the waterfall in a canoe of fire" as the Indians fall prostrate on the ground. In the final act of *Nick of the Woods* Telie explains that she is the lost child of Major Forrester; Nathan, having been overpowered by Indians, gains his freedom by a ruse, accomplishes his revenge and is recognized as Reginald Ashburn; Telie intercepts the bullet which Braxley fires at Roland, leaving Roland and Edith free to enjoy their legacy; Stackpole then kills Braxley, and the audience is allowed to watch Nathan die in "peace," a word he shouts frequently, and for rather obscure reasons, throughout the play.

By most standards *Nick of the Woods* is not a good play, although it was revived almost yearly for half a century. The exposition, for example, is confusing; the dialogue is typical of the strained stage speeches of the period. Ro-

Woodcut of Act II, Scene 5 of *Nick of the Woods* (1838) by Louisa Medina.

land describes his feeling about a maiden: "My brain turns; my senses reel!"
At another time Ralph Stackpole saves Telie from a panther while Roland describes the action: "He nears the beast; Gracious Heaven! A moment and the
child is lost; the panther turns and dashes toward the rapids; Ralph raises his
gun; he fires! He is hit! He falls; the child is saved! (Settlers shout.)" (I,3). As
a character Stackpole is particularly interesting in that he sounds a bit like Nimrod Wildfire and clearly illustrates the popular backwoodsman of that era. "Who's
for a fight?" he says. "Where's your old coon can claw the bark off a gum
tree? Where's your wolf of the rolling prairies? . . . Ain't I the old snag to
shake off a saddle—can go down Old Salt on my back and swim up the Ohio!
Hurray for a fight!" (I,3). Mainly, the play epitomizes the kind of melodrama
for which Medina had outstanding talent: action, adventure, mystery, disguises,
romantic love, strong and determined characters and scenes that took advantage
of the spectacle-producing skills of theatre managements at this time. In a brief
five-year period Louisa Medina wrote a substantial number of plays (at least
eleven and perhaps as many as thirty-four) and achieved a popular success that
no woman and few men would surpass or equal during the Age of Jackson. Her
career is particularly noteworthy in that her total exposure to the theatre appears
to have been limited to that five-year period.

Numerous playwrights took advantage of the scarcity of plays in America
and tried to fill this acknowledged void by adapting the latest popular English
or American fiction and by promoting nationalism with dramatized events from
American history. Mainly these were actors, keyed by profession to be sensitive to society's needs and trends. Ever on the lookout to enhance his value
with a theatre manager or promote his career with a comic novelty or spectacular melodrama, the actor was the logical person to accept the challenge presented by some American critics who would have scorned him as a dramatist.
His ambitions were, of course, more practical than they could have imagined
and his spirit more cavalier than inspired. Writers as well as many other literary-minded individuals attempted to fill this vacuum in American literature but,
without a knowledge of practical theatre, stood little chance of success. Actors,
on the other hand, even if their use of language was weak, frequently understood the value of dramatic structure and action and the needs of an audience
for spectacle and novelty. Unfortunately, neither by nature nor intent were these
casual actor-playwrights—James Rees, Henry J. Finn, James S. Wallace, Charles
Saunders, Walter Leman—thoughtful or probing, and their work was as ephemeral
as a season's bills. They wrote without pretense, and in the main their names
and the titles of their plays have been forgotten. If they attracted some attention, their horizons expanded, and their subsequent work showed a broader attempt to dramatize America.[54]

James Rees (1802–1885), a dramatist and critic who sometimes wrote over
the pseudonym of Colley Cibber, is best known to historians of American drama
and theatre as the author of *The Dramatic Authors of America* (1845). Strongly
nationalistic, Rees bemoaned the "decline of drama" in the preface to his work

and blamed the "melodramatic and pantomimic character of the stage" which had been spoiled by the "gross and licentious dishes" from France and the "flood of folly" from England.[55] Theatre fare, however, more generally reflects the tastes of a society than reforms such tastes. Spectacular melodrama, wherever it originated, attracted theatre audiences, and James Rees, the playwright, although contributing to the "decline" by following the impulse of the commercial theatre, had only moderate success.

Like most of the actor-playwrights, Rees adapted such popular fiction of the time as Cooper's *The Headsman* in 1834 and *Charlotte Temple*, the enormously successful novel written by Susannah Rowson in 1791. Neither had much success; in fact, few of his plays came to New York, although as might be expected, Rees emphasized nationalism in his works. *Washington at Valley Forge* (1832) was a "national drama in three acts" which, as Rees asserted in *Dramatic Authors*, was successful at the Camp Street Theatre in New Oleans. He also wrote *Washington Preserved* (1836); *LaFitte, the Pirate of the Gulf* (1837, a year after Louis Medina's play, and mainly produced in New Orleans); *Mad Anthony Wayne* (1845, for which he claimed a success in New York); and *Patrick Lyon; or, The Locksmith of Philadelphia* (1843), based on an actual event in 1798 when Lyon was victimized by bankers and jailed, although eventually acquitted and awarded damages. Among his other plays—such as *The Miniature* (1834), *The Squatter* (1838), and *The Brigand's Daughter* (1842)—only *Mike Fink, The Last Boatman of the Mississippi* (n.d.) seems at all interesting, and Rees remains a reasonably prolific but mediocre supplier of melodrama for theatres west of the Alleghanies.

Charles Weston Taylor first came to the American stage from England in 1819 and was still acting in New York in 1852, according to Wemyss. Odell, noting Taylor's version of *Eugene Aram* (1832), identifies him as "the almost official stage adaptor of popular novels for the Bowery."[56] Odell, unfortunately, identifies the American authorship of very few plays, but Taylor would have attracted his attention as an actor and manager who wrote for both the Richmond Hill Theatre and the National Theatre. James S. Wallace was an actor of light comedy who wrote *Love and Literature* (1832), and adapted Cooper's *The Water Witch* (1832), as well as James Kirke Paulding's *Westward Ho!* (1833), which according to James Rees played fifty nights in Boston.[57] An elusive person in theatre history, Wallace was a comic actor in 1837 at the Franklin Theatre in New York, for which he wrote *Spy in Washington* (1837) and *Sabotier; or, The Fairy of the Wooden Shoemaker* (1837). Augustus W. Fenno joined Joseph S. Jones at the Tremont Theatre in Boston for the 1839–1840 season and eventually returned to New York, where he wrote *The Campaign of the Rio Grande* (1846) for the Bowery management and *The Scourge of the Ocean* for the Chatham Theatre, where he was considered a starring actor.

Charles H. Saunders (1818–1857) first acted at Hamblin's Bowery Theatre during the 1843–1844 season and immediately became a writer of such farces and melodramas as *The Dancing Feather; or, The Maid's Revenge*, adapted from James H. Ingraham's novel (November 13, 1843); *The Mysteries of Paris*, another adaptation from current fiction (November 27, 1843); *The Pirate's Legacy; or, The Wrecker's Fate* (December 18, 1843); and *The Council of Blood; or, The Butchers of Ghent* (February 26, 1844). That same season his Irish farce, *Bumpology*, was a popular vehicle for Barney Williams. Indicative of his greater productivity are the following titles of Saunders' plays: *The Gambler* (1844), *Our Flag* (1845), and *Mary Martin; or, The Money Diggers* (1846).

Arriving at the Bowery Theatre as an actor at about the same time as Charles Saunders, Walter M. Leman (1810–1887?) wrote briefly for the New York stage and then migrated westward. By mid-century he was in California. His contribution to American theatre is more evident in his *Memories of an Old Actor* than in either his acting or playwriting, but his comments on his own playwriting are revealing as a general observation on the activity of the actor-playwright. He wrote *Rangers; or, The Battle of Germantown* (1845) for the Bowery management at the prompting of a friend and considered it a "passable medium of expression for the exuberant patriotism of Americans on an American holiday."[58] Later that year he wrote a one-act play entitled *Freedom's Last Martyr*, dealing with the death of Colonel Ledyard at the surrender of Fort Griswold during the Revolutionary War.

Leman claimed to have written *The Campaign of the Rio Grande* in May of 1846, a play which he confessed showed "more patriotic sentiment than real dramatic merit." His claim that this two-act play was produced just one month before Fenno's three-act patriotic drama of the same title, however, may show collaboration, antipathy or just plain confusion in an old actor's mind. *Prairie Bird; or, A Child of the Delawares* (1847), a dramatization of George A. Murray's novel, was one of Leman's "most pretentious efforts," he recalled, but it did not last long on the American stage. When the Pennsylvania Regiment of Volunteers returned home from the Mexican War, Leman was moved to create a mixture of tableaux in a one-act sketch called *Volunteers' Departure and Return* (1848). That same year James S. Wallace wrote a "happy prologue" for Leman's *Millionaire* (1848), a five-act comedy in which Leman remembered that he tried to follow the unities and ended with too much dialogue and too little action. Leman continued to write plays after going to California, where he claimed that he found audiences as capable of judging an actor or an author as any in New York or Boston. Not an outstanding actor, and certainly not an accomplished playwright, Leman illustrates the casual approach to playwriting that most of the minor dramatists of this period assumed: There was a need for plays. Why not write one?

For a brief period, Stephen E. Glover, captain of the *Tallahassee*, wrote for the American theatre. His first play, an adaptation of Cooper's *Lionel Lincoln* entitled *The Cradle of Liberty; or, Boston in 1775*, played first at the Tremont Theatre in Boston in 1832. This patriotic melodrama concentrated on the confrontation of a father and son—Major Lincoln of the British army and his son, Ralph, a native of Boston—and their concern for law, honor and individual obligations. Such minor characters as Job Pray who "don't love crowns," Mike Mainsail, a sailor whose language and native sentiments made him a favorite with audiences, and Seth Sage, a Yankee innkeeper, jack-of-all-trades and captain of the militia, provide good humor and a sense of theatricality which the basic patriotic argument lacks. When Hamblin produced the play at the American Theatre in New York, the reviewer praised only its patriotic appeal.[59] Another nationalistic play by Glover, *The Banished Provincial; or, New York in 1776*, appeared on the Bowery Theatre stage in 1834.

American Indians were another popular topic for dramatists, and the form and style of the resulting work is clearly revealed in this burlesque review of J. H. Hall's *Eagle Eye*:

Like all other Indian dramas, it abounds with pistol shooting, blood, murder, and tremendous acts of vengeance, for all the world knows the stage Indian is a most resolute, blood-thirsty and successful assassin. He commences his career by scalping the chief of the opposite tribe, who in some former dispute about religion or hunting grounds had the misfortune of slaying the Indian's father; he next gets on top of a rock and favors the friend of the defunked head of the other side with a rifle ball which, strange to say, always finds its way to the center of the heart. After this display of valor, he grows melancholy and takes to mountain streams, and then and there registers a vow to murder the entire contents of a good sized village, and lets his horse drink the blood of the foes of his father—Indian horses, according to dramatic authority, are as much given to blood drinking as their owners are to the consumption of bad whiskey.[60]

The horse, the scenery, the stage arrangements such as cataracts and mountain trails for the horse to leap or run—all had equal billing in this style of melodrama which, with different heroes and stage machinery, was enjoyed with equal seriousness by later generations.

A cursory glance through Odell's *Annals of the New York Stage* illustrates the great popularity of the American Indian during the 1830s: Louisa Medina's *Wacousta* (1833); Jonas Phillips' *Oronaska* (1834); Medina's *Kairrissah* (1834); *Outallissi* (an example of a playwright's humor?) *How Tall Is He?* (1834); *The Indian Heroine* (1835); *Sassacus* (1836); Robert Dale Owen's *Pocahontas* (1837); *Nick of the Woods* (1838); and all of the adaptations of Cooper's novels. Quinn lists twenty-six Indian plays from this decade. Some were produced; a few were published; several had strange origins. *Oceola* (1837) was written by L. F. Thomas, a junior editor of the Cincinnati *Evening Post*. Owen (1801–1877)— an Indian fighter, enthusiastic reformer with Frances Wright, and dedicated supporter of Jacksonian democracy—attracted some attention with the published version of *Pocahontas*, but the play lasted for only one performance on the New York stage. "It adheres to historical truth," wrote the editor of the *Federal American Monthly*, "and exhibits, in an instructive light, the vices and virtues of both savage and civilized society."[61] The poetic language of the Indians, however, bothered critics as well as the unorthodox dramatic techniques for which Owen argued in his introductory essay with no more success than the production of the play achieved.[62]

Among the playwrights who frequently exploited the public interest in the Indian, those existing at some distance from the theatre seemed most enthralled by the Red Man, whom they identified as a noble savage. Owen illustrates this point, as does General Alexander Macomb. Such writers usually had issues to argue and chose, for unknown reasons, the dramatic form for their argument. In *Pontiac; or, The Siege of Detroit* (1835), Macomb blames "the poisonous liquor" and the white man's abuse.

Tecumseh; or, The Battle of the Thames (1834), a national drama in five acts, was the first and only attempt at playwriting of Richard Emmons. Primarily a play of battles, rural scenes and a love interest, it also includes the poular song "The Hunters of Kentucky" and ends with a band playing "Hail Columbia!" Tecumseh's first speech—"Ah! Methought you Proctor was! Me, they told that I should find him at your wigwam here" (I,1)—suggests the tenor of the piece, and Tecumseh's death ends it: "The Red man's course is run; I die—the last of all my race." An avid supporter of the vice-presidential candidacy in 1836 of Richard M. Johnson, who presumably killed Tecumseh, Emmons offered this play as part of the campaign. When the play opened in Baltimore in January of 1834, the actor playing Tecumseh wore the "identical dress" in which the Indian chief had died, while the actor performing the part of Colonel Johnson used the same pistols which sent Tecumseh to his happy hunting ground.[63] The play evidently constituted good patriotic politics, as the war hero himself acknowledged the applause of the audience when the play came to Washington.

Theatre records show that history, particularly American history, was more popular on the stage of Jacksonian America than at any other time, although the authors of most of these plays have been long forgotten, if ever they were recognized. As people worked toward that future in which the promise of good fortunes seemed ever present, audiences appeared interested in hearing about the struggles and victories of the developing nation. Washington, Lafayette, Jackson, the independence of Texas, the war with Mexico—all appeared upon the stage with some regularity during Jackson's administration and the extended period of his influence. Texas was a popular topic: *Crockett in Texas; or, The Massacre of the Alamo* (1839); *Shot in the Eye; or, The Regulators of Texas* (1849); *The Lone Star* (1849); *The Texas Struggle* (1850). Not all interest in Texas, however, was purely theatrical, according to William B. Wood, who remembered a benefit in 1835 "in aid of the oppressed people in Texas."[64] Plays such as Mordecai Noah's *She Would Be a Solider* (1819), depicting a fictional heroine of the War of 1812, were produced frequently; and Noah, with his social and political prestige, maintained some influence in the American theatre.

As usual, history for the commercial playwright was largely a matter of depicting war or violence, permitting the melodramatic spectacle that audiences craved. *The Battle of Mexico; or, The Capture of the Halls of Montezuma* (1848) by Thomas Barry, a respected but ultimately unsuccessful theatre manager in Boston, was a military spectacle featuring Generals Scott, Worth, Shields and Twiggs, plus views of San Juan d'Uiloa and the American squadron. George Lionel Stevens' *The Patriot; or, Union and Freedom* (1834) presumed to treat "glory" and teach that "tyrant minds may not at freedom scoff." A spectacle, mainly in prose interspersed with insipid blank verse, its action took place in the shadow of Bunker Hill, with dances, songs and patriotic sentiment. There was also a slight love plot, an Irishman for atmosphere and a Negro, Sambo, who reminded people of Dan Rice and "Jump Jim Crow": "Weel about—turn about—do just so, an eb'vy time weel about jump Sambo—." A final statement drove home the point of the play: "Tell the world your Patriot Fathers died—to make their homes their son's and daughter's pride!" (V,3).

Joseph Breck's dramatization of Ingraham's romance of American history, *West Point; or, A Tale of Treason*, a historical drama in three acts, was published in Baltimore in 1840 and probably not produced, although it appears no less stageworthy than many other such plays. Breck stated in a prefatory note that he wrote it "to counteract the personal malevolence of one or two contemptible individuals whose insignificance is hardly worthy of even this attention" and thus separated himself from production-oriented playwrights. For its time, *West Point* had a number of the essential ingredients for success: Yankee and Negro characters with appropriate dialects, military spectacle and a ball, a slight love interest, a stirring historical event and sufficient patriotic sentiment. Its major dramatic asset is the development of André's heroism in contrast with Arnold's greed and pathetic fears. Even Mrs. Arnold's dramatic attempt to save André from the gallows in the final act, however, could not compensate for the heavy moralizing in the play.

In Jacksonian America a strong feeling for reform was basic to the beliefs and actions of those people who founded utopian societies, wrote manuals of instruction on diverse topics and promoted various movements for the betterment of mankind. With many of the reform leaders there was a determination bordering on mission, which onstage translated into melodrama. Charles Saunders' *Rosina Meadows, The Village Maid; or, Temptation Unveiled* (1843) was only one of many plays that upheld Jackson's preference for rural life and warned the unwary against the terrors of urban corruption. As a melodrama, it epitomized for David Grimsted "the dramatic form that dominated the stage in the period."[65] Rosina, the rose of country virtue, is crowned queen of the May before she leaves home to seek her fortune in Boston. Although she is warned by her father and her country lover of the vice that pervades city life, she is resolved to go. Alas! In Boston she is deceived by the city youth she trusted and lured into a false marriage ceremony; her honor is destroyed, her innocence lost. Returning home, she begs forgiveness of her father: "O, God! what are all earthly woes, compared to the feelings of a disgraced, broken-hearted and doting father?" (III,3). When the drunken city youth is apprehended, however, and accused by Rosina, her father relents, forgives her and strangles the villainous city youth as Rosina dies in the arms of her country lover. Such was the moral melodrama of the 1840s. Later American playwrights such as Bronson Howard were far less forgiving of the women who sinned, knowingly or unknowingly.

Frederich Stanhope Hill's best-known play ran the gamut of the immoral activities to which the youth of America might be tempted. Hill (1805–1851), a Boston native whose professional life included work as a newspaperman, theatre critic, poet, essayist, actor and, for some years, playwright and manager for William Pelby at the Warren Theatre in Boston, wrote *The Six Degrees of Crime; or, Wine, Women, Gambling, Theft, Murder and the Scaffold* (1834), adapting his work from *Les Six Degrés du Crime* by Theodore Nezel and Benjamin Antier. His other plays include *The Shoemaker of Toulouse; or, The Avenger of Humble Life* (1834), from *Le Savetier de Toulouse* by Pierre Cadmus and Francis Cornu; *Konrad of Rheinfeldt; or, The Widowed Bride*, and *Love and a Bunch* (1837). Along with Joseph Field, James Rees and Nathaniel Bannister, Hill spent a good part of his career in the theatre at New Orleans during the mid-1830s.

Six Degrees of Crime was a popular melodrama which achieved some distinction by displaying onstage the *maisons de plaisance* and seducing some contemporary critics to see the closing scene of the play as deeply tragic which, indeed, it was—in the same sense that *The London Merchant* was tragic. Odell dubbed Julio Dormilly, the major character in the play, the George Barnwell of the Bowery Theatre. A thorough bounder, wealthy, idle and abusive to his elders, particularly a black parson named Michael, Julio, under the influence of wine, succeeds in luring Louisa away from Francis, the man she is to marry. It is Louisa's destiny to mark the degrees of Julio's criminal acts: gambling, bank robbery and finally her own murder. "The sixth," shouts Michael, who reveals himself as the Executioner of Paris, "is the punishment of crime—the scaffold" (VI). There Julio, a convict, too weak to kill himself, is stabbed by Michael. Although there is a line of action in this melodrama, there is no satisfactory plot, no character development, no real motivation. Mainly, the play provided a moral lesson, perhaps stimulated by the activity of the American Temperance Society, which was established in Boston in 1826, and by the rapid spread of the temperance crusade during the next few years. The play's popularity depended mainly upon the violent and spectacular nature of its successive scenes.

Of all the social movements and causes popular at this time in America, none should have struck a more vibrant and tender chord among the actors and actor-playwrights than the temperance movement. Crusades by definition have a theatrical quality, and the pictures, pamphlets and platform lecturers who supported the temperance crusade tended to be spectacular, wisely in step with the melodramatic tendencies of the age and the form of entertainment the people enjoyed. Playwrights had only to transform narrative into dialogue and story into dramatic plot. Soon the theatre became a popular place for the temperance story, although the exact number of these plays, as well as their authors, may never be known. Most of the memorable temperance plays were produced during the 1850s, but scattered efforts appeared much earlier. In June of 1838, the National Theatre in New York advertised *The Drunkard's Warning. Another Glass; or, The Horrors of Intemperance* appeared at the Chatham Theatre in the fall of 1845. *Life; or, Scenes of Early Vice* (1848) was adapted from the illustrations of George Cruikshank by I. Courtney specifically for the Bowery Theatre management. According to the critic for the *Spirit of the Times*, the play had "a deep moral lesson, depicting the gradual fall from the gin shop to the felon's deathbed." [66] About this same time, Harry Seymour, that actor and "reckless daredevil," if one can believe Harry Watkins' journal entry, who always attempted "outrageous feats from a morbid desire to make himself notorious," wrote *The Temperance Doctor* and *Aunt Dinah's Pledge*, a "Temperance moral drama." [67]

For reasons that may be more easily explained by the psychologist than by the historian, the acting profession has been plagued by alcoholism. Spectacular illustrations are legion from Mrs. Hallam through Junius Brutus Booth and John Barrymore to the latest example of anyone's choice. The story of Mrs. Mowatt's first confrontation with a drunken actor without understanding the situation—she had never before seen a drunken person—illustrates a naivete that has probably never been repeated in the theatre. Harry Watkins repeatedly mentions the problem of drunkenness among actors. "A. A. Addams, tragedian, died last week in extreme poverty," Watkins wrote. "Had his great talent been coupled with prudence, he might still be living and occupying the very front rank in the Profession. It is the oft repeated tale: too long an association with John Barleycorn." An actor named Linden, Watkins complained, was seldom sober. "Tonight he had another attack of delirium tremens. I was obliged to cut some parts and change others. Troubles never end. Oh, this curse of drunkenness in my profession!" [68]

One of the most popular and frequently revived temperance dramas was *The Drunkard; or, The Fallen Saved*, which after opening at the Boston Museum on February 12, 1844, ran for 140 performances. Watkins, the traveling actor, provides this information about the play: "Mr. W. Smith, an actor who had been a hard drinking man, signed the pledge of total abstinence. This play was written for him; in fact, he wrote the greater portion of his own part himself. People looked upon it as a portrait of himself. He was playing his own life." [69] The role Smith performed was that of Edward Middleton, the fallen who was saved. Born with the surname Sedley in North Wales, he assumed the name of Smith for his first appearance in Philadelphia in 1827; sometimes he was called William Sedley Smith. Beginning in 1843, he was a memorable stage manager at the Boston Museum. On leaving Boston in 1859 he became a wandering actor, eventually arriving in San Francisco where he worked as an actor and stage manager. If Smith (1806–1872) wrote other plays, they have been lost.

Like many of the popular plays of the nineteenth-century American theatre, *The Drunkard* is a first-rate melodrama with many of the features that attracted audiences. Mainly, of course, it is a moralizing play, following the life of Edward Middleton through five acts (divided into twenty-three scenes) from happiness to drunken misery to happiness again. The villain, Cribbs, clearly identifies himself in a monologue at the beginning of the second scene of Act I. When the heroine, Mary, and Edward fall in love and the villagers prepare for their wedding with songs and dances, Cribbs vows to make Edward a drunkard. The scene of wedded bliss which closes the first act introduces the audience to Old Miss Spindle, a humorous character who tries unsuccessfully throughout the play to vamp William, a strong, nondrinking Yankee. William's sister, Agnes, is mentally deranged because of Cribbs' influence upon her fiancé. There has also been a vague mention of a will. In Act II, Cribbs has influenced Edward to drink, even on Sunday, and boasts of his scheme. Edward, well on the road to ruin, leaves home and family for New York where Cribbs tempts him to forgery, always a dastardly crime in nineteenth-century American melodrama, and mentions a "scheme on the house of Rencelaw." Meanwhile, Mary and her child are cold and hungry, living in a garret where Mary repulses Cribbs' attempt to seduce her and hears him boast: "Nay, then, proud beauty. You shall know my power" (III,5). But William arrives just in time to save Mary.

The tide of virtue over vice begins to flow. In a delirious and distraught condition, Edward is now confronted by Rencelaw—"You have been drinking," says the reformer (IV,1)—who identifies himself and presents a pledge for Edward to sign. By the end of this act, William has seen Cribbs forging a check on Rencelaw and Company, and the mysterious will of Edward's grandfather is somehow related to the past villainy of Cribbs, who now tries to escape the pursuing authorities. In Rencelaw's house, Mary, Julia and Edward are united: the fallen has been saved, and the temperance thesis is complete. Act V dispatches the villain. Agnes regains her sanity; the will and the forgery are linked; Cribbs is captured but refuses to repent; and the final tableau shows Edward with a happy family.

The mysterious will, the deranged person and the chase are all typical aspects of melodrama as is the thesis of *The Drunkard*: Saved! The moral propaganda against drink is well structured in particular speeches, the fights that result from drinking, the work of Rencelaw as a reformed drunkard, the use of religion and the sentimental scenes and tableaux. Popular theatrical devices served to create excitement, pathos, rhythmic changes and entertainment: dances, songs, references to rural people and local customs, fights, Spindle's humor, William's Yankee dialect. As a stage Yankee, William is shrewd, honest, good and occasionally humorous, but he functions mainly in the play as a Yankee deus ex machina to save people: Edward, in fights in New York and in the country; Edward, from himself as he tries to choke the landlord (IV,1); Mary, from Cribbs in New York; Agnes, from Cribbs (V,2). Although the language of the play is unwieldy, Spindle has some colorful phrases. For what it attempted to do, and for the audiences it served, *The Drunkard* was well written and successful, and considering the seriousness of the problem of alcoholism in Jacksonian America, the play's success is hardly surprising.

Although Horace's dictum "to delight and to instruct" frequently appeals to lecturers and beginning playwrights, any attempt at instruction must usually be introduced into a play with great finesse. This fact was not recognized in the forthright reform-oriented society of nineteenth-century America, and the popular acceptance of moralistic plays reveals something about that society. Other plays were presented in an equally forthright fashion, and a study of the theatres in which they were produced provides eloquent commentary on the interests of particular levels of urban society. By performing Shakespeare and the best of English and European dramas and contemporary plays, the Park Theatre pretended to be above melodrama and to cater to aristocratic society. The Bowery Theatre was the home of spectacular melodrama, and for more than a decade the Olympic Theatre provided a distinctive form of entertainment that came mainly from the pens of American playwrights.

Under the management of William Mitchell, the Olympic Theatre opened in New York on December 9, 1839—advertising "the production of Vaudevilles, Burlesques, Extravangazas, Farces, Etc."—and closed on March 9, 1850, having served its stated purpose well. An accomplished comedian from English provincial theatres as well as Covent Garden in London, Mitchell had come to the National Theatre in New York in 1836 and probably wrote *The Roof Scrambler*, a burlesque of *La Sonnambula* that opened at the Olympic Theatre on December 16, 1839.

As the manager of the Olympic Theatre, Mitchell began serving New Yorkers an exciting brand of entertainment that identifies his theatre and his own contributions to American drama. To help him, Mitchell employed a stable of writers at various times: William K. Northall, Alexander Allan, Joseph M. Field, Charles Walcot, Henry Horncastle, and Ben Baker. His object, however, was always the same: spectacular and interesting entertainment that exploited current happenings in and around New York. For his first season, he introduced *Billy Taylor* (1840), presumably written by Mitchell himself, and described the title character in a program note: "William Taylor, fanatically called Billy Taylor, a perfect gentleman, though living in a state of cannibalism—viz. upon his father—a gay young fellow attached to Mary Wagstaff, and occasionally to other ladies." Horncastle adapted Charles Dickens' *Nicholas Nickleby* as *The Savage and the Maiden* for the Olympic in January of 1840. *Asmodeus in New York*, a "new, local extravaganza" opening in April, was written for Mitchell by Alexander Allan, a company actor and a playwright. Born in London in 1806, Allan came to New York in 1822 and began to write plays in 1827. At the time of his interview with George Seilhamer in 1882, he could not remember the names of any of the plays he had written at the Olympic Theatre because they were created so quickly, and he was ashamed of them. A constant writer for years, he confessed to having many manuscripts which would probably "serve for a bonfire when I have passed away."[70]

In the fall of 1840 Mitchell opened three plays, one an anonymously written piece entitled *Sparring with Specie; or, The War of the Shinplasters*, which reflected the current banking problems in America, and featured President Eagle, Vice President Dollar, Shinplaster (played by Mitchell) and "a squad of very light characters, sometimes Good for a Drink and quite as often Good for Nothing." The two other pieces were extravaganzas written by Allan: *1940; or, Crummles in Search of Novelty*, which ran for thirty-five nights, and *The New World; or, The House of Liberty*, an allegory with such characters as Destiny, Liberty, Justice and Exile. By the spring of 1841, *1940* had become *1941* as Mitchell kept pace with the times, and Crummles had become such a popular character that Henry Horncastle, another English actor and playwright who had come to America in 1837, made him the center of a new sketch called *Old Olympian*. This played for a week in September of 1841, and the following week Horncastle wrote a burletta entitled *The Wreck; or, The Isle of Beauty*. When Boucicault's *London Assurance* played at the Park Theatre in October, Mitchell responded quickly with *Olympic Insurance*, "a lady and a gentleman in a peculiarly perplexing predicament." By January of 1842, Mitchell was producing *1942; or, Crummles in Search of Novelty*.

With the beginning of the 1842–1843 season Mitchell produced farce after burlesque after extravaganza by Field, Mitchell, Allan, Northall and Charles Walcot (1815–1868), that "good author," according to Wemyss, "but better actor who chooses to wrap his theatrical career in mystery."[71] During the 1843–1844 season Walcot wrote *Fried Shots*, a burlesque of *Der Freischutz*, *The Imp of Elements; or, The Lake of the Dismal Swamp* and *Old Friends and New Faces*. Walcot, Sr., whose son, Charles Melton Walcot, Jr., was also an actor, came to America in 1839 and was first successful as an eccentric comedian and playwright at Mitchell's Olympic Theatre. A prolific writer, he was to create his best plays during his tenure at Wallack's Theatre from 1853 to 1861.

Mitchell is memorable as a manager and actor because he was shrewd enough to catch the right topics of the day and to hire clever playwrights to help him dramatize them, playwrights such as W. K. Northall, another productive member of Mitchell's playwriting staff. Northall's burlesques of *Virginius* and *Macbeth* were very successful in 1843, particularly the latter, which lampooned the acting style of the English actor William Macready, then on tour in America, and gave Mitchell one of his better burlesque roles. Says Lady Macbeth: "What a beast you are! When you told me first your plan / I though you were quite an enterprising sort of man." (I,2) After murdering the king, Macbeth speaks:

> If the same knife which cuts poor Duncan's life supporters
> could only cut the throats of common news reporters
> and thus make dumb the press—it's pretty clear
> this cut would be the be-all and the end-all here. (I,4)

The burlesque form also stimulated Mitchell's interest in the famous Macready-Forrest feud that eventually culminated in the Astor Place Riot in 1849. In 1847 Northall described the setting for the future confrontation in *Uproar House in*

Disaster Place, and Mitchell wrote *Who's Got Macready; or, A Race to Boston* in 1848, the same year that he produced Walcot's *Le Mouchoir et l'Épée*, a burlesque of Forrest's Edinburgh hiss of Macready. The previous year (1847) Northall had also burlesqued the gargantuan peculiarities of Barnum and his fakeries in *Chinese Junk*.

Mitchell was obviously a very alert manager who took advantage of city events, visits by foreign dignitaries such as Charles Dickens (with *Boz*) and any activities at the Park Theatre that seemed popular enough to burlesque. Some of his pieces played for several nights, but generally they were entertainments of the moment and illustrate only the great capacity of the nineteenth-century theatre to consume plays and sketches. For the 1845–1846 season at the Olympic, Odell lists 107 pieces. Walcot was still prominent during the final season of the Olympic Theatre (1849–1850), with *Britania and Hibernia; or, Victoria in Ireland* and *Frank McLaughlin*, which the *Spirit of the Times* said was "founded upon the current joke of the day." The *Spirit* found Walcot "a very amusing writer, a very amusing actor, and a man of considerable talent."[72] As slight as some of these plays appear, they kept the Olympic Theatre open during one of the worst decades in American theatre history. Farces, extravaganzas and spectacles of every variety, they were, for the most part, written by Americans particularly to entertain Americans. The playwrights were professionals and wrote not only for Mitchell but for any theatre manager who would pay for their services. If after reading a number of their plays one finds that they all begin to sound a bit alike, it only indicates that playwrights had learned how to write the formula play that audiences enjoyed.

People's interests at the theatre as well as elsewhere move in cycles. Satire, burlesque and travesty had always been popular on the American stage because here was a large country with small pockets of peculiarities that people could ridicule. Oddities and extravaganzas were part of America. People did not mind being different because risks or chances were an acceptable part of life, and as people pulled this way and that to establish themselves, they succumbed to extremes that could lead to success or failure, either one a subject for the stage. A motto for the age was "work and succeed," and if pleasures were few, one found pleasure as close to home as possible by seeing humor in everyday experiences. Even success could be seen as funny. John Brougham was simply following the patterns of the day in burlesquing *Metamora* in 1847. When some beautiful Arab girls performed on the stage at the Adelphi Theatre in New York in 1848, they were followed the next month by *Mose's Visit to the Arab Girls* in three episodes—the Interior, the Dance and the Muss. Brougham's *Socialism; or, Modern Philosophy Put in Practice* (1849) burlesqued Charles Fourier, the French social philosopher whose ideas captured the imaginations of many Americans during the 1840s, and Horace Greeley, a major follower of Fourierism. The scene of this farce is a dinner party at which a discussion of socialism puts everyone to sleep while the dream of the socialists disappears with the awakening to reality. This was fortunate, for during the dream Fourier Grisley was president; a man's wife, children and property belonged to the state; there was no money, only barter; and the city was deserted. After the Fox sisters from Rochester, New York, had educated the country in 1848 about spirit-rappings and table-turnings, an alert playwright wrote *Mysterious Knockings* (1849). Later, at Burton's Theatre, T. D. Rice produced a burlesque called *Rochester Knockings*.

As observers, historians, moralists and entertainers of Jacksonian America, these playwrights were interested in make-believe, in fun and in jokes, in spectacle upon the stage. Basically, they were concerned with their own lives and careers, and their motivations for success were rooted in their own self-interests. If, as they wrote, they captured something of "the intellect, senses and feelings of man," as Parke Godwin described the potential of drama, or more likely, caught something of the "inspiration of popular life," they were pleased—but only if audiences reacted favorably and gave them good benefits. For the same reasons—the social and intellectual response of audiences—the historian can benefit from the work of these playwrights who, for their livelihood, tried to respond to the pulse beat of the developing nation.

NOTES

1. E. C. Stedman and Ellen M. Hutchinson, eds., *A Library of American Literature*, vol. VII (New York: Charles L. Webster, 1892), 315–17.

2. *Spirit of the Times*, VII (August 5, 1837), 1.

3. A burlesque review entitled *The Hatchet of Horror; or, The Massacred Mermaid* (*Spirit of the Times*, VII [March 11, 1837], 2) appears to refer to the hatchet murder in New York of Helen Jewett in June of 1836, for which the accused, a man named Robinson, was judged not guilty.

4. Quoted in George C. D. Odell, *Annals of the New York Stage*, vol. III (New York: Columbia University Press, 1928), 449.

5. *Ariel*, IV (November 27, 1830), 127.

6. Odell, *Annals*, V, 343.

7. William Knight Northall, *Before and Behind the Curtain; or, Fifteen Years' Observations Among the Theatres of New York* (New York: W. F. Burgess, 1851), 90, 92.

8. "Benjamin A. Baker," in George O. Seilhamer, *An Interviewer's Album: Comprising a Series of Chats with Eminent Players and Playwrights* (New York: Alvin Perry, 1881), 97–103. Unless otherwise identified, all quotations concerning Baker are from this essay.

9. Odell, *Annals*, IV, 650.

10. New York *Dramatic Mirror*, September 13, 1890, 2.

11. *Theatrical Biography of Eminent Actors and Authors* (New York: Estate of Wm. Taylor, n.d.), n.p.

12. Odell, *Annals*, V, 364.

13. *Spirit of the Times*, XVIII (April 22, 1848), 108.

14. Effie Ellsler Weston, ed., *The Stage Memoirs of John A. Ellsler* (Cleveland: The Rowfant Club, 1950), 41.

15. Odell, *Annals*, V, Bowery Theatre, 1848–49, February 12, 1849, beginning of twelve week run.

16. *Spirit of the Times*, XIX (February 24, 1849), 2.

17. William W. Clapp, Jr., *A Record of the Boston Stage* (Boston: James Monroe and Company, 1853), 432.

18. Eric Wollencott Barnes, *The Lady of Fashion* (New York: Charles Scribner's Sons, 1954), 108.

19. Anna Cora Mowatt, *Fashion; or, Life in New York* (London: W. Newbery, 1850), Preface.

20. *Spirit of the Times*, XV (March 15, 1845), 32.

21. *Spirit of the Times*, XV (March 29, 1845), 56.

22. *Spirit of the Times*, XV (April 5, 1845), 68.

23. *Broadway Journal*, I (March 29, 1845), 203, 205.

24. *Broadway Journal*, I (April 5, 1845), 219.

25. *Arthur's Ladies Magazine*, II (June 1845), 287.

26. Revivals of *Fashion* in New York and elsewhere (1914, 1924, 1959) have produced little memorable criticism.

27. *Broadway Journal*, II (July 19, 1845), 29.

28. *Spirit of the Times*, XIX (February 24, 1849), 2.

29. *Spirit of the Times*, XXI (August 23, 1851), 324.

30. Letter, May 21, 1854, Harvard Theatre Collection.

31. Letter, March 3, 1870, Harvard Theatre Collection.

32. *Spirit of the Times*, XIX (February 24, 1849), 2.

33. Unidentified article, dated 1856, Harvard Theatre Collection.

34. In Allardyce Nicoll, *A History of English Drama 1660–1900*, vol. VI (Cambridge: Cambridge University Press, 1959), 119. *Did You Ever Send Your Wife to Brooklyn?* Mr. Honeybun sends his wife to Brooklyn to beg money from Aunt Jewel, who eventually resolves both the farcical situations that confront Honeybun and his financial difficulties.

35. See George Rogers Taylor, "Gaslight Foster: A New York Journeyman Journalist of Mid-Century," *New York History*, LVIII (July 1977), 297–312.

36. *Spirit of the Times*, XVIII (October 21, 1848), 420.

37. James E. Heath, *Whigs and Democrats; or, Love of No Politics* (Richmond, Va.: T. W. White, 1839), iii.

38. *The Complete Works of Edgar Allan Poe*, Virginia Edition, vol. 14 (New York: Thomas Y. Crowell & Co., 1902), 241.

39. *Spirit of the Times*, I (November 3, 1832), 2.

40. *Spirit of the Times*, XXI (March 29, 1851), 67.

41. *Spirit of the Times*, II (July 27, 1833), 247.

42. *Spirit of the Times*, VII (February 25, 1837), 4.

43. See "Thomas S. Hamblin," *Spirit of the Times*, XXI (March 29, 1851), 67; "Death of Thomas S. Hamblin," *Spirit of the Times*, XXII (January 15, 1853), 576.

44. Rosemarie K. Bank, "Theatre and Narrative Fiction in the Work of a Nineteenth-Century American Playwright, Louisa Medina," *Theatre History Studies*, III (1983), 54–67.

45. Lester Wallack, *Memories of Fifty Years* (New York: Charles Scribners, 1889), 90.

46. Document in the Billy Rose Theatre Collection, New Public York Library at Lincoln Center identified "N.P.W. December 1845."

47. Bank, "Theatre . . . Louisa Medina," 57.

48. Odell, *Annals*, IV, 39.

49. *The Ladies Companion and Literary Expositor*, April 1837, 30.

50. *Spirit of the Times*, XVI (April 18, 1846), 96.

51. New York *Mirror*, XV (April 28, 1838), 351.

52. *Spirit of the Times*, IX (April 27, 1839), 96.

53. *Spirit of the Times*, IX (June 29, 1839), 204.

54. The more prolific playwrights who developed American characters and American ideas rather than make occasional references to passing or past events in America will be discussed in the next chapter, "America Dramatized."

55. James Rees, *The Dramatic Authors of America* (Philadelphia: G. B. Zieber, 1845), Preface.

56. Odell, *Annals*, III, 575.

57. James Rees, *Dramatic Authors*, 139.

58. Walter Leman, *Memories of an Old Actor* (San Francisco, Cal.: A. Roman Co., 1886), 184. All quotations in this discussion are from this book.

59. *Spirit of the Times*, I (November 3, 1832), 2.

60. *Spirit of the Times*, XIX (March 17, 1849), 48.

61. *Federal American Monthly*, X (August 1837), 180.

62. *The American Monthly*, December 1837, 489.

63. Arthur M. Schlesinger, Jr., *The Age of Jackson* (Boston: Little, Brown and Company, 1950), 212.

64. William B. Wood, *Personal Recollections of the Stage* (Philadelphia: Henry Carey Baird, 1855), 399.

65. David Grimsted, *Melodrama Unveiled, American Theatre and Culture, 1800–1850* (Chicago: University of Chicago Press, 1968), 241–48.

66. *Spirit of the Times*, XVIII (November 4, 1848), 444.

67. Maud and Otis Skinner, eds., *One Man in His Time, the Adventures of H. Watkins, Strolling Player, from His Journal* (Philadelphia: University of Pennsylvania Press, 1938), 100.

68. *One Man in His Time*, 99, 116.

69. *One Man in His Time*, 70.

70. Seilhamer, 121.

71. Francis C. Wemyss, *A Chronology of the American Stage from 1752–1852* (New York: W. Taylor, 1852), 154.

72. *Spirit of the Times*, XIX (December 22, 1849), 528.

6

AMERICA DRAMATIZED

Writing about an "American Drama" for the *American Quarterly Review* in 1827, James Kirke Paulding stressed the need for plays not only created by native Americans but plays that appealed to national feelings. Like historians and critics since his time who fret about the nationality of a Dion Boucicault or a T. S. Eliot, Paulding concerned himself with the attitude of the playwright toward his subject matter. During the Age of Jackson, theatre artists constantly came to America, some to visit for a few years and some to spend their lives. Few literary people, however, immigrated to America, and some who did were not well received. Lorenzo da Ponte, for example, an Italian who had written librettos for Mozart, immigrated to New York where he taught Italian, wrote a play entitled *Almachilde* in 1829 and even attempted to build an opera house. He died in 1838, poor and forgotten. At this point in history, da Ponte might have fared better had he written about America. Paulding, on the other hand, wanted more than painted scenes and hollow characters. An American drama, he contended, should be founded on a just appreciation of dramatic incidents and should reveal the distinguishing features of America in both the locale presented and the characters to be delineated by the actors. His was an ambitious request and few would meet its requirements, but it was also a logical and astute criticism of most pre-1827 American drama and showed clarity of thought and perception. Eventually, that American drama would be written, and some remarkable beginnings were made by Jacksonian Americans.

About 90 percent of the plays written in America during the 1829–1849 period were by actor-playwrights or journeyman playwrights who were commercially interested in offering a product for the American stage. Few of them, however, were Americans. Most wrote as they had been trained in England or influenced by their reading, and some of these visitors reacted as did Anthony

Aston who in 1703 "turn'd Player and Poet, and wrote one Play on the Subject of the Country." [1]

William Barrymore (d. 1847) represents one type of dramatist in America. According to Odell, Mr. and Mrs. Barrymore were brought from England to the Park Theatre in 1831 to produce dramas similar to those acted under his supervision at the Drury Lane Theatre.[2] Barrymore also acted in New York as well as in Boston, where he was stage manager of the Tremont Theatre and manager for the Lion Theatre. After his death in Boston, his wife returned to England. During the sixteen years he lived in America, Barrymore wrote at least a dozen plays. With the possible exception of *Old Jonathan and His Apprentices* (1832), which took advantage of the Yankee popularity and was written for the Bowery Theatre management, they did not reflect knowledge of or feeling for America. Another play, *The Cabin Boy and His Monkey Who Had Seen the World* (1832), helped to establish the career of an actor named Charles Parsloe, who acted the role of the monkey. Other plays by Barrymore simply show the fluffy nature of farce and sentiment that entertained theatre audiences on both sides of the Atlantic: *The Man In the Moon* (1834); *Lillian, the Show Girl* (1837); *Eva, the Lass of the Mill* (1838); and *The Busy Bee* (1844).

John Brougham (1810–1880) represents another kind of immigrant actor-dramatist. After gaining experience in England as an actor with Mme. Vestris and as a manager, he came to America in 1842, acting first at the Park Theatre in New York. During his lifetime he wrote 126 dramatic works and was dubbed the "American Aristophanes" by Laurence Hutton, author of *Curiosities of the American Stage* (1871). Of Brougham's many plays, some twenty were written before mid-century, not counting his claim that he was a substantial coauthor with Dion Boucicault of *London Assurance*. During his eight years in Jacksonian America, Brougham made a strong beginning for his long career in the American theatre, interrupted only by a five-year stay in England from 1860 to 1865.

Upon Brougham's arrival in New York, critics immediately singled him out as a "lively actor" with a "rich brogue" and "truly Irish countenance" which "never fails to bring out the rollicking fun and humor of the character which he represents."[3] As a playwright, Brougham quickly struck the pace of the plays that a large part of America enjoyed. *Jupiter Jealous; or, Life in the Clouds* appeared at the Olympic Theatre in October of 1842, along with the plays of Field, Mitchell, Allan and Walcot. Typically described in terms of his personal charm, grace and humor, Brougham was a happy-go-lucky man who enjoyed the American theatre scene, took chances and had his share of success and failure. A fine actor, he was a miserable theatre manager. Both vocations, however, forced him to write plays—the first to provide vehicles for his particular acting talents, generally in Irish roles; the second, to keep his theatres open. On both accounts he left some memorable plays. Farce and burlesque were areas of expertise in which he revealed an inexhaustible supply of wit and a tongue that matched the sharp fancy of his mind.

After losing all his money in a Mississippi riverboat poker game during a starring tour in the fall of 1843, Brougham started his playwriting career in earnest with *Life in New York* (1844) and *Declaration of Independence* (1844), slight works that followed the popular trends of the time. In 1846 he acted the lead in another play, *Franklin*—notable mainly in that the young Franklin was played by a female—which he wrote before going to Boston where he took over the management of the Adelphi Theatre in the spring of 1847 and failed after a year. Back in New York Brougham became stage manager of Burton's Theatre in Chambers Street and began to adapt some of the stories of Charles Dickens, a task he apparently enjoyed throughout his playwriting career. Reviewing *Dombey and Son*, a popular work which opened in July of 1848, the *Spirit of the Times* praised both Burton and Brougham for "leaving sacred to the imagination, in so far as they could, the purely imaginative creating of Mr. Dickens' pen, and contenting themselves with presenting to their audience the strongly marked and more every-day personages who figure in the tale."[4] In September of 1848, Brougham again went to Dickens for *The Capture of Captain Cuttle and Barnaby's Wedding*, a play frequently repeated that season.

During the 1848–1849 theatre season Brougham showed his skill at writing the popular farces that audiences enjoyed for the moment and then forgot: *The Revolt of the Sextons; or, The Undertaker's Dream* (October 1848); a burlesque of *Don Ceasar de Bazan*; an unnamed burletta touching upon the "California fever, that thirst for gold which threatens to carry off one half the population who, before that date, thirsted rather upon liquids than solids"; and a travesty upon the popular air which he called "Oh! Carry Me Back to Old Manhattan!"[5] Brougham also collaborated that year with Ben Baker at the Olympic Theatre on *Love and Murder*. One of his best efforts of the season, however, was *Romance and Reality; or, Silence Gives Consent*, which opened at the Broadway Threatre in April after playing in London the previous year. Critics tended to be enthusiastic about his contrasting the extreme absurdities of romantic notions with a life as real as his sense of reality would allow but did not find his work "of high dramatic superiority." "This gentleman," wrote the critic for *The Literary World*, "in the matter of actor-authorship, is to America what Buckstone is to England, writing and representing with equal facility and exellence. . . . As a humorous poet and tale-sketcher Mr. Brougham is also excellent."[6] *Temptation; or The Irish Emigrant*, opening at Burton's Theatre in September 1849, was a melodrama carefully structured to appeal to temperance workers and the church-going moralists. O'Bryan, the Irish ne'er-do-well acted by Brougham, like many of the Yankee characters in other vehicle plays, was comically entertaining but generally peripheral to the plot.

The most important play that Brougham wrote during these years relates to America's developing drama by burlesquing both the subject matter of Stone's achievement, *Metamora; or, The Last of the Wampanoags*, and the acting techniques of Edwin Forrest. *Met-a-mora; or, The Last of the Pollywogs* opened in Boston on December 9, 1847, at Brougham's Adelphi Theatre, where W. W.

Clapp reported that Brougham "was the life of the place." In his poetic address for the opening of the Adelphi, Brougham gave an appropriate cue to his managerial approach: "Let us then hope, in this our iron age, / When universal raildom is the rage, / You'll not forget this new established 'stage.' "[7] *Met-a-mora* remains an exceptional illustration of Brougham's talent and wit as well as a landmark in the development of satiric comedy in America.[8]

Brougham's play is basically Stone's, but he adds or omits action, changes characters' names and parodies speeches. Metamora becomes "the ultimate Pollywog, an aboriginal hero, and a favorite child of the Forrest." Lord Fitzarnold becomes Lord Fitzfaddle, a foppish Anglo-Saxon, "a highly-to-be-envied individual, who has the honor to die by Metamora's knife." Properties and references also change. Stone's majestic dying panther becomes a lowly and frightened pig, a vicious wolf becomes a dozing weasel. Stone's Metamora gives Oceana an eagle's plume, but Brougham's Metamora calls the heroine to him and says, "Here, take this tail, plucked from a mongrel rooster." Acting the role of Metamora, Brougham burlesqued Forrest's manner and delivery, changed Forrest's "Hah!" to "Ugh!" and ridiculed Forrest's well-known demand for exit speeches. At the end of Act II, scene 2, for example, Metamora sends his Indians off to raid the town and then pauses to speak to the audience:

> It's very probable you'd like to know
> The reason why the Pollywog don't go
> With his red brethren. Pray take notice, each,
> He stays behind to have an exit speech.

When Metamora asks his wife, Tapiokee, La Belle Sauvage, played by Mrs. Brougham, if she wished to die, she says:

> I rather guess I wouldn't. I'll tell you why.
> You've often told me never to say die.
> If it amuses you my blood to shed,
> Don't say another word, but go ahead. (II,3)

The English then appear, snap their pistols at Metamora, who jumps at each sound, and finish him off with pop guns as the chorus sings "We're all dying." It was an evening of broad farcical entertainment that Brougham further enlivened with one-liners and minstrel show humor. As the Indians approach at one point in the play, Oceana says to Vaughn, "Think! He may scalp you!" Vaughn responds: "Can't. I wear a wig!" Asked by Tapiokee if he would like a cup of tea, Metamora says: "No, my love, no! My nerves are too refined! / They cannot bear excitement of that kind." Brougham's later Indian burlesque, *Pocahontas*, is a more carefully and consistently constructed work, but *Met-a-mora* created a sensation when it played at the Chatham Theatre in the winter of 1848. As an actor whose talents supported his playwriting skills, Brougham was firmly establishing himself in 1849 as a force in American theatre. As a contributor to American dramatic literature, he is the only major playwright whose career began in Jacksonian America and continued to expand beyond mid-century.

Barrymore was an Englishman who remained English apparently in both temperament and artistry; Brougham accepted his new country and contributed to its theatrical art and literature, responding to Paulding's concern mainly in his satiric farces. There are a few American playwrights, however, who clearly agreed with Paulding's interest in a national drama, showed an understanding of America and dramatized American ideas, events and idiosyncrasies through American characters. The most important of these dramatists are George Washington Parke Custis, Joseph M. Field, Silas Steele, Cornelius Mathews and H. J. Conway. Inasmuch as records are available, these playwrights appear to have devoted their energies exclusively, or nearly so, to American topics and views. There were also American playwrights who emphasized American acts and attitudes in their work—Nathaniel Deering, Thomas Chivers, Charlotte Conner, George W. Harby, and Nathaniel H. Bannister, whose achievements make him one of the outstanding actor-dramatists of Jacksonian America.

Among the oddities sprinkled throughout any period in American history are the works of the amateur playwrights with a mission. Mrs. Margaret Botsford wrote *The Reign of Reform; or, Yankee Doodle Court* for a purpose: "To check, if possible, the violent spread of Reform, now so indiscriminate and so alarming to the interests of the country."[9] A biting satire, the play pictures Colonel Hardface and Major Dauntless, two Revolutionary patriots who in December of 1829 discuss Hickory (Andrew Jackson), the Duke of Intrigue (Van Buren) and the Prince of Influence (J. H. Eaton), among others. Obviously more of a dialogue than a drama—and published in six chapters—the work shows Mrs. Botsford's vengeful condemnation of Andrew Jackson, who evidently had not shown the appropriate gratitude for an earlier play eulogizing him as a hero which she had written and produced in Cincinnati in 1825.

George Washington Parke Custis (1781–1857) was that typical educated person, born into a distinguished southern family, who tried his hand at writing—prose, verse, drama—and showed some talent in answering the needs of his country's theatres but maintained a dilettante's point of view. There is evidence that he wrote nine plays, two that achieved some success in the theatre. After *The Indian Prophecy* (1827), Custis dramatized his admiration for Andrew Jackson in *The Eighth of January; or, Hurrah for the Boys of the West*. First produced at the Park Theatre on January 8, 1828, to commemorate Jackson's military victory in New Orleans and his bid for the presidency, this play is the least effective of three—Smith's work of the same title and C. E. Grice's *The Battle of New Orleans* (1815), which was occasionally produced to promote Jackson's popularity.

Custis' next play, *The Rail Road*, shows his interest in using the drama to make Americans aware of their heritage and the continuing development of the nation. In a colorful ceremony on July 4, 1828, the first important railroad line was begun by the Baltimore and Ohio Company. In October Custis' "New National Drama" opened at the Baltimore Theatre with scenes including "a distant view of the city of Baltimore," "a View of Fort McHenry" with different ships passing the fort and "a Distant View of a Rail Road in full Operation." This production came a month before Dunlap's scenic *Trip to Niagara* and made the most of spectacles including a locomotive steam carriage that whistled as it disappeared into the wings. That same year the Chesapeake and Ohio Canal, linking Washington and Cumberland, was begun, and when Custis' play came to the Washington Theatre in March of 1829, it was called *The Rail Road and the Canal*. It is revealing of Custis' serious attitude toward this nationalistic spectacle, the most successful of his plays, that he revised his work before it opened at Philadelphia's Walnut Street Theatre in May.

Pocahontas; or, The Settlers of Virginia, typically advertised as a "National Drama," first appeared at the Walnut Street Theatre in January of 1830, for a run of twelve nights, an achievement at this time, and was widely produced thereafter. Concentrating his efforts on the well-known love of Rolfe and Pocahontas, Custis succeeded in embellishing the story without excessive complication while generally increasing the intensity of the play's action. As might be expected, Captain Smith delivers appropriate patriotic speeches in the early scenes of the play, but Custis used Act I mainly to show the gentle and insightful character of Pocahontas, who finds her Indian suitor, Matacoran, brave but lacking "the best attribute of courage—mercy"(II, 2), and to dramatize her first meeting with Rolfe. Powhaton is a weak and cowardly king, afraid of the English and completely in the control of the wily Matacoran, an effective villain, as crafty and unscrupulous as he is strong and determined. Overhearing Matacoran prompt Powhaton to attack the English, Pocahontas vows to save Rolfe and enters the English camp by honestly, if accidentally, speaking the password that night—" 'tis Pocahontas comes—Pocahontas, the friend of the English" (III,1).

With the crisis of the battle foreshadowed at the end of Act II, the final act provides most of the spectacular action. Although the language of the play is not impressive, the battle scenes could have been very exciting, and physically demanding: "Smith with an Indian tied to his left arm, uses him as a buckler" (III,3). The final scene in Powhaton's palace allows Pocahontas the opportunity of shielding Smith from the executioner's sword before Powhaton prepares for the union between Rolfe and Pocahontas—between England and Virginia—and for the times when the "wild regions shall become the ancient and honour'd part of a great and glorious American empire" (III,5). As other playwrights have discovered, the love story of Rolfe and Pocahontas is difficult to dramatize, if the role of Smith is preserved. After warning the English in the second scene of Act III, Pocahontas has only five more speeches in the play; Rolfe is a mere shadow. Although Matacoran is the most consistent character, Smith takes over the action and most of the dialogue in Act III while Powhaton is somehow transformed into a king with a nationalistic curtain line. The love story is all but lost in the final act, but audiences did see some of the spectacle they enjoyed.

Custis wrote two more Indian plays; neither attracted attention. *The Pawnee Chief*, written before 1830, was presented at least once, on February 22, 1832. Custis was evidently writing *Monongahela* in 1836, but of this work all that is known is that he sent it to Edward Everett in 1839 with the idea that Everett might assist in getting it produced. Apparently, this did not happen.

Custis wrote *Northpoint; or, Baltimore Defended*, a celebration of the famous battle of the War of 1812, in nine hours at the request of the manager of the Baltimore Theatre, where it was produced on the anniversary of the engagement, September 12, 1833. With a heroine named Marietta who disguises herself as a soldier and runs away from home to fight, the play brings to mind Noah's *She Would Be a Soldier*. There was also a Negro veteran of the Revolution named Cully, and Custis included two songs as well as a climax that featured the British troops' bombardment of Fort McHenry. Three years later Custis again asserted his patriotism in a musical piece entitled *The Launch of the Columbia; or, America's Blue Jackets Forever*, which was commissioned to celebrate the launching of a "noble frigate" at Washington's shipyard. Performed on February 22, 1836, at the Washington Theatre, it was, according to reviewers, entertaining mainly for its spectacle and national sentiment.[10]

The only play that Custis attempted that was not apparently written from a nationalistic impulse was *Montgomerie; or, The Orphan of a Wreck*, a "Dramatic Romance" concerned with the clan Montgomerie in fourteenth-century Scotland. With Scottish castles, caverns by the sea, the songs of the clansmen of Montgomerie and a sword dance along with Highland games, the play had considerable spectacle frequently touched with gothic gloom and a suggestion of the supernatural in the person of a prophetess with second sight and a pirate chief identified as the "Mysterious Being."[11] Straightforward melodrama, this play moves quite rapidly through some twenty-seven scenes to a happy and expected conclusion, but it was not successful onstage. During the only production recorded (Washington, April 11, 1836), the audiences kindly endured a three-hour performance, probably because of their high regard for the author whose dramatic talents had shown some promise but who was now absorbed in managing estates he had inherited from his father (John Parke Custis, the stepson of George Washington) and his grandfather. For Custis, writing plays was strictly an avocation which lasted for only a brief period in his life, although he did have some gratifying success with performances of *The Eighth of January*, *The Rail Road* and *Pocahontas*.

Very different from Custis in social background and career, Joseph M. Field (1810–1856) was one of those itinerant writers and theatre people who are pulled here and there by whim or thoughtful interest. Born in Dublin, Field was brought to America at the age of two and lived in Baltimore and New York before his debut as an actor in Boston's Tremont Theatre in the fall of 1827. Soon after playing the title role in John Augustus Stone's *Tancred* at the Park Theatre in

March of 1831, Field went west, acting at various times under the management of Sol Smith and Noah Ludlow—in Cincinnati, St. Louis, Mobile and New Orleans—returning haphazardly to New York City and the East Coast theatres. In New Orleans he contributed poems and humorous sketches under the pseudonym of Straws to the *Picayune* (1839–1840), which sent him to Europe as a correspondent. As a lesser star in the American theatre firmament, Field enjoyed the system which encouraged brief engagements by a variety of actors. In 1837 he married Sol Smith's leading actress, Eliza Riddle, and afterwards acted with her and wrote plays in which she was featured. His best years were spent in the South and Midwest, particularly in St. Louis where he helped found a newspaper, *The Reveille* (1844) and managed Field's Variety Theatre from 1852 to 1853. Neither his theatre management nor his writing and playwriting, however, brought him the distinction he deserved. He died in Mobile, Alabama, in late January 1856, of consumption, leaving his wife and a daughter, Kate Field, who became a celebrated lecturer.

It was as a comic actor that Field was most appreciated, and his enactment of Dazzle in *London Assurance* was considered superior to any but that of John Brougham. During his peripatetic years in what was then the Southwest, Field tried all types of roles on the stage but finally "settled down to what he was really clever in—eccentric comedy."[12] James Rees described Field as an actor who was "universally admired,"[13] and when Field was hired by William Mitchell at the Olympic in New York for the 1842–1843 season, he was paid the highest salary of $25 a week plus one-third of the receipts of one benefit. Mitchell, however, the astute manager of the only theatre in New York making money that season, wanted Field for other reasons and specified that all plays written by Field and produced at the Olympic would be his property, entirely and exclusively.

The astute Boston theatre critic and correspondent for the *Spirit of the Times*, Acorn (James Oakes), provided some personal observations in his sentimental obituary on Field in 1856. "Mr. Field possessed fine literary ability and extraordinary taste and tact in his dramatic profession. . . . He was a witty poet and a remarkable humorist as a prose writer."[14] Unfortunately, except for essays and poems in the *Reveille* and the *Picayune*, Field left very little published work for later critics to consider. The two volumes of Field's prose sketches, *The Drama in Pokerville; or, The Great Small Affair Company* and *The Bench and Bar in Jurytown and Other Stories*, appeared first in 1847 as written by Everpoint and were reprinted in one volume in 1850. Beginning with the representation of a playbill, *The Drama in Pokerville* is a relatively dull story of a production of *Pizarro* embellished with a rehearsal of company problems concerning an actress, love affairs, fights and a duel.

As far as American theatre is concerned, Field published a far more interesting item in 1841: a poem describing an actress, *La Déesse, an Elssler-Atic Romance*. It was an obvious burlesque of the European dancer, Fanny Elssler, who performed at the Park in 1840–1841, was widely popular and made a fortune through her exorbitant demands upon the theatre management for $500 a night and a clear benefit. At the Olympic Theatre before Field joined the company, Mitchell had burlesqued Fanny Elssler's famous dance of *La Tarentule* with a production called *La Musquitoe*. Field's poem describes Gotham's reaction to La Déesse (rhymes with "guess"): "And La Déesse! She smiles away, / A bliss in ev'ry dimple's play." The dancer prepares for the evening, performs, receives a proposal of marriage, and hears the next morning from the critics that she had no "soul and heart." Field's clever poem undoubtedly reflected the views of many readers.

The exact number of plays Field wrote will probably never be known. Eugene R. Page, the editor of volume XIV of *America's Lost Plays* in which *Job and His Children*, Field's only extant play, is published, lists eighteen, but it is possible that he wrote many more. He was a man of his times, responding to current happenings and situations in *Nervo the Vitalics; or, The March of Science (or, What Next?)* (1842), or a burletta entitled *Antony and Cleopatra* (1843). *Family Ties*, which Field prepared in collaboration with J. S. Robb, a journalist in St. Louis who wrote under the pseudonym of Solitaire, won a $500 prize from Dan Marble but failed in its opening at the Park Theatre in 1846. James Rees declared that Field "signalized himself as a dramatist in the production of several excellent pieces: the best of which in our opinion is *The Tourist. Tod's Pilgrimage* by this gentleman is also spoken of very highly by the Southern critics."[15] Yankee Hill acted the part of Ebenezer Fish in *The Tourist; or, Tourists in America* (1839), in which Field ridiculed the foreign visitors who wandered across America and later recorded their thoughts.

Field was very much aware of the politics of his time. While the Oregon Controversy was being resolved with the British offer of the 49th Parallel as a treaty line, Field's *Oregon; or, The Disputed Territory* was produced in Mobile on January 26, 1846. A decade earlier several congressmen had reacted to abolitionist pressure by passing the so-called Gag Resolution, which required all anti-slavery appeals to be tabled. John Quincy Adams spearheaded an eight-year fight to appeal the rule, and Field evidently responded to the arguments in his typical fashion. "J. M. Field—*alias* 'Straws,' the poet-laureate of the *Picayune*—has written a new, romantic, antic, vocal, local sketch in verse called *G-A-G; or, The Starving System* which was produced for his wife's (late Miss Riddle's) benefit on the 20ult. It drew a good house, and drew down shouts of laughter. Mitchell needs such a man as 'Straws' to write farces for Mrs. Timm and himself."[16] Evidently, Mitchell agreed; he hired Field for the next season.

Although evidence is limited, it appears that Field took his art seriously and could profit from criticism while not presuming anything more than ephemeral delight. When *Such As It Is* failed at the Park Theatre in 1842, a critic for the *Spirit of the Times* suggested that a strong plot and more extravagant incidents would have helped.[17] Later, at the St. Louis Theatre in June of 1845, Field presented a version of *Such As It Is* with the title *Foreign and Native*. Neither play is extant, but a review in the *Missouri Reporter* indicates that Field might have been influenced by the success of Mowatt's *Fashion*, produced in March of 1845:

[*Foreign and Native*] is intended to give some insight into fashionable life in the American metropolis, and the characters are drawn accordingly. . . . There is a happy vein of satire running through this drama, designed to rebuke, by exposure, the foolish fondness of American *fashionables* for doing homage to every European nobleman or author who visits our shores. That folly is well exposed in the "Flare" Family; the father seeking for an indiscriminate ministration to national vanity, the mother for a *titled* husband for her daughter. Hence they fall an easy prey to any crafty adventurer, who is willing to avail himself of their foibles, and sometimes they take great pains to make themselves ridiculous and sacrifice the happiness of their children.[18]

The critic goes on to praise Field's attention to "character drawing" and to suggest a more careful attention to plotting. Some slight revision accomplished, the critic thought that Field had "in him the genius required for success in the most difficult department of literature." Whether Field attended to this advice remains a question, but his play was popular, paticularly in Western theatres.

One of the last plays that Field wrote had a serious tone embedded in a melodramatic plot: *Job and His Children* (1852). Job is an arrogant and self-righteous father who tries to control the lives of his grown children, all the time assuming piety and a Job-like stance. Refusing his blessing to his daughter, Faith, who wants to marry a worthy sailor, Job condemns himself to misery at the hands of an undeserving son, but Field allows sentiment and a change of heart to bring a happy conclusion for all but the conniving son. Fortunately, the Jobian moralizing is enlivened throughout by Oby Oilstone, a Yankee whose physical awkwardness and sense of humor provide some vitality for the play. "You ain't all-killin' pooty," he tells his girlfriend, "and you don't know much, but then, you've com-com-bustibility of character—putty in the hands of the artist, you know!" (I,1). With reference to a performance at Field's theatre in St. Louis, the *Spirit* noted the religious tone of the play and the effective acting of Mrs. Field in the role of Faith whose "heart-searching" words "penetrate every heart."[19]

Although *Job and His Children* is not representative of Field's best work, which was satirical farce, it may suggest the kind of dialogue he wrote. From all accounts, his sense of humor gave distinction to his plays, and that, with the exception of Oby Oilstone, is lacking in *Job and His Children*. Among the actor-playwrights in Jacksonian America who concentrated upon America's people, their follies and triumphs, Field seems to have been well liked by critics and a popular figure wherever he went. It is unfortunate that more of his work has not survived to allow a more accurate assessment of his contribution to American drama.

Silas S. Steele (b. 1812), a Philadelphia native, began acting in 1829 but discovered that his forté was writing, and twenty-odd years later was identified by Wemyss as one of the most prolific dramatists of the American stage. Although seldom produced in New York, his plays, the exact number of which will remain an uninteresting mystery, were popular in Philadelphia and in other East Coast theatres. Only *The Brazen Drum; or, The Yankee in Poland* (1841) was printed during Steele's lifetime, and *The Crock of Gold; or, The Toiler's Trials* (1845) was eventually published in *America's Lost Plays* (vol. XIV), which lists twenty-five plays and some fifteen of Steele's burlesques.

An enthusiastic proponent of the theatre—amateur and professional—of his day Steele tried to entertain the society he knew. In 1859 he published a *Book of Plays: For Home Amusement (Being a Collection of Original, Altered, and Selected Tragedies, Plays, Dramas, Comedies, Farces, Burlesques, Charades, Lectures, Etc. Carefully Arranged and Specifically Adapted for Private Representation, With Full Directions for Performance)*. A thick volume of about 150 items, it begins with *The Well of Death; or, The Brothers of Padua*, "a play in one act and one scene" from Steele's *The Matricide*, and ends with a patriotic recitation by Steele, "Our Union, Right or Wrong." Other signed works by Steele include a variety of Irish, Yankee and minstrel sketches or monologues and "a tale of the late attack on China" entitled "The Lamp-Lighter of the Pagoda; or, The Chinaman's Revenge," which reflects both the current interest in the Orient and Maria Cummins' extremely popular novel, *The Lamp Lighter* (1854). He may also have been responsible for an extravaganza entitled *Opera Mad; or, The Scream-A-Donna*, which featured "Miss Jenny Leatherlungs, alias Lind."

Silas S. Steele's work clearly illustrates the efforts of the journeyman playwright to catch the current topic of conversation and to dramatize the daily interests of the American public: the Canadian rebellion of 1837 (*Rebellion in Canada*, 1841), the campaign of William Henry Harrison in 1840 (*The Battle of Tippecanoe*, 1840), the problems relating to free banking by state-chartered institutions beginning in 1840 (*The Bank Monster* [1841] and *St. Dollar and the Monster Rag* [1841]) and Thomas W. Dorr's Rebellion in 1842 which reacted against a 1663 law of Rhode Island, created a people's constitution and attempted to establish an illegal state government in Providence (*Rhode Island; or, Who's the Governor?*, 1842). Sometimes the topicality of an issue could be a problem, and *The Battle of Tippecanoe*, performed at the Chestnut Street Theatre, had to be "withdrawn in consequence of the political excitement which raged in the city at that period."[20]

Alert to the ebb and flow of public enthusiasm, Steele adapted fiction, burlesqued stage successes and wrapped himself in the American flag when it was popular to be patriotic. Soon after Edgar Allan Poe published *The Gold Bug* with considerable success, Steele wrote *The Gold Bug; or, The Pirate's Treasure* (1843). Dion Boucicault's *London Assurance* was first performed at the Covent Garden in March of 1841, and opened at the Park in New York in October of that year. Two months later, about ten days before *New York Assurance* was produced at the Chatham Theatre, Steele's burlesque entitled *Philadelphia Assurance* appeared at the Arch Street Theatre and was described as "the best thing of its kind we ever witnessed—the very scenery and furniture were parodied. It is full of wit and humor, abounding with tart sayings and local hits which were received by a good house with shouts of applause. . . . The burlesque was decidedly successful, and adds another wreath to the brow of the author, Mr. Silas S. Steele." [21] Earlier that fall the Arch Street Theatre had mounted Steele's *The First Fleet and The First Flag*, founded on an event in the life of Captain Biddle of the American Navy during the Revolution. Evidently, the management at the Arch Street did a spectacular job, and James Rees took the occasion to promote American nationalism. "We have here," he wrote, "another apt illustration of the fact that our own country affords ample material for the poet, the painter, the historian, and the dramatist, without the absolute necessity of resorting to foreign lands for the means of preserving the genius of their art." [22] By 1840 Steele had written *The Lion of the Sea; or, Our Infant Navy*, a nautical drama in three acts, and had celebrated America's first president in *Washington and Napoleon* (1841) and *Washington's Birthday; or, The New York Boys* (1846).

The Crock of Gold; or, The Toiler's Trials (1845) was Steele's four-act dramatization of a currently popular tale by Martin Tupper dealing with poverty, oppression, temptation, intemperance, greed, crime and the comforts of religion and piety. Moralistic melodrama, indeed! The villain is Simon Jennings, a steward in Hurstley Manor, also a butler, bailiff and extortionist, who steals the money of his Aunt Quarles from its hiding place, "the honey crock— the precious crock of gold," and strangles her when she catches him in the act of theft (I,1). The good man of the play is Roger Acton—"a pious man, still hoping for the reward promised by his divine employer" (I,2)—a man loved by his wife, Mary, and his daughter, Grace, who turns wild with ecstasy when he accidentally finds Jennings' hoard. At a trial in the last act, however, the villain confesses, and the good man recovers his goodness.

With less spectacle than strong moral quality, Steele displayed some of the writing techniques that brought him popularity. There is, for example, a young fisherman named Peter Perch whose language, ever in imagery, always reflects his vocation: "Poor pious, and industrious Roger Acton—a fry as far above the pike Jennings, as the sky's above water—a little rough about the scales but a pure gold fish within" (I,1). There is also an appropriate Yankee, Jonathan Floyd, in addition to a few silly aristocrats of the manor, Lord Silliphant and the Honorable C. Silkhair. All parts of the play, from the stiff language to the obvious moral, bear the weight of a heavy hand, but the play is notable for the manner in which all characters are individually conceived and contribute to the plot, providing opportunities for change of pace. Although mainly associated with theatres in Philadelphia, Steele concentrated his attention upon American incidents and historic figures, and on this relatively superficial level responded to Paulding's plea.

Cornelius Mathews (1817-1889) dramatized America in a much more thoughtful and thought-provoking manner. One of the bright young men of American letters rapidly gaining stature in New York during the 1840s, he was a lawyer, a poet, an essayist, novelist, critic and editor. He was also a dramatist of some reputation, and when he died, the writer for the New York *Clipper* noted that he was sometimes called the "Father of American Drama."[23] There was a bitter irony in that title which has since disappeared in a cloud of indifference. It would appear that Benjamin Franklin was wrong: life may be longer than the art it creates. At the end of an interview with Mathews in 1881, George Seilhamer wrote: " . . . it was difficult to believe that this excellent and scholarly old man, whose name is now almost, if not entirely, unknown in the theatres of New York was, in fact, the most promising and successful American dramatist of the last generation."[24] But it was true. For the generation preceding Augustin Daly, Bronson Howard and Steele Mackaye, Mathews wrote at least five plays, two of them acted in New York with some success, and for American dramatic literature in the late 1830s and 1840s he would rank with Epes Sargent, N. P. Willis and Nathaniel H. Bannister as dramatists of considerable promise.

After graduation from New York University in 1835 and admission to the bar two years later, Mathews began a prodigious career in which he promoted an American literature, a realistic national literature, as untiringly as he contributed to it. In 1840 he founded *Arcturus*, one of the better journals of the period, with E. A. Duyckinck; he also founded *Yankee Doodle*, a journal of satire and humor, and edited, for the four issues that were printed, a drama periodical called *Prompter* in which he wrote about actors and dramatists. He impressed critics and readers with *The Motley Book*, *Behemoth: A Legend of Mound-Builders* and *The Career of Puffer Hopkins*, a "scourer" whose adventures gave Mathews the opportunity to comment on the "characteristic and national" features of America. He could be philosophical in his essays but his tongue seemed frequently in his cheek. "I see the Naked Age approaching," he wrote in "A Serious Argument Against the Use of Clothing: Addressed to Tailors," in which he suggested that man could not be man without clothes.[25] In addition to his writing, he is remembered as a strong advocate of both copyright protection in America and the establishment of a national literature that turned its back on the old world and accepted the mission of promoting democratic America. As part of that group of writers identified as Young America, including the Duyckinck brothers and Parke Godwin, Mathews reflected ideas that epitomized Jacksonian America. He was young, ambitious, masculine America. At the same time he eventually found himself in opposition to people such as Willis, Graham, Lowell and Longfellow who attacked the Young Americans and especially their "centurion," Cornelius Mathews.

"Casting an eye upon the field of letters in America," Mathews wrote to James Russell Lowell on October 15, 1842, "we find an intolerable hubbub prevailing—out of which I yet hope to see order and beauty springing[?] in every direction. . . . False as are many of the conditions under which American Literature is struggling, I am not the one to despair of it all together. I see a vast community of readers."[26] As he continued with his writing and his speeches, his idealism and the brash certainty of his own part in the struggle seemed never to be daunted, although he obviously learned that attackers would be attacked. Harper Brothers published *The Various Writings of Cornelius Mathews* in 1843 with a preface by the author noting the difficulty of keeping a good name in literature and the scarcity of journals whose authority could be trusted. The problems of literature in America offer a perplexing riddle, he confessed, but one worth the solving. "Literature, a patient youth, sits now on the verge of the horizon."[27]

Mathews obviously wanted to use the drama to help that "patient youth" into a world of glorious sunshine. His first effort, *The Politicians*, a comedy in five acts, was not acted, and Mathews published it first in 1840 and again among his *Various Writings*, where he described theatre managers in his preface as "the sworn foes to dramatic writers." His play was written for "the cause of a true National Literature," he said.[28] In this satire on the election of an alderman, Mathews pits Brisk, an intriguing schemer who wants only to add to his own wealth, against Gudgeon, an idealist who secretly believes his own imaginings. Although the jibes at election procedures are clever and well written, Mathews gave more attention to message than to action and his dialogue is more descriptive and narrative than dramatic. In its review of the published play, the *New York Review* took occasion to declare that "two of the most important desiderata for our comedies are a great poet and a great humorous writer."[29] At the age of twenty-three, Mathews showed promise as a "humorous writer" but could not yet marshal his talents for the stage.

For his next drama Mathews abandoned his comic pose and wrote a tragedy that ranks among the best American plays written before the Civil War: *Witchcraft; or, The Martyrs of Salem*. Not only was this play—first performed at the Walnut Street Theatre in Philadelphia on May 5, 1846, with James Murdock as Gideon—staged successfully in major American cities, it was published by Samuel French and a London publisher in 1852 and translated into French by Philarete Chasles. W. W. Clapp, who was not one to give unwarranted praise to American plays, mentioned the translation as "an honor never before extended to American work of its kind."[30] Although the reviewer of the London publication despaired of the French translation in *Revue Contemporaine* as lacking "a single trait of our old Puritan society," he found the play "a spirited work, the production of intellect and poetical genius."[31] Some critics of the early performance in America faulted the play for too little action and too much conversation—generally an accurate assessment of Mathews' plays—but later viewers would not demand the melodramatic spectacle that obsessed the average theatregoer of 1846 and would find greater satisfaction in the sensitivity of Mathews' dramatic concept and the beauty of many of the speeches.

In dramatizing the terrors of the Salem witch-hunts, Mathews was able to exercise his belief that there was something special about America as a land of beauty and freedom where the brave-hearted must not succumb to corrupt au-

thority. The main character around whom the tragedy revolves is Gideon Bodish, a young man who lives with his mother, Ambla Bodish. Their reclusive
ways set them apart from their neighbors in ways that Topsfield, an old friend
of Gideon and a believer in witches, understands:

> Ambla and Gideon, though with us, walk not
> Our path-but always more apart and bear
> With them, in gesture, greeting, look and voice,
> The memory of a life greater than ours.(I,1)

It is this distinction, explained as a sensitivity to the beauty of the physical world
as well as to the mysteries of the spiritual world, which makes them ready tar-
gets for gossip and envy.

Mathews immediately defined the lines of conflict and his plot. Deacon Gidney is that self-righteous fool who builds his own importance by promoting the
Salem hysterics. Ambla, the troubled and gloom-ridden woman who enjoys long
walks in the woods and appears to talk to herself, is vulnerable to his evil
machinations. With increasing anxiety for his mother's frailty, Gideon stays close
to her: "Oh, mother! the fields are, somehow, very dark / Today, and I came
back, because I had not heart / To wander far away from you." (I,2). During
one of Gideon's absences Deacon Gidney questions Ambla about the spirit of
a recently condemned woman that was seen going over Ambla's house "in a
white flame, at midnight." Interrupted in his interrogation by an angry Gideon,
Deacon Gidney delights in what he terms a discovery: "Ha, ha, you feel me
on your hip, Satan / Thou evilish woman, and young man no less" (I,2). As
the plot develops, Gideon emerges as a hero with an inner struggle in which he
questions the forces which influence his mother. He also has external conflicts
involving Susanna Peache, the girl who loves him, and Jarvis Vane, her persistent and jealous suitor whose part in Gideon's inevitable disaster is foreshadowed at the end of Act I. "Look to thyself," Jarvis mutters after Gideon has
left him, "thy doom has now begun."

From the beginning of Act II, the action of the play moves steadily toward
catastrophe. Distinctive characters help to pace the action of the play and provide a contrast with the more intimate conversations of Gideon and Susanna.
The tone and atmosphere, however, remain serious and foreboding, and Mathews did not intrude his celebrated sense of humor. When the gossips complain of strange events, the villain, Jarvis, intervenes: "Ambla Bodish does all
this mischief" (II,3). Hearing his mother called a witch, Gideon fears that her
honesty will get her into trouble. When Justice Fisk confronts Ambla with the
gossip and adds that "I am told, you threaten me, too, Mistress," Ambla responds in a frank manner that angers him.

> *Ambla*:   You've earned a hundred acres of this town,
>   By holding of its offices, and when
>   You have eaten the hungry in all

> Its beeves and wheaten loaves, and drunken up
> Its current wines, and ciders—
> *Fisk*: Enough; write down, Master Pudeater [his assistant]
> that she admits
> The charge, in all fullness and great depth. (III,1)

Now the Bodishes have another enemy, and the act ends with an angry confrontation between Jarvis and Gideon.

One of the most poignant moments of the play comes in Act IV when Gideon finds his mother on one of her nightly meanderings and questions her action. His lack of faith is, to her, the "sharpest dagger yet," as he begs her to drive away the specter that haunts her. But she must follow where it leads:

> It passes by the murmuring tree, it stops
> Now fast by the sweet brook, but not to drink!
> It shapes its way—Gideon—oh, heaven be merciful,
> Toward our house, toward my sad roof and see,
> It enters in! (IV,2)

As they enter their house, a breeze flutters the pages of the Bible, and Gideon reads, "Set thine house in order, for thou shalt die!" Shaken to his roots by incidents he can understand only as witchcraft, he now feels that his mother is a witch, and he acts in fear and consternation: "Your son no longer— / The thunderbolt has struck. Heaven deserts you! / Behold the damning evidence of guilt—a witch! a witch!" (IV,3). And the act ends.

By his own experience and the tales of others, Gideon has been forced to a conclusion which must be reversed in Act V. With a fine sense of dramatic timing, Mathews has reserved for this moment the full explanation of Ambla's behavior that has been only suggested in past scenes. Gideon's father had wrongly suspected her of being unfaithful with a man he eventually challenged to a duel in which he was killed. Because pride and indignation kept her from stopping the fight, she has lived with her guilt and agony—"an ever-living dagger / To my heart" (V,1). With this new understanding, Gideon now swears to defend her "against the world, and all / The world, in its wickedness, can bring!" (V,1). The authorities come for Ambla, and the atmosphere of her trial is clearly established by the deacon's preparatory remarks to those assembled:

> When enters Ambla Bodish, turn you
> A steadfast gaze on her, in which be shot
> Your whole soul's strength as against one who dooms
> Your soul to the red fire. (V,2)

In an effective trial scene Mathews marshals the evidence of the gossips and adds a telling blow with the testimony of Susanna Peache, who feels that Ambla has diverted Gideon's love from her. At the place of execution, under a tree from which Ambla must hang, Gideon defies the court:

> . . . She shall not die a witch's
> Death. No hangman's infamous hand shall fret
> Away her holy life: she is no witch
> But my dear mother still to whom is due
> All this arm's strength. (V,3)

But the people attack Gideon, and Jarvis, having discovered that Susanna has taken her own life, stabs Gideon to avenge her death. As Deacon Gidney reminds the court of its duty, Ambla dies of shock and Gideon of his wound.

In parts of *Witchcraft*, there is considerable power, both for the reader and for an audience, although the printed version has a significant number of lines that were never spoken onstage. More than any other play, *Witchcraft* reveals Mathews' ability to structure his ideas well for his contemporary stage and to present well-developed characters moving inevitably toward dramatic climaxes. Writing about witchcraft more than people, he lacked a strong hero whose tragedy was a consequence of his actions, but his play was surely an effort in which serious critics could see promise for an American drama and historians find another landmark in its development. After Mathews' death, the *Dramatic Mirror* (June 14, 1890) noted that he had dreamed of a revival which never came and quoted William Cullen Bryant's statement that *Witchcraft* was worthy to be a "corner-stone of an American drama."[32] Particularly impressive is Margaret Fuller's recognition of his play as "a work of strong and majestic lineaments" with "fine originality" and an aged heroine whose effect upon other characters is "depicted with force and nobleness."[33]

For his next play Mathews again chose a topic from American history, the story of Jacob Leisler, the penniless German soldier who came to America in 1660, and as a Protestant champion during a period when Catholics were feared, gained military control of part of New York and assumed the office of governor. Eventually, forced to surrender by troops under Colonel Henry Sloughter, Leisler was hanged as a traitor in May of 1691. Leisler's power, however, was such that decades after his execution political factions in New York were identified as Leislerian and anti-Leislerian. It would appear to have been a topic worthy of mid–nineteenth-century American theatre. Calling his work *Jacob Leisler, the Patriot Hero; or, New York in 1690*, Mathews again wrote for James Murdock, who opened the play on April 13, 1848, in Philadelphia. The next month it was performed at the Bowery Theatre in New York, where the *Spirit* found the dialogue "patriotic, sentimental and jocular by turns" and commented favorably on the tableaux of Indian scenery but found little interest in the patriotism and politics, regretting "that the author did not employ his talents upon a subject the embodiment of which would have created more pageant."[34] Although Mathews' nationalistic touch was evident, the spectacle was missing, and Murdock, who was supposed to be costumed as an old Dutch merchant, preferred romantic robes and long hair, much to Mathews' distress. *Jacob Leisler* ran for a week at the Bowery Theatre but was never published.

Mathews claimed to have written many plays. If so, they are lost to history. *Broadway and the Bowery; or, The Young Mechanic and the Merchant's Daughter* played at John Brougham's Bowery Theatre in November of 1856, with Brougham in the leading role. Boasting the usual mixture of New York society that was popular during the years following *A Glance at New York*, the play appears quite similar in character to Mathews' fiction entitled *Big Abel and the Little Manhattan* (1845) and *A Pen-and-Ink Panorama of New York City* (1853).

He wrote *False Pretenses; or, Both Sides of Good Society*, a satire on New York society, for Thomas Barry who performed it at Burton's Theatre in New York on December 3, 1855. Jacob Milledollars, a bank president, and Adam Crockery, a merchant, are brothers-in-law, and Mathews intended to use their respective daughters to show social conflicts. Poor and honest versus rich and corrupt, the two families could provide Mathews with any situation he wanted to discuss, but his plot—concerned with a lost will and intruded upon by comic characters and scenes of New York—seemed to have little to do with his purpose in writing the play.

Whether concerned with witchcraft in New England, politics in New York or the contrast of societies in America, Mathews' plays always showed him to be a man of strong opinions. In 1853, he published his most bitter attack upon the injustices he found in America in *Calmstorm, the Reformer*. He called his work a "Dramatic Comment," and it is hardly a play, although it is written in dialogue (an irregular iambic pentameter) and divided into five major parts in which there are numerous scenes. The hero, Calmstorm, is the ultimate reformer and who perhaps like Mathews late in his life, finding his influence waning, can only "stand in silence endless and so die" (V,4).

During his active years, Mathews was associated with theatre and drama as critic, commentator and playwright, and constantly urged the protection of dramatists through proper copyright laws. His essays include comments on James Fenimore Cooper's *Upside-Down; or, Philosophy in Petticoats*, produced in 1850, and E. S. Gold's *The Very Age* (1850), which he considered one of the best comedies on fashionable life written by an American. In its June 14, 1890 essay on Mathews the *Dramatic Mirror* noted that he had been writing for that newspaper for the past two years and was rewriting the libretto of his comic opera entitled *The Great Mogul*. He was, as the article concluded, "patriotic, lofty in principle, able in literary composition and skillful as a conversationalist." That he should have been called the "Father of American Drama," however, stimulates the imagination. Yet, for his devotion to the America in which he believed and his strong support of American writers and playwrights, he seems as deserving as any of this title, which perhaps should be given to a dramatist writing during this age of national emphasis. His play of *Witchcraft*, in conception and execution, is one of the outstanding plays of early nineteenth-century America. In addition, Mathews wrote a history play and an undetermined number of comedies and satires on society, mainly during the early 1850s. Both the reality of life and the idea of romantic escape from life appealed, as they do in most societies, to Jacksonian Americans, and Mathews, ambitious for a national literature, stressed both concepts. Although he lacked great popular success and lost influence in literary circles soon after he was forty years old, he had the wit, a sufficient knowledge of theatre and a philosophy of creativity during his most productive years that distinguished him from his playwright colleagues and pointed to the developing dramatic art of distant and future generations of which his work gave promise.

H. J. Conway (1800–1860) was associated with theatres in Philadelphia, Boston and New York for his entire life—as prompter, as treasurer, and as playwright. If he made a living in this fashion, he was one of a kind. Eugene Page, editor of *America's Lost Plays* (vol. XIV), which includes Conway's *The Battle of Stillwater; or; The Maniac* (1840), lists twenty-nine plays by Conway. Eight were written and produced by 1843, but only two, *The Battle of Stillwater* and *Charles O'Malley; or, The Irish Dragoon* (1842), an adaptation of Charles Lever's popular novel of 1841, achieved marked success.[35] According to the *Spirit of the Times*, *Charles O'Malley* was "immense fun. . . . A story so full of bustling scenes and ludicrous situations could hardly fail to please upon the stage; and excepting a most deplorable forgetfulness of the text on the part of some of the actors, the piece went off with éclat."[36] After this thematically eclectic beginning, Conway showed a decided interest in dramatizing America and is the only dramatist in Jacksonian America, other than John Brougham, whose career became more successful after 1849.

The Battle of Stillwater, celebrating the famous Revolutionary War battle of October 1777, had all of the necessary ingredients for a popular melodrama—spectacles of battles, burning buildings and rocky passes, patriotic speeches, a love plot, a fine Yankee character, a maniac heroine, and a climax with the surrender of General Burgoyne beneath the American flag. Although much of the appeal of the play rested upon the vigorous action onstage, the character of Uzzial Putnam added an appropriate tone and is central to the plotting of the story. Soldiering does not appeal to him, but honor does:

By Satan, if it warn't for two or three things, I'd be off like a streak of lightning acrost a New Hampshire logging chain. One thing is sartin, I mustn't sneak off and leave Miss Rose and that poor critter, her sister, chin deep in a quagmire without a soul to help 'em out. No, I swough, it ain't Uzzial Putnam that lets such nasty notions to get the upper hand of him. By Judas, Luce Lambson wouldn't like that and she is one of the loveinest and slickest critters I've seen since Ben Hannaford's darter, Jerushy, died eatin' artichokes when she had the hipenudins. (II,1)

Conway would develop his Yankee character further in *Hiram Hireout* (1851), but at this early stage he could do little better than add patriotism to Yankee humor and a lovely heroine protected by the maniac. Harry Cotton is an American soldier whose capture by the British allows him the opportunity to speak:

"No, rebel I am none! I fight for my country and if we are true to her, the whole world will soon behold Liberty shake off her gatling chains! Our country will be free! I have done—lead me to death! (folds his arms)" (III,2). These were the strong emotions to which many Americans eagerly responded as they flexed their muscles against England and Canada in border disputes, reacted to an influx of Irish and German immigrants, and made determined stances against the social fettering brought on by slavery, intemperance and ignorance.

In Jacksonian America, these were the playwrights who appeared to be contributing most specifically to a new national drama in the terms of Paulding's plea: Custis, Field, Steele, Mathews and Conway. As they presented distinctive American characters whose idiosyncrasies reflected both their emotional responses to the society around them and their curiosity about the newly developing expanse of America in contrast to a more ordinary but changing urban life, these playwrights developed scenes and themes that helped to define the temper of the age. It might be foolhardy to argue that any of them—with the exception of Custis and Mathews—wrote with any purpose other than to entertain and make a living, but consciously or unconsciously, their awareness helps explain the belief in that special destiny embraced by many Jacksonian Americans. Their inclinations and practical sense, as well as the theatres for which they wrote, directed their efforts. Numerous other dramatists did the same, if on a lesser scale. As they tried to write for American theatre audiences, these dramatists sometimes responded to the same drummer that seduced Paulding and wrote of people, places and incidents that Americans, curious about their self-identity and their place in the larger framework of life, wanted to hear and to see.

Nathaniel Deering (1791–1881) lived in Maine and evidently enjoyed it. When William Cullen Bryant offered him a job with the New York *Evening Post* he declined. A lawyer, editor of the *Independent Statesman*, and a popular orator in Portland, he seemed satisfied with the considerable amount of very average prose and verse which he contributed to newspapers and periodicals of northern New England. He claimed to have written several plays, but the names of only three have survived. *Carabasset; or, The Last of the Norridgewocks* (1831) has a familiar ring to its title and was performed at least once in Portland. It is a long and labored tragedy in five acts, and Deering probably gathered his information during his brief law practice in Skowhegan, Maine. Using events surrounding the life of Sebastian Rasles, a Jesuit priest who worked some thirty years with the Norridgewock Indians before he was killed by the English in 1724, Deering developed the heroic qualities of the Indian leader Carabasset by dramatizing the events which led to what he termed a massacre. Deering's comedy, *The Clairvoyants*, acted in Portland and in Boston in 1844, was a slight piece which took advantage of the current interest in spiritualism.

Deering's most ambitious play, a five-act tragedy in blank verse entitled *Bozzaris* (1851) was yet another of those dramas stimulated by the Greek War of Independence against the Turks (1821–1832). Although the topic had considerable romantic appeal in America, Deering was neither historically accurate in recreating the Greek patriarch, Marco Bozzaris (c. 1788–1823), nor effective in adapting the character for the stage. As Bozzaris carries out attacks on the Turks, using the dead to inspire the living, he must contend with a traitor in his own camp and the disturbance caused by his daughter's love for one of his men. The plot could have held dramatic potential, but Deering was unable to dramatize his ideas effectively. He did manage, however, to intrude those nationalistic ideas which are also featured in his other known plays. Just before the ultimate battle for the sacred cause of Christendom, Bozzaris thanks those men who have come from far countries: "And from that distant land across the seas / Freedom's last home—the land of Washington" (IV,3).

In August of 1829, another Maine author, Henry W. Longfellow (1807–1882), returned from three years study in Europe. Ten years later he published his first collected volume of verse, *Voices of the Night*. Of his interest in writing plays, only *The Spanish Student* (1842) is generally mentioned, always with the apologetic claim that it was essentially a closet drama and never produced in America. Drama, however, held a certain fascination for Longfellow, who could write dialogue quite consistent with that produced by poetic dramatists during his lifetime and superior to the work of many of them. Longfellow also seemed to channel his creativity in terms of dramatic action, situations into which events intrude and crises mount to their inevitable climaxes.

Although there was little theatre in Portland and Brunswick, where he attended Bowdoin College, Longfellow became aware of its attractions early in his writing career. Edward Wagenknecht has suggested that Longfellow's "juvenile drama, *The Poor Student*, 1824, deserves immortality if only for its final stage direction: '*A corpse is precipitated over the waterfall*'. Whereupon the Second Peasant cries' 'Tis she! 'tis she!'—she being our broken-hearted heroine." [37] Such a climax fuses the gruesome nature of Pixerécourt's late plays with the American's interest in gothic gloom and the spectacles produced on American stages during the 1830s and 1840s. His youth past, Longfellow did not continue in this writing style, but he did continue to think in terms of dramatic form throughout his life, a fact clearly demonstrated in his "Book of Suggestions," a journal of ideas.

Spotlighted by Edward Wagenknecht in his *Portrait*, this "Book of Suggestions" shows that Longfellow had many ideas for works, not in poetry, but in fiction and drama. [38] On July 19, 1843, for example, he jotted down at some length an idea for a play concerned with "Some of the evil deeds done in the world by the supposed agency of the fairy personages." His outline indicates a play in three parts concerned with a search for the elixir of life, the Salem witchcraft persecutions and slavery. Certain contemporary events—that real life to which Jacksonian Americans eagerly responded and which was always a source for stage plays at this time—spurred Longfellow to consider several prose tragedies: "The Mormon Elder," suggested by a letter in the New York *Tribune* (February 9, 1835); "George Hammon," an issue raised by a trial at London's

Old Bailey (1840); "Elizabeth Wharton, a Tragedy in prose" (1850), to be based on the memoir of Hannah Foster, author of *The Coquette* (1797). Longfellow also thought of dramatizing Hawthorne's short story "The Birthmark," and among his entries there is a note about a Mexican drama called *Don Serafin; or, The Marquis of the Seven Churches*, in which he proposed to include scenes from the cockpit and the circus. Finally, there is the item dated May 25, 1839, in which Longfellow contemplates a play called *Jabez Doolittle; or, The First Locomotive*, in which he would use "The Dragon of Yankeeland" as a spectacle for sensation in every scene. Although conservative in taste, opposed to the "young Americans" and frequently reticent, Longfellow held an appeal for the common man through his narrative poems which, given other circumstances, might have been written for stage.

The play that Longfellow did write for the American stage was never produced there.[39] A note in Longfellow's diary for March 27, 1840, recalls his enthusiasm for the plays of Lope de Vega and, the following day, a determination to write a comedy himself, *The Spanish Student*. Spain and its literature would be a strong source of inspiration for Longfellow, although Wagenknecht states that Fanny Elssler, who was in 1840 the tyrannical darling of the American theatre, may have stimulated Longfellow to write the play.[40] The recent success in the theatre of Nathanial Parker Willis also attracted the attention of Longfellow who, at this time, praised Willis' efforts.

A romantic melodrama, primarily in blank verse, *The Spanish Student* has a plot of somewhat common intrigue, supplemented by songs, dances and opportunities for scenic splendor. The hero is Victorian, an inordinately romantic fellow in the fashion of the fictional hero of the period, who falls madly in love with Preciosa the Gypsy dancer.

> Goodnight! [he says]
> But not to bed; for I must sit and read awhile,
> Must read, or sit in revery and watch
> The changing colors of the waves that break
> Upon the idle seashore of the mind! (I,5)

The villain of the piece is the Count of Lara, a man who arrogantly assumes that he can seduce Preciosa. To complicate matters, Preciosa's father has promised her to Bartolome. Although there is considerable action in this play—a dance, a duel, a riot—much of it resulting from misunderstandings, there is no strong conflict left to be resolved in the last act, only some clarifications to be made. These accomplished, the couple ride off to happiness through a mountain pass, escaping an ambush by Bartolome, who is killed in the brief encounter. The best part of the drama is Longfellow's use of language.

In her essay on modern drama, Margaret Fuller listed *The Spanish Student* with Maturin's *Bertram* and Talford's *Ion* as somewhat between good acting drama and closet drama. She explained that "*The Spanish Student* might also be acted, though with no great effect, for there is little movement in the piece, or development of character; its chief merit is in the graceful expression of single thoughts or fancies."[41] Edgar Allan Poe also caused Longfellow some agony with his repeated accusations of plagiarism. The play, however, can boast some witty scenes, particularly in the first act in which Lara and Don Carlos talk about the Gypsy girl. With the villainy divided between Lara, whose death is only reported in Act III, and Bartolome who is poorly conceived, the play suffers from a lack of conflicting action and ends abruptly with the lovers' galloping through the symbolic mountain pass. Longfellow's efforts as a dramatist, in any event, do not warrant much attention. He was, after all, a poet, and would have had great difficulty writing for the mid–nineteenth-century American theatre. It is his interest in the dramatic form that is worthy of some consideration, and there is evidence that he had opportunity to make a greater impression upon American drama had he so wished. When Augustin Daly opened his New Broadway Theatre in November of 1873, for example, he offered the poet a "very handsome sum" to write an address for the opening night, but the offer was not accepted.[42] Prior to 1860, when William Winter (1836–1917) was interested in his own poetry, he had a lengthy correspondence with Longfellow, but the creative interaction between a major poet and a major theatre critic never came to pass.[43]

Among the major southern writers in Jacksonian America, two—Edgar Allan Poe (1809–1849) and Thomas H. Chivers (1809–1858)—attempted to write for the theatre, but their efforts brought little response or interest from theatre audiences. Poe published his first volume of poetry in 1827, *Tammerlane and Other Poems*, and began his career in earnest in 1831 when he left West Point. His single effort in drama was a poetic play entitled *Politian*, written in 1835 and published in fragmentary form. His source was the Kentucky tragedy of ten years earlier, which he transferred to seventeenth-century Rome while changing the heroine's avenger from husband to lover. Such a change, of course, was perfectly consistent with the times and with Poe's philosophy of poetic composition in which pleasure rather than truthfulness or reality, was the objective. Only Poe's subsequent reputation in American letters has kept this title in history books, and by publishing the fragments of a work he never felt inclined to complete, Poe revealed his own lack of interest in dramatic writing.

As a critic of American drama, however, Poe has a substantial place in the history of dramatic literature. He was, according to Cornelius Mathews, "one of the few iron-fisted critics in this country."[44] Through the years Poe's reputation as a stern critic did not falter, although his tendency to follow a certain narrow approach and mistake his own opinions for reality sometimes limited his overall effectiveness. After seeing *Fashion* through several performances, he became more aware of the actor's and the designer's contributions to a production and commented intelligently upon the actor's work, but he persisted in seeing the drama only from that idealized position in the theatre of the mind. He demanded substance as well as entertainment, showed little tolerance for masked silliness and tended to prefer plays that were good literature, rather than plays structured for a viewing audience. Even with this approach, which was intolerant of most plays written at this time, Poe made some astute observations—on *Fashion*, on *Tortesa the Usurer*—for the history of American dramatic criticism. Like another influential poet, essayist, and critic, Walt Whitman, Poe was particularly sensitive to the developing character of American drama.

Thomas Holley Chivers, a friend of Poe who shared something of his morbid point of view, was the first to dramatize the famous Kentucky tragedy involving Ann Cooke, who was seduced by Colonel Solomon P. Sharpe, a state legislator. When her brothers did not avenge her honor, Ann went to Bowling Green, fascinated Jereboan Beauchamp with her story and agreed to marry him if he would kill Sharpe. They were married in June of 1824, and on November 6, 1825, Beauchamp called on Sharpe, who had previously refused his challenge to a duel, and stabbed him to death. Trial brought conviction. Allowed to spend one night with Beauchamp in his cell, Ann brought laudanum and a caseknife for a double suicide, but when the laudanum did not work, she stabbed herself. Beauchamp was hanged after writing a flamboyant confession. From this history, Chivers devised a play in five acts—Seduction, Vow, Murder, Trial, Execution—with stereotypical characters, somewhat confused dialogue and excessive use of metaphor. Ann became Eudora, Beauchamp became Conrad and Sharpe became a thoroughly detestable villain called Alonzo. Chivers first published his work as *Conrad and Eudora; or, The Death of Alonzo*, "a tragedy in five acts founded on the murder of Sharpe by Beauchamp in Kentucky, 1834." Later, in 1838–1839, Chivers rewrote the play as *Leoni; or, The Orphan of Venice*, taking his title from the two best-known Otway plays and publishing his new version in the *Georgia Citizen* on May 17, 24 and 31 and June 7 and 14, 1851. Ann now became Leoni and Beauchamp became Alvino, her childhood sweetheart. The play, which was somewhat improved in verse, remains erratic in action and ends with a double suicide.

Samuel Foster Damon, Chivers' biographer, states that Chivers wrote several plays but that none were acted, and only two were published.[45] Chivers himself appears to have been a strange and unpredictable man—ambitious, gloomy, egotistical, yet a man of his time, caught up in phrenology, spiritualism and hypnotic healing. William G. Simms called Chivers "the Wild Mazeppa of letters," and in *Graham's Magazine* (December 1841) Chivers was referred to as one of the best and one of the worst poets in America.[46] The strange character of his work is revealed in a late publication entitled *The Sons of Usna: Tragi-Apotheosis*, a five-act play written before 1854 and published in 1858. It deals with Coffa, the grandfather of Daidra of the Milesian legend, his defeat of Lucifer and apotheosis through love of man and God. Although some of the poetry is exciting, there is little action to relieve the moralistic tone of this complicated story, so filled with the mysterious meanderings of Chivers' mind.

Charlotte Barnes Conner (1818–1863) was the daughter of Mr. and Mrs. John Barnes, popular comic actors who came to America in 1816. Although she found the material for some of her plays in America, she understood that the Jacksonian American was also fascinated by unfamiliar people and places. Brought up in the shadow of theatres and first presented onstage at a young age, Conner enjoyed a long acting career, marrying an actor herself, E. S. Conner, in 1847. Her experiences in the theatre were an obvious advantage in developing the technical skills of dramatic construction, but although she considered herself a writer, she frequently lacked facility in language.

Her first play, *Octavia Brigaldi; or, The Confession*, was performed in New York in November of 1837, and according to the author, was played more than fifty times in America and England. In her preface to the published "laboriously revised" version in her *Plays, Prose and Poetry*, Conner noted that her youthful age of nineteen years and her parents' reputation clearly helped the play's reception. She also indicated that many of the incidents in the play— Castelli's desertion of Octavia, her subsequent marriage, the challenge, the slander and murder at Octavia's instigation, the climax in which both she and Brigaldi die—were based on actual events occuring in Frankfurt, Kentucky, in 1825.[47] This was the celebrated Kentucky tragedy of passion, which has inspired the creation of more literature than any other American crime. Thomas H. Chivers' *Conrad and Eudora* (1834) was available to Conner, as well as Poe's *Politian* (1835). While Chivers did not disguise his source, Conner, like Poe, preferred the camouflaged foreign scene.

The published version of *Octavia Brigaldi*, the best of her work, is a well-structured play with some excellent scenes. Set at Brigaldi's mansion in Milan sometime near the end of the sixteenth century, the play opens with Octavia's explanation of her unfortunate marriage to Castelli, the news of his death in battle and her subsequent happiness with Brigaldi. But Castelli lives and is re-married, and Octavia's tragedy begins as she pleads with Castelli to recant the lie he has told about her wantonness in an attempt to defend his past actions. Angered by his weakness, she curses his stubborn refusal:

> May thy wife's fame unjustly be destroyed,
> And thou be scorned, unable to refute
> The falsehood!—Oh, may children bear thy name
> And break their father's heart, as I for thee
> Broke mine. May every plague, save madness, haunt
> Thee! Mayst thou pray, like me, for madness, as
> A blessing! May death, though sought, long shun thee,
> And when he doth approach bring ling'ring anguish
> Great as the pangs that torture my brain now! (II.3)

Although not comparable to Metamora's curse, or many great curses in literature, Octavia's curse has an energy that shows the character of the heroine. After accomplishing the murder urged by Octavia, Brigaldi confesses and kills himself in prison, and Octavia, the traditional heroine of heroic tragedy, dies insane. Conner built her action carefully, and as an indication of her faith in her work, opened her engagement at London's Surrey Theatre in 1844 with *Octavia Brigaldi*.

Among Charlotte Barnes Conner's plays that exist only by title are *La Fitte*, a dramatization of J. H. Ingraham's novel, a popular source for adaptation, which opened at the New Orleans Theatre in 1837 with Conner herself playing the young romantic male lead; *A Night of Expectations* (1848), an adaptation of a French novel; and *Charlotte Corday* (1851), from Lamartine's *Histoire des Girondins* and Dunamoir and Clairville's *Charlotte Corday*. *The Forest Princess; or, Two Centuries Ago*, a historical play about Jamestown and the Pocahontas legend published in *Plays, Prose and Poetry*, was first acted in Liverpool in 1844.[48] Conner was pleased with her research in the British Museum for this play, and the result is interesting mainly for the final act, which takes place in 1617 England. Having failed in his expedition, Raleigh must answer to King James, and Rolfe becomes involved. Through the pleading of Pocahontas, however, and the help of Charles (who will be Charles I), Rolfe is released. The plays ends as Pocahontas, wanting to return to America where "rich redundant nature reigns alone," has a vision of Time and Peace, the Lion and the Eagle and Washington with the Genius of Columbia. Combining romance, sentiment and patriotism, Conner climaxes her play with the death of Pocahontas. Both of her plays are typical of the poetic drama of the period, made more stageworthy than the usual fare through Conner's combined knowledge of practical theatre and poetic expression.

Records of theaters in New Orleans are scattered with references to native dramatists, and one of the most successful during this period was George Washington Harby (1797–1862). Originally from Charlestown, the brother of Isaac Harby who was also a playwright, Harby appears to have spent much of his adult life as a schoolteacher, mainly in New Orleans after 1828. During his mature years Harby wrote at least ten plays, none of which was published. *Tutoona; or, The Battle of Saratoga* (1835), his best-known play, exists in manuscript form as *Tutoona; or, The Indian Girl*.[49] At the play's premiere in the American Theatre of New Orleans (February 22, 1835), a reviewer for the *Louisiana Advertiser* commented on the beauty of the prologue as well as the extravagant Indian scenes and spectacular escapes that distinguished contemporary melodrama. James Rees considered *Tutoona* one of the best American melodramas, superior even to that very popular play, *She Would Be a Soldier* by Mordecai Noah.[50]

Tutoona has a dual plot concerned with (1) the retaking of Fort Edward and the defeat of the British General Burgoyne at Saratoga by the American General Gates and (2) the revenge of an Indian chief, Copper Snake, upon an Indian named Mantogo who attempted the life of his daughter, Tutoona. These two actions are merged through the device of Indian warriors who fight on the side of the Americans with the assistance of a backwoodsman called Doyle or Old Hunter. Interestingly enough, patriotism is served before the Indian revenge theme reaches it climax. Scene 3 in Act V shows the last of the military action as the British and American troops fight, and the victory is celebrated in a speech by General Gates: "Let us hope that the day is not far distant when the whole world will acknowledge the Independence of the United States of America, and when peace and prosperity shall preside o'er 'Columbia's happy land.' " Scene 5 dramatizes the Indian revenge and reveals Harby's skills in creating the kind of Indian melodrama that Jacksonian audiences enjoyed. The scene is a holy place, "the red stake," where Mantogo comes in his canoe to mull over his problem:

This is the last time Mantogo will look upon the grave of his father. Their bones should lie in the same earth, but a panther is on Mantogo's track—the mighty Copper Snake will follow him. Fool, why did I not take surer aim? Tutoona lives and my disgrace is on me. A woman struck a warrior and she lives! The time will come when Mantogo will have revenge.

Silently, Copper Snake enters, watches Mantogo, refusing to kill him while he is praying. Then, they recognize each other, agree to use only knives and fight until Copper Snake hurls Mantogo to the earth, disarms him and holds him there:

Copper Snake: The panther has the false-heart now. He would have killed his young! Beg not for mercy. He never parts with his prey alive.

Mantogo: Mantogo can sit in the panther's den although he knows the beast will tear him to pieces.

Copper Snake: Has he sung his death-song?

Mantogo: His death-song is sung—strike, chief, strike.

(Copper Snake plunges his knife into Mantogo's heart, who falls prostrate, dead.)

Copper Snake: (Kneeling upon the body.) Ha! Ha! Ha! The vision is true!

(At this moment, enter Tutoona, Mary, Major Scott, Colonel Thomas and Doyle.)

See Tutoona is revenged.

(Rising. The company form a picture and the play closes.)

With this climax Harby brought his plot to a conclusion that would satisfy his audience by revealing the romance of savage passions in noble conflict. Good Christian that he is, Copper Snake embodies many of the admired characteristics of the Jacksonian hero. Although this play is hardly of the stature that Paulding envisioned, it is thoroughly in tune with the romantic American vision that inspired the painters of American wilderness, the composers of folk songs and romantic outbursts and the novelists who created western heroes and frontier romances.

Harby received excellent reviews for his adaptation of Bird's *Nick of the Woods*, which became one of the most successful plays of the 1837–1838 season at the American Theatre in New Orleans. Reviewers saw it as superior to the novel in plot and character and praised Harby's imagination. It is one of those strange coincidences that Harby's version opened in Natchez just a few days before Medina's extremely popular adaptation was premiered at Hamblin's Bowery Theatre in New York. The *Spirit of the Times* took note of Harby's work: "A new play is to be brought out shortly at New Orleans. . . . Mr. George W. Harby, favorably known to the community as the successful author of *Tutoona*, has dramatized, with some happy alterations, Dr. Bird's novel of *Nick of the Woods*, and placed it in the hands of Mr. Parsons for performance. . . . The ability with which Mr. Harby's first play was written, offers us a pleasing guarantee of the success of the present effort."[51] Later produced in Philadelphia, St. Louis and other American cities, Harby's *Nick of the Woods* became his best-known work.

On April 1, 1838, the St. Charles Theatre in New Orleans produced James Rees' *The Squatter* and Harby's *The Deceived*, a domestic drama which the *Louisiana Courier* (April 14, 1838) described as "a sorrowing tale, well told."[52] Other plays recorded as written by Harby include *Minka; or, The Russian Daughter*; *Mohammed*; *Stephanie, the Robber Girl*; *Azzo*; *Abou Hassan*; *The Gentleman in Black* and *Twenty Years' Life as a Courtesan*—titles that suggest the eclectic nature of Harby's interests. He appears to have had no particular mission as a playwright, nor was he a pretender to great dramatic literature, although he seems to have been well read. Reflecting the curiosity and temper of the time, Harby wrote to please a passing public with foreign fancies, romantic trifles and local views.

The actor-playwright of this period who made the most significant contributions to American dramatic literature was Nathanial H. Bannister (1813–1847), unquestionably American in his outlook and professionally trained to take advantage of the various and fickle fashions of the American theatre. Born in Baltimore, Bannister began his acting career in 1829, eventually performing at the Chatham and Bowery theatres in New York during the 1830–1831 season and in Philadelphia at the Arch Street Theatre the following season. In the fall of 1834 he joined the acting company at the American Theatre in New Orleans and was asked to deliver the address that opened the theatre that season. The following year he wrote at least five plays, married an actress, the widow of John Augustus Stone, and became established as a major writer and actor in New Orleans. During his final season in that city, he joined his wife at the St. Charles Theatre. By the fall of 1837, however, the Bannisters were in Philadelphia at the Walnut Street Theatre and in New York acting at both the Bowery Theatre, until it was destroyed by fire on February 18, 1838, and the Franklin Theatre, where Bannister remained throughout the 1838–1839 season. For the following season he was associated with the Chatham Theatre before returning to the new Bowery, where he wrote plays and acted until his death in 1847.

Although an active playwright, Bannister was not well paid during his short life, nor has he been adequately evaluated by historians. Presumably, he received no payment for many of the plays he wrote in New Orleans, and he sold his most popular play—*Putnam, The Iron Son of '76*—for $50. Like so many of his profession, he died a poor man. One wonders about the thoughts of Mrs. Bannister, twice widowed in poverty. Theatre historians record the titles of more than forty plays that Bannister wrote during a period of about twelve years. Undoubtedly, he wrote more plays, and in many of them acted with distinction. At least one of his plays was written for Forrest, and several were written for the actor and tragedian Charles B. Parsons. Although Joseph Ireland, a historian of the American theatre, questions Bannister's "judgement" as a playwright, he noted that his work was "always powerful, vigorous and original"[53]—qualities typically attributed to and admired by Jacksonians.

A thoughtful, well-read and intelligent man, Bannister was distinctively American among the actor-playwrights. Did he reflect Jacksonian America? A letter in the Historical Society of Pennsylvania includes a poem by Bannister (October 27, 1842) that reveals his answer:

> Say is the drama useful to mankind?
> Doth it corrupt or cultivate the mind?
> That question answered during ages past
> By Milton, Pope, Gay, Congreve, Shakespeare, last
> Their merits granted e'en Fanatics will say
> Good acts must hallow e'en the Sabbath day.
> Mark well the poets' words and we've no choice
> "The stage but echoes back the Public Voice."[54]

With few exceptions, Bannister tried always to follow the "Public Voice" that was America. Satisfaction, however, frequently eluded him. Although his achievements were not judged fairly by East Coast critics, who disdained theatre from any other parts of America, his plays are generally superior to those of his contemporary actor-playwrights and equal or superior to much of the work of the literary dramatists.

The year before Bannister's death, a reviewer for the *Spirit of the Times* described him as "a gentleman who claims the paternity of more plays of every class, than any previous writer. He possesses peculiar powers for arranging terrific plots and for disposing spectacles to the best effect, and is therefore a valuable adjunct to the Bowery management whose facilities for presenting plays of this nature are so immense."[55] The play under consideration was Bannister's *Arasapha*, an Indian drama featuring real horses and real water, and the reviewer placed Bannister accurately among the best of the creators of stage spectacle. Those critics who did not enjoy his plays generally did not enjoy the kind of theatrical entertainment produced at the Bowery and comparable New York theatres. In 1844 a critic for the *Spirit* had—ironically, as it turned out—commended Bannister on his ability to write plays that attracted audiences and made money for him. This critic compared Bannister unfavorably to such English writers as Jerrold, Planché and Lemon whose plays were freely stolen by American managers. "But," he recanted somewhat, "by a merciful providence

British writers do not dramatize Bunker Hill and the Taking of Cornwallis, and these sole subjects were instantly monopolized by the author of *Putnam*, and we will say, we have seen worse pieces than his even on the Park stage.''[56] Perhaps the most telling point is Bannister's success. *Putnam, the Iron Son of '76*, for example, first ran for seventy-eight nights and remained a favorite stage attraction for years. Also, six of Bannister's plays were published, one, *Gaulantas*, in a collection of four plays with Planché's *The Brigand*, Sheridan's *Pizarro* and Payne's *Brutus*.

Theatre and drama historians have not been any kinder to Bannister than were theatre managers of his day. Montrose Moses makes no judgment; Quinn dismisses him as the author of hastily written melodramas. For some reason historians have refused to acknowledge Bannister's career in New York theatres, but records indicate that he arrived at the Bowery in September of 1837, and maintained a connection with it and other New York theatres until his death ten years later. Although largely ignored, Bannister's plays reveal him as a writer of the spectacular melodrama that people flocked to see as well as of traditional and experimental plays. In both his acting and writing he dared to attempt new and different approaches. During a career that lasted only seventeen years—he was thirty-four when he died—he established an excellent reputation in the South and West as well as a popular presence in New York.

In contrast to most of his contemporary actor-playwrights, Bannister wrote mainly original plays. Occasionally, he adapted current fiction. *Rookwood* (1844), a dramatization of William Harrison Ainsworth's famous novel of the same name and date, was described as abounding ''in startling incidents and clever stage effects,'' probably referring to Dick Turpin's famous ride on his mare, Black Bess.[57] Another Bannister play which featured a horse, *Conaneheotah; or, The Indian's War Horse* (1838, 1841), was based on a story in *Blackwood's*. Although such adaptations were not usual with Bannister, they were successful. Commenting on *Conaneheotah*, the critic for the *Dramatic Mirror* declared that ''Bannister as an *actor* and *author* ranks deservedly high, and one more indefatigable in either profession it would be difficult to find.''[58] Clearly a hardworking professional in the theatre, Bannister took chances in good Jacksonian tradition. In what must have been a fascinating melodrama, Bannister's *Destruction of Jerusalem* (1837), in which he portrayed Judas, contrasted good and evil spirits in ways that so disturbed audiences that the theatre manager, Francis Wemyss, withdrew it after six nights. He also rearranged and adapted *Titus Andronicus*, playing the lead character; his version of *The Wandering Jew* consisted of fifteen acts. He was not easily· daunted, nor is the scope of his imagination easily described.

Most of Bannister's plays are known by title only, but those that do exist suggest his broad interests, his determination to respond to that ''Public Voice'' as well as his ambition to write serious plays and use the language of the poets. The history of Rome has provided the stimulus for a number of plays by American writers, and Bannister also responded to that ancient drummer. *Caius Sil-*

ius; or, The Slave of Carthage (1835), a tragedy, gained some popularity in the Midwest; *Rathaimus the Roman* (1835), a five-act tragedy, premiered in New Orleans; another title, *The Roman Slave*, Rees identifies as a five-act tragedy written for Charles B. Parsons;[59] *The Saracusan Brothers* appeared in 1838. *Gaulantus the Gaul* (1836), a five-act tragedy in poetry first produced in Cincinnati, was one of Bannister's early attempts to write plays that could be read with as much pleasure as they could be watched in the theatre. Although the verse is of uneven quality, the play has both a moving spirit and exciting scenes, particularly in the final act. As the effort of a twenty-three-year-old playwright, the story of Gaulantus, heroic leader of the Gauls, was worthy of encouragement.

Filled with despair at his defeat by the Romans and the loss of Leonida, his wife, to Carmitus, the Roman leader, Gaulantus plans his revenge while Carmitus, concerned with winning the affection of Leonida, loses his taste for battle. The slowly developing situation changes, however, in Act V when Carmitus, in a fit of anger against a comrade who has called him a "love-sick girl," repents his weakness and marshals his forces. Although he is the villain of the play, Carmitus has a sense of honor that makes his hand-to-hand fight with Gaulantus a scene of moving pathos as Gaulantus struggles with Leonida's adoring tormentor and then dies of his battle wounds. With its traditionally heroic protagonist and sensitive antagonist, *Gaulantus the Gaul* held more promise than many of the works by better known writers that frequently received the eager indulgence of the Park Theatre management and its puffers.

An experimenter and an imaginative writer, Bannister was still a man of the theatre, always eager to please audiences and management. When Yankee actors wanted vehicles, he wrote *The Yankee Duelist; or, Bunker Hill's Representative* (1838). When national issues erupted, such as the argument between the United States and Canada which threatened violence concerning the northern border of Maine, Bannister wrote *The Maine Question* (1839). He also dramatized national and local issues in *Murrell the Western Land Pirate*, *The Land Pirate; or, Yankee in Mississippi*, *Texas and Freedom* and *The Fall of San Antonio; or, Texas Victorious* (1836). In this last play a company of United States troopers appeared onstage and two characters did an Indian war dance. Two of his titles that catch the imagination are *The Bushwhacker* and *The Old Waggoner of New Jersey and Virginia*. Understanding his audiences' unwaning curiosity about heroes from distant lands and times past—heroic romances of faraway places—Bannister wrote *Two Spaniards* (1838); *Alvara of Spain*; *Chief of the McIvor*; *Robert Emmett* (1840); and *Psammelichus; or, The Twelve Tribes of Egypt*. He was also capable of writing light comedy as in *Infidelity; or, The Husband's Return* (1837), and a farce entitled *The Three Brothers; or, Crime Its Own Avenger* (1840), as well as farces on city themes such as *Life in New Orleans* and *Life in Philadelphia; or, The Unfortunate Author* (1838).

England's Iron Days, a five-act tragedy dedicated to "Edwin Forrest Esq. (Comedian)," was published in New Orleans in 1837. Having arrived in New

Orleans "some five years back," Bannister noted in a preface that he used this publication to thank his friends for their support and to pray that "the literary and commercial interests of this country may continue to flourish," appropriate sentiments of a serious dramatist.[60] As Lord Edgar, a bastard son and a villain, waits to be crowned king of England with Elgina as his bride, he senses impending disaster. Challenged by Alaster, the man Elgina loves, he makes plans to kill Wilfred, his half-brother, who has returned to England in disguise. Lord Edgar's paid ruffians, however, are overcome by the combined efforts of Wilfred and Alaster. In tournament battle Wilfred, disguised as Alaster, disarms Edgar who, although Wilfred forgives him, kills himself in agony over his own guilt. As an attempt to dramatize a page from English history, the play's strength lies mainly in a few well-structured scenes. Bannister evidently wanted to write for Forrest, as he did for Parsons, but neither this play nor *Psammelichus*, which Rees says was intended for Forrest, was destined to become part of that actor's repertory.[61]

The Gentleman of Lyons; or, The Marriage Contract (1838) is a melodrama in five acts, dedicated to "James H. Caldwell, the founder of the drama in the southern states," where Bannister and his wife played leading roles in the theatres. He undoubtedly took the title from Bulwer-Lytton's *The Lady of Lyons*, which first appeared in London that same year, but claimed in his preface that when he first saw *The Lady of Lyons* he already had in a "crude unfinished state" a brief drama entitled *The Jeweller's Son* that resembled Lytton's work.[62] Bannister's plot follows the progress of Julian, a poor but ambitious jeweller's son who is bitter toward the world. Unfortunately, Julian loves above his station, the object of his adoration being Adelaide, the daughter of the Count of Valcour. A secondary plot is concerned with Dorval, who has been contracted by his father to marry a rich heiress whom Dorval thinks must be ugly, although he has never seen her. An exuberant fellow, Dorval falls in love with Ernestine, a friend of Adelaide, without realizing that she is, in fact, his betrothed. Although the still youthful Bannister frequently indulged in stiff and heroic prose and poetry, the play includes some very witty scenes such as the following in which Dorval and a friend, Captain Dupuis, visit the young ladies.

Adelaide: Captain, you are welcome back to Lyons. My dear Ernestine, Captain Dupuis.

Captain: 'Tis an honor I am proud of. From Paris, I believe? A glorious and animated city. I'm afraid that you will find Lyons very dull.

Ernestine: So are our spirits; yet they may be rendered keen by wheting, and to your skillful hands we commit them.

Captain: The school of mirth is now the assembly of beauty, and here I consider myself a pupil.

Adelaide: What news have you, Captain?

Captain: None, Lady—the world is still in its beggarly costume, and it seems that neither the eloquence of morality, nor the misery of the tailors can persuade her to buy a new suit. Poverty is as meager as ever—charity, as cold as a Russian winter—and mercy as lean as a skeleton.

Ernestine: How does talent stand in the market?

Captain: It is not marketable at all—and yet scarce, for it has been nearly all starved to death. Honesty is likewise very scarce—modesty is stored away as unavailable—but vice and folly are abundant and still looking up. (II,3)

Among these characters only Dorval is ignorant of Ernestine's true identity and, of course, she is determined to punish him for his impudent assumption concerning her appearance.

Captain: Dorval was my companion. Poor fellow, Cupid and his followers have been battering at his breast, and his heart is entirely gone, and if I mistake not, this Lady has charge of it.

Ernestine: I have charge of it! I wouldn't have such a fickle thing as a man's heart in my possession for the world. (II,3)

Bannister's skill in creating dialogue and character in *The Gentleman of Lyons* shows remarkable improvement over his past work. He was prudent in disclaiming Bulwer-Lytton's play as his model, and a comparison of the two works reveals the Englishman simply as a more sophisticated writer of melodrama.

In Act III Dorval discovers his "angel" while the villain of the play, Valmont, kidnaps Adelaide after she refuses his suit. At this point a new character is introduced: the once banished brother of the Count of Valcour, the Duke of Valcour, philanthropist and "gentleman of Lyons" who escaped Lyons with his daughter while leaving his son with a friend. The scene changes to Italy, where Julian, disguised as a shepherd, has rescued Adelaide and won her love before the Duke of Valcour presses reality upon the lovers. Back in France (Act V) years later, Julian discovers a "mystery document" in which his mother, now dead, reveals that she was not his mother and that his real mother and father were rich and noble. By this time Valmont is dead and Ernestine has become Lady Dorval. The final scene of the play is a grand ball at which everyone hears the lute song that Julian, disguised as a shepherd, once played for Adelaide. Masked, Julian approaches Adelaide and explains that Julian is "no more." Then the "mystery document" is read: Julian is the son of the Duke of Valcour, the "gentleman of Lyons." Julian then throws off his disguise, receives Adelaide from the count and, without regard for their family ties, expostulates on the impartial fate that brought about a happy ending.

At various times throughout the play, in keeping with Jacksonian views and Paulding's plea, Bannister emphasizes the theme of democratic man, an idea suggested again in the final scene: Julian's comment that little distinguishes those who build the throne from those who sit upon it. Julian, originally played by Bannister, is a reasonably well-defined character, and Ernestine, originally played by Mrs. Bannister, is a pert and witty young woman. Clearly not an imitation

of Bulwer-Lytton's work, *The Gentleman of Lyons* stands by itself as one of
the more skillfully crafted plays written by an American during this period.

Consistent with the popular craving of Jacksonian theatre audiences for glimpses
of American history on stage, Bannister's best-known and most successful work
is *Putnam, The Iron Son of '76*. To achieve his success Bannister combined
two techniques employed by playwrights that were certain to attract theatregoers: a patriotic theme and horses on stage. The first, of course, properly ma-
nipulated along with God and motherhood, has a rich history in the theatre. The
second might be traced either to the Roman circus or the Mongolian dancing
horses and had recently proved to be exceedingly popular in America—the brief
success of the Lafayette Equestrian Theatre, the use of the horse in *Mazeppa*,
the occasional appearances of a stud of horses on stage or Bannister's own use
of the United States troopers in his play about San Antonio. It is fair to say,
however, that *Putnam*, a military drama in three acts, inspired a tradition in
American theatre that held audiences fascinated for several years, and Bannister
deserved credit for his imagination and sense of theatricality. *Putnam* was immediately successful upon its opening at the Bowery Theatre on August 5, 1844,
and theatre pirates began their work within two months. The Bowery manager,
Thomas Hamblin, was moved to publish a notice stating that the original national spectacle of *Putnam* was his exclusive property, "made so by Copy-Right,
having been acted at no other than the Bowery Theatre, for which establishment it was written." [63] Although Hamblin's bold assertion had no legal backing as far as copyright was concerned, he had paid for the play and the playwright had little recourse but to humor his authority,[64] even if pirates flaunted
it.

Putnam begins with a vision showing the Goddess of War and the Goddess
of Liberty in Roman chariots. As the curtain opens with the chorus singing "our
tyrant shall tremble, we will be free," a lion and an eagle descend from the
flies and the goddesses point to tableaux showing Benjamin Franklin and others
signing the Declaration of Independence and Washington meeting with Generals Putnam, Cadwallander and Greene. The chorus then sings "Hail our Chief,
the Mighty Washington"; the clouds are drawn away, and an American flag
appears. The play now begins.

The scene is a village where William is preparing to leave his beloved Clara
to fight for his country. As she gives him little mementos and he sings of wanting a wife, guns sound and all go "upstage as Putnam dashes on horseback,
leaps the gate, and falls on stage covered with blood. William secures the horse."

Clara: Dear uncle, you are wounded.

Putnam: A mere flea-bite. Arm, boys, arm! the white skins and red skins are upon us!
the war kettle boils! Three cheers, and upon them!

(Music. Indians rush on; one seizes Clara and is shot by Naragantah. Renegade seizes
Clara who is saved by Putnam. As British appear, he mounts his horse.) (I,1)

As the battle rages, William is captured by the Indians, while Putnam carries Clara away on his horse.

Having assaulted the audience with strong action, Bannister now used his next two scenes in Act I for comic relief. A henpecked Cabbageall complains bitterly as he is forcibly inducted into the army by a Yankee officer, Jedidiah, who addresses Cabbageall as a "red-nosed, hatchet-faced, sneaking son of a racoon" and marches him off to join Putnam (I,4). (In the original stage version the husband was a timorous tailor named Hadaway, and the Yankee captain, played by Hamblin, was called Davenport.) The third element of the plot involves the Indians, who are presented sympathetically, perhaps in deference to the popularity of *Metamora* and Edwin Forrest, on whom J. R. Scott, the impersonator of Bannister's Indian chief, Oneactah, is reported to have modeled his acting.[65] Oneactah has taken Clara from the Renegade who had somehow captured her. "I once had a plant like thee," Oneactah says, "and as it bloomed and opened the leaves of its loveliness, it withered beneath the smooth skin's smile and died" (I,5). Dignified and mighty, Oneactah protects Clara from the man who would kill her—"Tempt not the fury of the panther, or his claws will be dyed in thy blood"—only to be told that Putnam has stolen his son. A chase now begins as Putnam on Black Vulture races across the bridge with the Indian boy, followed by Oneactah riding Maneto. (Bannister's sense of humor may be showing in the name he gave his Indian hero—One act ah!)

The first scene of Act II dramatizes the confrontation between Oneactah, who fights for the British, and Putnam, who changes his attitude toward the Indian chief and confers with him over a bottle of whiskey and some venison. Scene 2 introduces Oneactah's daughter, Naragantah (called Violetah in the original production), now a prisoner of the British, who explains that it was the Renegade who persuaded her father to fight the Americans. She impresses her captors with her sophistication, gained, she reveals, "from the universal book of nature, bound by the green sward of my native hills, paged by the leaves of my native forests, and imprinted on my memory by the god of my people" (II,2). In Act II Bannister disposes of the evil Renegade, whose attempt to kill General Washington and his staff is thwarted by Clara and Naragantah. Oneactah then arrives in time to save his Indian followers and condemn the Renegade they once served. By his action Oneactah is united with his son and Naragantah and is awarded the Renegade who, marched off by Jedidiah, soon hangs from a tree: "Behold a traitor's doom!" Maintaining his interest in the noble Indian, Bannister uses the first scene of Act III to show Washington apologizing to the Indians before riding off to rally his army.

The seven scenes in Act III allow a great deal of diverse action while challenging the skills of the stage carpenters and machinists. This act features Putnam, who executes a clever and exciting escape from the British. As a prisoner, Putnam refuses to give his name and is approached by Cornwallis, who offers him £1,000 and his freedom if he will help capture Putnam. Delighted with the prospect, Putnam makes a bargain to which all drink: "The continental flag that waves over the sons of freedom'' (III,2). Cabbageall and Jedidiah, by now prisoners, provide some humor at this point, and Putnam saves Clara from some lascivious British soldiers who are also reprimanded by Cornwallis for being ungentlemanly. Putnam then escapes on a horse provided by Oneactah.

Scene 5 presents the major spectacle of the play: ''The whole extent of the stage runs from Paintroom, L.H. to R.H.; a rocky hedge from flies to E.R.H., down on to stage C., for Putnam to descend on horseback during scene, with tree on it to cut down.'' When Cornwallis discovers that the British guns have been spiked, he orders the soldiers to cut the tree and block Putnam's route. ''Putnam dashes down the hedge from the flies R.H.U.E., leaps the tree and off.'' Even after this spectacular scene there was plenty of excitement. Washington addresses the soldiers—''Yorktown is before us''—and Putnam again dashes across the stage on Black Vulture as Oneactah swears to protect Clara (III,6). Scene 7 is set on the battlefield: ''Red fire for the whole scene, and drums and trumpets.'' Finally, Washington appears on horseback, and the stage scene recreates the celebrated painting of the surrender of Cornwallis: ''Happy Termination Of The War Of The Revolution And Triumph Of The American Arms!''

Putnam well illustrates the spectacular melodrama of the period. Audiences enjoyed it nightly, particularly the famous run on horseback from the top of the theatre, 150 feet in height, down the rocky steps of Horse Neck. With sentiment, Indians and a plot in which a traitor is hanged and the villainous British are both duped and defeated, Bannister provided an exciting evening in the theatre. Although Putnam is the title character and is constantly dashing across the stage, he has fewer lines than Washington, who is clearly a major force in the play. With certain skill, Bannister created the necessary action for his contemporary theatre and carefully wove into his patriotic plot popular secondary themes of love and adventure. Characterization was not a strong point, but neither was it necessary. Although Bannister did not show exceptional facility with language in this play, he used dramatic irony well, carefully regulated the pace of his play and was particularly sensitive to the kind of action and tableaux that audiences wanted to see.

The success of the play immediately encouraged imitations on other American stages. Such past equestrian spectacles as *Saint George and the Dragon*, a hit at the National Theatre in the spring of 1837, and *Mazeppa* had started the fad. Bannister himself had exploited the horse in *Conaneheotah* (1838). With some insight, critics declared that the real hero of *Putnam* was Black Vulture, and this trained horse was, indeed, at the beginning of a spectacular career. In mid-November of 1844, a play entitled *Revolution; or, The Yeoman of '76* opened at the Bowery. A ''soul stirring and enthusiastically written production'' in four acts with ''a goodly number of skirmishes, one or two downright battles and a half-dozen prison escapes,'' the anonymous play followed the life of General Marion. A contemporary critic declared that ''the celebrated horse, Black Vulture, is a prominent actor in those scenes of battle and foray, and performs many bold and daring feats, alike creditable to his rider and trainer."[66] On February 12, 1845, James Rees' *Mad Anthony Wayne* was produced at the Park Theatre, that bastion of legitimate drama that on occasion bowed to box office demands. Another patriotic equestrian spectacle, according to the *Spirit of the Times'* reviewer, it began "with a mother's whine and ended off a shower of red fire and a bloody battle."[67] Six weeks later it played at the Bowery Theatre where it was more appreciated. Again Black Vulture was the attraction, "making a rapid and dangerous descent from the ceiling of the theatre down to the very footlights—a feat unequalled in the annals of equestrianism."[68]

"There was always more or less novelty about equestrian dramas, and the visitors of the Bowery are just the people to appreciate them; no class know more about horses, or have a greater admiration of their sagacity. A well trained horse to the mass is a subject of a very grateful contemplation."[69] This was the opinion of a reviewer for the *Spirit of the Times* in the late spring of 1849 as he watched a grand equestrian drama entitled *Mike Margin, the Bold Robber and Highwayman*. Earlier that spring, J. H. Hall played the hero, Otahontas, and rode his famous steed, Arbaces, in *Eagle Eye*, a play he also had authored. In spite of the inevitable mishaps, such as the one noted in the *Spirit* of March 12, 1853, when "the noble charger was guilty of an indiscretion," the rage for horses onstage continued for many years. In 1874, for example, Kate Foster and her horse, Wonder, performed in *Mazeppa*, *Eagle Eye*, *Three Fast Men*, *Putnam* and another great spectacle entitled *The Catarach of the Ganges*.

Bannister inspired much of this popularity, but his contribution to the development of American drama does not end here. Although he was an actor who wrote plays for his own talents, the kind of plays he wrote suggests his ambitions for the theatre in America. Obviously creating plays for the moment, he always tried to respond to the "Public Voice" with themes and approaches that illustrate an interest in contributing substantially to a new tradition of distinctively American drama. All of Bannister's extant plays include dramatic scenes and stirring situations, necessary for the stage of this time, while *Putnam*, *The Gentleman of Lyons* and the last act of *Gaulantus* show Bannister as exemplary among his contemporary actor-playwrights and one from whom still better things might have been expected had he lived longer.

The concern for nationalism that swept through Jacksonian America was nothing new to the pages of literary and society journals or to the lips of lecturers and politicians. In previous decades, however, the calls and pleas had been less numerous, less determined. Now the emphasis was strong and the interest emphatic. Emerson's Phi Beta Kappa address on "The American Scholar" at Harvard College in 1837, rejecting the "courtly muses of Europe," is only the best-known declaration. There were many other advocates of a national literature—William Ellery Channing in "On National Literature" (1830); Longfellow in "Defense of Poetry" (1832); Paulding in "National Literature" (1835); William Gilmore Simms in "Americanism in Literature" (1844); James Fenimore Cooper, John Neal and numerous critics and editors of journals. From the 1820s on there was also an ever-increasing pressure upon Congress to enact adequate copyright laws. Although the drama did not always figure prominently in these essays and comments, it was a vital part of a national literature, one which critics recognized for its particular problems and occasionally went out of their way to encourage. The pursuit of that national interest on America's stages was a challenge haunted by trailing ghosts from past traditions and present prejudices. Yet there were strong advocates of plays portraying Paulding's nationalistic ideas. Generally seated in the pit or the gallery rather than the dress circle, they applauded the work of these playwrights who by choice or by conviction dramatized America.

In concert with painters, musicians and other writers, American playwrights presented a cross section of themes and scenes that reflect the social pressures, exultations and fears of the times. Projecting a fetish for individuality and a sometimes pathetic yearning for self-identity, the Jacksonian American was portrayed onstage as a Yankee, a backwoodsman and a city tough, among other recognizable types. This was man pictured in his natural environment. With the introduction of photography to America soon after its invention in 1839, portraiture in art became less popular, and landscape painting seduced the public fancy. As a population eager to see and hear about itself searched for identity, it showed vivid curiosity about the landscape that was America and the contrast that land presented to exotic, foreign and ancient lands and people. Even the popular emotional responses to poetry, music and fiction, equated with the Romanticism that flourished in Jacksonian America, became fused with an interest in scenery that dominated stages and was already prominent in the writings of Longfellow, Hawthorne and the novelists of the frontier who followed the lead of Cooper. Painters such as Thomas Cole with *The Notch of the White Mountains* (1840) and other members of the Hudson River School soon capitalized on this fascination of Americans to see their own destiny, which they found symbolically represented on canvas. Like the more serious critics and literary dramatists, however, Cole complained bitterly about a lack of public taste when his paintings of *Childhood, Youth, Manhood,* and *Old Age,* so highly detailed and romantically allegorical, were not well received by people who wanted to see American wilderness.

With their articulated awareness of American idiosyncrasies, American dramatists responded to the desires of the people for a vivid scenery as well as an understanding of a national character. William Dunlap's *A Trip to Niagara* (1828) provided a beginning that was exploited by the popular dioramas and the spectacular theatre settings from *Nick of the Woods* to the numerous scenes of city life in *A Glance at New York* and many other plays. Generally, Jacksonian Americans did not care to be thoughtful; they wanted only to know what they looked like, individually and as a country. Parke Godwin was particularly acute in his observations about man's attractiveness to man. America *was* curious, and the playwright along with the painter, the songwriter and the storyteller of the time, although in a fashion more momentary than lasting, helped define the temper of that age.

NOTES

1. [Anthony Aston], *The Fool's Opera, or The Taste of the Age* (London, 1731), 20–21; Walter J. Meserve, *An Emerging Entertainment* (Bloomington: Indiana University Press, 1977), 37–38.

2. George C. D. Odell, *Annals of the New York Stage*, Vol. III (New York: Columbia University Press, 1928), 544.

3. "The Drama," *The Knickerbocker*, XX (November 1842), 493.

4. *Spirit of the Times*, XVIII (July 29, 1848), 276. To compete with Brougham's popular play the Park Theatre management hired Charles Walcot to adapt the same work, but his effort failed.

5. *Spirit of the Times*, XVIII (December 23, 1848), 528.

6. *The Literary World*, May 12, 1848, 417.

7. William W. Clapp, Jr., *A Record of the Boston Stage* (Boston: James Monroe & Company, 1853), 476.

8. See Laura McKernan, "A Study of John Brougham as a Writer of Burlesque," MA thesis, Indiana University, 1976, chapter 1.

9. *The Reign of Reform; or, Yankee Doodle Court* (By a Lady) (Baltimore: Printed for the Authoress, 1830), Preface.

10. *Daily National Intelligencer*, February 24, 1836, 3.

11. *Montgomerie; or, The Orphan of a Wreck*, A Dramatic Romance in Four acts, exists as a manuscript, identified as H.M. 598, in the Huntington Library, San Marino, California. In this discussion of Custis I am indebted to an unpublished paper entitled "The Indian Prophecy" written by Professor Billy J. Harbin, Louisiana State University.

12. Noah Ludlow, *Dramatic Life As I Found It* (St. Louis: G. J. Jones, 1880), 436.

13. *Dramatic Mirror* I (September 11, 1841), 33.

14. *Spirit of the Times*, XXV (February 9, 1856), 619.

15. *Dramatic Mirror*, I (September 11, 1841), 33; *Tod's Pilgrimage* is not listed by Page.

16. *Spirit of the Times*, XI (March 6, 1841), 12; *G-A-G* is not listed by Page.

17. *Spirit of the Times*, XII (September 10, 1842), 336.

18. Reprinted in *The Spirit of the Times* XV (June 21, 1845), 200.

19. *Spirit of the Times*, XXII (September 11, 1852)), 360; (October 9, 1852), 404.

20. James Rees, "Dramatic Authors of America," *Dramatic Mirror*, I (October 16, 1841), 72.

21. *Dramatic Mirror*, I (December 11, 1841), 141.

22. *Dramatic Mirror*, I (October 23, 1841), 87.

23. New York *Clipper*, April 6, 1889, n.p. Harvard Theatre Collection Clipping File.

24. George O. Seilhamer, *An Interviewer's Album: Comprising a Series of Chats with Eminent Players and Playwrights* (New York: Alvin Perry, 1881), 32.

25. *Knickerbocker Magazine*, IV (November 1836), 549–52.

26. Letter, Harvard Theatre Collection.

27. *The Various Writings of Cornelius Mathews* (New York: Harper Bros., 1843), v.

28. *Various Writings*, 119.

29. *New York Review*, VII (October 1840), 430.

30. Clapp, *A Record of the Boston Stage*, 404.

31. *Brownson Quarterly Review*, I (October 1853), 547.

32. New York *Dramatic Mirror* (June 14, 1890), n.p., Harvard Theatre Collection Clipping File.

33. Margaret Fuller, "The Modern Drama," in *Papers on Literature and Art*, vol. I (New York: Putnam, 1846), 391.

34. *Spirit of the Times*, XVIII (May 13, 1848), 144.

35. His other six plays were: *The Arab Chief; or, Pirate of the East* (1834); *A Miser's Miseries* (1835); *The Spanish Pirates; or, A Union of the Flags* (1835); *Fatal Prophecies; or, The Smuggler's Daughter* (1835); *Ida Steppanoff* (1836); and *The Black Douglass* (183?).

36. *Spirit of the Times*, XII (March 5, 1842), 12.

37. Edward Wagenknecht, *Longfellow: A Full-Length Portrait* (London: Longmans Green, 1955), 186.

38. Wagenknecht, *Longfellow*, 315–20.

39. Henry W. Longfellow, *The Spanish Student*, reprinted in *Poetical Works*, vol. 1 (Boston: Houghton Mifflin Company, 1904), 119–201. Introductory note, pp. 115–18, quotes diary entry and provides publication information. *The Spanish Student*, in three acts, appeared in the September, October and November 1842 issues of a new periodical, *Graham's Magazine*. In the summer of 1843 the play was revised slightly and published in book form. A dozen years later, January 28, 1855, a German version, *Der Spanische Student*, was produced at the Ducal Court Theatre in Desau, Germany. See Lawrance Thompson, "Longfellow Sells *The Spanish Student*," *American Literature*, VI (1934), 141–50.

40. Wagenknecht, *Longfellow* 215.

41. Margaret Fuller, "The Modern Drama," in *Art, Literature, and the Drama* (Boston: Robert Press, 1875), 112.

42. Wagenknecht, *Longfellow*.

43. There are seventy-one letters from Winter to Longfellow in the Harvard Theatre Collection.

44. Letter, Cornelius Mathews to Rufus Griswold, December 27, 1841, Gratz Collection, Case 6, Box 7, Historical Society of Pennsylvania.

45. Samuel Foster Damon, *Thomas Holley Chivers, Friend of Poe* (New York: Harper & Brothers, 1930), xviii.

46. Damon, *Thomas Holley Chivers*, 267.

47. Charlotte Barnes Conner, *Plays, Prose and Poetry* (Philadelphia: E. H. Butler, 1848), iii–v.

48. Conner, *Plays, Prose and Poetry*, 145–270.

49. American Jewish Archives, Cincinnati, Ohio.

50. Bertram Wallace Korn, *The Early Jews of New Orleans* (Waltham, MA: American Jewish Historical Society, 1969), 185.

51. *Spirit of the Times*, VII (January 6, 1838), 4.

52. Quoted in Nelle Smither, *A History of the English Theatre of New Orleans, 1806–1842)*. (1944; rpt. New York: B. Blom, 1967), 152. A confusion that follows playwrights may be illustrated with a play by Harby which Quinn lists as *Hard Times in*

New Orleans; or, The Gentleman in Black (p. 451), Nelle Smithers identifies as *Hard Times in New Orleans* (p. 340), performed at the American Theatre on April 17, 1837, while Bertram Korn, *The Early Jews of New Orleans* (1969), uses both titles to identify different plays (p. 186). *The Gentleman in Black*, by William Barrymore, was produced in Boston in 1839.

53. Joseph Ireland, *Records of the New York Stage*, vol. II (New York: J. H. Morrell, 1866), 205.

54. The Simon Gratz Collection, Historical Society of Pennsylvania.

55. *Spirit of the Times*, XVI (February 28, 1846), 12.

56. *Spirit of the Times*, XIV (December 21, 1844), 516.

57. *Spirit of the Times*, XIV (November 9, 1844), 444.

58. *Dramatic Mirror*, I (December 4, 1841), 134; *Spirit of the Times,* VIII (October 13, 1838), 244.

59. *Dramatic Mirror*, I (August 28, 1841), 18.

60. Nathaniel H. Bannister, *England's Iron Days* (New Orleans: W. McKean & Co., 1837), Preface, n.p.

61. *Dramatic Mirror*, I (August 28, 1841), 18.

62. Nathaniel H. Bannister, *The Gentleman of Lyons; or, The Marriage Contract* (New York: Levison & Brothers, 1838), i.

63. *Spirit of the Times*, XIV (October 5, 1844), 384; a play by George Hielge with the same title, incidents and characters opened at a Philadelphia theatre in September.

64. Harry Watkins complained bitterly that Hamblin made from $15,000 to $20,000 with *Putnam* and allowed Bannister to die in poverty in a city hospital. Maud and Otis Skinner, eds., *One Man in His Time* (Philadelphia: University of Pennsylvania Press, 1938, 106.

65. *The Albion*, N.S., III (August 10, 1844), 337–38.

66. *Spirit of the Times*, XIV (November 23, 1844), 468.

67. *Spirit of the Times*, XV (February 15, 1845), 612.

68. *Spirit of the Times*, XV (April 5, 1845), 68.

69. *Spirit of the Times*, XIX (June 9, 1849), 192.

7

AMERICAN DRAMATIC LITERATURE AND THE LITERATI

American dramatists writing during much of the nineteenth century rather neatly divided themselves into two camps. With some notable exceptions these were opposing camps. Such a division was, perhaps, a logical or at least an understandable distribution of labor in a new country that had not yet established traditions, but it was also a consequence of the two seldom reconciled approaches to playwriting that developing societies generally experience. The love of theatre came to America in the hearts of its early settlers who eventually built the theatres in which plays would be performed. Who would write these plays? There were those who worked in and understood the demands of the theatre; and there were the writers, those who used their pens to express their thoughts in poetry or fiction. Both groups of writers, those primarily concerned with theatricality and those interested in language and literature, were equally determined to entertain America. When the talents necessary for each approach were bestowed upon one playwright, the American audiences reaped the rewards, but this did not happen frequently.

The number of native plays produced in New York theatres each year would approximately double during the Age of Jackson, from nearly twenty in 1828 to as many as forty in 1849, depending upon the season and the kind of entertainment that might be identified as a play. Beyond New York there were undoubtedly many more native plays produced. By far the greater number of these plays came from the minds and pens of people working in or with the theatre, ephemeral and theatrical plays rather than literary, without pretense and written solely to entertain. The remainder were composed by people with formal education and intellectual as well as aesthetic interests who considered themselves writers by profession or whose careers in politics, law, journalism, education or the clergy allowed them time to pursue their literary inclinations. Other than having read plays, they might have no interest in theatre, and few had any knowledge of the practical stage. As the century progressed, these playwrights encountered the scorn of the theatre people while having ample opportunity—as editors of the journals that reviewed the contemporary stage—to comment on the paucity of American dramatic literature. Both sides collected abundant evidence to support their prejudices, and neither produced a great number of memorable plays. Obviously, they had different objectives. Nathaniel H. Bannister's *Putnam* opened with seventy-eight consecutive performances. Although Nathaniel Parker Willis' *Tortesa the Usurer* has much to recommend it, it was not well received. One play reached the people, the other did not. Both were published. How were they to be evaluated? A critic might approach his task with Henry James: allow the writer his donnée. But the theatre is always "now," and the merciless audience or reviewer passes judgment at the moment—thumbs up, thumbs down!

As time passes and transitory life encounters examples of lasting art, any generalized division of creations or creators to the right or left hand of God is a serious act of presumption on the part of the literary historian. Eventually, there would be a merging of the two camps of American playwrights as each became more tolerant of the other's point of view. In awe or through contempt a reciprocal education began. Although individual interests relative to theatricality and literary equality remained, later actor-playwrights such as James A. Herne began to write plays that could be read with enjoyment, and literary people such as William Dean Howells began to satisfy the demands of actors. Near the turn of the century Americans would read the plays of Clyde Fitch, who admired Howells with painful enthusiasm, and at one time had five plays on the New York stage. Although it is unfortunate that this necessary fusion of talents was so long in the making, class consciousness in Jacksonian America was as much a problem in the struggle to produce an exemplary dramatic literature as any faced by the aspiring playwright, whether he found greater comfort in the theatre or the library.

The impulse of most of the literati—literary people whose reputations as poets, editors or essayists encouraged them to write for the theatre—was to adapt a classical or traditional theme or to dramatize a historical event or romantic myth. In this endeavor they readily imitated their English forebears or peers, thus following an established American practice while satisfying the romantic tastes of many Americans. Occasionally, they—Robert Montgomery Bird, Robert J. Conrad, Richard Penn Smith, Nathaniel Parker Willis, or Epes Sargent—wrote for actors and reached varying degrees of success in an art form for which they were ill-prepared at the outset. Among them only Jonas B. Phillips and Isaac Pray managed to ride both horses and maintain a balance that gave them dual, if moderate, reputations in literature and in theatre. Mainly, however, these poets and editors with literary inclinations wrote a play or two and left the scene. In retrospect, a few of them clearly had potential for greater accomplishment—potential that was not encouraged.

David Paul Brown (1795–1872), a friend of Richard Penn Smith and fellow member of the bar in Philadelphia, wrote two plays in 1830: *Sertorius; or, The Roman Patriot* and *The Prophet of Saint Paul's*. He based *Sertorius* on information in Plutarch's *Lives* and concentrated on Sertorius' victory over Pompey and Metellus in Spain during the Roman Revolution—and on his death, triumphant and honorable at the hands of Perpenna, the villainous conspirator. Throughout the play, one Roman is pitted against another, a wronged Roman of high honor against a base Roman selfishly motivated to destroy greatness. In his writing, Brown remained faithful to his subject, respected the unities and presented interesting and bold characters in moving poetry, aspects of the drama that were appreciated by literary critics. Even the usually vituperative editor of the *Irish Shield and Literary Panorama* appeared impressed. "There are in [*Sertorius*]," he wrote, "some strokes of nature and touches of tenderness to please upon the stage; . . . In situation, plot and character, and even in energy of language and flowing versification [*Sertorius* is] equal to the *best effort* of American genius." He concluded, somewhat contradictorily but with his usual deflating thrust, that the play "though sterile in character and monotonous in incident has the merit, a rare quality among American dramatists, of being original." [1]

Scenes from Brown's play also suggest his comedic skills, especially in the first act with a schoolmaster, a cobbler and a carpenter:

Flavius: Ay, ay, Mucius is a rare one, and not the less so for being commended by thee, who art also a rare one—seeing you are the opposite of each other, or should be, judging from your mysteries.

Mucius: Mystery me no mysteries—come demonstrate.

Flavius: Why, the mystery is to supply furniture for the head, being a schoolmaster, or pedagogue; and his is to furnish the feet being a shoemaker or cobbler.

Mucius: And thine to accommodate the neck, being a carpenter or gallowsmaker—therefore, it is that thou art ever between us twain, as alike an enemy to both head and feet.

Flavius: Fie on't, fie! You are only chafed because my trade is the more prescriptive and honorable of the three.

Caiphus: Why more prescriptive?

Flavius: Because the gallows was in use before schools were taught, or shoes mended; and not before the world required it either—mankind having a natural itch for elevation.

Mucius: But why more honorable?

Flavius: Because it is the end of guilt and dishonor—whereas your arts are too frequently the credentials and lures of both. Calfskin from top to toes thrives best as the times run;—it is a most vendible commodity.

Mucius: Hang thyself to prove thy first position, and I care not to admit the *last* for the sake of the service. (I)

It is unfortunate that only sparse excerpts remain from a play that appears to deserve a better fate than to be completely ignored. The theatre at this time, however, was an actor's theatre, in fact, a single actor's theatre, and if actors did not find a play suitable to their talents, it would not be produced. Brown made the mistake of providing not one, but two good roles in Sertorius and Perpenna.

James Rees characterized *The Prophet of St. Paul's* as "better calculated for the closet than the stage," and most would agree.[2] It is basically a static play, mainly conversation, although the jester is well used. Dedicated to the members of the Philadelphia Bar in its published version (1836), the play tells the story of Mary, Henry VIII's sister, who is forced to marry the king of France although she loves Suffolk, Henry VIII's foster brother, who returns this love. Cardinal Wolsey explains the situation and foreshadows the action:

> Like the devout astronomer who gazed
> With naked eye upon the effulgent sun
> In close communion with the *earthly* planets,
> I am struck blind with light.
> Savoy's proud princess, the fair Margaret,
> In lineage scarcely rivaled by the King,
> Was too high, so Henry thought, for Suffolk;
> And when, to captivate her haughty eye,
> A dukedom was confered on humble Brandon,
> Fledged by that bounty, the ambitious youth,
> Now, like the falcon, circling in the air,
> Pursues another lure—and foils his master. (I,1)

For her part, Mary, advised by a necromancer, the Prophet of St. Paul's, goes to live with Louis XII, who treats her as a daughter. Eventually, Louis dies, and Suffolk, disguised as the Prophet of St. Paul's, steals Mary away and marries her. Mainly in blank verse, the play can boast some well-phrased speeches and ideas, but it lacks dramatic excitement, even in the tournament scenes in Act IV, which should have provided the popular spectacle. Brown's prologue, however, treating beauty and love, reveals a dramatic muse bound by tradition. Without an actor advocate to encourage it, the work of even a playwright of such potential was doomed to disappear from the American stage.

Theatre managers in Philadelphia at this time looked to native dramatists with a particularly understanding and sympathetic eye. Even George Pepper, the fearless editor of the *Irish Shield and Literary Panorama*, who was so determined to hold native playwrights to his high critical standards, wrote plays. His *Kathleen O'Neil; or, A Picture of Feudal Times in Ireland*, concerned with the invasion of Ireland by Prince Edward Bruce in 1316, had been performed in New York in 1827. It was probably another version of this play that was produced at the Walnut Street Theatre in Philadelphia in early 1831, entitled *Captive Princess; or, Feudal Times in Ireland* and having the added attraction of original songs composed for the Irish harp by Dr. C. Conwell of Philadelphia and sung by a Miss Rock who performed the part of the princess of Ulster.

Another Irishman and citizen of Philadelphia since 1816, Dr. James Mc-

Henry (1785–1845), was no less forthright in his opinions but more persistent as a playwright than Pepper and equally important as an editor of the *American Monthly Magazine* (owned by Robert Walsh) and as a critic. McHenry was a singular individual. After his play *The Usurper* (1827), caused considerable discussion upon its unsuccessful debut on stage, McHenry was surely abused when the strict Presbyterian Church in Philadelphia, of which he was a member, "Resolved, that Dr. James McHenry be, and he is hereby suspended from the Communion of the Church until he gives satisfactory evidence of his repentance." There is no evidence that he either repented or was released from the church's censure.[3] In fact, McHenry continued to write for the theatre.

Love and Poetry; or, A Modern Genius, McHenry's five-act satiric comedy, was produced in late 1829 as a kind of release of venom on the part of its author. The critic for the *Ladies' Literary Port Folio* classified it as an attempt to "satirize the mad extravagancies of modern genius, poetical, political, and pathetical. This is done with considerable bitterness and effect."[4] The audience was highly entertained, however, and the reviewer faulted only the length of the play and references (whatever they were) to "Lord Byron, to Sir Walter Scott, and especially to Miss Landon." After this attack upon "unfledged" poets and "unlearned" political economists, McHenry wrote *The Maid of Wyoming* (1831) and a frivolous musical interlude, undated, entitled *Which Shall I Marry?; or, Who Does Best?*, in which the heroine must choose among Tom Trifle, Dick Desperate and Harry Heartfelt. As a critic of literature and society, McHenry was a strong but reasonable voice. His condemnation of all poetry that puzzled or wearied the reader caused a storm among critics, but no less than his consistent adverse criticism of American poetry which he reviewed for different journals throughout much of his professional life. In 1842 he was appointed consul at Londonderry, Ireland, and died in the country of his birth in 1845.

The Maid of Wyoming, acted at the Arch Street Theatre, is a dramatization of McHenry's novel, *The Wilderness; or, Braddock's Times* (1823). A pretentiously patriotic work praising Washington, the play dramatizes the massacre of the inhabitants of Wyoming by the Tories and Indians under the English General Butler and the Indian leader Brandt. Although Pepper saw flashes of "eloquence and passion," he missed the "bussle of incident" and the attraction that comic relief would have brought to the plot.[5] Evidently, Pepper felt some guilt in commending any part of a play by his fellow countryman and in a second review compared it unfavorably to *The Usurper* and condemned it to "the nettles and hemlock of oblivion."[6] A phlegmatic playwright, one whose single-minded passions drove him to write, McHenry was also a fair poet and a man actively involved in theatrical and literary circles as well as the medical profession. When Sheridan Knowles visited America in 1834, McHenry served on the reception committee and composed a song entitled "The Drama of Britain," which was sung at a dinner for the English actor-playwright. That same year the *North American Review* published an essay on McHenry, ridiculing his work in poetry and drama, particularly *The Usurper*, in a mass of acrimonious commentary.[7] Doubtless, McHenry's own condemnation of American poets and poetry stimulated such attacks. Certainly, he got as he gave in the sharp-tongued literary-theatrical world of Jacksonian America.

Charles Jared Ingersoll (1782–1862) was another poet and professional man from Philadelphia who contributed briefly to American dramatic literature. A lawyer who served two terms in Congress and one of the intellectuals converted to Jacksonian causes—a strong leader against corporations and paper money after 1833—Ingersoll appeared to show some promise in American letters in 1831, when he published *Julian, a Tragedy*. Thirty years previously his youthful tragedy of *Edwy and Elgiva* had been produced and published. For *Julian* Ingersoll took Gibbon as his source and attempted to dramatize the monomania of Julian, the Apostate, a Roman leader whose thirst for fame drove him mad. The major action of the play, however, follows the machinations of Zopyrus, the Persian patriot, who fulfills his vow to destroy Julian. Killed by a poisoned arrow, Julian dies as he lived:

> For fame, not pleasure—for renown, not ease—
> Studying life's noblest lesson—how to die
> Earning its richest heritage—renown.
> Grateful and glorious I depart.

Although, as pointed out by a writer in the *North American Magazine* who extolled the play,[8] parts of *Julian* show the strengths of Ingersoll's verse, the editor of the *Irish Shield and Literary Panorama* provided a more balanced criticism:

As a literary composition, possessing the graces of style and the attributes of poetry, the tragedy before us, we have no hesitation to aver, is superior to any essay of the American tragic muse that has fallen under our observation. The poetry of *Julian* germinates its fantasy and blossoms out luxuriantly, as it ought, in imagination and passion. But though the characters of this play speak courtly language and lofty sentiments, they do not *act* with dramatic effect; they fail in stimulating our feelings, or winning our sympathies. A drama, to succeed, must be like the magic mirror in the fable, capable of reflecting dissimilar characters, as well as their various passions and foibles. . . . We omen that a gentleman of Mr. Ingersoll's accomplished talents, expanded reach of thought, and lofty fantasy, will *yet write* a tragedy that will insure him lasting fame, and confer honor on the American drama. Let him study dramatic effect, and he will reach the sum of his success.[9]

No better advice could have been offered to Ingersoll or to other writers who wished to create for the stage, but none of his generation would accept the challenge. Ingersoll never resolved the problems of the play nor wrote more for the theatre.

By the late 1830s American theatrical endeavor had firmly established a home for itself in New York where opportunities were greater than in other cities— more theatre, more actors, more potential for audiences. Although at this time not the center of literary activity in America—an honor resting with Cambridge and Boston, where it would remain until late in the century—New York experienced a burgeoning of writing enterprises, propelled in part by the establishment of numerous cultural and literary periodicals. The poet William Cullen Bryant became editor in chief of the New York *Evening Post* in 1829 and for a generation exerted his influence. Other editors asserted their opinions on the writing of the period—editors such as George Pope Morris, Sarah Josepha Hale, Rufus W. Griswold, Nathaniel Parker Willis and Cornelius Mathews—and in the process, created a variety of contretemps pertaining to the New York literati.[10] With the establishment of the *Spirit of the Times* in 1831 William T. Porter raised the public awareness of American drama and theatre with a more organized assessment of all theatre than had existed previously, although with some bias for legitimate theatre and literary drama. It would be these editors and critics, frequently with strong nationalistic prejudices, who brought attention not only to a developing American literature of poetry and fiction but to a struggling American drama. Sometimes they tried to remedy the situation themselves; occasionally, their criticisms stimulated other writers.

None of these writers—editors, poets, essayists—who tried to create a literary drama for America had substantial and continuing success in the theatre, although Willis probably could have written more memorable plays had his spirit so directed him, and Cornelius Mathews had a much greater contemporary reputation in the theatre than an ungenerous history has accorded him. By and large, however, American theatres experienced brief visits of various effect by numerous literary people of high ambitions but few of the skills necessary to write successful drama. Occasionally, the theatrical event attracted only a single note by a reviewer and was lost. On June 26, 1834, for example, *The Venetian Bride*, written by "one of the literati of New York," was performed at the Bowery Theatre. If the playwright had been better known, or perhaps, equal to claiming his composition, a review might exist.

Giordano; or, The Conspiracy was written by James Lawson, a New York editor and poet. First produced at the Park Theatre in 1828, it was performed at the Arch Street Theatre in Philadelphia in 1830 and again in 1832, always a failure. The reviewer for the *North American Magazine* sympathized with the "small and suffering audience" watching *Giordano*, a play that was "neither original nor effective in plot, incident or language."[11]

Park Benjamin (1809–1864), born in British Guiana of a New England family, was another poet and editor, in Boston and New York, who tried his hand at playwriting. His work as a magazine editor and poet, however, absorbed most of his writing career.[12] Starting in 1831 on the *New England Magazine* with the Buckinghams, Benjamin edited the *American Monthly Magazine* (1836–1838), the *New World* (1839), and the *New Yorker* (1836–1841). His interest in theatre began in Boston, where on the occasion of a benefit for John Howard Payne (April 3, 1833), he wrote an address in poetry: "The author, bringing forms to life and light / Which here reflected you may see to-night. . . . "[13] Benja-

min's only play was a farce called *The Fiscal Agent*, which opened at the Park
Theatre on February 28, 1842. Dealing with stockbrokers and the exchange,
the play had a theme which should have been popular at this time in New
York, but the *Spirit of the Times*, prepared to be enthusiastic about the work
of a brother journalist, was disappointed: "The farce of *The Fiscal Agent*,
written by Park Benjamin, Esq., was not what we expected from this gentleman's ready pen, and except for a few local allusions there was little to pro-
voke a laugh."[14]

Some writers were satisfied merely to publish their plays. Sarah Josepha Hale
(1788–1879) was a poet, novelist and editor. Her powerful and energetic work
for *Godey's Lady's Book* was as influential in New York as in Philadelphia,
and among her varied publications—the lightest yet most memorable being
"Mary's Lamb"—are five plays. One was a tragedy entitled *Ormond Grosvenor* (1839); another was *The Judge* (1851), "a Drama of American life."
Romantic melodrama of rather dull variety, *The Judge* is not so much a story
of a judge as of a girl, Isabelle, who turns out to be the judge's ward. Eventually, Isabelle will marry the judge's son but not before she is caused great
trouble by two suitors whom she spurns. The plot turns on revelations of switched
and abandoned babies and appears quite remote from any "American life" existing outside that of the current extravagant fiction.

Presumably, Hale did not pursue production possibilities. Nor did Delia Salter Bacon (1811–1859), who explained in the preface to the publication of *The
Bride of Fort Edwards* (1839) that it was "not a play . . . not intended for the
stage and . . . not capable of representation."[15] When such plays were reviewed as literature, however, their authors were frequently praised and encouraged. This was true of the *New York Review*'s comments on G. P. R. James'
(1801?–1860) *Blanche of Navarre* (1839), and H. H. Locke's *Harold, King of
Norway*, which impressed the editor of the New York *Evening Journal* as
"destined to eclipse many things of the kind that have been produced on this
side of the Atlantic."[16] Sometimes, these stories in dialogue, or closet dramas,
were identified as "dramatic poems," even by such dramatists as Jonas B. Phillips
and James Rees, who knew how to write for the stage. *Hannah, the Mother of
Samuel, the Prophet and Judge of Israel* (1839), by Louisa Jane Hall (1802–
1892), was labeled in this manner and did not impress the critic for the *New
York Review*, who described it as a work "whose most distinguished trait is
that unendurable mediocrity, which, without the faults or the merits of unripe
genius, contains nothing for the present, or of promise for the future."[17] Such
a comment could be repeated for most of the plays that were published rather
than produced onstage during this period.

A number of editors and publishers actively promoted American drama. The
editor of the *North American Magazine*, for example, was particularly interested in hailing Dr. T. A. Ware, author of *Dion, the Patriot of Syracuse* (1833),
as a successful American dramatist.[18] Attracted by the poetry of the play, he
passed lightly over the admittedly complicated plot concerning Dion's patriotic

designs for his country and the treacherous actions of the ultimately evil Callippus who destroys Dion. It was a futile attempt, however, and the play was rejected by J. R. Scott, the actor for whom it was written.

A minor poet of his day, Rufus Dawes (1803–1859) has been virtually forgotten with passing time, in spite of his literary ambitions, which in 1839 included a series of novels illustrating the growth of American civil liberty.[19] Although his single contribution to the drama, *Athenia of Damascus*, was never staged, it was praised by the *New York Review* as the work of a "man of genius, and a true poet." The critic found "beautiful thoughts and exquisite passages" of genuine poetry in the play, but also noted that Dawes' "talents were less suited to the drama, than to some other forms of poetic creation."[20] There is little to commend the work, however, either as drama or poetry. Set in 634 A.D. in the city of Damascus, under siege by the Saracen chief, Kaled, the play deals with the problem of Calous, the leader of the city, who is persuaded by Euphorn, the prefect and father of Athenia, to allow the Saracens to take Damascus for "a greater good" that will come later. Although in the hands of a good dramatist the story of treachery which fails could have made an exciting play, Dawes promised few skills as a dramatist and was scarcely a good poet.

Waldimar (1831) was apparently the only play of John J. Bailey (d. 1873), a native New Yorker, and was acted with some success by Charles Kean in New York and Philadelphia. Like most plays by writers not well versed in dramatic techniques, *Waldimar* has little action to follow the usual rush of exposition in a confusing first act. It does, however, have a strong plot line and a hero whose stern beliefs, though not well developed, thrust him toward his ruin. It is only in the fifth act that Bailey shows any real talent for dramatic composition, although he had strong support for his attempt with a prologue of special pleading by Robert C. Sands:

> Would you behold the native drama rise?
> .   .   .   .
> Try, then, our author's argument and cause,
> By patriotic feeling, not by tyrant laws;
> And let not justice hold the balance, *blind*,
> But poise the scales, determined—*to be kind*!

And from the epilogue by the popular writer Theodore S. Fay: "Let him but once *your* bounteous favor share / And then—ye critics!—touch him if ye *dare*!" They dared, of course. Bailey's uncertain and loaded approach, however, shows both an amateur spirit and a lack of dignity touched, perhaps, with appropriate fear of the critics whose numbers included the paid puffers and the never-daunted martinets. It is little wonder that animosity developed between the practical journeyman playwright and the literary pretender to the stage.

The scene of *Waldimar* is Thessalonica at the close of the fourth century during the reign of Theodosius the Great. Stern and ambitious, Waldimar, the tyrant hero who undertands only military power leading to fame, will sacrifice his daughter, Hersilia, to increase his fortune and favor with the emperor. When Claudius, Hersilia's lover, refuses to be bribed to do Waldimar's shadowy work, Waldimar has him thrown in prison, stating:

> Then meet thy fate—
> For know, that ere the Emperor shall come,
> And with his clemency can stay the arm
> Now lifted to destroy, the gushing blood
> Of thousands shall in wide libations flow,
> To appease the ashes of my soldiers slain. (IV,2)

Then Theodosius appears, frees Claudius and finally confronts Waldimar, who yields to his own fate "but unsubdued by man" (IV,6). Only in Act V does the play move quickly and forcefully and with well-devised action to suggest the motivations of a tyrant hero whose ambitions for power are frustrated by his love for his daughter and loyalty to his emperor. It is in this suggestion of potential rather than in accomplishment that Bailey's importance lies. Charles Kean might find some power in the play, but Waldimar falls short of the hero who would have excited nineteenth-century audiences.

Although this was a time when self-reliance and individuality were praised, it was also a time when results were the major criteria for that praise. Dramatists needed nurturing, especially by those from inside the mysterious and revered circle of theatre artists, but there was little sympathy or time for that nurturing. The literary dramatist, the person who pursued a career or avocation in letters and wanted to write for the stage, seemed ever on the edge of the theatre world. Nevertheless, an impressive number of poets, novelists, essayists and journal editors took it upon themselves to write plays. Many had their plays produced, occasionally with some momentary success as friends and admirers and occasionally an editor with nationalistic views would keep a play on the boards, at least through the author's benefit. Few plays by these literary dramatists, however, went beyond the meager point of acceptance in American theatres where English plays and melodramatic spectacles were the vogue.

The plays of both Nathaniel Parker Willis and Epes Sargent illustrate this point. Although both were initially encouraged by literary critics, they did not speak clearly and forcefully to the people who supported popular theatre, while the legitimate theatre lacked the power and the inclination to encourage American dramatists. Willis' plays, for example, would seem to have shown that recognizable dramatic talent on which patrons of serious drama should have insisted. His objectives, however, were not always clear, and he clouded his genius in *Bianca Visconti* by allowing a potentially inspiring heroine to expire through traditional insanity while concentrating his energies upon the delightful scenes with Fiametta and Pasquali. His insight is more apparent in the character of Tortesa, for here is a moneylender who is neither the traditional villainous Jew nor unscrupulous social climber. True, he would trade money for a high-born wife, but he only does it for spite. His love is reserved for Zippa. As the curtain falls in the final act, the high-born Isabella marries the poor painter for love, and Tortesa the rich man is delightfully satisfied with the common-born Zippa. This representation of realistic and powerful emotions of common humanity shows a perception for dramatic construction uncommon during this period in American theatre history. Yet Willis was not successful as a dramatist.

The number of writers who tried to write for the theatre and either failed or otherwise became discouraged must remain a mystery. But the range of their backgrounds and attitudes is wide. James M. Kennicott of New Orleans was a young schoolteacher in western New York when he wrote *Irma; or, The Prediction* (1829) for the opening of James Caldwell's American Theatre in New Orleans. Based on an old Welsh legend about a woman who allowed her life to be destroyed by a prediction that she would be a murderess, the play won Caldwell's prize of $300 and was produced in New Orleans and Cincinnati. Both A. H. Quinn and James Rees wrote favorably of Kennicott's play.[21]

Associated as a writer of both New York and South Carolina, Mrs. Elizabeth Fries (Lumis) Ellet (1812–1877) was a strong advocate of women, a historian of society in America and of woman's place in that society. A critic, essayist, poet, translator, anthologist and dramatist, she was a determined and ambitious woman, not overly burdened with scruples, who would not tolerate abuse from the pens or those free-swinging journalists and editors of the 1840s in New York—as Rufus W. Griswold discovered after publishing *The Female Poets of America* (1848).[22] Among her writings are *The Pioneer Women of the West* (1852) and *The Women of the Revolution* (3 volumes, 1848–50) which she wrote to show the importance of women in the establishment of the new nation. Unfortunately, her interest in women and America was not reflected in her interest in writing drama, which waned after 1853. Although as a young woman she translated *Euphemio of Messina* (1843) from the Italian of Silvio Pellico, the play which insures her a place among America's literary playwrights is *Teresa Contarini*, first performed at the Park Theatre on November 19, 1835. Odell identified the author as part of the literary set of the 1830s in New York and quoted the *Knickerbocker Magazine* (April 1835): the play was "received with decided favor by a crowded house. It abounds in language rich in poetic beauties and possesses many sterling scenes."[23] Performed without distinction in other theatres across America, *Teresa Contarini* is a traditionally conceived drama that suffers from a lack of action.[24]

A second play by Ellet to be performed in New York was entitled *Wissmuth and Company; or, The Noble and the Merchant*, an adaptation of a novel by Franz Dingelstadt, which appeared at the Park Theatre on April 13, 1847. As its author, Ellet was identified as "an American lady of distinguished literary reputation . . . who has shown great cleverness in her various prose and poetical contributions to the magazines."[25] Mr. Wissmuth's young wife has a lover whose discovery on the premises excites a chase and an accusation that the young man has stolen $30,000. Ellet was apparently more interested in skulduggery in the business world than in romance, and when the real robber, the head clerk, is revealed, the play ends abruptly with Mr. Wissmuth's death. The production, according to the reviewer, was not successful, although the author was "commended for her cleverness." Unlike many clever young writers of this generation who wrote a play or two and then lost interest in the theatre, Ellet did not abandon her playwriting no matter how unsatisfactory the results. Moreover, her reviews of Italian drama and her analysis of *The Characters of Schiller* (1839) add to a body of dramatic criticism.

George H. Calvert (b. 1803) first attracted some attention with his translation of Schiller's *Don Carlos*. His *Count Julian*, published in Baltimore in 1840, inspired the critic for the *New York Review* to puff this "noteworthy event" because few talented poets attempted "dramatic productions."[26] Calvert would write tragedies and comedies for the next thirty-odd years, but seemingly with little knowledge of dramatic technique or interest in the theatre. *Count Julian*, set in Bavaria in the fifteenth century, explores the countess' desire to have her niece and her son wed amid complications arising from a mysterious past which eventually cause Julian to go mad. The long, involved speeches and drawn-out story become dull, but the countess could have been a formidable villainess. When in the final scene of Act II, Ada, the niece, appears to love another man, the countess reacts:

> So liberal of her presence! Palm to palm!
> Poor child! Ere thy quick senses have drunk in
> The maddening poison, I must pluck thee back—
> Will then no plan move smoothly to its end?
> Impediments rise ever in my path.
> Aye, but they rise only to be thrust down.
> Young man, come not 'twixt me and a fixed purpose.

With stiff and ponderous dialogue, however, the clichés of heroic adventures and an insensitivity to dramatic representation other than a strict adherence to the so-called unities, *Count Julian* is no more than another of the many dramas or "dramatic poems" published during the nineteenth century.

Not all writers of literary pretension either failed as playwrights or left the theatre with bitter memories. Their names may well be forgotten and their contributions meager in both literary and theatre worlds, but a few held some status among their contemporaries in literature and in theatre. Jonas B. Phillips, a poet and playwright who left little behind him that has lasted, was a productive and steady writer of popular melodrama in New York during the 1830s. Some dozen or more of his plays, for which productions are listed by theatre historians, show the several approaches he used to capitalize on the tastes of his day. *Telemachus; or, The Enchanted Isle*, was an extravaganza, a vehicle for scenery and costumes featuring Mentor and Telemachus shipwrecked on an island after a storm at sea, a burning ship and a visit to the submarine palace of Neptune. Among the spate of Indian plays at the Bowery Theatre, where most of Phillips' plays were produced, his *Oronaska* was acted in 1834. He also created a number of slight entertainments such as *The Polish Wife* (1831); *Cold Stricken* (1833); and *The Widow's Curse* (1837); and two "vaudevilles," *Ma Femme et Ma Parapluie* and *Le Chevalier d'Industrie* (1837). For his benefit at the Bowery Theatre in September of 1840, Phillips wrote *Ten Years of a Sailor's Life*, an effort to take advantage of the current popularity of nautical plays. Clearly, Phillips was a professional playwright, a journeyman playwright, who wrote for the commercial theatres of his day. At the same time, as a poet, he was sometimes interested in writing more substantial drama than the usual ephemera which flowed from his pen.

Phillips achieved sufficient stature with the New York theatres to present the opening address for the 1836–1837 season at the National Theatre. He gave a similar welcome speech at the Chatham Theatre to open the 1842–1843 season, and wrote the address delivered by Harry Eytinge at the opening of the Metropolitan Theatre in 1854. Such addresses were popular, and Louisa Medina opened the Broadway Theatre in the fall of 1837 with an address "in the form of a dramatic masque."[27] These were difficult times in the American theatre, it must be remembered, and novelty in any form was eagerly seized upon by nervous managers. During the spring of 1837, for example, the Brooklyn Theatre advertised a lecture by an Indian on "Wars and Treaties With Whites and Indians." Phillips' address was part of a standard practice and diversion for audiences, but he also brought prestige as a published author with *Tales for Leisure Hours* (1827) and *Zamira, a Dramatic Sketch and Other Poems* (1835). Although Phillips considered himself a man of letters, his only effort at serious and thought-provoking drama was *Camillus; or, The Self-Exiled Patriot* (1833). No better than his literary peers in his poetic drama, Phillips was yet different. He had the skill and knowledge to write successfully for the contemporary theatre, and two of his works held the stage for many years.

The Evil Eye, a two-act melodrama written with George Jones (1810–1879) and first performed at the Bowery Theatre on April 4, 1831, was based on a story by the same title set in Greece and published in the *London Keepsake* in 1830. The Greeks were involved in a struggle for independence from the Turkish Empire (1821–1832), and numerous volunteers of romantic inclination from England, France and Russia went to their aid, the most notable being Lord Byron. A spectacular melodrama revealing the intricate patterns of lineage that created problems among the Greeks, *The Evil Eye* features Demetri, the Klepht of the evil eye. "Ruin has been said to follow where his glance has rested in anger" (I,1). This is the power of Demetri, who becomes involved in a dispute between two brothers, Katusthius and Cyril, and uses his power to defend Cyril's son, Constans, whom he eventually identifies as his grandson. With music, songs, dance, fights and a spectacular water scene, the play was obviously more exciting than the plot suggests and reached its climax with a bloody fight in which Demetri kills Katusthius. With such spectacle, *The Evil Eye* was one of the popular melodramas of the period.

An even more popular work by Phillips was his adaptation of Harrison Ains-

worth's *Jack Sheppard* (1839), a novel of gothic intrigue that rivaled the popularity of *Oliver Twist*, the novel that Charles Dickens published that same year.
Ainsworth's work dealt with the exploits of an eighteenth-century robber, noted
for his prison escapes, who ended his life at Tyburn with a noose around his
neck. Two months after the novel was published, Phillips' *Jack Sheppard; or,
The Life of a Robber*, a melodrama in three acts, opened at the Bowery Theatre
(December 30, 1839). Although the first act of this play is weak and extremely
complicated, once past the awkward exposition the action moves rapidly and
clearly toward a spectacular climax. Jack and Thames Durrell are apprentices
of a benevolent carpenter named Owen Wood. They are opposites. Thames is
the good, loyal worker, loved by Winifred, Owen's daughter, while Jack, a
profligate lad of gin and gambling, loves Winifred. The mysterious character
throughout the play is Jonathan Wild, a villain sworn to corrupt Jack and see
him hanged and a person of considerable knowledge who provides periodic revelations throughout the play. As one part of the plot dramatizes the violent career of Jack Sheppard, the other traces the social rise of Thames, whose inheritance of a title and estate is periodically thwarted by Jonathan in the employ
of Sir Rowland Trenchard. Act I ends as Thames discovers his mother, Lady
Trafford, and her relationship to Sir Rowland, but not the name of his father.
"Too Late—too late!" she cries, "I die—my son, my son!"

Act II begins five years later. Captain Thames Durrell has returned to Winifred from military service in France. Jack has become a celebrated house-
breaker with a price on his head whose crimes have driven his mother, Constance Sheppard, to madness. Although Jack promises that he is through with
crime, he is his father's son and must contend with his father's corrupter, Jonathan Wild. Having revealed that Constance Sheppard is Sir Rowland's sister,
Jonathan is paid by Sir Rowland to destroy Thames, and takes villainous pleasure in controlling the vast estate which legally belongs to Mrs. Sheppard or to
her heir. The last scene of Act II is typical of the play's melodramatic action.
As Jack asks forgiveness of his mother, Jonathan Wild appears at the window.
He will save Jack, Jonathan says, if Mrs. Sheppard will become his wife. At
last Wild's motivations have become clear, but Mrs. Sheppard refuses. There
is a fight which is interrupted by the arrival of Thames and Wood, and Jonathan, frustrated in his attempt to abduct Mrs. Sheppard, sees his difficulty, and
"throws" Mrs. Sheppard at her rescuers as he escapes through the window.

By the end of Act II Jack has increased his reputation as a criminal in direct
proportion to Thames' advance as an honorable man. Jonathan, meanwhile, remains obdurate in his villainy. Jack returns to the carpenter's room where his
life of crime started six years previously: where the shrewish Mrs. Wood struck
him and made him a criminal, where he twice robbed Wood and witnessed Mrs.
Wood's murder, where he left a friend and broke his mother's heart. He now
regrets his life as he receives from a strange character named Kneebone a packet
of materials establishing his birth, his inheritance and his parent's intention that
he should marry Winifred. There he stands, as handsome as the company cos-

tumer could make him: "enveloped in a handsome roquelaire which on enter-
ing he throws off—his dress-coat of brown flowered velvet laced with silver—
richly embroidered white satin waistcoat—shoes with red heels and large diamond buckles; pearl colored stockings—a muslin cravat edged with lace ruffles
of the same material and a handsome sword" (III,2).

The last scene of the play takes place at the gallows.

(Music. Procession.)

Jonathan: Hark, lose no time—a hundred pounds if you do it quickly.

Executioner: Rely on me! Any last words, Jack?

Jack: Nothing—I am ready—Jonathan Wild—in less than a year you will hang from this
same gibbet!

(Music. Blueskin cuts rope, is wounded. Wild's house appears in flames. Thames rushes
to take Jack as Blueskin falls. Jonathan tries to get Jack, and Blueskin fires, killing him.
Both die.)

Jack: True, faithful friend! Thames Durrell, you will have your rights. Tell Winifred
Wood that Jack Sheppard blessed her—as he died.

(Dies. Shouts. Curtain.)

This was early nineteenth-century melodrama at its best: intrigue, sentiment,
fights, escapes and pursuits, music and extravagant costumes and scenery designed to provide visual pleasure.

Phillips wrote the play for the Bowery Theatre, but *Jack Sheppard* in one
form or another remained popular on the American stage for the next fifty years.
As any knowledge of American theatre or other entertainment immediately reveals, managers and playwrights do not allow a popular stage character to fade
away. Instead, that popularity is always exploited, and Jack Sheppard continued onstage through several metamorphoses. In 1862, for example, *Harlequin
Jack Sheppard* appeared. The following year John F. Poole, a very productive
English actor, theatre manager and playwright who spent much of the later part
of his life in America, prepared a new and more romantic version of Ainsworth's novel entitled *Knights of the Mist; or, Jack Sheppard from His Cradle
to His Grave*. For novelty's sake, apparently, one production of this subject
was called *Jack Sheppard and His Dog*. In 1876, an anonymous playwright
decided to emphasize a nationalist theme and wrote *The Highwayman of 1776;
or, The Jack Sheppard of America*. Given the interests of the nineteenth century, there were also the inevitable burlesques, one which was produced as late
as 1889 and entitled *Little Jack Sheppard*. Harry Watkins mentions playing Jack
Sheppard for the first time, recalling that the part was generally played by a
woman "which is truly an absurdity, for no woman could go through what
Sheppard did, escaping from jails, etc. The piece went well, and I was called
before the curtain. This drama does not tend to elevate public morals but if it
does no real harm, managers can hardly be blamed for presenting it."[28]

Like most of the playwrights who gained any acceptance in the American theatre, Phillips achieved his greatest successes with adaptations from current fiction. His higher aspirations for dramatic composition appear in *Camillus; or, The Self-Exiled Patriot*, which he wrote in 1830 and dedicated to Mordecai M. Noah and "the interest you have ever manifested in the cause of the dramatic literature of our country, and the zeal with which your efforts have always been directed to its advancement." [29] This was an appropriate gesture, for Noah's presence was felt among the theatre people of New York throughout Jacksonian America. The dedication also suggests Phillips' ambitions.

Camillus, a five-act tragedy in blank verse, is not, unfortunately, a well-written play no matter how patriotic its theme or how noble its hero. It was, however, performed in Philadelphia at the Arch Street Theatre in 1833 and at the Bowery Theatre in New York in 1835. The plot revolves around the love that Camillus, tribune and later dictator of Rome, has for Rome and for his daughter, Camilla. Her rejection of the villain early in the play precipitates the internal and external strife that Phillips dramatizes. Her death in the fifth act determines Camillus' final action as he kills the villain and falls prostrate on Camilla's body. Patriotism is the main thread of the play whose hero has all the qualities that Jacksonians should admire, and the audience is asked in an epilogue to adopt similar attitudes and thoughts:

> Then were you marshalled for your native land—
> To-night you're not a less efficient band;
> By freedom's banners you were then combined—
> To-night you join the banners of the mind.

A romantic and sometimes melancholy writer whose poetic talents appear extremely limited, Phillips also wrote a dramatic sketch entitled *Zamira* in which the heroine waits for her lover who escapes his country's tyrant, aided by a mist created by the Spirit of the Lake. "Why comes he not? I long have tarried / By this silv'n lake, upon whose verdant banks / We have oft wander'd at the moonlight hour." Phillips wrote for both passing worlds—that of literature and of theatre—but he was clearly better prepared for the latter, where his work was a prominent part of New York entertainment for a decade.

Isaac Pray (1813–1869) was a Boston-born journalist, poet, dramatist, critic, actor and theatre manager. Although not a major figure in either literary or theatre circles, he represents that tertiary level of the literati who, as a journal editor, was constantly aware of the progress of literature in America and of his contributions to it while achieving some success in the theatre. In a letter to R. Shelton MacKenzie written late in 1835, Pray showed this awareness along with a sense of humor: "The literary world is rather dull here—there are no new works in press of any consequence. One of the most remarkable works, lately published, is 'Vita Washingtorin' by Francis Glass—a man who thought in Latin." [30] At this time, Pray, just beginning his career, described the literary scene, accurately, and while his dramatic work added little to his status, his efforts are part of that greater activity which would eventually produce memorable nights in the theatre.

Beginning his playwriting career at the youthful age of fourteen, Pray presumably wrote a play called *The Prisoners*, which was produced at the Albany Theatre. Later, in Boston, he edited *The Pearl* and was the owner and editor-in-chief of the *Daily-Herald*. In 1836 he moved to New York, where he managed the National Theatre and at the request of William Pelby wrote a five-act tragedy entitled *Julietta Gordini; or, The Miser's Daughter*. During the late 1830s Pray dramatized from the *Sunday Morning News* (which he also edited) his very popular story entitled *The Old Clock; or, Here She Goes, There She Goes*, which was first produced at the Park Theatre and later in other New York theatres. Pray appears to have been an extremely busy and influential person in both literary and theatre circles in Boston and New York. During the early 1840s in New York, for example, he edited the *Dramatic Guardian*, a daily paper, as well as a monthly called the *Ladies' Companion* and wrote dramatic criticism for the *Express* and other newspapers. His acting career began in 1846 during a visit to England and to Cork, Ireland, where he managed the Theatre Royal. Upon his return to New York, he continued acting and by 1849 was back in Boston, where he helped to open the Beach Street Museum. At this theatre he produced his tragedy *The Broker of Florence*, which played for thirty-six consecutive nights. It was also for this theatre that he wrote *The Female Forty Thieves* (1849), his most successful play, and with the help of Charles T. P. Ware, another burlesque entitled *The Model Modern Aladden*. Returning to New York in 1850, he wrote music and drama criticism for the *Herald* and published *The Book of the Drama* (1851), which shows his interest in Italian opera.

Clearly a man of considerable energy, Pray appears to have been one of those bridging the gap between literature and theatre more consistently than any of his colleagues but without marked success in either field of endeavor. His acting career was of brief duration, but he managed a number of theatres and gained some reputation as a tutor of such actors and actresses as Charlotte Cushman, Agnes Ethel, Augustus A. Addams and Charles Thorne. He also published a respectable number of books. The first, entitled *Prose and Verse from the Portfolio of an Editor* (1836), included a brief dramatic sketch entitled *Idiot Boy*. A volume of *Poems* appeared in 1837. *Memoires of James G. Bennett* was published in 1855. The number of his dramatic works—tragedies, comedies, farces, burlesques, librettos—will probably never be known. After becoming stage manager for Laura Keene in 1854, he produced *Electra* at the Broadway Theatre, showing his deep interest in classical drama. He is also listed as having translated some fifteen French operas and several of the plays made popular by the Italian actress Adelaide Ristori after her 1855 Paris success—*Judith, Mary Stuart, Deborah of Steinmark*.

Most of Pray's original plays were of a character and quality comparable to the work of his contemporary editors and writers rather than that of actors and theatre managers. Apparently, he did not write primarily for the nonsensical pleasure of audiences but had more serious motives. Of his works, a prompt copy of *Julietta Gordini* has been preserved along with some scenes from *Caecinna, the Roman Consul*, a play written for McKean Buchannan that was produced at the Astor Place Opera House in October of 1850, and later successfully performed by that actor on tour in 1851. This was evidently a later version of Pray's 1837 play described by the *Spirit of the Times* as "a new Roman tragedy nearly ready."[31] In March of 1837, the New York *Mirror* printed the first scene from *The Noble Romans*, an "unpublished tragedy of Isaac Pray, Jun." The following speech of Caecinna to Thraseus, his daughter's fiancé, suggests the quality of Pray's poetry:

> And love would have a lifelong holiday!
> Think not too much of love. In evil times
> Like these, to whom his native land is dear,
> At most, his love should be a second purpose.
> Rank weeds possess the ground where grows that flower
> They rooted from the soil, 'twill quicken it
> To grow, to blossom and delight, while spring
> Around it others, like itself; but this
> Undone, the beauty of the plant is lost—
> Its Virtues lost—concealed amid the growth
> Of tangled shrubs that draw its strength away
> Infecting it, ofttimes, with poison! Let
> Thy soul wed first its hope for liberty;
> Thy country needs thy thought, thine act. Our life
> In the low slavery borne which now we feel
> Is death—or, at the best, a sleep which knows
> No dreams, and wakens only when Minerva,
> By Jove's indignant wrath, all panoplied,
> Is seated mid the clouds, with frowning face,
> Lighted by lightnings, while his voice resounds
> Over heaven's wide arch, and shakes the eternal hills
> Whose every peak sends back the shout they hear
> Of "Liberty!"[32]

Concerned, as were his contemporaries, with classical and nature imagery, Pray wrote reasonably flowing lines in which he reveals his acceptance of the popular rule of heroic tragedy by which love must give way to honor and patriotism.

The play begins near the end of the reign of Tiberius Claudius who sends for Caecinna, consul in Illyria, to answer for his attempt to dethrone the emperor. In choosing his conflict, Pray took advantage of Caecinna's wife, Arria, whose determination to help her husband is as strong as Caecinna's ill-fated attempt to rescue his country from its repulsive licentiousness. Patriotism, family and romantic love confront Claudius' cruelty in Pray's attempt to create a good acting role from the ruins of the Roman Empire. Man needs heroes, a fact exploited by Emerson and Thomas Carlyle, and for writers of heroic tragedy in America and elsewhere the past history of Rome appeared to be an irresistible attraction. They wrote of Spartacus, of Caius Marius and of Sertorius but expected the audiences to think of Washington, Andrew Jackson and John Jacob Astor or even the mythical Jonathan. Whether or not it was an effective technique, Pray was simply falling in step with his literary peers in an endeavor to satisfy the expectations of American theatre audiences.

In that division of prejudices that fettered critics during much of the nineteenth century, only the efforts of the literati seemed to hold any real promise for the national dramatic literature that seemed necessary for the new nation. There were few words of critical enthusiasm or recognition of serious potential for such playwrights as Joseph S. Jones, Louisa Medina, Nathaniel H. Bannister, John Augustus Stone, George Washington Harby, Joseph Field or scores of others. Instead, George Pepper and like critics would spend considerable energy on the efforts of a Charles Ingersoll and argue that he had the talent to write a great tragedy that would "confer honor on the American drama."[33] For Ingersoll and other such aspiring playwrights as David Paul Brown, Rufus Dawes or Elizabeth Ellet, critics took the time to urge them to study dramatic effect and improve their works. That these playwrights neglected to follow this excellent advice only reemphasizes the division of interests and the arrogance that worked against the developing literature. Although few in number—Nathaniel Parker Willis, Robert Montgomery Bird, Richard Penn Smith, Epes Sargent, Cornelius Mathews, George Washington Parke Custis—some literary dramatists deserved a great deal more attention than they received. Had the times been different, several might have accomplished more, and writers like Phillips and Pray might have been influential. While the commercially oriented American playwright supplied the theatre fare that the star system and the prejudices of the time would allow, the literati in America entered the theatrical arena, contending many times with favorable critics but indifferent audiences, and then withdrew without the success they had anticipated. Class-conscious audiences, a haunting antagonism between the literati and the theatre artists, and all of the other problems facing any playwright in Jacksonian America combined to nullify any advantage a talented writer might have as a dramatist. Those who succeeded did so on the terms established by the popular theatre of the day.

NOTES

1. *Irish Shield and Literary Panorama*, III (February 18, 1831), 76–77.
2. *Dramatic Mirror*, I (August 21, 1841), 9–10.
3. See Robert E. Blanc, "James McHenry (1785–1845), Playwright and Novelist," Ph.D. diss., University of Pennsylvania, 1939, p. 19.
4. *Ladies' Literary Port Folio*, I (December 9, 1829), 1.
5. *Irish Shield and Literary Panorama*, III (February 11, 1831), 62.
6. *Irish Shield and Literary Panorama*, III (March 11, 1831), 127.
7. *North American Review*, IV (May 1834), 53–57.
8. *North American Magazine*, I (December 1832), 127.
9. *Irish Shield and Literary Panorama*, III (February 18, 1831), 77.

10. See "The Literati of New York City" (1846), in *The Complete Works of Edgar Allan Poe*, vol. XV (New York: Thomas Y. Crowell & Company, 1902), 1–126.

11. *North American Magazine*, I (December 1832), 127–28.

12. Merle M. Hoover, *Park Benjamin, Poet & Editor* (New York: Columbia University Press, 1948).

13. Printed in William W. Clapp, Jr., *A Record of the Boston Stage* (Boston: James Monroe and Company, 1853), 302–3.

14. *Spirit of the Times*, XII (March 5, 1842), 12.

15. Delia Salter Bacon, *The Bride of Fort Edwards* (New York: S. Colman, 1839), ii.

16. *New York Review*, V (October 1839), 518; New York *Evening Journal*, quoted in the *Spirit of the Times*, I (April 14, 1832), 3.

17. *New York Review*, IV (April 1839), 497.

18. *North American Magazine*, I (January 1833), 1.

19. Other than *Athenia of Damascus*, Dawes' only claim for attention in the theatre is a manuscript copy of a play entitled *The Battle of Stillwater; or, The Maniac* in the Billy Rose Theatre Collection, New York Public Library of Lincoln Center, once owned by John B. Wright, the prompter of the Boston National Theatre where the play was produced for his benefit on March 16, 1840. Mysteriously, Dawes' name appears on the manuscript along with the titles of plays written by another author. Records show, however, that H. J. Conway wrote a play entitled *The Battle of Stillwater* as well as plays with the other listed titles. Moreover, there is nothing to suggest Dawes' poetic style in *The Battle of Stillwater*, which was obviously written by a person familiar with both the theatre and the nationalistic interest of the common man.

20. *New York Review*, IV (April 1839), 490–493.

21. Arthur Hobson Quinn, *A History of the American Drama from the Beginning to the Civil War* (New York: Appleton-Century-Crofts, Inc. 1943), 263–64; *Dramatic Mirror*, I (September 18, 1841), 47.

22. For details of Griswold's quarrel with Mrs. Ellet, see Joy Bayless' *Rufus Wilmont Griswold* (Nashville, Tenn.: Vanderbilt University Press, 1943)), 137–60.

23. George C. D. Odell, *Annals of the New York Stage*, vol. IV (New York: Columbia University Press, 1928), 17.

24. Published the same year it opened in New York, in Mrs. Ellet's *Poems, Translations from the French & Italian, Some Original* (1835), *Teresa Contarini* is based on Nicolini's *Antonia Foscarini* and illustrates that dark period in Venetian history when state decrees and the judgment of the inquisitors degenerated into scenes of private revenge. Although a writer in the *American Monthly Magazine* found "the tragedy superior to anything that has appeared since *The Gladiator*, of native talent," he felt that a revision would make the play "as good an acting play as it is now a beautiful poem" (IV, [1835], 157–58).

25. "The Drama," *The Literary World*, April 24, 1847, 281.

26. *New York Review*, VI (April 1840), 503.

27. Odell, *Annals*, IV, 184.

28. Maud and Otis Skinner, eds., *One Man in His Time, the Adventures of H. Watkins, Strolling Player, 1845–1863, from His Journal* (Philadelphia: University of Pennsylvania Press, 1938), 183.

29. Jonas B. Phillips, *Camillus; or, The Self-Exiled Patriot* (New York: E. B. Clayton, 1833), Dedication.

30. Letter to R. Shelton MacKenzie, December 2, 1835, Gratz Collection, Case 6, Box 33, Historical Society of Pennsylvania. Robert Shelton MacKenzie (1809–1881) is of far greater importance to American writers and dramatists than has been recognized. An Irish author and journalist, appointed the English correspondent for the New York *Evening Star* in 1834, MacKenzie came to New York in 1852 where he worked for five years as a music and drama critic. Moving to Philadelphia, he became literary and foreign editor and dramatic critic for the Philadelphia *Press*. His correspondence with American authors was voluminous even before he came to America.

31. *Spirit of the Times*, VII (February 25, 1837), 1.

32. New York *Mirror*, XIV (March 25, 1837), 310.

33. *Irish Shield and Literary Panorama*, III (February 18, 1831), 77.

8

THE LEGACY OF THE AGE OF JACKSON

"Man is a singular creature. He has a set of gifts which make him unique among the animals: so that, unlike them, he is not a figure in the landscape—he is a shaper of the landscape." [1] In that class-conscious society of Jacksonian America many people relished that "singular" quality, accepted a manifest destiny and saw themselves as shapers of the landscape. Largely white, Anglo-Saxon protestants and fascinated by a male-oriented world, they came from different levels of society to assert their beliefs as leaders or followers in that development of a "more perfect union." A huge landscape, America would undergo drastic changes during that twenty-year period. Demographic changes, for example, would play havoc with the struggling social structure, while the political upheaval created by Jacksonian democracy was reflected in most aspects of American life. Contending with these changes, man the "shaper of the landscape," the shaper of his art and literature, his work and his play, encountered difficulties. In the development of a national dramatic literature, however—in spite of the problems inherent in his social structure and regardless of his inability to encourage or properly recognize sustained artistry—he created far better than he realized, better than what had come before and, with the single exception of G. H. Boker's *Francesca da Rimini*, better than anything that would be written for the American theatre until well after the Civil War.

Profit-minded, risk-taking, reform-oriented, bold and adventurous, hardworking and idealistic, many Jacksonians sought material gains or expansive dreams of power with a single-mindedness that frequently clouded or eliminated any interest in the arts or leisure-class activities. They crossed the continent, expanded their political rights, increased their technological knowledge, changed the speed and volume of transportation over their landscape, and sent clipper ships around the world. In 1830 there were only twenty-six cities in America with over 8,000 citizens, while their aggregate number was only 6.72 percent of the total population of the country. Ten years later the number of such cities had jumped to forty-four, and to eighty-five in 1850. On August 8, 1829, in northeastern Pennsylvania Horatio Allen made a trial run of a seven-ton locomotive called the Sturbridge Lion, and during the following decade the miles of railroad track in America increased from 39.8 to 2,755.2. To travel from Philadelphia to Pittsburgh in 1834 took nearly four days; twenty years later the distance could be covered in thirteen hours. Such changes were reflected in the American's style of living, in his beliefs and dreams as well as in his struggle to maintain balance, create stability and form pleasurable habits in a recognizable society.

In this fast-moving society, literature and art, music and theatre, in fact all social and artistic events, were forced to develop by their own merit or not at all. Although the social aristocracies of Tidewater Virginia, Boston's Beacon Hill and Knickerbocker New York maintained their cultural interests, they were not the moving majority that put Jackson in the White House. If the common people were not interested in art, literature or intellectual pursuits, it was because they had no time or saw no advantage to them, and advantages in their minds generally meant material gain. Writers, to mold their work into the current philosophy of the 1829–1849 period, needed a ready market for their products. By the same reasoning, playwrights should have been able to support themselves by supplying interested theatre managers with plays which they, by adroit management of performers and physical theatres, could sell nightly to an eager public. Such, of course, has always been the argument of a commercially oriented society. Theoretically, it can work. In that best of all possible societies art should satisfy a basic need of mankind.

The Age of Jackson was not a period that recognized many literary achievements, although a number of major poets and novelists published their works during the period. Washington Irving wrote *The Conquest of Grenada* (1829) and *The Alhambra* (1832) while abroad and published three other works during the 1830s. Cooper returned to America in 1833 and published more than a dozen books before his death in 1851. Among the lesser but popular novelists of that period were James Kirke Paulding, Robert Montgomery Bird, John Pendleton Kennedy, William Caruthers and William Gilmore Simms. In the field of poetry, Edgar Allan Poe's entire career was encompassed by these years and Longfellow was beginning to gain a reputation. Emerson wrote his best essays during this period; Hawthorne and Melville had also begun writing and publishing their work before 1850. The most popular writer, however, was Nathaniel Parker Willis, and the most widely read poet was James Gates Percival. With very few exceptions, none of these, nor scores of lesser writers, made a living writing poetry or fiction. Generally, they worked as teachers, lecturers, editors and journalists to support themselves and their avocations. Historians have made much of Poe's dire poverty, but he was hardly alone in this plight. All writers were necessarily risk-takers in the true Jacksonian sense, and the odds were ingloriously mounted against them.

For many literary-minded individuals the editorship of a journal was some stay against financial hardship, although the establishment of any publishing venture was itself a great risk. Many fine journals, however, were established during the Age of Jackson—the *New England Magazine* (1831–1835), *Knickerbocker* (1833–1865), *United States Magazine and Democratic Review* (1837–1859), *Southern Literary Messenger* (1834–1869), *Graham's Magazine* (1840–1855), *Godey's Lady's Magazine* (1830–1898), *The Democratic Review* (1837–1859), *The Dial* (1840–1844) and *The New York Review* (1837–1842). There were also magazines particularly related to the theatre, carrying such titles as *The Drama*, *The Dramatic Mirror*, *The Prompter*, *Dramatic Miscellaneous*, *Dramatic Rights* and *Dramatic Sketches*. The number of magazines published during these years is legion. Most did not last long; a number printed all types of poems and essays plus criticism of the theatre and drama. In the extremely competitive world of entrepreneurship pressured by the inhuman philosophy of "root, hog, or die!" the life of a magazine—and its editor—could be very brief. Jacksonians believed in markets in which profit depended upon selling, and selling depended upon the product. What did American writers and playwrights have to offer?

With the exploitation of democratic capitalism on a new level of experience, writers had to contend with Tocqueville's prediction that writing would be looked upon as a "mere trade." It is the adjective that would irritate the Jacksonian American who saw trade as a worthy ideal, but the practical playwright took no offense. He understood completely the flawed humanity that always perverted the ideal that the best of literature and the best of theatre entertainment should appeal to all people at all times. Additionally, the playwright had far less opportunity than the writer of fiction or poetry to reach this ideal, for the latter might publish and still go unread, only to be preserved for later generations. On the other hand, the playwright whose plays are not produced generally joins the closet dramatists or tries another literary genre, and plays will be produced only if they provide immediate satisfaction for actors, theatre managers and audiences. Tocqueville notwithstanding, the playwright by definition *is* a tradesman. This does not mean, as Shakespeare and many others have illustrated, that he or she must create inferior works of literature, but it does mean that a paying public must be pleased.

The American public-to-be-pleased expanded considerably during the 1830s and 1840s. Although New York continued to strengthen its reputation as the center of theatre in America, as men made their way across the continent, they took their theatre with them. After the mid 1830s Chicago grew as a center for theatre, while the Mississippi River brought theatre to towns in eastern Iowa, St. Louis and down to New Orleans where a number of American playwrights—Rees, Bannister, Field and Harby—were active in the theatres. Between the Atlantic Coast, where there were major theatres from Washington to Boston, and the great river, there were many cities that could boast more than a casual interest in theatrical entertainment. The theatre managers in these areas such as Noah Ludlow, Sol Smith and James Caldwell frequently advertised for "Ladies and Gentlemen of the Histrionic Profession" to work at their establishments.[2]

The character of this public, which a theatre manager must understand to be successful, was as diverse as might be expected, and the stage reflected distinctive tastes from ribald farce to grand opera. Theatres in the eastern cities purposefully determined their clientele by their offerings, and traveling stars from England mainly played in those theatres in which English plays, foreign adaptations and the classics were the usual fare. Because constant change of the evening's entertainment was standard practice, these theatres would also arrange for performances by American actors and actresses of star quality when necessary. Other theatres in the East kept their doors open with varied entertainment that included spectacular melodrama, burlesque and farce, a theatre fare increasingly produced by Americans as the period progressed. The offerings of theatres springing up in mid-America depended entirely upon the finesse and persuasive powers of their managers to attract touring stars and to mount spectacular entertainment. Frequently, these managers would produce any novelty they could find, consistent with the tastes of their known audiences, when they did not have a touring star.

In attempting to appeal to this diverse public the native American playwright was limited by his social background and occupation as actor or writer. Without either some reputation as a writer or editor or acceptance into a certain social level, a playwright could not presume to write for certain theatres. Assuming those conditions, any playwright could generally be assured of a production and an audience for a night or two. After that, philanthropy gave way to commercial instinct. Most playwrights wrote for the less pretentious houses, where they made little or no money, and constantly took the chance of having their work stolen or perhaps slightly changed in another production to create an illusion of originality. Unless the production was spectacular or there was little competition on other stages, these were the plays that got a line or two from reviewers between comments on some traveling star. The exceptions are the plays discussed in this study. When the author of the "Decline of the Modern Drama" wrote in 1830 that "it is to the pit and the gallery that he [the playwright] must appeal," he was describing the road to success for the popular playwrights as well as bemoaning the paucity of sophisticated audiences in America.[3] In either event it was advice that many American playwrights followed, although their part in providing theatre entertainment for Jacksonian America remained woefully small. With few and scattered exceptions, English playwrights, past or present, were most popular with American theatre audiences.

In 1829 there had been at least eight American playwrights who could be termed active in the American theatre. In 1849 there were slightly more than a dozen comparably active playwrights. Of these, only two, John Brougham and H. J. Conway, could be considered on the upward swing in their playwriting careers, while J. S. Jones steadily maintained his long and productive life in the theatre. That is not a great improvement over a generation, but the latter figure does not take into consideration the greater activity of those writing plays in 1849, including the vastly increased number of actor-playwrights who wrote a play or two or the anonymously written plays that may be presumed of American authorship. Moreover, there were another dozen or more Americans who wrote plays, showed definite talent as playwrights, and then, for one reason or another, essentially stopped writing for the stage. Bird is the outstanding example because he appears to have had such excellent opportunity, writing for the foremost American actor of the period. Smith and Brown were also worthy of encouragement as were Conrad and Custis—all of whom chose other careers. Willis and Sargent contracted some of Bird's bitterness although for different reasons. It would have been interesting to see what Longfellow might have accomplished, given a theatre that supported the work of fledgling playwrights. The same might be written of Ellet or Conner. Mowatt cannot be faulted for choosing the more lucrative career of acting, and Steele eventually became an anthologizer. Stone committed suicide, and two of the most successful writers of popular plays, Medina and Bannister, died young. The dramatist who was recognized by the next generation as the "Father of American drama," Cornelius Mathews, dropped out of the theatre a few years after mid-century.

These were the Heralds of Promise—the playwrights of Jacksonian America! With the plays they wrote during this twenty-year period they prepared the way for the greater accomplishment of American dramatists who would follow. Whether literary or commercial playwright, each strove for a certain level of achievement in his or her art, even if that level was constrained by the mediocrity of a manager's taste. By sheer weight of numbers the American playwrights, though not substantially better off than those a generation earlier, were forcing themselves upon the attention of audiences as well as managers and actors. With the first annual dinner of the American Dramatic Fund Association in April of 1849, at the Astor House in New York, there was both expressed and implied interest in the American playwright. "We were rejoiced," wrote the critic from the *Spirit,* to see among the patrons and supporters of the project, gentlemen of the highest respectability and of literary fame. . . . We were equally delighted to perceive the fraternal commingling of the actor, the author, and the man, and more than all did it gratify us to hear the sentiment of harmonious coalition and devotion in a good cause." Major Noah attended—"No one more conversant with theatricals before and behind the curtain"; Hamblin condemned the evils of the "star system," and James T. Brady spoke of the Association bringing "the members of the dramatic profession in union with the rest of the community."[4] With such sentiments, there did, indeed, appear to be real promise for the future of American drama.

To create that sense of promise, the playwrights of Jacksonian America had both imitated their English colleagues and struck out onto new paths of theatrical creativity. Like his European and English contemporaries, the American dramatist of literary pretensions wrote plays on classical themes, took his heroes from ancient Rome and created romantic tales set in mythical and faraway places. He did this as much to satisfy acknowledged desires of theatre audiences as to continue in his traditional writing style. The work of the popular actor-playwright Sheridan Knowles also influenced the American literati and encouraged actors who would be playwrights. Just as the English stole from the French theatres, the Americans stole from both and adapted English and American popular fiction in the fashion of the day. Douglas Jerrold's *Black-Eyed Susan,* for example, inspired nautical dramas in America although, strange to say, Americans never appreciated the dramatization of the novels of James Fenimore Cooper in any way comparable to their popularity in England. The tremendous attraction of melodrama and spectacle, however, spread rapidly across the Atlantic. Pixerécourt's art was widely imitated while the French interest in detailed scenic displays appeared in their *Livrets Scéniques.* Following the lead of their literary and theatre colleagues across the Atlantic Ocean, Americans provided entertainment that occasionally in Jacksonian America and certainly in later decades surpassed the melodrama of England and Europe in excitement and splendor. At the same time they made contemporary society in the new nation more aware of the need for an American dramatic literature.

There existed, throughout the period, an intricate relationship between English and American actors and playwrights which can be explained, or forgiven, mainly in terms of human frailties and strengths. As opportunists, the English came to America to act, write and return to England or to remain to promote theatrical art in their adopted country. Quite logically, they brought English plays and appealed to the aristocratic levels of American society. For the common man in Jacksonian America, however, they offered little. Consciously or unconsciously, they controlled the theatres, drove American actors out of the large cities and essentially discouraged American playwriting. This is, of course, not a fair assessment of all English theatre people; Thomas Hamblin, for commercial reasons, promoted American drama, and William Burton along with certain others does not deserve this assessment, which is, however, as true as any generalization. The English clearly helped establish theatre in America; at the same time, they clearly delayed the development of a distinctive American dramatic literature.

The first original contributions of American playwrights appeared in the characters they created, the points of view they dramatized and the theatrical forms they devised. Although English critics sometimes saw the Yankee as a variation of the crude Yorkshireman—and the English actor Charles Mathews must be given his due for his portrayal of Jonathan—American actors and playwrights developed and perfected the characterization. The fashion for city plays undoubtedly owes something to Egan's *Tom and Jerry*, but Mose came from

New York, and the backwoodsman and the stage Indian are American innovations. *Fashion*; *Putnam, The Iron Son of '76*; and *Witchcraft* are basically American in thought and sentiment. Diverse as these are in structure and purpose, there were obviously many other such plays with American points of view. Although theatrical forms are not the province of this study, American playwrights helped establish the minstrel show that sprang up in the early 1840s and provided much material for the creation of spectacular melodrama.

In an article entitled "Obstacles to American Literature," published in *The Knickerbocker* in 1833, Timothy Flint noted that the public fascination with politics was stronger than an interest in literature. He also condemned the habit of many critics to puff American writing whatever its merits and the prevailing assumption that English works were always superior to American efforts.[5] This last comment was a fair generalization and one that would remain appropriate for generations, for dramatic literature as well as other literary genres. For dramatists, however, any list of obstacles should have included the lack of copyright protection, the nature of dramatic criticism in America, the religious and social adversaries, and the conditions in the theatre which ignored or irritated the playwright. These obstacles remained prominent, to be duly recognized, bemoaned or explained by people of varied humors. In his *Notions of the Americans* Cooper noted that the theatres in America, though numerous, were decidedly English in both plays and players. "Of dramatic writers there are none, or next to none," he wrote; yet in spite of the "baldness of the ordinary American life," which he found hostile to "scenic representation," he held some hope that America would have a drama in the future.[6] That was in 1828, and Cooper was living in England and Europe and not one to be trusted completely as a critic of American drama. At least, William Gilmore Simms thought not. Denying that American literature was basically English, he took Cooper firmly to task for his views.[7] Both Cooper and Simms, it should be noted, attempted unsuccessfully to write for the theatre.

In a very perceptive observation, Margaret Fuller declared that neither the age nor the country favored the writing of drama. She went so far as to recommend that attempts to write plays be abandoned and that people be satisfied with opera, ballet and pantomine.[8] Other writers, even Nathaniel Parker Willis in the *Broadway Journal* of June 11, 1845, seemed less interested in promoting good American drama than in complaining that there were no American dramatists, that the stage was English in character and thought and that speeches in plays were delivered by actors with English accents. Although drama critics suggested revisions for the plays reviewed, none inspired American dramatists to greater heights of creativity, nor did they exert any real influence upon the kind of drama written. Clearly illustrating an ignorance of American drama that must have been disheartening to American nationalists is a contemporary publication entitled *The British and American Theatre*, "A choice collection of the most popular dramatic pieces of both nations."[9] Of the thirteen plays collected, not one is by an American author. Yet an American drama of marked accomplishment did exist.

The legacy that the Age of Jackson left to American drama was one of hope—
a promise demonstrated by a dozen or more playwrights whose work overcame
seemingly insuperable obstacles to reveal qualities of distinction. Stone's *Metamora*, Conrad's *Jack Cade*, and *The Gladiator* and *The Broker of Bogota* by
Bird—these helped bring Edwin Forrest his reputation. The long and distinguished career of Joseph S. Jones and the brief and intensive success of Louisa
Medina were determined by conditions inherent to the Age of Jackson. Although the contributions of Joseph Field have been neglected because he was
not long a major figure in Eastern theatres, his contemporary reputation suggests a greater importance to American drama than existing evidence can support. On the other hand, Nathaniel H. Bannister had six of his plays published,
a considerable achievement at this time, while *The Gentleman of Lyons* and
Putnam, The Iron Son of '76 are distinctive contributions to American drama.
Nathaniel Parker Willis' *Tortesa the Usurer* is a substantial comedy for any
period in history, one that still reads and plays well. Although neither of Epes
Sargent's romantic tragedies, *The Bride of Genoa* nor *Velasco*, has much appeal for modern audiences, both showed a promise that deserved encouragement, as did the work of Richard Penn Smith and David Paul Brown, whose
lighter plays indicate talents that were never developed. Finally, there is Cornelius Mathews' *Witchcraft*, the major work of the man identified by his generation as the "Father of American Drama." In addition to these outstanding
contributions to a developing American drama, there was the growing number
of American playwrights ready and eager to promote the novelties or features
that would either keep theatres open during the absence of touring stars or help
some of the American stars establish careers.

In the work of these dramatists lay promise for an American drama of the
future. There is another characteristic of the Jacksonian legacy to America drama,
however, one equally distinctive if not as praiseworthy, and related to the first
as a confirmation of these playwrights as heralds of promise. Margaret Fuller
was right: neither the age nor the country favored the writing of great drama.
Perhaps the problem extended to the entire Western world where dramatists of
stature either did not exist or were not appreciated during their lifetimes. Jacksonian America, however, had its particular obstacles. Although a respectable
number of people wrote plays, for a number of reasons—contests, the star system, an aggressive interest in money, nationalistic ambitions—they were not
properly rewarded. At a time when the nation appeared to thrive on hard work
and to believe in the right to receive just recompense, dramatists found themselves painfully abused, with the result that the potential for playwriting exhibited by a remarkable number of them was never developed. Literary playwrights did not understand the situation in the theatre and departed in bitterness,
although critics frequently applauded their efforts and begged for national encouragement. Commercial playwrights did understand and accept, but they also
despaired. Conditions placed upon both kinds of playwrights were not conducive to the creation of great art. Even considering the increasing number of plays
written over this period and the remarkable achievement of certain dramatists,

it was still not a good time for dramatists in America. In spite of the prevailing conditions, however, they brought a distinction to American dramatic literature that would not be equaled until another generation had passed. The legacy of the Age of Jackson was distinctly one of hope and promise, but it was forged in an atmosphere of disappointment and frustration.

The theatre was moving westward in 1849 and American literature moved with it. In a letter to Robert Dale Owen in January of 1845, James Kirke Paulding wrote: "The people of the West are too busy . . . to be fully conscious of their powers, but it has long been my opinion that it is from thence our national literature will finally divine its distinctive character. They do not feel every gale that blows across the Atlantic."[10] There was a fine perception in this comment that was more relevant metaphorically than actually to theatre and drama. During the previous twenty years critics and playwrights had complained that literary and dramatic efforts had been stymied and progress infinitesimal. In a bitter comment in 1849 on the progress of American drama, the *Spirit* blamed the playwrights: "If there is any talent for dramatic literature in the country, it is a pity that it is so niggardly hoarded."[11] It was a thoughtless comment, not only reflecting the writer's indignation toward the Mose fad but his short memory for past achievements and ignorance of past and current conditions. Yet such quickly written opinions colored contemporary views as well as the judgment of future generations concerning American drama during the Age of Jackson. America needed to move away from such conditional responses, but it would take more than one generation to accomplish this.

Playwrights will write. They will create for fame, for money, for vanity, for a sense of romance they find in the theatre, for an opportunity to express ideas, to persuade others. America from 1829 to 1849 was, in fact, an era of hopeful persuasion. Throughout this Age of Jackson a surprising number of critics had commented on the American drama and theatre in an attempt to influence the kind and quality of plays written, to bring audiences to higher levels of artistic appreciation, to create an interest in a national drama. Achievements had been made, but playwrights went unrecognized, and lacking great persuasive effect, critics could only look to the future. During the next two decades, however, the progress of American drama would be even slower; attempts to change existing conditions would be fewer. Then, given the right time and the right people, the bright future, which was anticipated by the distinctive accomplishments of the dramatists during the Age of Jackson, would appear.

NOTES

1. J. Bronowski, *The Ascent of Man* (Boston: Little, Brown, 1974), 19.
2. *Spirit of the Times*, V (August 8, 1835), 7.
3. "Decline of the Modern Drama," *New England Magazine*, VIII (February 1835), 105.
4. *Spirit of the Times*, XIX (April 21, 1849), 108.

5. *The Knickerbocker*, I (1833), 161–70.

6. *Notions of the Americans: Picked Up by a Travelling Bachelor*, 2 vols. (London: Henry Colburn, 1828), I: 150.

7. William Gilmore Simms, "The Writings of James Fenimore Cooper," in *Views and Reviews in American Literature, History and Fiction* (New York: Wiley and Putnam, 1845), 210–38.

8. Margaret Fuller Ossoli, "American Literature; its position in the Present time, and Prospects for the Future," in *Art, Literature, and the Drama* (Boston: Roberts Press, 1875), 310; see also discussion of Margaret Fuller's criticism in John Paul Pritchard, *Criticism in America* (Normam: University of Oklahoma Press, 1956), 65.

9. H. Croll, ed., *The British and American Theatre* (Stuttgart: Hallberger's Library, 1842–1855).

10. Letter, Paulding to Robert Dale Owen, Dreer Collection, Historical Society of Pennsylvania.

11. *Spirit of the Times*, XVIII (February 3, 1849), 600.

APPENDIX A

AMERICAN PLAYWRIGHTS, 1829–1849

J. P. Addams
Alexander Allan
George H. Andrews
Delia Salter Bacon
John J. Bailey
Benjamin Baker
Nathaniel H. Bannister
Thomas Barry
William Barrymore
Park Benjamin
William Bayle Bernard
Robert Mongomery Bird
Margaret Botsford
Joseph Breck
John Brougham
David Paul Brown
William E. Burton
George H. Calvert
William P. Chapman
Thomas H. Chivers
Charlotte Barnes Conner
Robert T. Conrad
H. J. Conway
James Fenimore Cooper
I. Courtney
George Washington Parke Custis
Rufus Dawes
Nathaniel Deering

William Dunlap
John E. Durivage
Oliver Everett Durivage
Elizabeth Fries Ellet
Richard Emmons
Thomas Dunn English
Augustus W. Fenno
Joseph M. Field
Henry J. Finn
Stephen E. Glover
E. S. Gold
Sarah Josepha Hale
J. H. Hall
Louise Jane Hall
George Washington Harby
James E. Heath
Caroline Lee Hentz
Frederick Stanhope Hill
Henry Horncastle
Charles Jared Ingersoll
G. P. R. James
Joseph Steven Jones
James M. Kennicott
James Lawson
Walter M. Leman
H. H. Locke
Cornelius A. Logan
Henry W. Longfellow

James McHenry
Alexander Macomb
Cornelius Mathews
George H. Miles
William Mitchell
John Neal
Mordecai M. Noah
William K. Northall
Robert Dale Owen
James Kirke Paulding
John Howard Payne
George Pepper
Jonas B. Phillips
Henry W. Plunkett (H. P. Grattan)
Edgar Allan Poe
Lorenzo da Ponte
Isaac Pray
James Rees
Anna Cora Mowatt Ritchie
Epes Sargent

Charles Saunders
Harry Seymour
Richard Penn Smith
William Smith
Silas S. Steele
George Lionel Stevens
John Augustus Stone
Charles Weston Taylor
L. F. Thomas
Amira Thompson
E. H. Thompson
Zouch S. Troughten
Charles M. Walcot
James S. Wallace
T. A. Ware
Harry Watkins
Nathaniel Parker Willis
Samuel Woodworth
Frances Wright

APPENDIX B

AMERICAN PLAYS, 1829–1849

(Title, playwright, and year of first performance or publication)
Abou Hassan, Harby, n.d.
The Actress of Padua, R. Smith, 1836.
The Adventure; or, The Yankee in Tripoli, Jones, 1835
The Adventures of a Yankee, Jones, 1836
Almachilde, da Ponte, 1829
Altorf, Wright, 1819
Alvara of Spain, Bannister, n.d.
Amy Lee; or, Who Loves Best?, Baker, 1843
The Ancient Briton, Stone, 1833
Another Glass; or The Horrors of Intemperance, Anon., 1845
Anthony and Cleopatra (burlesque), Field, 1843
The Arab Chief; or, Pirate of the East, Conway, 1834
Arasapha, Bannister, 1846
Armand, the Child of the People, Mowatt, 1847
Asmodeus in New York, Allan, 1840
Athenia of Damascus, Dawes, 1839
Aunt Dinah's Pledge, Seymour, 1848 (?)
Aylmere; or, The Bond Man of Kent, Conrad, 1841
Azzo, Harby, n.d.
The Banished Provincial; or, New York in 1776, Glover, 1834
The Bank Monster, Steele, 1841
Batkins at Home; or, Life in Cranberry Center, Jones, 1858
The Battle of Mexico; or, The Capture of the Halls of Montezuma, Barry, 1848
The Battle of New Orleans; or, Lafitte the Pirate, Anon., 1829
The Battle of Stillwater; or, The Maniac, Conway, 1840
The Battle of Tippecanoe, Steele, 1840
Beulah Spa; or, Two of the B'hoys, Anon., 1834

Bianca Visconti; or, The Heart Overtasked, Willis, 1837
Billy Taylor, Mitchell, 1840
The Black Douglass, Conway, 183?
Blanche of Navarre, James, 1839
Blud Da Nouns; or, The Battle of the Frogs, English, 1843
Blue Laws; or, Eighty Years Ago, Woodworth, 1835
The Bombardment of Algiers, R. Smith, 1829
The Borderers, Anon., 1829
Bozzaris, Deering, 1851
The Brazen Drum; or, The Yankee in Poland, Steele, 1841
The Bride of Fort Edwards, Bacon, 1839
The Bride of Genoa, Sargent, 1837
The Brigand's Daughter, Rees, 1842
Britania and Hibernia; or, Victoria in Ireland, Walcot, 1849
Broadway and the Bowery; or, The Young Mechanic and the Merchant's Daughter, Ma-
    thews, 1856
The Broker of Bogota, Bird, 1834
The Broker of Florence, Pray, 1849
Brutus, Payne, 1818
Bumpology, Saunders, 1843
The Bushwacker, Bannister, 1838
The Busy Bee, Barrymore, 1844
The Cabin Boy and His Monkey Who Had Seen the World, Barrymore, 1832
Caecinna, the Roman Consul, Pray, 1850
Caius Marius, R. Smith, 1831
Caius Silius; or, The Slave of Carthage, Bannister, 1835
Camillus; or, The Self-Exiled Patriot, Phillips, 1833
The Campaign of the Rio Grande, Fenno, 1846; Leman, 1846
The Cannibals; or, The Massacre Islands, Woodworth, 1833
Captain Kidd; or, The Wizard of the Sea, Jones, 1839
The Captive Princess; or, Feudal Times in Ireland, Pepper, 1831
The Capture of Captain Cuttle and Barnaby's Wedding, Brougham, 1848
Carabasset; or, The Last of the Norridgewocks, Deering, 1831
Caridorf, Bird, 1828
The Carpenter of Rouen; or, The Massacre of St. Bartholomew, Jones, 1840
The Celestial Empire; or, The Yankee in China, Logan, 1846
Change Makes Change, Sargent, 1845
Charles II, Payne, 1824
Charles O'Malley; or, The Irish Dragoon, Conway, 1842
Charlotte Corday, Conner, 1851
Charlotte Temple, Rees, 1836
Le Chevalier d'Industrie, Phillips, 1837
Chief of the McIvor, Bannister, n.d.
Chinese Junk, Northall, 1847
Chloroform, Logan, 1849
The City Looking Glass, Bird, 1828
The Clairvoyants, Deering, 1844
Cold Stricken, Phillips, 1833

Conaneheotah; or, The Indian's War Horse, Bannister, 1838, 1841
Conrad and Eudora; or, The Death of Alonzo, Chivers, 1834
Conrad, King of Naples, Conrad, 1832
Conrad of Naples, Conrad, 1832
The Council of Blood; or, The Butchers of Ghent, Saunders, 1844
Count Julian, Calvert, 1840
The Cowled Lover, Bird, 1827
The Cradle of Liberty; or, Boston in 1775, Glover, 1832
Crockett in Texas; or, The Massacre of the Alamo, Anon., 1839
The Crock of Gold; or, The Toiler's Trials, Steele, 1845
Cut and Come Again, O. Durivage, 1841
The Dancing Feather; or, The Maid's Revenge, Saunders, 1843
The Daughter, R. Smith, 1836
The Deceived, Harby, 1838
The Declaration of Independence, Brougham, 1844
The Deformed; or, Woman's Trial, R. Smith, 1830
DeLara; or, The Moorish Bride, Hentz, 1831
The Demoniac; or, The Prophet's Bride, Stone, 1831
The Destruction of Jerusalem, Bannister, 1837
Did You Ever Send Your Wife to Brooklyn?, Anon., n.d.
Dion, the Patriot of Syracuse, Ware, 1833
The Disowned; or, The Prodigals, R. Smith, 1829
The Divorce; or, The Mock Cavalier, R. Smith
Dombey and Son, Brougham, 1848
Don Caesar de Bazan (burlesque), Brougham, 1845
The Don Not Done; or, Giovanni From Texas, Walcot, 1844
The Doom of the Drinker, English, 1844
Down South; or, A Military Training, Field, 1829
The Drunkard; or, The Fallen Saved, W. Smith, 1844
The Drunkard's Warning, Anon., 1838
Eagle Eye, J. Hall, 1849
The Eighth of January, R. Smith, 1829
The Eighth of January; or, Hurrah for the Boys of the West, Custis, 1828
Ellen Wareham, Burton, 1833
England's Iron Days, Bannister, 1837
Ernest Maltravers, Medina, 1838
Eugene Aram, Jones, 1832; Taylor, 1832
Eva, the Lass of the Mill, Barrymore, 1838
The Evil Eye, Phillips, 1831
The Fall of San Antonio; or, Texas Victorious, Bannister, 1836
False Pretenses; or, Both Sides of Good Society, Mathews, 1855
Family Ties, Field and Robb, 1846
Fashion; or, How to Write a Comedy, Burton, 1845
Fashion; or, Life in New York, Mowatt, 1845
Fatal Prophecies; or, The Smuggler's Daughter, Conway, 1835
Fauntleroy; or, The Fatal Forgery, Stone, n.d.
The Female Forty Thieves, Pray, 1849
Fifteen Years of a Fireman's Life, Anon., 1841

The Fireman's Frolic, Anon., 1831
The First Fleet and the First Flag, Steele, 1841
The Fiscal Agent, Benjamin, 1842
Foreign and Native, Field, 1845
The Forest Princess; or, Two Centuries Ago, Conner, 1844
The Forest Rose, Woodworth, 1825
The Foundling of the Sea, Woodworth, 1833
Franklin, Brougham, 1846
Frank McLaughlin, Walcot, 1849
Freedom's Last Martyr, Leman, 1845
Fried Shots, Walcot, 1843
G-A-G; or, The Starving System, Field, 1841
The Gambler, Saunders, 1844
Gaulantus the Gaul, Bannister, 1836
The Genoese, Sargent, 1837
The Gentleman in Black, Harby, 1839; Barrymore, 1839
The Gentleman of Lyons; or, The Marriage Contract, Bannister, 1838
Giordano; or, The Conspiracy, Lawson, 1828
Giovanni in Gotham, Walcot, 1843
The Gladiator, Bird, 1831
A Glance at New York, Baker, 1848
A Glance at Philadelphia, Burton, 1848
The Glory of Columbia, Dunlap, 1817
The Gold Bug; or, The Pirate's Treasure, Steele, 1843
The Great Mogul, Mathews, 188?
The Green Mountain Boy, Jones, 1833
Gulzara; or, The Persian, Mowatt, 1840
Guy Rivers; or, The Gold Hunters, Anon., 1834
The Gypsy Wanderer; or, The Stolen Child, Mowatt, 1837 (?)
Handy Andy, English, 1844
Hannah, the Mother of Samuel, the Prophet and Judge of Israel, L. Hall, 1839
Hard Times in New Orleans; or, The Gentleman in Black, Harby, 1837
Harold, King of Norway, Locke, 1839
The Headsman, Rees, 1834
The Highwayman of 1776; or, The Jack Sheppard of America, Anon., 1876
Ida Steppanoff, Conway, 1836
The Imp of Elements; or, The Lake of the Dismal Swamp, Walcot, 1844
The Indian Heroine, Anon., 1835
The Indian Prophecy, Custis, 1827
The Indian Wife, Anon., 1829
Infidelity; or, The Husband's Return, Bannister, 1837
The Inquisitive Yankee; or, A Peep in All Corners, Anon., 1832
Irma; or, The Prediction, Kennicott, 1829
Is She a Brigand?, R. Smith, 1833
Jack Cade, Conrad, 1835
Jack Sheppard; or, The Life of a Robber, Phillips, 1839
Jacob Leisler, the Patriot Hero; or, New York in 1690, Mathews, 1848
Job and His Children, Field, 1852

Job Fox; or, The Yankee Valet, Anon., 1834

Josh Horseradish; or, The Lying Yankee, Anon., 1842

The Judge, Hale, 1851

Julian, Ingersoll, 1831

Julietta Gordini; or, The Miser's Daughter, Pray, 1836

Jupiter Jealous; or, Life in the Clouds, Brougham, 1842

Kairrisahi; or, The Warrior of Wanachtihi, Medina, 1834

Kathleen O'Neill; or, A Picture of Feudal Times in Ireland, Pepper, 1827

The Kentuckian; or, A Trip to New York, Bernard, 1833

The Kentucky Heiress, Willis, 1837

The Knight of the Golden West; or, The Yankee in Spain, Stone, 1834

Konrad of Rheinfeldt; or, The Widowed Bride, Hill, 1834

The Lady of the Lions, O. Durivage, 1842

La Fitte, Conner, 1837

Lafitte, Pirate of the Gulf, Medina, 1836

Lafitte, the Pirate of the Gulf, Rees, 1837

Lamorah; or, The Western Wild, Hentz, n.d.

The Lamp-Lighter of the Pagoda; or, The Chinaman's Revenge, Steele, n.d.

The Land Pirate; or, Yankees in Mississippi, Bannister, 1835

La Rogue, the Regicide, Stone, n.d.

The Last Days of Pompeii, Medina, 1835

The Last Dollar, Jones, 1850

The Last Man; or, The Cock of the Village, R. Smith, n.d.

The Launch of the Columbia; or, America's Blue Jackets Forever, Custis, 1836

Leoni; or, The Orphan of Venice, Chivers, 1838–39

The Liberty Tree; or, Boston Boys in '76, Jones, 1832

Life in New Orleans, Bannister, 1837

Life in New York, Phillips, 1834; Bannister, 1839; Brougham, 1844

Life in Philadelphia, Anon., 1832

Life in Philadelphia; or, The Unfortunate Author, Bannister, 1838

Life; or, Scenes of Early Vice, Courtney, 1848

Lillian the Show Girl, Barrymore, 1837

The Lion Doomed, Medina, n.d.

The Lioness of the North, Anon., 1846

The Lion of the Sea; or, Our Infant Navy, Steele, 1840

The Lion of the West, Paulding, 1830

The Lone Star, Anon., 1849

Love and a Bunch, Hill, 1837

Love and Literature, Wallace, 1832

Love and Murder, Brougham and Baker, 1848

Love and Poetry; or, A Modern Genius, McHenry, 1829

The Lyre of Tioga, A. Thompson, 1829

Macbeth (burlesque), Northall, 1843

Mad Anthony Wayne, Rees, 1845

Ma Femme et Ma Parapluie, Phillips, 1837

The Maid of Wyoming, McHenry, 1831

The Maine Question, Bannister, 1839

Major Jack Downing; or, The Retired Politician, Anon., 1834

The Man in the Moon, Barrymore, 1834
Mary Martin; or, The Money Diggers, Saunders, 1846
Massachusetts Railroads, Finn, 1829
The Massacre; or, The Malay's Revenge, Woodworth, 1836
The Matricide, Steele, n.d.
Mazeppa; or, The Wild Horse of Tartary, Payne, 1825
Met-a-mora; or, The Last of the Pollywogs, Brougham, 1847
Metamora; or, The Last of the Wampanoags, Stone, 1829
Mike Fink, the Last Boatman of the Mississippi, Rees, n.d.
The Millionaire, Leman, 1848
The Miniature, Rees, 1834
Minka; or, The Russian Daughter, Harby, n.d.
A Miser's Miseries, Conway, 1835
The Model Modern Aladden, Pray, 1849
The Moderns; or, A Trip to the Springs, Anon., 1831
Mohammed, Harby, n.d.
Mohammed, the Arabian Prophet, Miles, 1851
Moll Pitcher; or, The Fortune Teller of Lynn, Jones, 1839
Moll Pitcher; or, The Pirate Priest, Jones, 1843
Monongahela, Custis, 1836
Montgomerie; or, The Orphan of a Wreck, Custis, 1836
Moonshine; or, Lunar Discoveries, Finn, 1835
The Mormons, English, 1858
Mose in a Muss, Chapman, 1849
Mose in California, Chapman, 1849
Mose in China, Baker, 1849
Mose, Joe and Jack, Anon., 1849
Mose's Visit to the Arab Girls, Anon., 1848
Le Mouchoir et L'Épée, Walcot, 1848
Murrell, the Western Land Pirate, Bannister, n.d.
The Mysteries and Miseries of New York, Plunkett, 1848
The Mysteries of Paris, Saunders, 1843
Mysterious Knockings, Anon., 1850
My Uncle's Wedding, R. Smith, 1832
Nature's Nobleman, the Mechanic; or, The Ship's Carpenter of New York, Watkins,
     1850
Nervo the Vitalics; or, The March of Science (or, What Next?), Field, 1842
New Notions, Anon., 1840
New York As It Is, Baker, 1848
New York Assurance, Anon., 1841
New York Directory; or, The Cockney in America, Burton, 1849
New York in 1848, Baker, 1848
New York in Slices, Anon., 1848
The New York Merchant and His Clerks, Anon., 1843
The New York Milliners, Anon., 1848
The New World; or, The House of Liberty, Allan, 1840
Nick of the Woods, Harby, 1838
Nick of the Woods; or, Telie, the Renegades' Daughter, Medina, 1838

The Night Hawk, Logan, 1830
A Night of Expectations, Conner, 1848
Nina Sforza, Troughten, 1842
1940; or, Crummles in Search of Novelty, Allan, 1840
1941; or, Crummles in Search of Novelty, Allan, 1841
1942; or, Crummles in Search of Novelty, Allan, 1842
The Noble Romans, Pray, 1837
Norman Leslie, Medina, 1836
Northpoint; or, Baltimore Defended, Custis, 1833
Nullification; or, The Yankee in Charleston, Anon., 1833
Oceola, Thomas, 1837
Octavia Brigaldi; or, The Confession, Conner, 1837
Of Age Tonight; or, Natur's Nature, Anon., 1842
The Old Clock; or, Here She Goes, There She Goes, Pray, 1837 (?)
Old Friends and New Faces, Walcot, 1844
Old Job and Jacob Gray, Jones, 1849
Old Jonathan and His Apprentices, Barrymore, 1832
Old Manhattan; or, Wall Street in an Uproar, Bannister?, 1840
The Old Olympian, Horncastle, 1841
The Old Waggoner of New Jersey and Virginia, Bannister, 1847
Olympic Insurance, Anon., 1841
O'Neil the Rebel, Medina, 1835
Opera Mad; or, The Scream-A-Donna, Steele, n.d.
Oralloossa, Bird, 1832
Oregon; or, The Disputed Territory, Field, 1846
Ormond Grosvenor, Hale, 1839
Oronaska, Phillips, 1834
Our Best Society, J. Durivage, 1854
Our Ephraim; or, The New Englanders, a What-d'ye-call it?, Neal, 1834
Our Flag, Saunders, 1845
Outallissi; or, The Indian Counsel Chamber, Anon., 1834
Ovid and Obid; or, Yankee Blunders, Anon., 1834
Patrick Lyon; or, The Locksmith of Philadelphia, Rees, 1843
The Patriot; or, Union and Freedom, Stevens, 1834
Paul Revere, and The Sons of Liberty, Jones, 1875
The Pawnee Chief, Custis, 1829 (?)
The Pelican, R. Smith, 1825
Pelopidas, Bird, 1830
The People's Lawyer, Jones, 1839
Peter Finn; or, A Trip to See the Sea, Finn, 1829
Peytona and Fashion; or, North Against South, Baker 1845
Philadelphia As It Is, Anon., 1841
Philadelphia Assurance, Steele, 1841
The Pirate's Legacy; or, The Wrecker's Fate, Saunders, 1844
Pocahontas, Owen, 1837
Pocahontas; or, The Settlers of Virginia, Custis, 1830
The Polish Wife, Phillips, 1831
Politian, Poe, 1835

The Politicians, Mathews, 1840
Pontiac; or, The Siege of Detroit, Macomb, 1835
The Poor Student, Longfellow, 1824
Prairie Bird; or, A Child of the Delawares, Leman, 1847
The Priestess, Sargent, 1855
The Prisoners, Pray, n.d.
The Prophet of St. Paul's, Brown, 1830
Psammelichus; or, The Twelve Tribes of Egypt, Bannister, n.d.
Punch in New York, Andrews, 1847; Northall, 1849
Putnam, the Iron Son of '76, Bannister, 1844
Quite Correct, R. Smith, 1828
The Rail Road, Custis, 1828
The Rail Road and the Canal, Custis, 1829
Rangers; or, The Battle of Germantown, Leman, 1845
Rathaimus the Roman, Bannister, 1835
Rebellion in Canada, Steele, 1841
The Reign of Reform; or, Yankee Doodle Court, Botsford, 1830
Removing the Deposits, Finn, 1835
Restoration; or, The Diamond Cross, Stone, 1824
The Revolt of the Sextons; or, The Undertaker's Dream, Brougham, 1848
Revolution; or, The Yeoman of '76, Brougham, 1844
Rhode Island; or, Who's Governor?, Steele, 1842
Richard Number 3, O. Durivage, 1842
Rienzi, Medina, 1836
Robert Emmett, Bannister, 1840
Romance and Reality; or, Silence Gives Consent, Brougham, 1847
The Roman Slave, Bannister, n.d.
The Roof Scrambler, Mitchell (?), 1839
Rookwood, Bannister, 1844
Rosina Meadows, the Village Maid; or, Temptation Unveiled, Saunders, 1843
Sabotier; or, The Fairy of the Wooden Shoemaker, Wallace, 1837
St. Dollar and the Monster Rag, Steele, 1841
Sam Patch in France; or, The Pesky Snake, Addams, 1848
Sam Patch; or, The Daring Yankee, E. Thompson, 1839
The Saracusan Brothers, Bannister, 1838
Saratoga Springs, Allan, 1843
Sassacus, Owen, 1836
The Savage and the Maiden, Horncastle, 1840
The Scourge of the Ocean, Fenno, 1846
The Sentinels; or, The Two Sargeants, R. Smith, 1829
Sertorius; or, The Roman Patriot, Brown, 1830
Shakespeare in Love, R. Smith, n.d.
She Would Be A Soldier, Noah, 1819
The Shoemaker of Toulouse; or, The Avenger of Humble Life, Hill, 1834
Shot in the Eye; or, The Regulators of Texas, Anon., 1849
The Silver Spoon; or, Our Own Folks: A Joiner's Job in Four Parts, Jones, 1852
The Six Degrees of Crime; or, Wine, Women, Gambling, Theft, Murder and the Scaffold, Hill, 1834

Socialism; or, Modern Philosophy Put in Practice, Brougham, 1849

The Solitary; or, The Man of Misery, Smith, n.d.

Solon Shingle, Jones, 1839

The Sons of Usna: Tragi-Apotheosis, Chivers, 1858

The Spanish Pirates; or, A Union of the Flags, Conway, 1835

The Spanish Student, Longfellow, 1842

Sparring with Specie; or, The War of the Shinplasters, Anon., 1840

Spy in Washington, Wallace, 1837

The Squatter, Rees, 1838

The Stage-Struck Yankee, O. Durivage, 1840

Stephanie, the Robber Girl, Harby, n.d

Such As It Is, Field, 1842

The Surgeon of Paris; or, The Massacre of the Hugenots, Jones, 1838

Tancred, King of Sicily; or, The Archives of Palermo, Stone, 1831

Tancred; or, The Siege of Antioch, Stone, 1827

Tecumseh; or, The Battle of the Thames, Emmons, 1834

Telemachus; or, The Enchanted Isle, Phillips, 1838

The Temperance Doctor, Seymour, 1848 (?)

Temptation; or, The Irish Emigrant, Brougham, 1849

Ten Years of a Sailor's Life, Phillips, 1840

Teresa Contarini, Ellet, 1835

Texas and Freedom, Bannister, n.d.

The Texas Struggle, Anon., 1850

Thérèse, the Orphan of Geneva, Payne, 1821

The Three Brothers; or, Crime Its Own Avenger, Bannister, 1840

Three Years After, Chapman, 1849

The Times; or, Life in New York, Anon., 1829

Timothy Lincoln's Visit to the Capitol of Nullification, Anon., 1833

Tod's Pilgrimage, Field, 1841 (?)

The Toodles, Burton, 1848

Tortesa the Usurer, Willis, 1839

Touretoun, Stone, n.d.

The Tourist; or, Tourists in America, Field, 1839

A Trip to Niagara, Dunlap, 1828

The Triumph of Plattsburg, Smith, 1830

Tutoona; or, The Indian Girl, Harby, 1835

Twenty Years' Life as a Courtesan, Harby, n.d.

Two Spaniards, Bannister, 1838

Uproar House in Disaster Place, Northall, 1847

Upside-Down; or, Philosophy in Petticoats, Cooper, 1850

The Usurper, McHenry, 1827

Velasco, Sargent, 1837

The Venetian Bride, Anon., 1834

The Vermonter; or, Love and Phrenology, Anon., 1842

The Vermont Wool Dealer, Logan, 1838

The Very Age, Gold, 1850

Virginus (burlesque), Northall, 1843

The Volunteers' Departure and Return, Leman, 1848

Wacousta; or, The Curse, Medina, 1833
The Wag of Maine, Logan, 1834
Waldimar, Bailey, 1831
Wall Street; or, Ten Minutes Before Three, Anon., 1819
The Wandering Jew, Bannister, 1837
Washington and Napoleon, Steele, 1841
Washington at Valley Forge, Rees, 1832
Washington Preserved, Rees, 1836
Washington's Birthday; or, The New York Boys, Steele, 1846
The Water Witch, Taylor, 1830; Wallace, 1832
The Water Witch; or, The Skimmer of the Seas, R. Smith, 1830
The Wept of Wish-ton-wish, Anon., 1834
Werdenberg; or, The Forest League, Hentz, 1832
West Point; or, A Tale of Treason, Breck, 1840
Westward Ho!, Wallace, 1833
The Wheelwright; or, Boston Pride, Jones 1845
Which Shall I Marry?; or, Who Does Best, McHenry, 1831
Whigs and Democrats; or, Love of No Politics, Heath, 1839
Who's Got Macready; or, A Race to Boston, Mitchell, 1848
The Widow's Curse, Phillips, 1837
A Wife at a Venture, R. Smith, 1829
The Wigwam; or, Templeton Manor, Field, 1829
William Penn, R. Smith, 1829
Wissmuth and Company; or, The Noble and the Merchant, Ellet, 1847
Witchcraft; or, The Martyrs of Salem, Mathews, 1846
The World's Fair; or, London in 1851, Burton, 1851
The Wreck; or, The Isle of Beauty, Horncastle, 1841
The Yankee at Niagra, Anon., 1843
The Yankee Duelist; or, Bunker Hill's Representative, Bannister, 1838
The Yankee in 1776, Anon., 1843
A Yankee in Time, Anon., 1838
The Yankee in Trouble; or, Zephanich in the Pantry, Anon., 1832
Yankee Land; or, The Foundling of the Apple Orchard, Logan, 1842, 1844
Yankee Peddler, Anon., 1834
The Yankee Peddler; or, Old Times in Virginia, Bernard, 1836
The Yankee Preacher, Anon., 1843
Yankees in China; or, A Union of the Flags, Anon., 1840
Zafari the Bohemian, Jones, 1856
Zara, Hentz, n.d.

SELECTED BIBLIOGRAPHY

These books, articles and microfilms are listed to provide the reader with selected sources used in preparing this volume and to suggest additional reading material. The reader is also referred to two other books by the author: *An Emerging Entertainment: The Drama of the American People to 1828* (1977) and *American Drama to 1900, A Guide to Information Sources* (1980).

COLLECTIONS OF PLAYS

The plays described and evaluated in this study have been found in a variety of collections in university and private libraries across the country. The best single major source, however, is the Readex Corporation's microprint collection of "American plays, 1831–1900," which is part of the *English and American Plays of the Nineteenth Century*. An invaluable tool for the use of this microprint collection is Don J. Hixon and Don A. Hennessee's *Nineteenth-Century American Drama: A Finding Guide* (Metuchen, N.J.: The Scarecrow Press, 1977). Other sources include the following:

Clark, Barrett, H., ed. *America's Lost Plays*, 20 vols. 1941. Reprint in 10 vols. Bloomington: Indiana University Press, 1963–1965; vol. 21, 1969.
Moody, Richard, ed. *Dramas from the American Theatre, 1762–1909*. New York: World Publishing Company, 1966.
Quinn, Arthur Hobson, ed. *Representative American Plays*. 7th ed. New York: Appleton-Century-Crofts, 1953.

CULTURAL AND HISTORICAL BACKGROUND

Bayless, Joy. *Rufus Wilmot Griswold*. Nashville, Tenn.: Vanderbilt University Press, 1943.
Bode, Carl. *The Anatomy of American Popular Culture, 1840–1861*. Berkeley: University of California Press, 1960.

Cawley, Elizabeth H., ed. *The American Diaries of Richard Cobden.* New York: Cambridge University Press, 1975.

Chevalier, Michael. *Society, Manners and Politics in the United States.* Boston: Weeks, Jordan and Company, 1839.

Cooper, James, F. *Notions of the Americans: Picked up by a Travelling Bachelor,* 2 vols. London: Henry Colburn, 1828.

Curti, Merle. *Human Nature in American Thought.* Madison: University of Wisconsin Press, 1980.

French, J.S. *Sketches and Eccentricities of Col. David Crockett of West Tennessee.* New York: Harper, 1833.

Greenleaf, Barbara Kaye. *American Fever.* New York: New American Library, 1970.

Grund, Francis, J., ed. *Aristocracy in America,* 2 vols. London: Richard Bentley, 1839.

Hamilton, Thomas. *Men and Manners in America.* Philadelphia: Carey, Lea & Blanchard, 1833.

Hart, James D. *The Oxford Companion to American Literature.* New York: Oxford University Press, 1941.

Knapp, Samuel L. *Lectures on American Literature with Remarks on Some Passages of American History.* Elan Bliss, No. 107 Broadway, 1829.

Mark, Irving and Eugene L. Schwaab, eds., *The Faith of Our Fathers.* New York: Octagon Press, 1976.

Marryat, Frederich. *A Diary in America with Remarks on Its Institutions.* ed. Sydney Jackman. New York: Alfred A. Knopf, 1962.

Martineau, Harriet. *Society in America,* 3 vols. London: Saunders and Otley, 1839.

Morison, Samuel Eliot. *The Oxford History of the American People.* New York: New American Library, 1972.

Nagel, Paul. *This Sacred Trust: American Nationality, 1798–1898.* New York: Oxford University Press, 1971.

Nevins, Allan, ed. *The Diary of Philip Hone, 1828–1851.* New York: Dodd, Mead & Company, 1936.

Parrington, Vernon Louis. *Main Currents in American Thought.* 3 vols. New York: Harcourt, Brace and Company, 1930.

Pessen, Edward. *Most Uncommon Jacksonians.* Albany: State University of New York Press, 1967.

———. *Riches, Class and Power Before the Civil War.* Lexington, Mass.: D. C. Heath, 1973.

Pope-Hennessey, Una, ed. *The Autocratic Journey, Being the Outspoken Letters of Mrs. Basil Hall, Written During a Fourteen Month's Sojourn in America, 1827–1828.* New York: G. P. Putnam's Sons, 1931.

Pritchard, John Paul. *Criticism in America.* Norman: University of Oklahoma Press, 1956.

———. *Literary Wise Men of Gotham.* Baton Rouge: Louisiana State University Press, 1963.

Quinn, Arthur Hobson, ed. *The Literature of the American People.* New York: Appleton-Century-Crofts, 1951.

Rathburn, John W. *American Literary Criticism, 1800–1860.* Boston: Twayne Publishers, 1979.

Rogers, Cleveland and John Black, eds. *The Gathering of the Forces.* New York: G. P. Putnam Sons, 1920.

Rozwenc, Edwin C., ed. *Ideology and Power in the Age of Jackson.* New York: Doubleday & Company, 1964.

Saum, Lewis O. *The Popular Mood of Pre-Civil War America*. Westport, Conn.: Greenwood Press, 1980.

Schlesinger, Arthur M., Jr. *The Age of Jackson*. Boston: Little, Brown and Company, 1950.

Simms, William Gilmore. *Views and Reviews in American Literature, History and Fiction*. New York: Wiley and Putnam, 1845.

Simpson, Henry. *The Lives of Eminent Philadelphians*. Philadelphia: W. Brotherhead, 1859.

Smith, Henry Nash. *Virgin Land*. Cambridge: Harvard University Press, 1950.

Spencer, Ben T. *The Quest for Nationality*. Syracuse, N.Y.: Syracuse University Press, 1957.

Spiller, Robert E., ed. *The American Literary Revolution, 1783–1837*. New York: Doubleday & Company, 1967.

Stedman, E. C. and Ellen M. Hutchinson, eds. *A Library of American Literature from the Earliest Settlement to the Present Time*, 10 vols. New York: Charles L. Webster, 1892.

Styan, J. L. *Drama, Stage and Audience*. New York: Cambridge University Press, 1975.

Trollope, Frances. *Domestic Manners of the Americans*. New York: Dodd, Mead & Co., 1827.

Tyler, Alice Felt. *Freedom's Ferment: Phases of American Social History from the Colonial Period to the Outbreak of the Civil War*. Minneapolis: University of Minnesota Press, 1944.

Ward, John William. *Andrew Jackson, Symbol of an Age*. New York: Oxford University Press, 1955.

Weber, Adna Ferrin. *The Growth of Cities in the Nineteenth Century*. 1899. Reprint. Ithaca: Cornell University Press, 1963.

Welter, Rush. *The Mind of America, 1920–1860*. New York: Columbia University Press, 1975.

THEATRE HISTORY

Briggs, H. E. and E. B. "The Early Theatre in Chicago." *Journal of the Illinois State Historical Society* XXXI (June 1946), 165–78.

Brown, T. Allston. *History of the American Stage*. 1870. Reprint. New York: Burt Franklin, 1969.

Clapp, William W., Jr. *A Record of the Boston Stage*. Boston: James Monroe and Company, 1853.

Clarke, M. *A Concise History of the Life and Amours of Thomas S. Hamblin*. Philadelphia: n.p., n.d.

Dorman, James H. *Theater in the Ante Bellum South*. Chapel Hill: University of North Carolina Press, 1967.

Fox, D. R. "The Development of the American Theater." *New York History* XVII (1936), 22–41.

Hill, George H. *Scenes from the Life of an Actor*. 1853. Reprint. New York: Benjamin Blom, 1969.

Hodge, Francis R. *Yankee Theatre, The Image of America on the Stage, 1825–1850*. Austin: University of Texas Press, 1964.

Hornblow, Arthur. *A History of the Theatre in America from Its Beginnings to the Present Time*, 2 vols. Philadelphia: J. B. Lippincott, 1919.

Ireland, Joseph. *Records of the New York Stage*. vol. 2. New York: J. H. Morrell, 1866.

Leman, Walter M. *Memories of an Old Actor*. San Francisco: A. Roman Co., 1886.

Ludlow, Noah. *Dramatic Life As I Found It*. St. Louis: G. J. Jones, 1880.

McVicker, J. H. *The Theatre: Its Early Days in Chicago*. Chicago: Knight & Leonard, 1884.

Murdock, James E. *The Stage, or Recollections of Actors and Acting from an Experience of Fifty Years*. Philadelphia: J. M. Stoddard, 1880.

Nicoll, Allardyce. *A History of English Drama 1660–1900*. vol. VI. Cambridge: Cambridge University Press, 1959.

Northall, William K. *Before and Behind the Curtain; or, Fifteen Years' Observations Among the Theatres of New York*. New York: W. F. Burgess, 1851.

————., ed. *Life and Recollections of Yankee Hill: Together with Anecdotes and Incidents of His Travels*. New York: W. F. Burgess, 1850.

Odell, George C. D. *Annals of the New York Stage*, vols. 3, 4, and 5. New York: Columbia University Press, 1928, 1928, 1931.

Power, Tyrone. *Impressions of America During the Years 1833, 1834 and 1835*, 2 vols. Philadelphia: Carey, Lea & Blanchard, 1836.

Skinner, Maud and Otis, eds. *One Man in His Time, the Adventures of H. Watkins, Strolling Player, 1845–1863, from His Journal*. Philadelphia: University of Pennsylvania Press, 1938.

Smith, Sol. *Theatrical Management in the West and South for Thirty Years*. New York: Harper, 1868.

Smither, Nelle. *A History of the English Theatre at New Orleans, 1806–1842*, 1944. Reprint. New York: Benjamin Blom, 1967.

Stone, Henry Dickinson. *Personal Recollections of the Drama* 1873. Reprint. New York: Benjamin Blom, 1969.

Stratman, Carl J. *American Theatrical Periodicals, 1798–1967*. Durham, N.C.: Duke University Press, 1970.

Theatrical Biography of Eminent Actors and Authors. New York: Estate of Wm. Taylor, n.d.

Wallack, Lester. *Memories of Fifty Years*. New York: Charles Scribners, 1889.

Wemyss, Francis C. *A Chronology of the American Stage from 1752–1852*. New York: W. Taylor, 1852.

Weston, Effie Ellsler, ed. *The Stage Memoirs of John A. Ellsler*. Cleveland: The Rowfant Club, 1950.

Wilson, A. H. *History of the Philadelphia Theatre, 1835–1855*. Philadelphia: University of Pennsylvania, 1935.

Wood, William B. *Personal Recollections of the Stage*. Philadelphia: Henry Carey Baird, 1855.

DRAMA AND DRAMATISTS: HISTORY, CRITICISM AND BIBLIOGRAPHY

Adkins, Nelson, F. "James K. Paulding's Lion of the West." *American Literature* III (November 1931), 249–58.

Amacher, Richard E. "Behind the Curtain with the Noble Savage: Stage Movement of Indian Plays, 1825–1860." *Theatre Survey* VII (1966), 101–14.

Auser, Courtland P. *Nathaniel Parker Willis*. New York: Twayne Publishers, 1969.

Bank, Rosemarie K. "Theatre and Narrative Fiction in the Work of a Nineteenth-Century American Playwright, Louisa Medina." *Theatre History Studies* III (1983), 54–67.

Barnes, Eric W. *The Lady of Fashion*. New York: Charles Scribner's Sons, 1954.

Bates, Alfred, ed. *The Drama, its History, Literature and Influences on Civilization*, vols. 19 and 20. New York: Smart & Stanley, 1903.

Beers, Henry A. *Nathaniel Parker Willis*. Boston: Houghton Mifflin, 1885.

Conner, Charlotte Barnes. *Plays, Prose and Poetry*. Philadelphia: E. H. Butler, 1848.

Dahl, Curtis. *Robert Montgomery Bird*. New York: Twayne Publishers, 1963.

Damon, Samuel Foster. *Thomas Holley Chivers, Friend of Poe*. New York: Harper & Brothers, 1930.

Dorson, Richard M. "Mose the Far-famed and World-renowned." *American Literature* XV (November 1943), 288–300.

Durang, Charles. *The Philadelphia Stage, From the Year 1749 to the Year 1855*. Philadelphia *Sunday Dispatch*; Third Series, 1830/1–1855, beginning July 8, 1860.

Enkvist, Nils Erik. *Caricatures of Americans on the English Stage Prior to 1870*. Commentationes Humanarum Litterarum, XVIII, 1. Helsingfors: Centraltryckeri och Bokbinderi ab, 1951.

Faust, Clement E. *The Life and Dramatic Works of Robert Montgomery Bird*. New York: Knickerbocker Press, 1919.

Felton, C. C. "Dramas of N. P. Willis." *North American Review* LI (1840), 141–58.

Fuller, Margaret [Ossoli]. *Papers on Literature and Art*, 2 vols. New York: Putnam, 1846.

———. *Art, Literature and the Drama*. Boston: Roberts Press, 1875.

Gafford, Lucile. "Transcendentalist Attitudes Toward the Drama and the Theatre." *New England Quarterly* XIII (September 1940), 442–66.

Grimsted, David. *Melodrama Unveiled, American Theatre and Culture, 1800–1850*. Chicago: University of Chicago Press, 1968.

Harris, Richard A. "A Young Dramatist's Diary: *The Secret Records* of R. M. Bird." *Literary Chronicle, University of Pennsylvania* XXV (Winter 1959), 8–24.

Hartman, John Geoffrey. *The Development of American Social Comedy, 1787–1936*. 1939. Reprint. New York: Octagon Books, 1971.

Havens, Daniel F. *The Columbian Muse of Comedy: The Development of a Native Tradition in Early American Social Comedy, 1787–1845*. Carbondale: Southern Illinois University Press, 1973.

Hawes, David S. "John Brougham as a Playwright." *Educational Theater Journal*, IX (1957), 184–93.

Hoover, Merle M. *Park Benjamin, Poet & Editor*. New York: Columbia University Press, 1948.

Jefferson, Joseph. *The Autobiography of Joseph Jefferson*. New York: The Century Company, 1889.

Korn, Bertram. *The Early Jews of New Orleans*. Waltham, Mass.: American Jewish Historical Society, 1969.

Lease, Benjamin. *That Wild Fellow John Neal and the American Literary Revolution*. Chicago: University of Chicago Press, 1972.

Lochemes, Sister M. Frederick. *Robert Walsh: His Story*. Washington, D.C.: Catholic University of America Press, 1941.

McCullough, Bruce Welker. *The Life and Writings of Richard Penn Smith with a Reprint of His Play, "The Deformed," 1830*. Menasha, Wis.: Banta, 1917.

McKernan, Laura. "A Study of John Brougham as a Writer of Burlesque." M.A. Thesis, Indiana University, 1976.

Mathews, Cornelius. *The Various Writings of Cornelius Mathews*. New York: Harper Bros., 1843.

Matthews, Brander. "The American on the Stage." *Scribner's Monthly* XVIII (July 1879), 321–33.

Meserve, Walter J. *An Outline History of American Drama*. Totowa, N.J.: Littlefield, Adams, 1965.

Moody, Richard. *America Takes the Stage*. Bloomington: Indiana University Press, 1955.

Moses, Montrose J. *The American Dramatist*. Boston: Little, Brown, 1925.

Moses, Montrose J. and John Mason Brown, eds. *The American Theatre as Seen by Its Critics, 1752–1934*. New York: Norton, 1934.

Mowatt, Anna Cora. *Autobiography of an Actress*. Boston: Ticknor, Reed & Fields, 1854.

————. *Mimic Life; or, Before and Behind the Curtain*. Boston: Ticknor and Fields, 1856.

Peavy, C. D. "The American Indian in the Drama of the United States." *McNeese Review* X (Winter 1958), 68–86.

Quinn, Arthur Hobson. *A History of the American Drama from the Beginning to the Civil War*. New York: Appleton-Century-Crofts, 1943.

Ramshaw, Molly N. "Jump, Jim Crow! A Biographical Sketch of Thomas D. Rice (1808–1860)." *Theatre Annual* XVII (1960), 36–47.

Reed, Perley I. *The Realistic Presentation of American Characters in Native American Plays Prior to 1870*. Ohio State University Bulletin, no. 26. Columbus: Ohio State University Press, 1918.

Rees, James. *The Dramatic Authors of America*. Philadelphia: G. B. Zieber, 1845.

Roden, Robert. *Later American Plays, 1831–1900*. New York: Dunlap Society, 1900.

Ryan, Pat M. "John Brougham: The Gentle Satirist." *Bulletin of the New York Public Library*, LXIII (1959), 619–40.

Seilhamer, George O. *An Interviewer's Album: Comprising a Series of Chats with Eminent Players and Playwrights*. New York: Alvin Perry, 1881.

Taylor, George Rogers. "Gaslight Foster: A New York Journeyman Journalist of Mid-Century." *New York History* LVIII (July 1977), 297–312.

Thompson, Lawrance. "Longfellow Sells the Spanish Student." *American Literature* VI (1934), 141-50.

"Uncle Ben Baker." New York *Dramatic Mirror*. 13 September 1890. p. 5.

Wagenknecht, Edward. *Longfellow: A Full-Length Portrait*. London: Longmans Green, 1955.

Westlake, Neda McFadden, ed. *Caius Marius, A Tragedy by Richard Penn Smith*. Philadelphia: University of Pennsylvania Press, 1968.

Wilson, Garff B. *Three Hundred Years of American Drama and Theatre* 2d ed. Englewood Cliffs, N.J.: Prentice-Hall, 1982.

Winter, William, ed. *Life, Stories and Poems of John Brougham*. Boston: James R. Osgood, 1881.

DISSERTATIONS

Blanc, Robert E. "James McHenry (1785–1845), Playwright and Novelist." Ph.D. diss., University of Pennsylvania, 1939.

Harris, Richard A. "The Major Dramas of Robert Montgomery Bird: A Critical Analysis of Their Structure and Development." Ph.D. diss., Indiana University, 1966.

Hawes, David S. "John Brougham as American Playwright and Man of the Theatre." Ph.D. diss., Stanford University, 1953.

Pagel, Carol Ann Ryan. "A History and Analysis of Representative American Dramatizations from American Novels, 1800–1860." Ph.D. diss., University of Denver, 1970.

Reardon, John. "Verse Drama in America from 1765 to the Civil War." Ph.D. diss., University of Kansas, 1957.

Salvaggio, Odette C. "American Dramatic Criticism, 1830–1860." Ph.D. diss., Florida State University, 1979.

Sitton, Fred. "The Indian Dramas in America, 1750–1900." Ph.D. diss., Northwestern University, 1962.

Todd, Hal J. "America's Actor-Playwrights of the Nineteenth Century." Ph.D. diss., University of Denver, 1955.

CURRENT PERIODICALS AND NEWSPAPERS, 1829–1849

The periodicals and newspapers listed below contained either criticism or reviews of American drama and theatre during the years covered in this volume or commentary on the playwrights. Except for some New York newspapers they are available in the microfilm reproductions of the American Periodical Series by University Microfilms, Inc.

Albion
American Masonic Register and Literary Companion
American Monthly Magazine
Anglo-America, a Journal of Literature, News, Politics, the Drama, Fine Arts
Ariel
Arthur's Ladies Magazine
Atlantic Journal and Friend of Knowledge
Boston Quarterly Review
Broadway Journal
Brother Jonathan
Brownson's Quarterly Review
Burton's Gentleman's Magazine and American Monthly Review
Critic
Dramatic Mirror and Literary Companion
Expositor
Federal American Monthly
Hopkinsian Magazine
Irish Shield and Literary Panorama
Irish Shield and Monthly Hilenan
Irish Shield and Monthly Milesian, A Historic, Literary and Dramatic Journal
Knickerbocker

Ladies' Literary Port Folio
Literary Examiner and Western Monthly Review
Literary World
New England Magazine
New York Mirror
New York Review
North American Magazine
North American Review
Parlour Review and Journal of Music, Literature and the Fine Arts
Spirit of the Times
Yankee; and Boston Literary Gazette

INDEX

About the Author

WALTER J. MESERVE, Professor of Theater and Drama and the Director of the Institute for American Theater Studies, Indiana University, is the author or editor of 12 books, among them *An Emerging Entertainment: The Drama of the American People to 1828* and *American Drama to 1900* and articles in *American Literary Scholarship, Theatre Survey, Theatre Journal, Modern Drama,* and *Theatre Quarterly.*

Recent Titles in
Contributions in American Studies
Series Editor: Robert H. Walker

The Bang and the Whimper: Apocalypse and Entropy in American Literature
Zbigniew Lewicki

The Disreputable Profession: The Actor in Society
Mendel Kohansky

The.Formative Essays of Justice Holmes: The Making of
an American Legal Philosophy
Frederic Rogers Kellogg

A "Capacity for Outrage": The Judicial Odyssey of J. Skelly Wright
Arthur Selwyn Miller

On Courts and Democracy: Selected Nonjudicial Writings of J. Skelly Wright
Arthur Selwyn Miller, editor

A Campaign of Ideas: The 1980 Anderson/Lucey Platform
Clifford W. Brown, Jr., and Robert J. Walker, compilers

Dreams and Visions: A Study of American Utopias, 1865–1917
Charles J. Rooney, Jr.

Mechanical Metamorphosis: Technological Change in Revolutionary America
Neil Longley York

Prologue: The Novels of Black American Women, 1891–1965
Carole McAlpine Watson

Strikes, Dispute Procedures, and Arbitration: Essays on Labor Law
William B. Gould IV

The Soul of the Wobblies: The I.W.W., Religion, and American Culture in the
Progressive Era, 1905–1917
Donald E. Winters, Jr.

Politics, Democracy, and the Supreme Court: Essays on the Frontier of Consti-
tutional Theory
Arthur S. Miller

The Supreme Court and the American Family: Ideology and Issues
Eva R. Rubin